From Obstacle to Ally

From Obstacle to Ally charts the history of psychoanalysis through a close look at its clinical practice. In this study, Judith M. Hughes succeeds in bringing alive the clinical struggles and theoretical contributions of the last century's most influential psychoanalysts, including Sándor Ferenczi, Anna Freud, Melanie Klein, Joan Riviere, Wilfred Bion, Betty Joseph, and Heinz Kohut.

Taking a cue from Freud's reflections on transference, Hughes traces a series of encounters in which psychoanalysts managed to negotiate obstacles to treatment and, on occasion, transform them into allies. Through an examination of the specific obstacles posed by particular diagnostic categories, she shows, in convincing detail, how grappling with such obstacles prompted advances in psychoanalytic practice.

As well as providing an excellent introduction to fundamental psychoanalytic concepts, *From Obstacle to Ally* offers a highly original account of their evolution. It is a book that will fascinate psychoanalysts and psychotherapists alike.

Judith M. Hughes is a professor of history at the University of California, San Diego and is on the faculty of the San Diego Psychoanalytic Institute.

Also by Judith M. Hughes

To the Maginot Line: The Politics of French Military Preparation in the 1920s (1971)

Emotion and High Politics: Personal Relations at the Summit in Late Nineteenth-Century Britain and Germany (1983)

Reshaping the Psychoanalytic Domain: The Work of Melanie Klein, W. R. D. Fairbairn, and D. W. Winnicott (1989)

From Freud's Consulting Room: The Unconscious in a Scientific Age (1994)

Freudian Analysts/Feminist Issues (1999)

From Obstacle to Ally

The evolution of psychoanalytic practice

Judith M. Hughes

Routledge
Taylor & Francis Group
LONDON AND NEW YORK

First published 2004
by Brunner-Routledge

This edition published 2012 by Routledge

2 Park Square, Milton Park, Abingdon, Oxon OX14 4RN
52 Vanderbilt Avenue, New York, NY 10017

Routledge is an imprint of the Taylor & Francis Group, an informa business

Copyright © 2004 Judith M. Hughes

Typeset in Times by RefineCatch Limited, Bungay, Suffolk

Paperback cover design by Hybert Design

British Library Cataloguing in Publication Data
A catalogue record for this book is available from the British
Library.

Library of Congress Cataloging-in-Publication Data
Hughes, Judith M.
   From obstacle to ally : the evolution of psychoanalytic practice /
Judith M. Hughes.– 1st ed.
      p.   cm.
   Includes bibliographical references and index.
      ISBN 1-58391-889-2 (hardcover)—ISBN 1-58391-890-6 (pbk.)
      1. Psychoanalysis—Practice—History. 2. Psychoanalysis—
History. I. Title.

RC506.H846   2004
616.89'17'09–dc22   2004003623

ISBN 13: 978-1-58391-889-0 (hbk)
ISBN 13: 978-1-58391-890-6 (pbk)

For my patients

Contents

Acknowledgments

It gives me great pleasure to thank those who have helped me along the way—including a number of the psychoanalysts who figure as protagonists in this study. Years ago, in connection with an earlier project, I had the good fortune to interview the late Herbert A. Rosenfeld. I have a vivid memory of him and of our long conversation. In connection with this work I had similarly extended talks with Betty Joseph, Otto F. Kernberg, and John Steiner. Their openness and encouragement have been much appreciated.

At an early stage, before I was ready to put pen to paper, I tried out ideas with two different groups: I gave a couple of most informal lectures to the Psychoanalytic Interdisciplinary Seminar at the University of California, San Diego; and I presented material that became the first chapter to the University of California Interdisciplinary Consortium. Both groups urged me to press on.

For steady support during and after my training at the San Diego Psychoanalytic Institute, I have relied on Alvin Robbins, Allan D. Rosenblatt, Alan Sugarman, and Robert L. Tyson. For intellectual companionship, I have turned, again and again, to Roy D'Andrade, Donald L. Kripke, and Edward Lee. Reva P. Greenburg and Melford E. Spiro have stood by me in the worst of times.

In previous books I invariably expressed my deepest gratitude to my husband, Stuart. He died as I was struggling with the second chapter of this one. Until the very end, he wanted to know how I was progressing and wanted to listen to my prose. His love and kindness have not been lost.

Abbreviations

F/Fer Correspondence	*The Correspondence of Sigmund Freud and Sándor Ferenczi*, vol. 1, *1908–1914*, ed. Eva Brabant, Ernst Falzeder, and Patrizia Giampieri-Deutsch, trans. Peter T. Hoffer, vol. 2, *1914–1919*, ed. Ernst Falzeder and Eva Brabant, with the collaboration of Patrizia Giampieri-Deutsch, trans. Peter T. Hoffer, vol. 3, *1920–1933*, ed. Ernst Falzeder and Eva Brabant, with the collaboration of Patrizia Giampieri-Deutsch, trans. Peter T. Hoffer (Cambridge, MA: Harvard University Press, 1993–2000)
IJP	*The International Journal of Psycho-Analysis*
JAPA	*Journal of the American Psychoanalytic Association*
SE	Sigmund Freud, *The Standard Edition of the Complete Psychological Works of Sigmund Freud*, translated under the general editorship of James Strachey (London: Hogarth Press, 1953–1974)

Introduction

> The scientific results of psycho-analysis are at present only a by-product of its therapeutic aims, and for that reason it is often just in those cases where treatment fails that most discoveries are made.

Freud made this observation in a footnote to his "Notes upon a Case of Obsessional Neurosis" (1909). He reckoned that analysis, of Ernst Lanzer (a.k.a. the Rat Man), a success—"the patient recovered, and his ordinary life began to assert its claims; there were many tasks before him, which he had already neglected for too long, and which were incompatible with a continuation of the treatment."[1] Other cases, Freud judged to be failures. Did they, as he supposed, promote the piecing together of new knowledge?

Failures—and successes as well—come in all sizes and shapes. So too they may be private or public; they may be considered a purely personal matter or they may become part of a disciplinary enterprise. If private, the individual therapist may gain something—people do learn from their mistakes; psycho-analysis profits not at all. The argument I am putting forward is that failures have been public enough to prompt major advances in psychoanalytic practice. Instead of failure, however, I have taken another cue from Freud and have opted for the word obstacle.

* * *

On December 31, 1900, Dora began her psychoanalytic session by asking Freud if he knew that today would be their last meeting. She thus signaled her intention to break off treatment. Her announcement came as a nasty surprise to her analyst; it came just when his "hopes of a successful termination . . . were at their highest." He consoled himself with the thought that anyone who summoned up "the most evil of those half-tamed demons that inhabit the human breast" and attempted "to wrestle with them" should be prepared for reverses.[2]

In the postscript to his report on Dora's treatment and in an effort to explain its abrupt end, Freud spelled out his understanding of the chief obstacle he had encountered: "transferences"—the "new editions or facsimiles of the impulses and phantasies which are aroused and made conscious during the progress of an analysis" and which "replace some earlier person by the person of the physician." In Dora's case Freud "did not succeed in mastering the transference in good time." Nonetheless he confidently concluded that to be forewarned was to be forearmed: "Transference, which seems ordained to be the greatest obstacle to psycho-analysis, becomes its most powerful ally, if its presence can be detected each time and explained to the patient."[3] Freud himself did not provide a detailed account of such a conversion from obstacle to ally.

Transference(s) proved to be only one among many obstacles psychoanalysts confronted. As I see it, historically as well as clinically, an obstacle had its locus classicus in a particular diagnostic category—though it was later met with across categories. (Freud, for example, initially came face to face with transference in treating hysterical patients; subsequently he found it turning up—albeit less blatantly—in his obsessional cases.) Psychopathology, it occurred to me, might serve as an organizing device. In tracing a series of encounters with different patient populations, I might focus on a particular obstacle presented by a specific category of patient. Beyond that I might focus on how psychoanalysts managed to get round the impediments, if not to convert them into allies, how they managed to resist the constant temptation to shout them down because they were "decidedly inconvenient" and appeared "inaccessible to treatment."[4]

Consequently, my study is arranged topically rather than chronologically. To each of five diagnostic categories—hysteria, obsessional neurosis, depression, paranoia, and narcissism—I have devoted a chapter. With the exception of narcissism, these categories have long pre-psychoanalytic histories. Psychoanalysts simply adopted the prevailing psychiatric nosology—after all most of them were initially trained as psychiatrists—and used it to determine the patients for whom psychoanalysis stood as the treatment of choice. Over time their ambitions grew. Freud demarcated a small number of conditions that he claimed could be alleviated by psychoanalytic means—principally hysteria, phobia (which he considered an anxiety-hysteria), and obsessional neurosis. It was his followers who attempted to push the therapy he had pioneered beyond his prescribed limits.

Who are the protagonists of my study? Freud, of course, figures in the text; in fact he appears at the start of every chapter. Yet he is more progenitor than protagonist. Having assigned that role to him, having chosen my five diagnostic categories—given the history of psychoanalysis, their selection was self-evident—I had no trouble determining the criteria for inclusion: the protagonists should be psychoanalysts who could be considered lineal descendants of Freud and who directly addressed the specific obstacle posed by a particular diagnostic category. Here is the line-up: hysteria—Sándor Ferenczi and Michael Balint; obsessional neurosis—Anna Freud and Ralph

R. Greenson; depression—Melanie Klein and Joan Riviere; paranoia—Wilfred R. Bion and Betty Joseph; narcissism—Heinz Kohut, Otto F. Kernberg, and Herbert A. Rosenfeld. Note that with the exception of the last trio, the members of the previous pairs had strong links with one another. As for Kohut, Kernberg, and Rosenfeld, these three rank as rivals rather than as collaborators.

*   *   *

What obstacles—other than transference—did psychoanalysts come up against as they started to treat a wide variety of patients? What followed from such encounters? It might be helpful for me to give a preview of the developments that lie ahead.

By 1900, by the time Dora's father "handed her over" to Freud for treatment,[5] Freud had already fashioned the distinctively psychoanalytic notion of the unconscious and thus provided a conceptual rationale for transference.[6] So too the unconscious provided a rationale for the interpretation of dreams. And Freud's initial approach to transference amounted to treating it as he treated dreams—as an instance of displacing feeling from one idea to another. His formulation of the Oedipus complex prompted him to think again, to think of transference as something more global, as actualizing *the* crucial childhood conflict. This is where I begin my first chapter—with Freud's botched analysis of Sándor Ferenczi, with his lack of success in analyzing the transference, and with his scant appreciation of a second obstacle: countertransference.

Resistance—a close cousin to dream censorship—comes on stage in the second chapter. "Have you ever seen a foreign newspaper which passed Russian censorship at the frontier?" Freud queried his great friend Wilhelm Fliess. "Words, whole clauses and sentences are blacked out so that the rest becomes unintelligible."[7] Resistance acted similarly: it blocked the verbalized recollection of pathogenic events, and thus the symptoms remained incomprehensible. Neither censorship nor resistance fit comfortably into Freud's topography of Conscious–Preconscious–Unconscious. Within the structural model of ego–id–superego, both found a home; both counted as functions of the ego. In its new location, resistance underwent a sea change: its defensive aspect came to the fore. And here Anna Freud made her signal contribution: she pioneered the analysis of defense.

The negative therapeutic reaction makes its appearance in the third chapter. There were certain patients, Freud wrote in *The Ego and the Id* (1923), who reacted to progress in treatment by immediately getting worse. There was something in them that set "itself against their recovery." This "most powerful of all obstacles," Freud attributed to what might "be called a 'moral' factor, a sense of guilt," which refused "to give up the punishment of suffering."[8] In sum, he attributed it to the superego. Klein took Freud's concept as her point of departure; she transformed his superego into a world of internal objects ("object" is the unfortunate term psychoanalysts use to talk about a person) and offered a rich account of depressive anxiety and/or guilt. As for the negative therapeutic reaction, both she and Riviere, with a measured optimism, continued to plumb its meaning(s).

At the end of Chapter 1, I examine Balint's attempt to grapple with countertransference—and express reservations. At the end of Chapter 2, I present, and implicitly demur from, Greenson's claim that patients who suffered from—using the idiom of American ego psychologists—an impaired "capacity for . . . conflict-free ego functioning" were not amenable to psychoanalytic treatment.[9] Their "ego weakness," understood as deficit or defect, constituted, in his view, an insurmountable obstacle. These two obstacles, countertransference and what Freud referred to as "abnormal changes in the ego,"[10] turn up again in Chapter 4. Klein's discussion of schizoid mechanisms—her notion of the ego splitting itself excessively—began to flesh out those "abnormal changes." Bion and Joseph carried on; they extended Klein's concepts in terms of both theory and technique. In so doing they came to view the analytic work as taking place not only in the transference, but in the countertransference as well.

The lack of capacity for transference, and, along with it, megalomania, Freud considered twin characteristics of those suffering from narcissistic neuroses. He regarded both as insuperable obstacles to psychoanalytic treatment. Kohut, Kernberg, and Rosenfeld disagreed. They rejected Freud's therapeutic pessimism: they spied transference at work and sought to describe it; they also discerned megalomania or grandiosity or omnipotence and offered opposing, indeed incompatible, accounts of what they perceived. It is fitting to end on a clashing note: it brings into the open the competition—in this case among conceptual variants—that is a crucial part of an evolutionary story.

*   *   *

One further issue needs to be addressed: the chapter by chapter division by diagnostic categories. To quote Stephen Jay Gould: "Taxonomy is always a contentious issue because the world does not come to us in neat little packages."[11] In certain academic circles it is now de rigueur to question the messy packages of mental illness. Rather than assume the role of epsitemologist, I would like to play ethnographer and look briefly at how psychoanalysts have used and continue to use classification systems.

Freud himself was not much interested in constructing categories. Hysteria, obsessional neurosis, melancholia, paranoia—the stuff of late nineteenth-century psychiatry, he took for granted. Yet "choice of neurosis" deeply concerned him. From the beginning of his career he had tried to explain why, for example, a patient developed hysteria rather than obsessional neurosis. In advancing his notorious seduction hypothesis, he had linked a traumatic sexual event, and the age at which it occurred, to a specific mental disorder. In retreating from it, in replacing childhood sexual trauma with infantile sexuality, he did not give up on etiology. He redefined his task: he now felt obliged to find a connection between sexual development and particular psychiatric illnesses.

Freud elaborated two distinct developmental lines. It took him until 1923 to work out his subsumption of human sexuality under erotogenic zones—the famous oral, anal, and phallic.[12] He outlined the unfolding of object love more than a decade earlier.[13] People, in his view, arrived late in an infant or child's sexual world—though he did acknowledge that the mother's breast, or its substitute, was there at the start. Between auto-erotism and object love, he interpolated a narcissistic phase—when the subject took his own person or his own body as his love object. Object love itself first appeared with the phallic stage; at one and the same time, the male child found his mother as love object and discovered his genitals as a source of sexual delight.

How did these sequences advance Freud's project—"to explain all neurotic and psychotic phenomena as proceeding from abnormal vicissitudes of the libido, that is, as diversions from its normal employment"?[14] Here Freud introduced a conceptual couple: regression—"a return of the sexual organization as a whole to earlier stages"; fixation—a lagging behind "of a part trend"; and the notion that "the stronger the fixations," the greater the likelihood of regression:

> Consider that, if a people which is in movement has left strong detach-ments behind at the stopping-places on its migration, it is likely that the more advanced parties will be inclined to retreat to these stopping-places if they have been defeated or have come up against a superior enemy. But they will also be in the greater danger of being defeated the more of their number they have left behind on their migration.[15]

A nice rhetorical flourish; yet scarcely an explanation.

The protagonists of my study accepted Freud's developmental perspective; they accepted the linking of specific mental disorders to something gone off track in a gradual progression. They also adhered to the maxim, the sicker the patient, the earlier the fixation. Beyond that—with Kernberg the lone excep-tion—they showed little interest in rethinking Freud's schema. So it lingered on, sounding both arcane and archaic.

All the while, psychoanalysts were becoming skeptical about standard diagnostic categories. Greenson captured the increasingly common attitude:

> There is no doubt that the clinical diagnosis can be of value in determin-ing a patient's suitability for analysis, but unfortunately it often takes a great deal of time to arrive at a definitive diagnosis. Sometimes the presenting psychopathology is merely a superficial screen for malig-nant pathology which is hidden and latent. The presence of hysterical

symptoms does not mean the patient is essentially a hysteric; or, vice versa, bizarre symptomatology may still have the structure of hysteria. Symptoms are not bound to specific diagnostic syndromes as we used to believe. Sometimes one can arrive at a reliable diagnosis only at the end of a long analysis.[16]

Still, the categories turn up in psychoanalytic training—at least in the United States. In what ways do analysts find them minimally helpful?

At this point let me bring in a distinction Ian Hacking makes between indifferent and interactive classifications or kinds. Indifferent kinds are those that are indifferent to their naming: "The classification 'quark' is indifferent in the sense that calling a quark a quark makes no difference to the quark." The notion of an interactive kind, in contrast, suggests "actors, agency and action." The "inter" signals "the way in which the classification and the individual classified ... interact": it matters a great deal to a child, for example, to be classified as hyperactive and attention deficient. Certain psychopathologies, Hacking argues, may be both an indifferent kind and an interactive kind: indifferent, because, like biological kinds, they are unaffected, as kinds, by what one knows about them; interactive, because they "exhibit a looping effect," that is, they "have to be revised because the people classified in a certain way change in response to being classified."[17]

Psychoanalysts, without being aware of these philosophical niceties, have behaved as if they have understood them full well. Freud, for one, had dreamed of discovering the solid organic grounds for his psychology; in waking like he was obliged to admit that he could not fit together the physiological and the psychological. As long as psychoanalysts entertain hopes similar to his—even if their fulfillment threatens to be long delayed—they implicitly view diagnostic categories as indifferent kinds. At the same time, as far as everyday practice is concerned, they treat such categories as interactive kinds. They employ a rough and ready diagnosis to form hunches—and nothing more than hunches—about three matters of concern: possible trouble spots in a patient's childhood; characteristic defenses to deal with the troubles; and the unfolding of the transference. The first two suggest past interactions between a classifier, say, a parent, and the classified, say, a child. The third, which ranks as the most important, hints at an interaction that is just beginning.

And here categories may appear in a different guise: as grist for the analytic mill. A patient of mine came up with a self-diagnosis of "obsessional, paranoid, and narcissistic." What was the meaning of offering that self-description at that very moment? What was going on between us? We were caught up, not in the logic, but in the dynamics of classification.

A final comment—aimed at preventing confusion or false expectations. Although hysteria, obsessional neurosis, depression, paranoia, and narcissism appear in the chapter titles, they are not topics in their own right. They serve simply as points of departure for the real quest: exploring how my protagonists attempted to convert obstacles into allies and how, in the process, they advanced the psychoanalytic enterprise.

*   *   *

In the summer of 1980, just as I was starting analysis, Janet Malcolm's articles, later published as a book with the title *Psychoanalysis: The Impossible Profession*, appeared in *The New Yorker*. I rushed to read them and came away quite unnerved. I did not like "Aaron Green," Malcolm's chief psychoanalyst-informant. He seemed like a wimp: on first meeting Malcolm, she reported with a touch of arrogance, "he subtly deferred to me, he tried to impress me. He was the patient and I was the doctor; he was the student and I was the teacher. . . . [T]he transference valence of the journalist was . . . greater than that of the analyst." He also seemed trapped in his own uncomfortable skin, trapped, as he told Malcolm, by his "selfishness and self-absorption and incapacity for immersion in another person." This piece of self-flagellation was prompted by a discussion of treating or, in Green's case, not treating, very disturbed patients. Here Malcolm discerned yet another—to me—unsettling characteristic: Green's "glum incuriosity about alternatives to classical technique."[18] I was primed to fasten on his negative features; I was primed to worry lest my analyst shared them.

Who, in reading about psychoanalysts at work is not quick to imagine herself a patient? Who is not inclined to make a mental note of which consulting room she would enter and which she would not? Who is not ready to judge which analyst would suit her and which would not?

What, then, of this study's protagonists? They were idiosyncratic enough to make generalizations risky. By and large, however, they were neither saints nor fools. Some may have been reluctant, as Ferenczi put it, "to give up even the most obstinate cases." Some may have joined with him in refusing "to accept verdicts . . . such . . . as . . . a patient's resistance was unconquerable, or that his narcissism prevented our penetrating any further, or the sheer fatalistic acquiescence in the so-called 'drying up' of a case."[19] No one promised a pain-free life. Freud spoke of a patient's neurotic misery being transformed into ordinary unhappiness.[20] Klein wrote of a patient's personality being enriched, by which she meant becoming better able to handle "the whole gamut of love and hatred, anxiety, grief and guilt."[21] And finally, all shared an intense commitment to exploring the mind and its depths.

Chapter 1

Hysteria: Transference

What was the "hysteria" that Freud set out to treat? Its distinctive characteristic was the existence of physical symptoms for which no demonstrable physical cause could be found. In the case of Anna O., the young woman who ranked as the first psychoanalytic patient, the symptoms were legion. Here is a partial listing:

> Left-sided occipital headache; convergent squint . . . markedly increased by excitement; complaints that the wall of the room seemed to be falling over . . .; disturbances of vision . . .; paresis of the muscles of the front of the neck, so that finally the patient could only move her head by pressing it backwards between her raised shoulders and moving her whole back; contracture and anaesthesia of the upper right, and, after a time, of the right lower extremity. . . . Later the same symptom appeared in the left lower extremity and finally in the left arm.[1]

Anna O. was not Freud's patient. Josef Breuer, Freud's mentor and senior by 14 years, was the physician in charge. The essential feature of his treatment, or rather the essential assumption on which it rested, was that the physical symptoms had psychological meaning, that they marked some prior significant happening—or as he and Freud jointly put it: "Hysterics suffer . . . from reminiscences."[2] Over the course of time Freud parted company from Breuer and elaborated an account of his own: the symptoms, he claimed, stood as a compromise between contending psychic forces, and hence their meaning was not immediately comprehensible; and then, he further argued, it was sexual fantasies, not traumatic events, that were being represented. Despite their disagreements, both Breuer and Freud—and Freud's early followers as well—subscribed to the view which Sándor Ferenczi summed up in pithy fashion: "Thinking with the body equals hysteria."[3]

In 1897 Freud wrote his confidant Wilhelm Fliess that he had been "through some kind of neurotic experience, curious states incomprehensible to Cs. [consciousness], twilight thoughts, veiled doubts." In his next letter he reported that "something from the depths of my own neurosis set itself against any advance in . . . understanding." A month later he confided that "the chief patient I am preoccupied with is myself. My little hysteria . . . has resolved itself further."[4] Freud's "little hysteria" seems to have included no "conversion"[5]: in his case psychical excitation was not transformed into somatic symptoms. In contrast Ferenczi complained of multiple physical ailments. He was not certain, as he wrote Freud in 1912, "how much of the *neurotic symptoms* in him" was "*dependent* on the organic substrate," and how much that was "apparently organic" was "psychogenic."[6] Whether or not Freud's and Ferenczi's self-diagnoses would win assent today— after all hysteria has been notoriously protean and elusive—is beside the point. Rather what should be emphasized is that they, the therapists, were personally implicated—and at risk.

In this chapter the treating physicians are Freud, Ferenczi, and Michael Balint. Freud needs no further introduction; Ferenczi and Balint do.

Ferenczi was born in 1873, 17 years after Freud.[7] He was the eighth of 12 children, one of whom died in infancy. His father had migrated from Poland to Hungary and had ardently supported Hungarian independence in 1848. Out of enthusiasm for the liberal cause, he had his German-Yiddish family name of Fraenkel legally changed to the Hungarian Ferenczi. After the defeat of the Hungarian insurrection, he settled in the provincial town of Miskolc, where he opened a bookshop and a publishing establishment. He died when Sándor was 15, and his wife took over running the enterprises— with great success. She later opened a second bookshop in a neighboring town and also served as president of the Union of Jewish Women in the area. Sándor considered himself his father's favorite; as for his mother, he claimed that from her he had received "too much severity . . . and [not] enough love."[8]

Ferenczi left Miskolc after completing his secondary education, and went to Vienna for his medical training. When he returned to Hungary, he settled in Budapest. For 13 years he worked in a number of different venues, in a clinic for prostitutes, in a hospital department of Neurology and Psychiatry, in a service for a cooperative health insurance plan, and finally in private practice as general practitioner and neuropsychiatrist, functioning, in addition, as a consultant psychiatrist for the judiciary. In 1910 he left general medicine to devote himself to psychoanalysis.

Two years earlier, in February 1908, he had met Freud. They were immediately drawn to one another. The following summer Freud invited Ferenczi to join his family during their summer holiday. Ferenczi did so—and for many years he either visited Freud and his family or traveled with Freud during the summer break. When his eldest daughter, Mathilde, married in 1909, Freud replied to Ferenczi's congratulatory telegram by confiding that "I would have liked to have seen you in the place of the young man who . . . has now gone away with my daughter."[9] Later that same year Ferenczi accompanied Freud on his one trip to the United States. There Freud was awarded an honorary degree by Clark University, in return for which he lectured on psychoanalysis.

As he described it: "In the morning, before the time had come for my lecture to begin, we [he and Ferenczi] would walk together in front of the University building and I would ask him to suggest what I should talk about that day. He thereupon gave me a sketch of what, half an hour later, I improvised in my lecture." In subsequent years the two men used their shared vacations for exchanging and elaborating ideas. "A number of papers," Freud commented, "that appeared later in the literature under his or my name took their first shape in our talks." Toward the end of Ferenczi's life—he died of pernicious anemia in 1933—Freud felt that the younger man had "drifted away" from him.[10] Drifted away, perhaps, but he did not desert him.

Nor did he desert the cause. In 1910 Freud prevailed on him to take the lead in establishing the International Psychoanalytic Association. In 1913 Ferenczi founded the Budapest Psychoanalytic Society. This was the year in which, as a response to Freud's break with Carl Gustav Jung, Ferenczi joined together with Ernest Jones, Karl Abraham, Otto Rank, and Hanns Sachs to form a tight, small organization of loyalists, a clandestine "Committee," to rally around Freud as his dependable palace guard. (It lasted into the 1920s.)[11] A year later Freud remarked: "Hungary, so near geographically to Austria, and so far from it scientifically, has produced only one collaborator, S. Ferenczi, but one that . . . outweighs a whole society."[12] (In subsequent years the Budapest society had a most impressive roster of members—including Franz Alexander, Melanie Klein, Sándor Radó, Geza Roheim, René Spitz, along with Michael Balint.)[13] After the First World War, psychoanalysis prospered briefly in Hungary. For a matter of months Ferenczi held the first university chair, anywhere, in psychoanalysis. Then in February 1920 the anti-semitic and anti-psychoanalytic Horthy regime took over. Forced to resign from the Hungarian Medical Society, Ferenczi became increasingly withdrawn, devoting himself to psychoanalytic research.

Given the political situation in Hungary, it is not surprising that Ferenczi should have thought of leaving. Berlin seemed attractive, and many of his co-workers moved to the German capital; the United States seemed even more so. Ferenczi decided to test the waters. In response to an invitation from the New School for Social Research, he spent the academic year 1926–1927 lecturing in New York. There he met a cool reception from members of the New York Psychoanalytic Society, with whom he (and Freud) disagreed about the psychoanalytic training of non-medical candidates. In Washington, DC, where he spoke in April 1927, he was warmly welcomed by Harry Stack Sullivan. At Sullivan's urging, his colleague, Clara Thompson, went to Budapest for treatment with Ferenczi in the summers of 1928 and 1929, and then continuously from 1931 until Ferenczi's death two years later.[14] Freud, for one, was relieved by Ferenczi's coming back to Europe; he had not wanted to lose him to "to the land of the dollar barbarians."[15]

How, then, did Ferenczi's drift away? As Freud saw it: after Ferenczi's return from America, "one single problem . . . monopolized his interest."

The need to cure and to help became paramount in him. He had probably set himself aims which, with our therapeutic means are altogether
out of reach to-day. [S]o long as he had not succeeded . . . , he kept apart,
no longer certain, perhaps, of agreement with his friends. Wherever it
may have been that the road he had started along would have led him, he
could not pursue it to the end.[16]

As Michael Balint saw it:

The tragic disagreement between Freud and Ferenczi, which caused both
of them so much pain, . . . considerably delayed the development of our
analytic technique . . . Ferenczi, because of his own uncertainty, could
not make use of Freud's well-meant and well-founded criticisms; he saw
in them only lack of understanding. Freud, for his part, . . . found in
Ferenczi's experiments nothing but confirmation of his cautiousness.
    The . . . disagreement between Freud and Ferenczi acted as a trauma
on the psychoanalytic world . . . [T]he shock was highly disturbing and
extremely painful. The . . . reaction to it was a frightened withdrawal.[17]

Despite Freud's belief that "the history of . . . [his] science" would never
forget Ferenczi, it came pretty close to doing so.[18] In Balint's view the forget-
ting amounted to repression: the psychoanalytic community adopted the
hysteric's classic defensive measure designed to ward off distressing ideas.
    In Balint Ferenczi found a keeper of the flame.[19] Born in Budapest in 1896,
the elder of two children, Balint came from a middle-class Jewish family
which had been fully assimilated for only a couple of generations—in fact,
his father had learned Hungarian in secondary school as a foreign language.
On reaching adulthood, Michael changed his family name legally from
Bergsmann to Balint; he also converted to the Unitarian faith. If his father
was dismayed by the name change and the conversion, he was pleased with
his son's decision to follow in his professional footsteps and enroll in medical
school. Shortly thereafter Michael was called up for military service in the
First World War. Thanks to a thumb wound, he was able to return to his
studies after a two and a half year hiatus and finish them by war's end.
    Balint first encountered psychoanalysis by way of reading *The Interpret-
ation of Dreams* and *The Psychopathology of Everyday Life*. He was critical
of both. At the age of 21, he changed his mind: "the *Three Contributions* and
Totem and Taboo . . . decisively and definitely conquered" him. *Totem and
Taboo* had been given to him by a "young girl who was studying pure mathematics . . . because there were no facilities for studying anthropology" in
Budapest. Her name was Alice Székely-Kovács, and she was the daughter
of Vilma Kovács, an analysand of Ferenczi and herself a psychoanalyst.
She became Balint's wife, and until her death in 1939, they "read studied,
lived and worked together."[20] Because of the political situation in Budapest,

the young couple moved to Berlin. Michael pursued his PhD in biochemistry and began treating psychosomatic cases at Berlin's Charité Hospital. Simultaneously he worked half-time at the Berlin Psychoanalytic Institute and went into analysis with Hanns Sachs. He was not happy with Sachs, and in 1924 he and Alice decided to return to Budapest and to seek out Ferenczi.

Balint stayed in the Hungarian capital for another 15 years—he and Alice emigrated to England at the beginning of 1939. In the intervening decade and a half, he had two years of analysis with Ferenczi—it was terminated when his analyst went to New York. He himself became an active member of the Budapest psychoanalytic community; he helped establish an outpatient clinic; he served first as deputy-director, then as director of the Budapest Psychoanalytic Institute. All the while the political situation was getting worse and worse:

> [W]e were ordered to notify the police of every one of our meetings with the result that a plain-clothes policeman attended each of them, taking copious notes of everything that was said. We could never find out what these notes contained or who read them. The only result we knew of was that on several occasions the detective, after the meeting, consulted one of us either about himself, his wife, or his children. This was quite amusing for us, but no proper discussions could develop under these circumstances.[21]

In England, after the Second World War, Balint became a member of the British Psycho-Analytical Society; he was elected scientific secretary for 1951–1953 and later president from 1968 until his death in December 1970. Within the British Society, both he and his new wife, Enid—they married in 1953—belonged to the Independent (Middle) Group, and he ranked as one of its training analysts. His psychoanalytic work during those years—both clinical and theoretical—"developed as a remarkably regular line."[22] And from his first papers written in the 1930s to his last last published four decades later, Ferenczi's influence made itself felt.[23]

*   *   *

Early on Freud recognized that transference had interfered with Breuer's treatment of Anna O:

> What really happened with Breuer's patient I was able to guess. . . . On the evening of the day when all her symptoms had been disposed of, he was summoned to the patient again, found her confused and writhing in abdominal cramps. Asked what was wrong with her, she replied: "Now Dr. B.'s child is coming!"[24]

In retrospect he realized that countertransference had also intruded:

It would seem that Breuer had developed ... a strong [attachment] to his interesting patient. At all events he was so engrossed that his wife became ... jealous. She did not display this openly, but became unhappy and morose. It was a long time before Breuer, with his thoughts elsewhere, divined the meaning of her state of mind. It provoked a violent reaction in him compounded of love and guilt, and he decided to bring the treatment to an end. He announced this to Anna O., who was now much better, and bade her good-by. But that evening he was fetched back to find her ... in the throes of an hysterical childbirth. ... Though profoundly shocked, he managed to calm her down by hypnotizing her, and then fled the house in a cold sweat. The next day he and his wife left for Venice to spend a second honeymoon, which resulted in the conception of a daughter.[25]

Se non è vero, è ben trovato. The point of my repeating this story is that Freud grappled, albeit fleetingly, with the first of these two obstacles; Ferenczi began where Freud left off and then felt himself obliged to take on the second obstacle as well. Here he floundered. And here Balint made his principal contribution: thinking about the role and the impact of the analyst in the analytic setting.

Freud, Ferenczi, and Elma

Children's relations to their parents, as we learn alike from direct observations of children and from later analytic examination of adults, are by no means free from elements of accompanying sexual excitation. The child takes both of its parents, and more particularly one of them, as the object of its erotic wishes. In so doing, it usually follows some indication from its parents, whose affection bears the clearest characteristics of a sexual activity, even though of one that is inhibited in its aims. As a rule a father prefers his daughter and a mother her son; the child reacts to this by wishing, if he is a son, to take his father's place, and, if she is a daughter, her mother's. The feelings which are aroused in these relations between parents and children and in the resulting ones between brothers and sisters are not only of a positive or affectionate kind but also of a negative or hostile one. The complex which is thus formed is doomed to early repression; but it continues to exercise a great and lasting influence from the unconscious. It is to be suspected, that together with its extensions, it constitutes the *nuclear complex* of every neurosis.[26]

So said Freud at Clark University in 1909. (Recall that he drafted his lectures with Ferenczi's assistance.) How did Freud fit together hysteria and the complex he named after King Oedipus?[27] The answer falls into two parts, which is in keeping with Freud's claim that the oedipal drama began when two separate currents converged, that is, stages of libidinal development and stages in the unfolding of object love. Hysteria, he wrote, was intimately related "to the final stage of libidinal development," which was "character-ized by the primacy of the genitals."[28] That stage had been reached, but the wishes demanding satisfaction (in a male, for penile activity) were repressed. In their repressed guise, such wishes could obtain satisfaction only in substi-tute forms: it was "quite usual for signs of stimulation, sensations and innervations, and even the processes of erection, which belong properly to the genitals, to be displaced on to other, remote regions of the body—as for instance, by transposition upwards, to the head and face."[29] Why the repres-sion? The hysteric had also reached the stage of object love, and if male, was discovering *both* mother *and* father as love objects and encountering father as castrator. The paternal threat of castration produced repression—and stagnation: the oedipal conflict remained unresolved, and, as a result, the sexuality of hysterical symptoms remained bisexual in nature.

When Freud thought the suffering of his hysterical patients stemmed from reminiscences, he regarded their "transferring . . . distressing ideas . . . on to the figure of the physician" as an obstacle to analysis, "but an external obstacle, and not one inherent in the material."[30] When he concluded that their misery derived from repressed oedipal wishes, he amended his view of transference: he now saw himself as "dealing with a phenomenon" that was "intimately bound up with the nature of the illness itself."[31] And he was in the course of making these revisions when he met Ferenczi, and when, on three separate occasions during the First World War, he took his younger friend and colleague into analysis.

*   *   *

In September 1910 Freud and Ferenczi traveled together once again, this time to Palermo. There an exchange took place which, in subsequent correspond-ence, they analyzed and re-analyzed, and which remained a reference point for both. In a letter dated Christmas 1921, Ferenczi gave an account of it to Georg Groddeck, a self-styled "wild analyst" and director of a sanitorium in Baden-Baden.[32]

> I could never completely be free and open with him; I felt that he expected too much . . . "deferential respect" from me; he was too big for me, there was too much of the father. As a result, on our very first working evening together in Palermo, when he wanted to work with me on the famous paranoia text (Schreber), and started to dictate some-thing, I jumped up in a sudden rebellious outburst, exclaiming that this was not working together, dictating to me. "So this is what you are like?" he said, taken aback. "You obviously want to do *the whole* thing

yourself." That said, he now spent every evening working on his own, I was left out in the cold.[33]

This letter was written more than ten years after the event and addressed to a man from whom Ferenczi was beginning to expect much in the way of support and comfort.

At the time, or rather immediately upon his return from Palermo, Ferenczi sounded anything but rebellious; he was quick to thank Freud for the trouble he had taken as "tour leader" and to express his fervent wish that what had happened in Sicily would not damage their "personal and scientific relations." After Freud answered him in a reassuring fashion, Ferenczi's relief was palpable:

> I was anticipating your letter with no slight tension—I almost write "anxiety." I have already tried to familiarize myself—in fantasy—with *all* eventualities and even prepared myself for the situation in which, with respect to the disappointment I caused you, you would no longer find it worthwhile to be interested in me. . . . My "heroic" plan was to remain loyal to you without consideration for our personal relations, that is to say, for *your* change of heart.

Ferenczi dispensed with the heroism; he did not dispense with the hero worship:

> [D]on't forget that for years I have been occupied with nothing but the products of your intellect, and I have also felt the man behind every sentence of your works and made him my confidant. Whether you want to be or not, you are one of the great master teachers of mankind, and you must allow your readers to approach you, at least intellectually, in a personal relationship as well. . . . I am convinced that I am not the only one who, in important decisions, in self-criticism, etc., always asks and has asked himself the question: How would *Freud* relate to this? Under "Freud" I understood his teachings and his personality, found together in harmonic unity.

Nor did he dispense with analyzing what he had done and not done and imparting to Freud "the confession of a man who exists in psychoanalytic torment."

> What made me inhibited and taciturn—and at the same time somewhat stupid . . . was longing for personal, uninhibited, cheerful companionship with you (and I *can* be cheerful, indeed, boisterously cheerful), and I felt—perhaps unjustifiably—forced back into the infantile role. To be sure, I did, perhaps have an exaggerated idea of companionship between

two men who tell each other the truth *unrelentingly*, sacrificing all consideration. . . . I believed that this, apparently cruel but in the end only useful, clear-as-day openness, which conceals nothing, could be possible in relations between two ψα-minded people who can really understand everything and instead of making value judgments can seek the determinants of their ψ. impulses. . . .

My dream in which I saw you standing naked before me (naturally without feeling the slightest conscious [indeed, also in the dream still unconscious] sexual arousal) was the transparent symbolization of 1) the usc. homosexual tendency and 2) the longing for absolute mutual openness.[34]

In Ferenczi's attachment to him, Freud appreciated the presence of "the strange phenomenon . . . known as 'transference.' "[35] Writing to Carl Gustav Jung, while still in Italy, he indicated as much:

My traveling companion is a dear fellow, but dreamy in a disturbing kind of way, and his attitude towards me is infantile. He never stops admiring me, which I don't like, and is probably sharply critical of me in his unconscious when I'm taking it easy. He has been too passive and receptive, letting everything be done for him like a woman, and I really haven't enough homosexuality in me to accept him as one.[36]

Freud also appreciated that he had not "overcome the countertransference." To Ferenczi's confessional letter, he replied:

It is remarkable how much better you can present yourself in writing than in speech. Of course, I knew very much or most of what you are writing about and now need to give you only a few clarifications pertaining to it. Why didn't I scold you and in so doing open the way to an understanding? Quite right, it was a weakness on my part; I am also not the ψα superman whom you have constructed . . . I couldn't do it, just as I can't do it with my three sons, because I like them and I feel sorry for them in the process.[37]

Freud was not Ferenczi's analyst—or at least not officially, or at least not yet. Emotionally, however, Ferenczi's analysis had begun—and with it Freud's simultaneous recognition of transference and countertransference and reluctance to do more than acknowledge their existence.

*   *   *

In Ferenczi's letter to Groddeck, dated Christmas 1921, he told his new confidant of his suppressed love for his wife's daughter Elma. The younger woman should have been his fiancée, he lamented, and was "in effect" his "bride until a somewhat disparaging remark of Freud's" prompted him "to fight this love tooth and nail—literally to push the girl away."[38]

The bare facts are these. From 1900 on Ferenczi was involved with Gizella Pálos, a married woman (separated but not divorced from her husband) eight years his senior. She was also the mother of two daughters and could not have any more children. In 1911 Ferenczi undertook the analysis of Elma, the older daughter, fell madly in love with her and with a view to becoming her husband instead of her analyst, succeeded in sending her, early the following year, to Vienna for treatment with Freud. The treatment lasted for three months, and at its end she returned to Budapest and to Ferenczi, who eventually opted for an analytic rather than a marital relation. For the next several years Ferenczi found himself torn between his love for Gizella, whom he regarded as capable of being a true companion, and his desire for Elma, who might give him children. In 1919, at long last, the marriage between Ferenczi and Gizella took place—on the very day that Gizella's ex-husband, Géza, dropped dead of a heart attack. As for Elma, she married someone else, but the marriage did not last, and Ferenczi's desire for her periodically resurfaced.[39]

Freud's involvement in the relationship between Ferenczi and Elma began when, in July 1911, Ferenczi informed Freud that he was taking his mistress's daughter into treatment. (Freud had already acted as consultant; the girl had been brought to see him earlier in the year.)[40] Freud sent back his good wishes for this "new enterprise." In December Ferenczi relayed the dramatic turn that had occurred:

> I was not able to maintain the cool detachment of the analyst with regard to Elma, and I laid myself bare, which then led to a kind of closeness which I can no longer put forth as the benevolence of the physician or of the fatherly friend.—I know and share your view of the Janus character of the neurotic, and it is precisely this conviction that toughened my resolve, again and again, to resist temptation. Perhaps in the end my sight was clouded by passion.

To which Freud responded: "[B]reak off treatment, come to Vienna for a few days . . ., don't decide anything yet, and give my regards many times to Frau G."[41] At the New Year Ferenczi, having returned from Vienna with his passion undiminished, conveyed sad tidings: he thought that he and Elma were virtually engaged; Frau G., displaying "incomparable love and kindness," gave her consent; Herr G.—Géza Pálos—proved less accommodating:

> At the last minute, when the already completed plan was presented to Elma's father, he made a few hesitant objections by alluding to Elma's earlier engagement, which had been called off a few years ago. At that, to my amazement, certain doubts crept into *Elma's* mind. That made me

suspicious. I inquired further and learned from her (what I certainly should have learned in her analysis) that *every time* she wishes something especially strongly, she inwardly feels an inability to wish . . . without reservation. *That* always made her so unhappy.

She then sought to soften the impression. . . . But . . . I had to recognize that the issue here should be one not of marriage but of the treatment of an illness. Of course, I myself cannot continue the treatment. After many bitter tears . . . she consented to go to Vienna and enter treatment with you.

Ferenczi refused, as he put it, "to spare" Freud "the effort and trouble" of treating her.[42]

Over the next several months it was Freud's turn to report on an analysis of Elma. And he did so from the outset, rather fully:

I can imagine how anxiously you are awaiting news from me. . . . She [Elma] is quite inhibited, obviously wants to be the good child, to please, to be treated with tenderness; fears loss of love if she admits something. . . . She is one of those children who, very spoiled by the father in the first years, have felt the unavoidable loss of intimacy as neglect. It seems that all her attitudes and desires go back to this factor. . . . Certainly her love for you is based on her attitude toward her father and the competition with her mother.

Two months into the treatment Freud thought that "real progress" had been made:

She is now herself. . . . She no longer plays the part of the good patient at all. . . . I would like to send her home for Easter. . . . When she comes back, I think it makes sense for both of you to resolve anew to consider everything that has happened before to be extinguished.

Within a week, however, his tone changed: matters had "come to a total halt," and his final report sounded the same discouraged note:

With Elma things continue to go gloomily. She has brought out several quite surprisingly intelligent insights, but she doesn't want to get into the experience with you and doesn't want to finish with me; i.e., because of the transference she wishes to extend her stay past Easter, which I don't want to do. . . . I am cooling off noticeably.[43]

So Elma returned to Budapest; but Ferenczi did not heed Freud's advice and consider his marital hopes a thing of the past. Indeed he took Elma back into analysis to pave the way for their realization. And again he sent news to Freud:

> If I were successful in educating her to be ruthlessly honest with me and with respect to herself, I would then have a certain guarantee that she will be reliable in marriage and not the plaything of dark drives, and then something could still come of the matter, provided that she wants it.

Less than four months later he announced:

> [I]t became quite clear to me that she is subjecting herself to analysis against her will, solely because of her hoped-for and impatiently anticipated marriage, and her tendency is to withhold from analysis everything that might impede this plan. I explained that to her, and she admitted everything and pressed for a decision. . . . I made it comprehensible to her that the affective relations between doctor and patient usually fall victim to the analysis, so that the prospects for a marital union between us were minimal, even in the event that the analysis should continue. I told her at the same time that, if she comes to me as a *patient*, I will always gladly be at her disposal.—
>
> I did this with somnambulistic certainty, paying no heed to the painful uproar inside me.

"A sentence from my reading of Voltaire," Freud wrote in reply, "stayed in my memory: 'en cas de doute abstiens-toi.' "[44] He himself refrained from further comment. None was necessary: his preference for the mother was amply apparent.

As for the relationship between Ferenczi and Gizella, Freud inserted himself into it in late 1911, when his friend was "turning away from the mother to the daughter" and "expecting him to recognize this trade" as one that held out "the promise of happiness." (Ferenczi's mentor and mistress had met for the first time earlier that year.) Freud wrote to Gizella directly, giving her his assessment of the unfolding "family romance." She showed this letter to Ferenczi, despite Freud's wishes to the contrary:

> When, years ago, I first learned of the relationship that he [Ferenczi] had lodged himself in, I made a face and made it very clear to him that I wished something else for him. When I then became acquainted with you, I quickly learned to esteem you and was able to concede to him that, in comparison to other husbands and lovers, he possessed incomparably more. . . . Since then, not a word or gesture has issued from me that could have weakened his attachment to you. . . .
>
> [I]f it had been the case that the girl had fallen in love with her mother's youthful friend, pined for him, and suffered in the process until both of the others discovered the secret, it would have been a beautiful novel with a touching conclusion . . . ; but neurosis would not have been allowed to play any role in it . . . [T]he girl should not have been allowed

to show so clearly that she wants to repress her mother just as she did when she was a child, and that she wishes nothing but this.

Six years after his initial communication to Gizella, Freud summed up the situation once again—this time addressing his remarks to Ferenczi:

> You emphasize that the signs of age in Frau G. have scared you away. They are undeniable, but are seen by you from a false perspective. Perhaps you think, since I myself have grown old and have no access to youth, that I am also wishing an old woman on you. No, I wouldn't have asked that of you, but it is not a matter of choosing a wife. She has already been that for fifteen years, became that when she was young and beautiful, has aged with you, and that should not be a motive for casting out one's wife after so many long years. It is now only a matter of transforming an uncomfortable marriage into a contented living together. Incidentally— she is today, with all the deficiencies of her—merely somatic—age, still worth incomparably more than most of the squeaky-clean and glossy women who get married. And finally—you know that yourself.[45]

Recall that in 1911–1912 Freud was not Ferenczi's analyst—at least not yet. Still, his bearing toward his friend can be compared with his stance vis-à-vis Sergei Pankejeff, better known as the Wolf Man, whom Freud had in analysis from 1910 to 1914. At the beginning of treatment, Freud wrote, his patient's "homosexual attitude . . . persisted in him as an unconscious force with . . . very great intensity" and, as a consequence, few of his "psychical trends were concentrated in his heterosexual object-choice." In these circumstances, that is, in light of what Freud regarded as his patient's "inhibited sexual development," he was prepared to sanction Pankejeff's "fight for the object of his masculine desires."[46] With Ferenczi Freud did more than sanction; he influenced the selection of the object as well[47]—and he did so knowing that he might incur his friend's "silent ill will."[48]

*   *   *

In December 1912 Ferenczi revealed his analytic hopes or rather plans to Freud. "I am," he wrote Freud, "a case in need of treatment. . . . It was and is my intention, if you can grant me time (hours), to go into analysis with you— perhaps two weeks (maybe three), for now." He then proceeded to provide Freud with a list of presenting symptoms; they were somatic, and Ferenczi assumed that they were neurotic as well—hence they should be treated by analysis. Here is an example:

> [T]here remains a peculiar symptom complex. . . . I wake up around 4–4:30 in the morning *usually* without anxiety, with a peculiar disturbance in breathing: I notice that my breathing is very shallow, and my breaths

are also very infrequent; my pulse is *very weak* and *slow*; my whole body
is cold (the thermometer recently showed 35.5° C), my belly inflated . . .
[by gas], my nose more or less stuffy (usually only on one side). Then I
can't go to sleep anymore, unless I consume something. This morning,
e.g., I was naturally washed out, depressed, and weak.

Ferenczi also proceeded to demonstrate his analytic aptitude; for Freud's
benefit he analyzed his own dreams, recording the manifest content and dili-
gently associating to them bit by bit. He ended on a note of triumph: "Please
forgive this *gratis analysis*, which I have gotten from you by sheer obstinacy
(if only in writing)!"[49]

Freud could be equally stubborn: "Will you believe or be angry about the
fact that I have read your autoanalytic letter, but I have not studied it as I
should? In so doing I have half frustrated your intention. So, get something
from me by sheer obstinacy!"[50] For the next year and a half Freud did not
budge. Shortly after the outbreak of the First World War, he changed his
mind. Why is unclear, but change it he did. Ferenczi's first stint of analysis,
two sessions a day, began on September 20, 1914; after 15 or 20 days it had to
be interrupted because Ferenczi was called up for military service, an eventu-
ality that had been anticipated. Not until 1916 did he have a chance to resume
what he regarded as unfinished. A second installment took place from June
14 to July 5, and a third between September 25 and October 9.[51] Thereupon
Ferenczi tried once again to coerce Freud into analysis by mail. And once
again he found Freud in a refractory mood. "Your long letter arrived today.
. . . I will say little about it. When I said the treatment was at an end, I did not
mean it was terminated, . . . but rather broken off because of unfavorable
circumstances."[52]

More than five years after his analysis with Freud had come to a halt,
Ferenczi reported to Groddeck:

> Prof. Freud considered my overall physical symptoms for one to two
> hours; he persists in his original view that the crux of the matter is my
> hatred for *him,* because he stopped me (just like her father did. . .) from
> marrying the younger woman (now my stepdaughter). Hence my mur-
> derous intentions towards him which express themselves in nightly scenes
> (drop in body temperature; gasping for breath). These symptoms are,
> furthermore, overdetermined by my memories of watching my parents
> having intercourse. I must admit it did me good to talk for once to this
> dearly loved father about my hate feelings.[53]

Eight years later he wrote to Freud himself:

> Now, in the relationship between you and me, it is (at least in me) a
> matter of the most diverse conflicts of feeling and attitude. First you were

my revered teacher and unattainable model, for whom I harbored the, as you well know, not completely unalloyed feelings of an apprentice. Then you became my analyst, but the unfavorable conditions did not permit carrying out my analysis to completion. I was especially sorry that you did not comprehend and bring to abreaction in the analysis the . . . negative feelings and fantasies. As is well known, no analysand can do that without help, not even I, with my years of experience with others. For that, a very laborious self-analysis was necessary, which I carried out quite methodically afterwards. Naturally, this was also connected to the fact that I exchanged my somewhat boyish attitude for the insight that I should not overestimate my significance for you. Little events on our trips together for their part also allowed a certain inhibition to arise in me, especially the strictness with which you punished my obstinate behavior in the matter of the Schreber book [on paranoia]. I still ask myself, even now: Would not leniency and consideration on the part of the bearer of authority have been more correct? On the other hand, I understand that you wanted to travel with a healthy person and not a neurotic. But do you believe that there are people without character difficulties?[54]

Freud, though reluctant to be "pushed back into the role of analyst," felt obliged to defend his treatment of Ferenczi:

[Y]ou reproach me for having neglected the foreseeable negative reaction in your analysis. Whereby you fail to consider that this analysis goes back fifteen years, and that at the time we were by no means so sure that these reactions should be expected in every case. At least, I wasn't. You yourself [should] consider how long this analysis would have had to last until the inimical impulses in our excellent relationship had succeeded in getting through.

Note the discrepancy between Freud's post-analytic self-justification and his obvious awareness of Ferenczi's mixed feelings during the first decade of their relationship as well as his obvious awareness of the immediate trigger to the hostile component. This discrepancy points once again to a slippage: Freud's recognition of the transference was not matched by a readiness to analyze it.

I will gladly admit to you that my patience with neurotics runs out in analysis, and that in life I am inclined to intolerance toward them. Especially earlier—so, fifteen years ago—I lived in the hope that one could rely on a kind of letting the not directly addressed abnormal reactions be swept along. Certainly, in so doing, I behaved like the less potent man who told his young wife after the first coitus of the wedding night:

So, now you have become acquainted with that; everything else is also only always the same.[55]

Ferenczi's experiments in technique

With Ferenczi, Freud had not managed to turn his transference(s) into an ally. How, in theory, did he imagine such a transformation taking place?

Repetition figured as the key term. Freud contrasted what went on in hypnosis with what went on in psychoanalysis. In hypnotic treatments the patient simply "put himself back into an earlier situation, which he seemed never to confuse with the present one, and gave an account of . . . it."[56] In analysis the patient did not remember the whole of what had been repressed, and what he did not remember might be "precisely the essential part of it":

> He [the patient] is obliged to *repeat* material as a contemporary experience instead of, as the physician would prefer to see, *remembering* it as something belonging to the past. These reproductions, which emerge with such unwished-for exactitude, always have as their subject some portion of infantile sexual life—of the Oedipus complex, that is, and its derivatives; and they are invariably acted on in the sphere of the transference, of the patient's relation to the physician. . . . It has been the physician's endeavour to keep . . . transference . . . within the narrowest limits: to force as much as possible into the channel of memory and to allow as little as possible to emerge as repetition. The ratio between what is remembered and what is reproduced varies from case to case. The physician as a rule cannot spare his patient this phase of the treatment. He must get him to re-experience some portion of his forgotten life, but must see to it . . . that the patient retains some degree of aloofness, which will enable him, in spite of everything, to recognize that what appears to be reality is in fact only a reflection of a forgotten past.[57]

With the aid of repetition in the transference, conflicts became accessible to the patient, both affectively and cognitively, or, as Freud put it, "relics of antiquity"[58] joined the category of the conscious and in so doing became subject to a process of wearing away.

This aid notwithstanding, Freud became increasingly pessimistic about the possibilities of psychoanalytic therapy. It was a pessimism that Ferenczi continually resisted:

> I have had a kind of fanatical belief in the efficacy of depth-psychology, and this has led me to attribute occasional failures not so much to the patient's "incurability" as to our own lack of skill, a supposition which

necessarily led me to try altering the usual technique in severe cases with which it proved unable to cope successfully.[59]

Yet for all his experimentation, until the last year of his life, Ferenczi held on to the framework Freud had established.

*   *   *

In September 1918 Freud delivered an address to the Fifth International Psychoanalytic Congress, meeting in Budapest, the main part of which was devoted to discussing a recent publication by Ferenczi. The question Ferenczi raised was whether psychoanalytic technique could be improved by introducing various forms of "activity." The paper dealt with a case of hysteria, a woman who had twice come to him for treatment, who had twice departed "uncured," and who had now turned up once again and was making no progress:

> In the course of her inexhaustibly repeated love phantasies, which were always concerned with the doctor, she often made the remark, as though by the way, that this gave her feelings "down there." That is, she had erotic genital sensations. But only after all this time did an accidental glance at the manner in which she lay on the sofa convince me that she kept her legs crossed during the whole hour. This led us—not for the first time—to the subject of onanism, an act performed by girls and women ... by pressing their thighs together. As on former occasions, she denied most emphatically ever having carried out such practices.

At this point Ferenczi felt compelled to give up the customary passivity of the psychoanalyst and to interfere energetically "in the patient's psychic activities." He told her to stop crossing her legs. That was not all. He forbade everything, both within and without the analytic session, that he regarded as a "larval form of onanism," including "playful squeezing and handling of the most varied parts of the body" as well as numerous practices the patient employed to eroticize her housewifely and maternal duties.[60] As Freud understood it:

> Cruel though it may sound, we must see to it that the patient's suffering, to a degree that is in some way or other effective, does not come to an end prematurely. ... He [the patient] continually finds new distractions ... into which the energy necessary to carrying out the treatment escapes, and he knows how to keep them secret for a time. It is the analyst's task to deflect these divergent paths and to require him every time to abandon them, however harmless the activity which leads to satisfaction may be in itself.[61]

Writing of another (or was it the same?) hysterical patient, Ferenczi reported ordering her, when she experienced erotic genital sensations, to turn "her attention consciously" to a particular fantasy.[62] The one Ferenczi had in mind—he had not hesitated to attribute and communicate it to her—was of "a (presumably) aggressive sexual act . . . with her father or his surrogate the physician."

> [S]he confessed to me later that she had experienced a phantasy of sexual intercourse, though not an aggressive one, and at the end of it had felt an irresistible impulse to make onanistic movements with the pelvis, where-upon the tension suddenly ceased with the feeling of orgastic ease. This . . . was repeated several times. The analysis showed clearly that the patient entertained the hope unconsciously that the analyst would on hearing the account of these phantasies give effect to them. However, the physician contented himself with making this wish clear to her and searching for the roots in her previous history. From then onwards the phantasy changed: she would then be a man with a conspicuous male member; she made me . . . into a woman. The analyst had then to make clear to her that by so doing she was only repeating the way in which as a child she had reacted to her father's disdain by identification with him (masculine attitude) in order to make herself independent of [his] favour. . . . There were other variations: phantasies of being teased by a man . . . , then phantasies of sexual occurrences with her older brother. . . . finally she had the quite normal feminine onanistic phantasies, full of resigna-tion, which were surely in continuation of the original loving attitude toward the father.

From first to last Ferenczi found himself obliged "to provide the direction in which she ought to force" her fantasies.[63]

The purpose of both prohibition and injunction, singly or in combination, was "to bring the patient to the point of tolerating the phantasies without onanistic discharge, and thereby make conscious the feelings of distress and painful affects related to them (longing, rage, revenge, etc.) without con-verting them into hysterical 'feelings of tension.' "[64] So far, so good. Since, Ferenczi continued, patients were not able to recollect everything that had been repressed, since many tendencies were for the first time intensely developed and actually experienced in the transference situation, and since conviction was acquired only through immediate experience, it followed that the analyst should promote experience. Ferenczi understood and referred to experience as repetition, and in this fashion he came to attribute *the chief rôle in analytic technique to repetition instead of to remembering*[65]—which prompted Freud to complain that it sounded like a "slogan."[66]

By the mid-1920s Ferenczi began to have doubts, not about repetition, but about "activity":

[D]ifficulties arose from my putting forward certain injunctions and prohibitions ... too strongly till I finally became convinced that these expressions themselves ... [constituted] a danger; they induce the physician forcibly to thrust his will upon the patient in an all too true repetition of the parent-child situation.[67]

Ferenczi thought of himself as an empiricist. He was discovering that "activity" frequently misfired. "Ideas," he wrote to Freud, "are always connected with the variations of the treatment of patients and find either rejection or confirmation in them."[68]

*   *   *

In 1928 Ferenczi gave a lecture to his Hungarian colleagues, taking as his title a phrase supplied by a patient: "the elasticity of analytic technique." The analyst, Ferenczi wrote, "like an elastic band, must yield to the patient's pull, but without ceasing to pull in his own direction, so long as one position or the other has not been conclusively demonstrated to be untenable."[69] The following day he sent a report to Freud:

I endeavored (and it didn't cost much effort to do so) to prove that there is essentially no difference between your conception and mine. I know that you occasionally told me that I strive all too much to produce complete identity between your views and mine. But I believe that this time I am in the right.[70]

Over the next half decade "identity" with Freud, whether perfect or imperfect, became increasingly difficult.

Ferenczi began to experiment anew, and in advocating "indulgence" and "relaxation" he elaborated on just how elastic "elasticity" might become— including practices which infringed one or another of Freud's precepts:[71]

For instance, my attempt to adhere to the principle that patients must be in a lying position during the analysis would at times be thwarted by their uncontrollable impulse to get up and walk about the room or speak to me face to face. Or again, difficulties in the real situation, and often the unconscious machinations of the patient, would leave me with no alternative but either to break off the analysis or to depart from the general rule and carry it on without remuneration. I did not hesitate to adopt the latter alternative—not without success. The principle that the patient should be analyzed in his ordinary environment and should carry on his usual occupation, was very often impossible to enforce. In some severe cases I was even obliged to let patients stay in bed for days and weeks and to relieve of the effort of coming to my house. The sudden breaking-off of the analysis at the end of the hour very often had the effect of a shock, and I would be forced to prolong the treatment until the reaction had spent itself; sometimes I had to devote two or more hours a day to a single patient.[72]

Then there was the case of Clara Thompson. Ferenczi initially refused to take her into treatment—he had earlier seen her "behaving quite improperly at a dance." Upon this rebuff, "she went straight to the apartment of a young man and lost her virginity." Why Ferenczi changed his mind and accepted her as a patient is unclear; but it is certain that the analysis proceeded in an unorthodox fashion. Thompson made use of his principle of indulgence: she "allowed herself to take more and more liberties, and occasionally even kissed" her analyst. Ferenczi offered no objection: he treated her kissing him "as something permissible in analysis and at most commented on [it] theoretically." Thompson moreover felt free to brag: she "remarked quite casually in the company of other patients, who were undergoing analysis elsewhere: 'I am allowed to kiss Papa Ferenczi, as often as I like.' "[73]

And so Ferenczi's "detail in technique" came to Freud's attention:

[P]icture to yourself what will be the consequence of making your technique public. There is no revolutionary who is not knocked out of the field by a still more radical one. So-and-so many independent thinkers in technique will say to themselves: Why stop with a kiss? Certainly, one will achieve still more if one adds "pawing," which, after all, doesn't make babies. And then bolder ones will come along who will take the further step of peeping and showing, and soon we will have accepted into the technique of psychoanalysis the whole repertoire of demiviergerie and petting parties, with the result being a great increase in interest in analysis on the part of analysts and those who are being analyzed. The new ally will, however, easily lay too much claim to this interest for himself, the younger of our colleagues will be hard put, in the relational connections that they have made, to stop at the point where they had originally intended, and Godfather Ferenczi, looking at the busy scenery that he has created, will possibly say to himself: Perhaps I should have stopped in my technique . . . *before* the kiss.[74]

The kissing came to an end but not the indulgence and/or relaxation.

Ferenczi continued to experiment—with Thompson and other patients—and produced unexpected results:

[A]fter we had succeeded in a somewhat deeper manner than before in creating an atmosphere of confidence between physician and patient and in securing a fuller freedom of affect, hysterical physical symptoms would suddenly make their appearance, often for the first time in an analysis extending over years. These symptoms included parathesias and spasms, definitely localized, violent emotional movements, like miniature hysterical attacks, . . . slight vertigo and a clouding of consciousness often with subsequent amnesia for what had taken place. . . . In certain cases these hysterical attacks actually assumed the character of *trances*. . . . Without any such intention on my part and without making the least attempt to induce a condition of this sort, unusual states of consciousness manifested themselves, which might also be termed autohypnotic.

Ferenczi considered such states a godsend: the trances enabled him to inquire about dissociated parts of his patients' personalities, while the bodily symptoms themselves served "as physical memory symbols." Until "then the patients had spoken only of possibilities or, at most, of varying degrees of probability and had yearned in vain for memories." Now "the reconstructed past had much more of a feeling of *reality and concreteness* about it than heretofore, approximated much more closely to an actual *recollection*." Until then Ferenczi, too, had yearned in vain for certainty. Now he had "a confirmation from the unconscious" that the "toilsome analytical construction" had "finally succeeded in drawing near to the aetiological reality."[75]

And here Ferenczi parted company with Freud. At the end of August 1932, on his way to the International Psychoanalytic Congress in Wiesbaden, Ferenczi stopped off in Vienna to read Freud the paper he was to deliver, "Confusion of Tongues between Adults and the Child." It was to be Ferenczi's last meeting with Freud, and it was a painful encounter. Freud disapproved of what Ferenczi had to say and demanded that he refrain from publication. He later maintained that the request was made in Ferenczi's interest:

> I didn't want to give up hope that in your continuing work you would still recognize the technical impropriety of your procedure and the limited correctness of your results. You seemed to agree with me, but I naturally relieve you of your promise and, of necessity, forgo any influence, which I don't possess anyway.[76]

The paper appeared in German in 1933; not until 1949 was it published in English.[77] In it, Ferenczi resurrected the claim, long considered discredited, that "trauma, specifically sexual trauma" could not be "stressed enough as a pathogenic agent." "Even children of respected, high-minded puritanical families," Ferenczi insisted, fell "victim to real rape much more frequently than one had dared to suspect."[78] He was convinced, for example, "that . . . as a child, Dm. [Thompson] had been grossly abused sexually by her father, who was out of control."[79] He offered the following description of a typical "incestuous seduction":

> An adult and a child love each other; the child has the playful fantasy that he will assume the role of the mother to the adult. The game may

also take on erotic forms, but always remains on the level of tenderness. This is not true of adults with a pathological disposition, particularly when their equilibrium and their self-control have been upset by some misfortune or by the consumption of intoxicating substances. They confuse the playfulness of the child with the wishes of a sexually mature person or let themselves be carried away to engage in sexual acts without consideration of the consequences. Actual rape of girls barely beyond infancy, similar acts of grown women with boys, even sexual acts of a homosexual character by force are commonplace.[80]

Ferenczi never abandoned his seduction hypothesis—despite the lack of identity between him and Freud.

*   *   *

Ferenczi's *Clinical Diary*, which covered nine months from January to October 1931 and which was published in English only in 1988, is filled with references to the patient R. N.—his code name for Elizabeth Severn. Born in 1879, in a small midwestern American town, she became a self-styled "metaphysician" and staunch believer in the power of positive thinking, dreams, visualization, and telepathic healing. In 1912 she set up a "psycho-therapy" practice in London; in 1914 she transferred her operations to New York, initially renting a Fifth Avenue hotel suite to use as an office. She herself suffered from multiple psychological and physical symptoms, including confusion and hallucination. She consulted numerous doctors, psychiatrists among them, and one psychoanalyst, Otto Rank, who was on a visit to New York. By late summer 1924 they had all given up on her; in a desperate state she traveled to Budapest and sought out Ferenczi.[81]

In his *Clinical Diary* Ferenczi cited R. N. as a case of "schizophrenia progressiva";[82] in *The Basic Fault* Balint described the difficult patients Ferenczi had attempted to treat as suffering from "severe hysteria."[83] There is no contradiction or incompatibility. The new diagnosis of schizophrenia, which had been introduced by Eugen Bleuler in 1911, incorporated "several components of the old hysteria."[84] No wonder that Anna O. and R. N.'s symptoms bore a family resemblance. And R. N. played as crucial a role in Ferenczi's understanding of analytic technique as Anna O. had in Freud's. His experience with R. N. prompted Ferenczi to supplement Freud's theorizing about repetition in the transference by including the analyst as a central player.

R. N.'s analysis lasted a long time, with frequent interruptions as she shuttled back and forth between Budapest and New York. It took years before analyst and analysand felt confident that they had broken through her infantile amnesia and recovered the details of early childhood sexual abuse. Ferenczi described the turning point (reminiscent of Breuer's work with Anna O.) as follows: "the patient conceived the plan, or reported her conviction, that in the course of the summer [1928], on the dates corresponding to her infantile trauma, according to the calendar, she would repeat and remember the whole event." She did so only in part. Here is Ferenczi's summary of what he and she pieced together:

> I. [T]he first shock occurred at the age of one and a half years (a promise by an adult, a close relative [her father?] to give her "something good," instead of which, drugged and sexually abused). . . .
>
> II. At the age of five, renewed, brutal attack; genitals artificially dilated, insistent suggestion to be compliant with men; stimulating intoxicants administered. . . .
>
> III. The last great shock struck this person . . . at the age of eleven and a half. . . . [A] form of adaptation to the unbearable situation had set in over the years. Being hypnotized and sexually abused became a style of life. . . . But there is also the unconscious awareness that behind the tortures of the adult are concealed loving—though distorted— intentions. . . . The combination of all these factors and others as yet incompletely explored may, therefore, have established a state—albeit a very precarious one of equilibrium.
>
> In this situation, sudden desertion by the tormentor strikes like a bolt of lightening. . . . The situation was made worse by the fact that the father, before the separation, as a kind of farewell, had cursed the child, and thus had used his influence . . . to make the child indelibly aware of her own filthiness, uselessness, and contemptibility.[85]

That was not all. In Ferenczi's view the pathogenic experience had a biphasic structure—the trauma first, lack of compassion second: "the most frightful of frights" was "when the threat from the father" was "coupled with simultaneous desertion by the mother." As therapist Ferenczi did not think he could undo the trauma; he hoped instead to provide the charitable attitude that had been absent:

> According to the . . . suffering people, a quantity and quality of love of an extraordinary kind, the most complete and perfect genital–moral– intellectual happiness, could revive . . . dead fragments of the psyche; that is, . . . physical and mental components of the personality could be regenerated to full functional capacity, no matter how badly they had been shattered. But such happiness is not to be had in reality (in the case of infantile rape, for example, marriage to the greatest man in the world, both physically and mentally, might still be too weak an antidote to be effective against the degradation and the narrowing—the mutilation—of the personality caused by the trauma). . . . It is my hope that with tremendous patience and self-sacrifice on my part, after hundreds of instances of enormous forbearance, sympathy, the renunciation of every authoritarian impulse, . . . it will be possible to make the patient

renounce that colossal wish-fulfillment and make do with what offers itself.[86]

With R. N., Ferenczi made heroic efforts:

[R]ight from the beginning the patient had claimed to be more important than the other patients, something that had not especially endeared her to me. When the case did not show any progress, I redoubled my efforts; . . . gradually I gave in to more and more of the patient's wishes, doubled the number of sessions, going to her house instead of forcing her to come to me; I took her with me on my vacation trips and provided sessions even on Sundays.

Ferenczi continued in this vein for more than two years:

The most trying of the demands on me arose from the fact that toward the end of the sessions the patient would have an attack, which would oblige me to sit by her for another hour or so, until the attack subsided. My conscience as a doctor and a human being prevented me from leaving her alone and in this helpless condition. But the overexertion appears to have provoked immense strain in me, which at times had rendered the patient hateful to me. It came to a kind of crisis.

And an about-face:

The . . . crisis forced me, against my sense of duty and probably my sense of guilt as well, to limit my medical superperformances. After a hard inner struggle I left the patient by herself during vacations, reduced the number of sessions, etc. . . . I maintained firmly that she ought to hate me, because of my wickedness toward her; she resolutely denied this, yet these denials at times were so ferocious that they always betrayed feelings of hatred. For her part she maintained that she sensed feelings of hate in me, and began saying that her analysis would never make any progress unless I allowed her to analyze those hidden feelings.[87]

How did Ferenczi and R. N. conduct the "mutual analysis" that he agreed to after roughly a year of resisting her request?

[T]here was a long struggle over priority: who should begin. Each offered to let the other go first. . . . Above all, I wanted to work over the old material and the impressions of the previous day, and feared that what I was about to communicate would provoke new material, and new emotions, before the old material had been worked through. . . . Taking into consideration the analysand's objection that she would be incapable of dealing with me objectively after the end of [her own] analytical session, . . . [her] wish had to prevail . . . , and now every double session begins with the analysis of the analyst. . . .

The first consequence of this decision was the flaring up of my hemicrania [migraine] on the left side. Persistent depression then led to the following modification of the scheme: the analysis of the analysand must not be interrupted, if only so that the tensions of the patient do not accumulate. The best thing would be, therefore, if on a day of analysis only one or the other is analyzed. . . . [T]he analysis would alternate from day to day.[88]

Once on the couch Ferenczi, to his "enormous surprise," conceded that R. N. had been "right in many respects":

I had retained from my childhood a specific anxiety with regard to strong female figures of her kind. I found and continue to find "sympathetic" those women who idolize me, who submit to my ideas and my peculiarities; women of her type, on the other hand, fill me with terror, and provoke in me the obstinacy and hatred of my childhood years. The emotional superperformance, particularly the exaggerated friendliness, is identical with the feelings of the same kind I had for my mother. When my mother asserted that I was bad, it used to make me, in those days, even worse. She wounded me by claiming that I was killing her; that was the turning point at which, against my own inner conviction, I forced myself to be good and obedient.

The patient's demands to be loved corresponded to analogous demands on me by my mother. In actual fact and inwardly, therefore, I did hate the patient, in spite of all the friendliness I displayed.[89]

After he had vented his antipathy, R. N. felt vindicated; after he "had openly admitted the limitations" of his capacities, "she began to reduce her demands." As a further consequence of "this manifest 'circulus benignus,' " he wrote:

I really find her less disagreeable now; I am even capable of transferring friendly and joking feelings onto her. My interest in the details of the analytical material and my ability to deal with them—which previously seemed paralyzed—improved significantly. I must even confess that I am beginning to be aware of the beneficial influence of this liberation from anxiety in relation to other patients as well, and thus I am becoming, not only for this patient but also for the others, altogether a better analyst. (Less sleepiness during sessions, more human interest in all of them; sincerely sensitive intervention in the analytic process when necessary.)[90]

"Now the question: must every case be mutual?" Ferenczi answered his query indirectly and in the negative. Scattered throughout his *Diary* is ample evidence that he appreciated the impracticality of replicating his daring experiment. (He actually engaged in several such treatments; R. N.'s he reported in the greatest detail.) When he came to assessing mutual analysis as a means for transforming the analyst's obstructive countertransference, he simply listed it as a "last resort! Proper analysis by a stranger," he added, "would be better."[91]

*   *   *

Severn's analysis did not terminate, rather it ended. Ferenczi's last diary entry about her, dated October 2, 1932, suggested that they were still *in medias res*.[92] By then Ferenczi was suffering from pernicious anemia and finding it necessary to conserve his strength.[93] Ferenczci's own analysis had also merely ended. As he saw it:

My . . . analysis could not be pursued deeply enough because my analyst . . ., with his strong determination to be healthy and his antipathy toward any weaknesses or abnormalities, could not follow me down into . . . [the] depths, and introduced the "educational" style too soon.[94]

Here Ferenczi was pointing to Freud's (unanalyzed) countertransference as an obstacle.

Years earlier Freud had remarked: "I have . . . good reason for asserting that everyone possesses in his . . . unconscious an instrument with which he can interpret the utterances of the unconscious in other people."[95] Freud was thinking of the analyst not the patient, of the analyst as interpreter of the patient's unconscious. Ferenczi turned this around—after all he had been an analysand, Freud had not:

Gradually I came to the conviction that patients have an extremely refined feeling for the wishes, tendencies, moods, likes and dislikes of the analyst, even should these feelings remain totally unconscious to the analyst himself. Instead of contradicting the analyst, instead of accusing him of certain misdemeanors or blunders, patients *identify with him*; only in certain exceptional moments of a hysteriod excitement, that is, when they are in a condition of near-unconsciousness, can they bring themselves to protest. Generally they permit themselves no criticism of us; such criticism does not even occur to them unless we expressly give them permission to do so, in fact directly encourage them to make such criticisms. Therefore we must, from the associations of patients, discern . . . not only . . . unpleasant things from their past; we must also, more than we have done until now, look for the . . . repressed or suppressed criticism of us.[96]

In this fashion the analyst would remain alert to the implicit supervision being offered by the patient. In this fashion the analyst's countertransference might cease to be a hindrance—even if it had not yet been transformed into an ally.

Balint: Regressions, malignant and benign

"The problem of hysteria," Balint wrote in 1938, "has been more and more neglected."[97] He regretted this neglect. Analytic technique, after all, had been invented and had been "mainly developed when working with pathological forms" that had "strongly cathected object-relations." And with hysteria, everything happened with an "eye on the objects." Take the case of Anna O.: "the many changes of her object-relations to Breuer . . . in turn compelled . . . [him] to ever new adaptations, i.e. changes in his technique." No wonder, then, that "the *psycho-analytical* situation, a situation where relations to one object—admittedly a very peculiar object"—were of "overwhelming importance," became "the true field of study."[98]

By the time Balint was worrying about the disappearance of hysteria from psychoanalytic literature—note that he was not worrying about the disappearance of hysterics from analysts' consulting rooms—hysteria as a category of mental illness was in the course of changing. The emphasis no longer fell on symptoms: they were "more and more. . . found to be products of a neurotic personality rather than pathological appendages to a 'normal' personality, requiring only amputation."[99] Freud had paved the way. In writing of Dora he claimed that hers was merely a case of " *'petite hysterie'* with the commonest of . . . somatic . . . symptoms"; but he also claimed that by the age of fourteen, that is, four years before he took her into treatment, she "was already entirely and completely hysterical." He would consider "a person hysterical in whom an occasion for sexual excitement elicited feelings that were preponderantly or exclusively unpleasurable"; and he would do so "whether or not the person were capable of producing somatic symptoms."[100]

Balint concerned himself with neither symptoms nor personality. Instead he focused on his patients' object relations. In a paper published almost four decades after Ferenczi's "Confusion of Tongues," he summed up his thinking about trauma, arguing that it had a triphasic structure. To the two phases Ferenczi had postulated—trauma and lack of compassion—Balint added another, a prologue to the trauma itself, which he reckoned the first phase: "In . . . [this] phase the immature child is dependent on the adult and, although frustrations in their relationship may occur which may lead to irritation and even to rage at times, the relationship between the child and the adult is mainly trusting."[101] Balint intended to elaborate on this loving and trusting relationship.

With what evidence? Initially, drawing on Ferenczi's phylogenetic fantasy *Thalassa* (1924), Balint accepted his mentor's notion of "passive object love" to characterize the primitive relationship between child and adult (now identified as mother). He grew dissatisfied with "passive"—on this point he extrapolated from analytic work with adult patients—and substituted "primary," writing of "primary object-love" or "primary object relationship." Again he grew dissatisfied—again he extrapolated from clinical experience— and postulated a phase prior to the emergence of primary objects. He called this "the phase of the undifferentiated environment, the phase of the primary substances, or—a somewhat clumsy phrase—the phase of the harmonious interpenetrating mix-up."

> [T]he best illustration of this state is the relationship we have towards the air surrounding us. It is difficult to say whether the air in our lungs or in our guts is us, or not us; and it does not even matter. We inhale the air, take out of it what we need, and after putting into it what we do not want to have, we exhale it, and we do not care at all whether the air likes it or not. It has to be there for us in adequate quantity and quality; and as long as it is there, the relationship between us and it cannot be observed, or only with very great difficulty; if, however, anything interferes with our supply of air, impressive and noisy symptoms develop in the same way as with the dissatisfied infant.[102]

Balint was in the course of taking two steps that distanced him from Freud and aligned him with Ferenczi. The first, already implicit in his notion of primary objects relationships, amounted to insisting that object relations existed from birth onwards. The second amounted to depriving infantile sexuality of its preeminent position. Neither Ferenczi nor Balint was ready to deny that sexual desire also had a history dating from birth; both were eager, however, to affirm that all was not sexuality that might look like it. As Ferenczi put it:

> The fact that infantile sexuality exists obviously remains undisputed, yet much of what appears as passionate in infantile sexuality may be a secondary consequence of the passionate behavior of adults, forcibly imposed on children against their will and, so to speak, artificially implanted in them. Even overpassionate manifestations of nongenital tenderness, such as passionate kissing, ardent embraces, affect the child in fact unpleasurably. Children want no more than to be treated in a friendly, tender, and gentle way. Their own movements and physical expressions are tender; if it is otherwise, then something has already gone wrong. One has to ask oneself how much of what is involved in the undying love of the child for its mother, and how much of the boy's murderous desire against the rival father, would develop in a purely spontaneous way, without the premature implantations of passionate adult eroticism and genitality.[103]

Balint provided a theoretical gloss:

> [U]ntil now we have regarded the development of the genital functions
> and the development of object-relations as two aspects of the same pro-
> cess. . . . It was tacitly assumed that the sequence of these phases is
> determined biologically, taking place, as it were, spontaneously, without
> being influenced in any way by the environment. Now I believe that these
> two developments—though frequently intertwined—are nevertheless two
> different processes; further, that the different object-relations do not suc-
> ceed one another according to biological conditions, but are to be con-
> ceived as reactions to actual influence of the world of objects—above all,
> to methods of upbringing.[104]

What should one make of Balint's speculations? One could subject them
to the kind of criticism that he leveled against Freud's concept of primary
narcissism, viz., that it stood as an example of a tendency common in psychoanalytic theorizing: to antedate, "to refer to still earlier phases of development, so early as to be beyond the reach of any clinical observation."[105]
What needs to be stressed here is how, taken together, Balint's two steps
helped him to rethink and to justify his rethinking of the analyst's role.

*   *   *

> For some years now we have organized research seminars . . . to study the
> psychological implications of general medical practice. In one of these
> seminars the first topic discussed was the drugs usually prescribed by
> the practitioners. In a very short time the discussion revealed—certainly
> not for the first time in the history of medicine—that by far the most
> frequently used drug in general practice was *the doctor himself*. It was
> not only the medicine in the bottle or the pills in the box that mattered,
> but the way the doctor gave them to his patient—in fact the whole
> atmosphere in which the drug was given and taken.[106]

In this fashion Balint addressed a wide variety of medical practitioners. His
remarks were bound to startle the psychoanalysts in his audience, to remind
them forcibly of their discipline's history. Freud, borrowing from the hypno-
tists in the 1890s, appreciated full well what it meant to make use of the
doctor-as-drug. Two decades later, having devised a psychoanalytic technique, he took care to distinguish his "scientific activity" from the "magic,
incantation and hocus-pocus" of the hypnotist.[107] The questions suggestion
raised about the scientific status of psychoanalysis was one issue; about its
efficacy was another. Both combined to prompt psychoanalysts to downplay
or ignore the issue of the analyst's participation. Balint's emphasis on object
relations and, along with it, his insistence on viewing the analytic situation as
a two-person drama, led him to confront that issue directly.

Psychoanalysts were not oblivious; they were simply silent. There were "many . . . personal elements," Balint wrote, "which, though often discussed by analysts in private circles and even with a very keen interest, have scarcely if ever been mentioned publicly." A typical detail of this kind was "the problem of the cushion."

> There are several solutions to this problem: (a) the cushion remains the same for every patient, but a piece of tissue paper is spread over it, which is thrown away at the end of the hour; (b) the cushion remains, but every patient is given a special cover, distinguishable from the others by its shade or design, and for each hour the cushion is put into the appropriate cover; (c) each patient has his own cushion and must use only his; (d) there is only one cushion or only two or three of them for all the patients and it is left to them to use them as they like. . . . Then there is the couch itself, which may be low, broad, comfortable, or quite the contrary; the chair of the analyst; the arrangement of the consulting-room—shall it be furnished as study or as a drawing room? or shall it be left totally unfurnished apart from the couch and the chair?

Another item was how the analyst announced the end of the session.

> Some analysts get up from their chairs, thus giving the signal. Others simply announce it in stereotyped words; others again try to invent new formulas for each session; some begin to move to and fro in their chairs and the patient has to infer from the sound that the time is over; others again use alarm clocks, or keep a clock in front of the patient so that he may himself see the time passing.[108]

And then there was the matter of the way the analyst handled a silent patient:

> [The] analyst might adopt the very early technique used by Freud in the *Studies on Hysteria*, i.e. urging and pressing the patient, demanding that . . . he . . . say what has come into his mind. Freud even used to put his hand on the patient's forehead, and in the early case-histories phrases frequently occur such as "under the pressure of my hand" or "in concentration," etc., the patient was able to speak. Nowadays . . . this method is seldom used, and, if at all, only in the case of minor obstacles. . . .
> There is another approach. . . . I propose to call it "*creating a proper atmosphere*" *for* the patient *by* the analyst, in order that the patient may be able to open up. If it is thought that this is too much to ask, I shall put it in a negative form: *avoiding* the creation of an atmosphere that shuts the patient up. Putting it in this way, it is obvious that silence is not due to the patient's transference, or to the analyst's counter-transference,

but to an interplay of transference *and* counter-transference, i.e. to an object-relation.[109]

From first to last, Balint argued, technique bore a personal stamp.

What, then, could be done to ensure the analyst's objectivity? How, on this question, did Balint differ from Freud? Initially Freud exhorted the therapist to practice self-analysis and more self-analysis.[110] It was not too long before he revised his recommendation. In 1912 he insisted that "everyone" who wished "to carry out analyses on other people" should himself undergo what soon became known as a training analysis.[111] And that he regarded as no easy task.[112] In 1937 he sounded an even more somber note: analysis, he maintained, did not offer a lifetime guarantee. The only recourse was for the analyst "to submit . . . periodically . . . to analysis once more, without feeling ashamed of taking this step."[113] An interminable analysis stood as Freud's final piece of advice. Balint sounded a similar note:

> [T]he analyst must be required to make himself conscious of every emotional gratification brought about by his individual technique. . . . Every advance in psycho-analysis has had to be paid for by an ever-increasing conscious control over the investigator's emotional life. We believe that our technique can be still further improved, if we are able to bear still further conscious control over our everyday analytical behaviour.[114]

Still there was a difference in emphasis. Where Freud was impressed, if not discouraged, by the analyst's difficulty in preserving "neutrality towards the patient,"[115] Balint was prepared to make a virtue of necessity. If analysts could not keep their countertransference completely in check, if the most that could be expected was for them to understand their countertransference and its impact on the patient, then they had license to heed Ferenczi's advice to be "elastic." They had room to experiment.

*   *   *

> At our research seminars on general medical practice doctors often used to report that they had explained to a patient very clearly what certain implications of an illness were; then, when the actual results of the explanation were compared with those intended, surprisingly often it emerged that the explanation was clear only to the doctor; to the patient it was not clear, often it constituted no explanation at all. . . . [N]ow, whenever a doctor reports that he explained something very clearly, the habitual question follows: "clearly, but to whom?" The reason for this discrepancy between the intention and the result is that the same words have a totally different meaning for the sympathetic but uninvolved doctor and his deeply involved patient.[116]

Psychoanalysts, Balint wrote, made similar observations. They might give a patient an interpretation that was "clear, concise, well-founded, well-timed, and to the point"; frequently to their "dismay, irritation, and disappointment," it had an effect quite different from what they had expected. How to account for this frustrating result? Analysts were assuming that the patient "was capable of taking the interpretation in, experiencing it as an interpretation, and allowing it to influence his mind. With the class of 'deeply disturbed' patients," this might not be the case—and it was these patients that Balint wanted to reach.[117]

So too had Ferenczi; and Balint's reflections on patients' differing responses to adult language, which he conceptualized in terms of two levels of analytic and therapeutic processes, constituted an effort to continue his mentor's "pioneer work." For the more adult level in which adult language was an "adequate and reliable means of communication," Balint opted for the name oedipal. For the more "primitive" level in which adult language was often "useless or misleading in describing events," he proposed "the level of the *basic fault*": "basic," because what happened at that level "belonged exclusively to a two-person relationship"; "fault," because this was "exactly the word used by many patients."

> The patient says that he feels there is a fault within him, a fault that must be put right. And it is felt to be a fault, not a complex, not a conflict, not a situation. . . . [T]here is a feeling that the cause of this fault is that someone has either failed the patient or defaulted on him; and . . . a great anxiety invariably surrounds this area, usually expressed as a desperate demand that this time the analyst should not—in fact—must not fail him.[118]

Regression to the level of the basic fault came in two varieties: malignant and benign. Freud, Balint argued, had encountered only the former. As evidence he cited the story of Breuer's Anna O., as well as a brief mention of "gross sexual" acting out by one of Freud's patients—she threw her arms around his neck as she awoke from a hypnotic trance.[119] The demand for sexual gratification, of "suspiciously high intensity," was, in Balint's view, the distinguishing feature of a malignant regression. The "gratification expected . . . by the patient" was "never auto-erotic"; it had to "come from the environment"; it had to be "initiated by an event in the external world," an event in which the analyst, whether "by passive consent or active participation," was "willy-nilly deeply involved." And should the patient's requests be met, a "vicious spiral" would develop: as soon as some of the patient's "cravings" were satisfied, new ones would appear, "leading eventually to a development of addiction-like states." As for Ferenczi, Balint claimed that he had encountered both types. His mentor had "some remarkable successes . . . [and] was so impressed that his well-known enthusiasm carried him away." He was slow to appreciate that the "unquestionable improvement of some of his patients would last only as long as he was able" to fulfill their demands. This realization did, however, dawn on him in early 1933, when because of increasing physical weakness, he had to give up his analytic practice. "A number of his patients reacted to this with confused despair or bitter resentment and a deterioration in their state."[120]

Not every regression, Balint insisted, brought "unending suffering or unending vituperation, or both together." With the benign type the accent fell not on gratification by an external object, but on recognition by the analyst of "the patient's internal life . . . and unique individuality." To illustrate this type Balint cited the following case:

> The patient, who at the time had been under analysis for about two years, remained silent, right from the start of the session for more than thirty minutes; the analyst accepted it and, realizing what was possibly happening, waited without any attempt whatever at interfering, in fact, he did not even feel uncomfortable or under pressure to do something. I should add that in this treatment silences had occurred previously on several occasions, and patient and analyst had thus had some training in tolerating them. The silence was eventually broken by the patient starting to sob, relieved, and soon after he was able to speak. He told his analyst that at long last he was able to reach himself; ever since childhood he had never been left alone, there had always been someone telling him what to do. Some sessions later he reported that during the silence he had all sorts of associations but rejected each of them as irrelevant, as nothing but an annoying superficial nuisance.

Here Balint's conjectures about primary relationships were put to use:

> The . . . [benign] type [of regression] . . . presupposes an environment that accepts and consents to sustain and carry the patient like [sic] the earth or the water sustains and carries a man who entrusts his weight to them. In contrast to ordinary objects, especially to ordinary human objects, no action is expected from these primary objects or substances; yet they must be there and must—tacitly or explicitly—consent to be used, otherwise the patient cannot achieve any change: without water it is impossible to swim, without earth impossible to move on. The substance, the analyst, must not resist, must consent, must not give rise to too much friction, must accept and carry the patient for a while, must prove more or less indestructible, must not insist on maintaining harsh boundaries, but must allow the development of a kind of mix-up between the patient and himself.[121]

Above all, the analyst in this phase of the work should be "unobtrusive." A key negative injunction followed: the analyst should avoid becoming or even appearing to be omnipotent in the eyes of the patient—and by extension, suggesting or even appearing to suggest that he will "compensate for the patient's early privations and give more care, love, affection than the patient's parents" had "given originally (and even if he tried, he would almost certainly fail)." On the positive side, Balint enjoined the analyst to gauge his patient's needs, to know why they were as they were, and why they fluctuated and changed; he must be felt to be present and at the right distance—"neither so far that the patient might feel lost or abandoned, nor so close that the patient might feel encumbered and unfree." Along the same lines, "the analyst must sincerely accept all complaints, recriminations," and grievances "as real and valid," allowing "his patient a sufficiently long, in some cases very long, period of violent aggressiveness" and resentment.

> Provided the analyst is able to fulfill most of the requirements . . . , a new relationship may develop which will enable the patient to experience a kind of regret or mourning about the original defect or loss which led to the establishment of the fault or scar in his mental structure. . . . The regret or mourning I have in mind is about the unalterable fact of a defect or fault in oneself which, in fact, has cast its shadow over one's whole life, and the unfortunate effects of which can never fully be made good. Though the fault may heal off, its scar will remain for ever; that is, some of its effects will always be demonstrable.[122]

Early in his career Balint wrote of a "new beginning." Over the following decades he held on to the term but changed its meaning—from a patient's newly acquired ability to express "long-forgotten, infantile, instinctual wishes"[123] to a patient's discovering "new forms of object relationship," experiencing them, and experimenting with them.[124] His final statement sounded like a slogan, "regression for the sake of progression": regression because the patient went "back to something 'primitive,' to a point before the faulty development started"; progression because at the same time the patient found a "new, better-suited" way of being in the world.[125]

*   *   *

To review: Freud was intent on mastering transference, on bending it to therapeutic purposes. For him repetition figured as the key to such a transformation: thanks to repetition in the transference, to the patient's repeating repressed material as a contemporary drama in which the analyst was assigned a role, the "relics of antiquity," as he put it, could become conscious and more manageable.[126] For Ferenczi, his efforts to promote repetition in the transference were aimed at making certain that it was accompanied by the "throb of experience."[127] That throb ranked as crucial to getting the patient to accept the reality of what had been repressed. "Experience" might get out of hand; it might overwhelm the patient. Ferenczi knew this full well. He was not on that account, however, prepared to abandon his experiments in technique. Instead he held himself responsible: something in him was acting as a hindrance in the treatment. In his mind countertransference stood as a second great obstacle. And in my view, his struggles to grapple with it, flawed though they were, show an increasingly refined and nuanced understanding of the psychoanalytic situation.

What about Balint's contribution? Transference, repetition, acting out, regression—all these concepts appeared in his work; he saw them as overlapping and frequently spoke of a "regressed transference." Could his benign regression, then, be considered the functional equivalent of Freud's transference neurosis—an artificial neurosis built around the relationship with the analyst? Perhaps. It would be a stretch. Could Balint's unobtrusive analyst be regarded as the functional equivalent of Freud's neutral analyst? I think not. Balint's notion opened up the prospect of the patient enjoying a new psychological experience, in the present, with the analyst. The experience itself promised to be therapeutic; it promised to be a new beginning. Was it promising too much?

> If this process [the new beginning] can develop in an undisturbed way a surprisingly uniform experience dominates the very last period of the treatment. The patient feels that he is going through a kind of re-birth ..., that he has arrived at the end of a dark tunnel, that he sees light again after a long journey, that he has been given a new life, he experiences a sense of great freedom as if a heavy burden had dropped from him. ... It is a deeply moving experience; the general atmosphere is of taking leave for ever of something very dear, very precious—with all the corresponding grief and mourning—but this sincere and deeply felt grief is mitigated by the feeling of security, originating from the newly won possibilities for real happiness. Usually the patient leaves after the last session happy but with tears in his eyes—I think I may admit—the analyst is in a very similar mood.[128]

Chapter 2

Obsessional neurosis: Resistance

"Persons suffering from a severe degree of obsessional neurosis," Freud commented in his "Notes upon a Case of Obsessional Neurosis," "dissimulate their condition in daily life . . . as long as they possibly can." They "often call in a physician only when their complaint has reached such an advanced stage, as had they been suffering, for instance, from tuberculosis of the lungs, would have led to their being refused admission to a sanatorium." What did the condition look like? Take the Rat Man, the subject of Freud's case history and a "moderately severe" obsessional neurotic. Ernst Lanzer, 29 years old and university trained, began treatment with Freud in October 1907 afflicted with myriad obsessional ideas. He mentioned, as an example, a compulsion to cut his throat with a straight razor. Just when "he was in the middle of a very hard piece of work the idea had occurred to him: 'If you received a command to take your examination this term at the first possible opportunity, you might manage to obey it. But if you were commanded to cut your throat . . . , what then?' He had at once become aware that this command had already been given, and was hurrying to the cupboard to fetch his razor."[1] Years of his life, he complained on meeting Freud, had been wasted fighting against such compulsions, commands, and prohibitions. Freud spent the better part of the next year trying to fathom these psychical structures, to distinguish among them, and to undo the distortions which they had undergone.

What stood out in Ernst's fragmented narrative was a conflict between love for his father and love for his "lady." Freud considered this conflict a "simplification." What stood out in his case history was the "*chronic* co-existence of love and hatred, both directed towards the same person and both of the highest degree of intensity"; his patient was "unmistakably victim to a conflict between love and hatred . . . in regard . . . to his lady and to his father" alike.[2] To account for this "ambivalence," a term Freud picked up from the Swiss psychiatrist Eugen Bleuler,[3] he postulated a developmental stage in which the object is external "to the subject's own self, but in which *the primacy of the genital zones has not yet been established. . . .* [T]he component instincts which dominate this *pregenital organization* of the sexual life are the anal-erotic and sadistic ones." It was in the anal-sadistic stage—whether never "completely surmounted" or "re-activated by regression"—that Freud located the disposition to obsessional neurosis.[4]

Early in his career hysterics had loomed large in Freud's practice. In mid-career obsessional neurotics came to rank as his most important analysands, and among his most discouraging. As far as "severe cases of obsessive acts" were concerned, he noted in 1919, their analyses were "in danger of bringing to light a great deal but changing nothing."[5] Others were soon to find themselves similarly taxed.

The others I have in mind are Anna Freud and Ralph R. Greenson. They along with Freud figure as the therapists in this chapter, and they need further introduction.

Anna was born in December 1895. Thus in July of that year, when Freud dreamt of his patient Irma and "submitted [the dream] to a detailed interpretation," his wife was already pregnant with Anna, their sixth and last child.[6] In her view she and psychoanalysis figured as twins—and rivals—competing for her father's attention. By the 1920s, by the time Freud had his first cancer operation, she had aroused his interest by becoming a psychoanalyst herself; by then she was also becoming his Antigone—his secretary, his liaison with the psychoanalytic movement, and his designated guardian of its future.[7]

The principal feature of Anna's psychoanalytic training was her analysis with her father. In recent decades the fact that Freud treated his own daughter has seemed shocking. To be sure, the taboo he flouted against mixing the personal and/or social with the analytic was not yet a taboo in 1918, when he took Anna into treatment. In the small psychoanalytic circle of the 1910s, analyses frequently crossed friendship lines. Though he had been reluctant to do so, Freud analyzed Ferenczi; and subsequently Ferenczi reproached him with having left the negative transference unanalyzed. In contrast Freud began his daughter's treatment with enthusiasm: he wrote Ferenczi shortly after it started that "Annerl's analysis is getting very fine."[8] For her part, Anna voiced no reproaches—perhaps because, as Freud commented, "she can't stand the demolition of her father complex."[9]

In her 1922 paper, "Beating Fantasies and Daydreams"—a disguised piece of autobiography[10]—Anna highlighted daydreams that dated from her putative patient's fourteenth or fifteenth year. She had accidentally come upon "a boy's storybook," which contained a short piece set in the Middle Ages, and from it, she had taken the following material: a medieval knight had been engaged in a long feud with a number of nobles who were in league against him; in the course of a battle a 15-year-old noble youth was captured by the knight's henchmen; he was taken to the knight's castle where he was held prisoner for a long time; finally, he was released. The daydreamer depicted the knight of the castle as "sinister and violent"; the noble youth was endowed "with all possible good and attractive characteristics." An "apparently irreconcilable antagonism between" one who was "strong and mighty" and another who was "weak and in the power of the former" thus took center stage.

[T]he knight in fact threatens the youth and makes ready to torture him, but at the last moment the knight desists. He nearly kills the youth through the long imprisonment, but just before it is too late the knight has him nursed back to health. As soon as the prisoner has recovered the knight threatens him again, but faced with the youth's fortitude the knight spares him again. And every time the knight is just about to inflict great harm, he grants the youth one favor after another.

Several years later, the patient used these daydreams to fashion a short story, which "began with the prisoner's torture and ended with his refusal to escape." In this way the private fantasies were transformed into "a communication addressed to others."[11] With their further transformation into any essay, with her presentation of it as a membership paper to the Vienna Psychoanalytic Society, Freud saw Anna taking "a decisive step."[12] It amounted to a resolve to remain in her father's castle.

Forming that resolve when she did, roughly in 1922 at the end of her first analysis (Anna had a second, briefer period of analysis with her father in the mid-1920s as well as a "discussion and consultation relationship" with Lou Andreas-Salomé)[13] her "Freud" was the Freud shifting from a topographic—Conscious–Preconsious–Unconscious—to a structural—ego, id, and super-ego—model of the mind. "Looking back," she commented years later, "I believe I felt half-hearted about the matter and that—even where I used structural terms in writing and talking—I continued still to visualize matters for myself . . . by means of the older topical terms." The turning point for her came in the 1930s. "Somehow things fell into place. . . . It seemed right to me to divide the mind according to id, ego, and superego each pursing their aim in life to the best of their possibility. This gave me a real sense for the purpose of life, or rather the conflicting purposes."[14] By then she herself had written *The Ego and the Mechanisms of Defense* (1936), which was hailed as inspiring "a further study of the ego and its activities," as offering "a method for . . . that study," and as opening up "fresh prospects for psycho-analytical exploration."[15]

The Ego and the Mechanisms of Defense was the subject of an extended, and favorable, discussion in the *International Journal of Psycho-Analysis*. Anna's first book, *Introduction to the Technique of the Analysis of Children* (1927), had been received with far less respect. In that book Anna took issue with Melanie Klein, and Klein, having recently settled in London, joined with members of the British Psycho-Analytical Society to hold a symposium on child analysis that served as a rebuttal. The heated debate about treating children led to a heated exchange of letters between Freud and Ernest Jones, president of the British Society.[16] In September 1927 Freud wrote:

In London you are organizing a regular campaign against Anna's child analysis, accusing her of not having been analyzed deeply enough, a reproach that you repeat in a letter to me. I had to point out to you that such a criticism is just as dangerous as it is impermissible. Is anyone actually analyzed enough? I can assure you that Anna has been analyzed longer and more thoroughly than, for example, yourself. [In 1913 Jones had had an analysis lasting a few months with Sándor Ferenczi.] The whole criticism . . . , with some good will, could have been avoided. . . . What does all this mean? I believe I may ask for an explanation. The difference[s] of opinion between two child analysts . . . are really not so drastic that one could not leave them to historical development, that they have to produce such a premature, passionate, and unfair reaction. Is this directed at me because Anna is my daughter? A nice motivation among analysts, who demand that others control their primitive impulses.[17]

After 1938 Anna Freud and Melanie Klein found themselves together in the British Psycho-Analytical Society, and its members barely managed to control the primitive impulses that were unleashed. The Freuds had arrived in London in June of that year, thanks to Jones's strenuous efforts to procure them British entry and work permits. A little over a year later, Freud was dead. Jones strove equally hard to get émigré analysts accepted into the British Society. As Anna subsequently remarked: to persuade the British "to open their doors to the influx of members from Vienna, i.e., to colleagues who held different scientific views from their own and [who] could only be expected to disrupt peace and internal unity" was no mean achievement.[18] Within four years, a strife-torn society decided to examine theoretical disputes over a number of meetings—a series that came to be known as the Controversial Discussions. The attempt at conceptual clarification proved inconclusive. The simultaneous effort to find a common ground in psychoanalytic technique proved contentious as well. When a majority of the Training Committee came to the conclusion that though differences in technique did exist, they could be contained within existing psychoanalytic practice, an intransigent Anna resigned from the committee. Before long the Society's new president approached her and elicited from her the conditions under which she and her supporters would take an active part in the training program. And so, in 1946, the Society introduced two parallel courses: Course A, organized as formerly on an eclectic basis, with a strong Kleinian element, and Course B, to be taught by Anna Freud and her adherents. A third—middle—group, who did not identify themselves as either Kleinian or Anna Freudian, also formed. "The society remained one, but divided into three separate groups with two training courses."[19]

In the decade following the end of war in Europe and of strife in the British Society, Anna established herself as the director of the Hampstead Child Therapy Clinic. Throughout the remainder of her long life—she died in 1982—she presided over an institution that combined treatment, research, and training. The clinic could not be counted as an annex to her father's castle; it had to be reckoned as Anna's own.

Money for the clinic—a constant worry—came largely from the United States, and Ralph R. Greenson figured as one of the benefactors. His Foundation for Research in Psychoanalysis, headquartered in Beverly Hills, proved to be an important source of funds. In 1968, for example, when the Clinic's budget was $60,000 in the red, the Foundation made up half the deficit. Anna had met Greenson almost a decade earlier; on a trip to California, she had been the guest of Greenson and his Swiss-born wife, Hildi, and soon included him in the circle of her friends. At his death in 1979, a grieving Anna wrote for his memorial service: "We are raising a new generation of psychoanalysts all over the world. Nevertheless, we have not yet discovered the secret of how to raise the real followers of people like Romi Greenson, namely, men and women who make use of psychoanalysis to its very limits: for the understanding of themselves; of their fellow beings; for communicating with the world at large; in short, for a way of living."[20]

Born in 1911, Romeo Samuel Greenschpoon was one of a set of fraternal twins. His sister was called Juliet, and despite his own later name changes, he was always addressed by those acquainted with him as Romi. Juliet excelled at music and had a career as a concert pianist. Greenson, unable to perform at his sister's level on the violin, followed his father into medicine. He did his undergraduate work at Columbia University, then went to Bern for his medical education—in that era Jewish students faced quotas that kept many from entering a medical school in the United States. In Switzerland he met his wife: they were married in 1935 and subsequently had two children, one of whom, Daniel, became a third-generation physician and a psychoanalyst as well.[21]

Greenson's analytic training took place in Vienna and Los Angeles. For nine months, in the mid-1930s, he worked "with Wilhelm Stekel in his 'active' psychoanalytic school."[22] He left Vienna with Stekel's assurance that he had been a very talented student. Greenson himself had misgivings. In 1938 he approached Ernst Simmel, president of the Los Angeles Study Group, and expressed a wish to re-enter treatment with an eye to becoming a Freudian psychoanalyst. It was Simmel's turn to have misgivings. He told Greenson: "We can't have people coming to our meetings who at least don't agree with certain basic principles, because we don't want someone . . . to give a paper and then [have] somebody like you get up and argue 'Is there an Oedipus complex? I don't believe in it.' "[23] Nonetheless, Simmel referred Greenson to Otto Fenichel, who had recently arrived from Czechoslovakia. Despite Fenichel's doubts about analyzing a "Stekelian," he started a trial analysis with Greenson, which turned into a four-year training analysis.[24]

Given his geographical location, given his love of performing,[25] it is not surprising that Greenson got involved with the movie industry. He even appeared, albeit disguised, as the hero of a motion picture—*Captain Newman, M.D.* Based on a novel about Greenson's wartime career—he had been stationed at the Army Air Force Convalescent Hospital in Fort Logan,

Colorado—the film starred Gregory Peck. Newman was portrayed as a sin-gularly gifted therapist. Beneath his brusque and offhand manner, his patients saw "their confessor, their life-line to sanity . . . their hope for salva-tion: that miracle of insight and intercession which could heal them."[26] If not quite a celebrity himself, Greenson grew accustomed to Hollywood figures: Peter Lorre, Frank Sinatra, Vivien Leigh—all sought his professional help.[27]

So too did Marilyn Monroe, who died—a probable suicide—from an over-dose of barbiturates in 1962. Greenson's treatment of her had followed a plan—a highly unorthodox one. He brought his new charge—Marianne Kris, a great friend of Anna Freud's, had referred her former patient to Greenson in January 1961—into his home life. He "hoped to expose Marilyn to the warmth and affection of a happy family. He hoped to compensate for the emotional deprivation she had suffered since childhood. He hoped to assuage her painful loneliness."[28] The intense daily contact that ensued began to take its toll on Greenson, and he longed for a break. In May 1962, he flew to Europe; Marilyn deteriorated; he cut short his stay and came home. He was now on call 24 hours a day, seven days a week. Still it was not enough.

Both before and after this terrible loss, Greenson was deeply concerned about psychoanalytic practice and psychoanalytic politics. The two came together in debates about the work of Melanie Klein that threatened to split the Los Angeles Psychoanalytic Society. Founded in 1946 when the Los Angeles Study Group was elevated to the ranks of a full-fledged society, it counted Greenson among its charter members. In 1947 he was appointed a training analyst. Over the next two decades he served as president of the society as well as dean of education. (Additionally he was clinical professor of psychiatry in the UCLA Medical School.) Starting in the late 1950s, younger analysts latched on to Klein, and in the course of the 1960s, the polarization within the Los Angeles Society came to mirror the polarization in London between the Anna Freudians and the Kleinians. Greenson led the anti-Klein forces: one senior analyst recalled him as remarking, "I can't wait to take on Kleinian psychoanalysis"; another recollected that at a dinner party Greenson had told him that "he had promised Anna Freud that he would destroy the Kleinian movement in the US. . . . He acted in all sincerity and he acted as if he had that as a mission."[29]

Greenson chose psychoanalytic technique as the grounds on which to fight. His textbook, *The Technique and Practice of Psychoanalysis* (1967) repre-sented 14 years of work. "Papers," he told his son, "are easy, they are for now; but books are for posterity."[30] His volume underwent numerous printings and appeared, year after year, in the bibliographies of American psycho-analytic training programs. To generations of candidates in the United States, Greenson came to represent mainstream psychoanalysis. An ironic fate for someone so experimental and unconventional.

*   *   *

Very early on Freud defined resistance as "*whatever interrupts the progress of the analytic work*."[31] (Transference certainly did that, and he counted it as a formidable resistance.) In 1910, he remarked: "Our work is aimed directly at finding out and overcoming the 'resistances,' and we can justifiably rely on the complexes coming to light without difficulty as soon as the resistances have been recognized and removed."[32] As for obsessional patients, they were notorious for their resistance:

> For a time . . . , these cases yield the clearest results and permit a deep insight into the causation of symptoms. But presently one begins to wonder how it is that such marked progress in analytic understanding can be unaccompanied by even the slightest change in the patient's compulsions and inhibitions, until at last one perceives that everything that one has accomplished is subject to a mental reservation of doubt, and that behind this protective barrier the neurosis can feel secure. "It would be all very fine," thinks the patient, often quite consciously, "if I were obliged to believe what the man says, but there is no question of that, and so long as this is so I need change nothing." Then, when one comes to close quarters with the motives for this doubt, the fight with the resistances breaks out in earnest.[33]

Freud battled against them for decades. Along the way their tenacity prompted him to turn his attention to the agency he deemed responsible and in doing so, to think systematically about the ego. His efforts marked only a beginning—in terms both of theory and of technique—and he acknowledged his daughter's work as having picked up from where he left off. She made the ego—a resisting ego—the object of analysis. Greenson also made the ego the focus of his concern—a cooperating ego. He fancied a working alliance between patient and analyst, a relationship that managed to exclude resistance in general and transference in particular.

Freud and his "grand patient"

> Over a long period I studied a woman patient whose neurosis underwent an unusual change. It began, after a traumatic experience, as a straightforward anxiety hysteria. . . . One day, however, it suddenly changed into an obsessional neurosis of the severest type. . . . The obsessional neurosis was not a further reaction to the same trauma which had provoked the anxiety hysteria; it was a reaction to a second experience, which had completely wiped out the first. . . .
>
> The content of her obsessional neurosis was a compulsion for scrupulous washing and cleanliness and extremely energetic protective measures against severe injuries which she thought other people had reason to fear

from her—that is to say, reaction-formations against her own *anal-erotic* and *sadistic* impulses.[34]

The woman in question, Elfriede Hirschfeld, whom Freud referred to as his "grand patient,"[35] provided him with the starting point for a "small fragment of theory": the connection between obsessional neurosis and the anal-sadistic stage of libidinal organization. Hers was a very serious case, and from the outset Freud expected "improvement . . . to be slow."[36] Her analysis, with a few interruptions, went on for more than five years, from the end of 1908 until 1914.[37]

Born around 1873, the eldest of five girls, Elfriede was raised in Frankfurt. Her mother had married relatively late, at the age of 30, and was older than her husband.[38] She was also less agreeable. "The little girl early developed an unusually strong attachment to her father. . . . But she could not long escape the discovery that her beloved father was not . . . so powerful or so distinguished as she had imagined. . . . He had to struggle against money difficulties. . . . [S]he could not put up with this departure from her ideal. Since, as women do, she based all her ambition on the man she loved, she became too strongly dominated by the motive of supporting her father against the world." And when she grew up this attachment to her father "was destined . . . to wreck her happiness."[39]

> One day a relative of her mother's appeared on the scene, considerably older than she was, but still (for she was only nineteen) a youngish man. He was a foreigner who lived in Russia as the head of a large commercial undertaking and had grown very rich. . . . He fell in love with his young . . . cousin and asked her to be his wife. Her parents put no pressure on her, but she understood their wishes. . . . [S]he felt the attraction of the fulfillment of a wishful phantasy of helping her father and rescuing him from his necessitous state. She calculated that her cousin would give her father financial support so long as he carried on his business and pension him when he finally gave it up, and that he would provide her sisters with dowries and *trousseaux* so that they could get married. And she fell in love with him, married him soon afterwards and followed him to Russia.[40]

For the first eight years of their marriage, everything went well. Elfriede developed "into an affectionate wife, sexually satisfied, and a providential support to her family. Only one thing was wanting: she was childless."

> She . . . now . . . lived in Germany, and after overcoming every kind of hesitation she went for a consultation to a German gynaecologist. With the usual thoughtlessness of a specialist, he assured her of recovery if she underwent a small operation. She agreed, and on the eve of the operation discussed the matter with her husband. It was the hour of twilight and

she was about to turn on the lights when her husband asked her not to: he had something to say to her and he would prefer to be in darkness. He told her to countermand the operation, as the blame for her childlessness was his. During a medical congress two years earlier he had learnt that certain illnesses can deprive a man of his capacity to procreate children. An examination had shown that such was the case with him. After this revelation the operation was abandoned. She herself suffered from a temporary collapse, which she vainly sought to disguise.[41]

As Freud saw it, "three paths were open to her, all equally impassable: . . . renunciation of her wish for a child, . . . separation from her husband, [and] . . . unfaithfulness." The first was excluded by the "strongest unconscious" reasons: "her whole childhood had been dominated by the . . . disappointed wish to get a child from her father";[42] the second was ruled out "for the best practical reasons"; as for the third, she "clearly suffered from being tempted."[43] Another possibility remained: when Elfriede learned that she would never have children by her husband, she fell ill of neurosis—in fact of two different kinds:

> The anxiety hysteria with which she reacted to this frustration corresponded, as she herself soon learned to understand, to the repudiation of phantasies of seduction in which her firmly implanted wish for a child found expression. She now did all she could to prevent her husband from guessing that she had fallen ill owing to the frustration of which he was the cause. . . . [But] her husband understood, without any admission or explanation on her part, what his wife's anxiety meant; he felt hurt, without showing it, and in his turn reacted neurotically by—for the first time—failing in sexual intercourse with her. Immediately afterwards he started on a journey. His wife believed that he had become permanently impotent, and produced her first obsessional symptoms on the day before his expected return.[44]

And they became entrenched. After her illness had lasted ten years, some of which she spent in institutions, Elfriede came to Freud.

Despite his strenuous efforts, her condition did not improve. She was not only Freud's "grand patient"; she was his "chief tormentor" as well.[45] When she interrupted her treatment in 1910 for a couple of months, a relieved Freud wrote: "I was saved just short of the final point of exhaustion by the departure of my main client for Frankfurt yesterday."[46] The following year he asked Oskar Pfister in Zürich to handle the case during his summer vacation. Pfister agreed, and when it became apparent to Freud that the two of them had begun a regular analysis, he was by no means eager to get Elfriede back.

*   *   *

In December 1911, Freud remarked: Frau Hirschfeld "has not been heard from for a fortnight. . . . Of course she is right, because she is beyond any possibility of therapy, but it is still her duty to sacrifice herself to science."[47] Soon thereafter Elfriede returned to Vienna, and her analysis resumed. In early 1912 Freud commented to Pfister that he was "determined to treat her very harshly";[48] to Jung he wrote that he kept "cruelly reminding her" that what she wanted most was "to forget her illness for a while."[49] A month later he issued a more positive bulletin: he was "on a much better footing with her than before," thanks to her "completely changed behavior."[50] Could it be that Elfriede had begun to obey the fundamental rule?

In this regard obsessional neurotics were famously recalcitrant. Their watchfulness, their constant struggle against "the manifestation of ambivalent trends,"[51] made it difficult for them to comply with the one injunction Freud issued to a patient before treatment got underway. For beginning practitioners he wrote the lines that he and they should deliver:

"One more thing before you start. What you tell me must differ in one respect from an ordinary conversation. Ordinarily you rightly try to keep a connecting thread running through your remarks and you exclude any intrusive idea that may occur to you and any side-issues, so as not to wander too far from the point. But in this case you must proceed differently. You will notice that as you relate things various thoughts will occur to you which you would like to put aside on the ground of certain criticisms and objections. You will be tempted to say to yourself that this or that is irrelevant here, or is quite unimportant, or nonsensical, so that there is no need to say it. You must never give in to these criticisms, but must say it in spite of them—indeed, you must say it precisely *because* you feel an aversion to doing so. . . . [S]ay whatever goes through your mind. Act as though, for instance, you were a traveller sitting next to the window of a railway carriage and describing to someone inside the carriage the changing views which you see outside. Finally, never forget that you have promised to be absolutely honest, and never leave anything out because, for some reason or other, it is unpleasant to tell it."[52]

Disobedience took various forms. An exchange with Ernst Lanzer offers a graphic example both of it and of Freud at work. During his second analytic session the young man recounted, in a disjointed fashion, the crisis that had led him to Freud's consulting room. A couple of months earlier, while doing his stint as an Austrian reserve officer, he had lost his pince-nez and had wired his optician in Vienna for a replacement. Having sent the telegram, he fell into conversation with a Czech captain who told him of a terrible punishment practiced in the East. At this point Ernst "broke off, got up from the sofa," and begged Freud "to spare him the recital of the details." Freud refused:

> I assured him that I myself had no taste whatever for cruelty, and certainly had no desire to torment him. . . . I went on to say that I would do all I could . . . to guess the full meaning of any hints he gave me. Was he perhaps thinking of impalement?—"No, not that; . . . the criminal was tied up . . ."—he expressed himself so indistinctly that I could not immediately guess in what position—". . . a pot was turned upside down on his buttocks . . . some *rats* were put into it . . . and they"—he had again got up, and was showing every sigh of horror . . .—". . . *bored their way in* . . ."—Into his anus, I helped him out.[53]

Disobedience, in whatever form, pointed to resistance. At the beginning of the session, when Ernst told Freud that "there was much in himself which he would have to overcome if he was to relate this experience of his," Freud "explained the idea of 'resistance' to him." In the midst of Ernst's fragmented speech, Freud interjected that "the overcoming of resistance was the law of the treatment, and on no condition could it be dispensed with." For Ernst to ask to forgo the details, Freud continued, was equivalent to asking Freud "to give him the moon." In a subsequent session Freud remarked that Ernst "must never lose sight of the fact that a treatment like ours proceeded to the accompaniment of a *constant resistance*." And he expected to be "repeatedly reminding" his patient of this[54]—and reminding his fellow analysts as well:

> The first step in overcoming the resistances is made . . . by the analyst's uncovering the resistance, which is never recognized by the patient, and acquainting him with it. Now it seems that beginners in analytic practice are inclined to look on this introductory step as constituting the whole of their work. I have often been asked to advise upon cases in which the doctor complained that he had pointed out his resistance to the patient and that nevertheless no change had set it. . . . The treatment seemed to make no headway. . . . The analyst had . . . forgotten that giving the resistance a name could not result in its . . . cessation. One must allow the patient time to become more conversant with this resistance with which he has now become acquainted, to *work through* it. . . .

The rest of this sentence reads: "to overcome it, by continuing in defiance of it, the analytic work according to the fundamental rule of analysis."[55] The patient was to carry on regardless of his reluctance to do so. "Do it anyway!" seemed to be what Freud enjoined.

The hopes, which he expressed when Elfriede returned to analysis in early 1912, proved fleeting. After she left treatment, he commented: "[S]he has been running away from me ever since I let her into the real secret of her illness."[56] Long before he had written Jung: Frau Hirschfeld "will probably be a hard nut to crack. Of course it is easy to see what ails her, but the other part of the problem, to make her understand and accept it, will no doubt be difficult. . . . She pins herself up at night to make her genitals inaccessible; you can imagine how accessible she is intellectually."[57]

*   *   *

In the paper he delivered to the Fifth Psychoanalytic Congress—"Lines of Advance in Psycho-Analytic Therapy" (1919)—Freud mentioned a new approach to severe obsessional cases. With such patients, "a passive . . . attitude" is not indicated: "there is little doubt that . . . the correct technique can only be to wait until the treatment itself has become a compulsion, and then with this counter-compulsion forcibly to suppress the compulsion of the disease."[58]

Here Freud was drawing on his experience with Sergei Pankejeff, otherwise known as the Wolf Man:

> The patient . . . remained for a long time unassailably entrenched behind an attitude of obliging apathy. He listened, understood, and remained unappproachable. . . . It required a long education to induce him to take an independent share in the work; and when as the result of this exertion he began for the first time to feel relief, he immediately gave up working in order to avoid any further changes, and in order to remain comfortably in the situation which had been thus established. His shrinking from a self-sufficient existence was so great as to outweigh all the vexations of his illness. Only one way was to be found of overcoming it. I was obliged to wait until his attachment to myself had become strong enough to counter-balance this shrinking, and then played off this one factor against the other. . . . I determined that the treatment must be brought to an end at a particular fixed date, no matter how far it had advanced. I was resolved to keep to the date; and eventually the patient came to see that I was in earnest. Under the inexorable pressure of this fixed limit his resistance and his fixation to the illness gave way, and now in a disproportionately short time the analysis produced all the material which made it possible to clear up his inhibitions and remove his symptoms. . . . [D]uring . . . this last period of the work, . . . resistance temporarily disappeared and the patient gave the impression of lucidity which is usually attainable only in hypnosis.[59]

In "Analysis Terminable and Interminable" (1937) Freud assessed the merits of the measure he had taken:

> There can be only one verdict about the value of this blackmailing device: it is effective provided that one hits the right time for it. But it cannot guarantee to accomplish the task completely. On the contrary, we may be sure that, while part of the material will become accessible under

the pressure of the threat, another part will be kept back and thus become buried, as it were, and lost to our therapeutic efforts. For once the analyst has fixed the time-limit he cannot extend it; otherwise the patient would lose all faith in him. . . . Nor can any general rule be laid down as to the right time for resorting to this forcible technical device; the decision must be left to the analyst's tact. A miscalculation cannot be rectified. The saying that a lion springs once must apply here.[60]

At one and the same time Freud claimed that "the working through of the resistances" distinguished "analytic treatment from any kind of treatment by suggestion,"[61] and sketched out a strategy for bypassing those resistances in order to gain direct access to the "pathogenic . . . pieces of the patient's childhood history."[62] The temptation was great to lean on the patient's attachment to the analyst to circumvent obstacles that proved troublesome. The temptation was great to exploit that attachment to escape from the impasse in which Freud had found himself with Elfriede Hirschfeld.

Anna Freud: The analysis of defense

On December 28, 1907, Freud noted, when Ernst Lanzer showed up for his analytic session, "he was hungry" and, Freud added, he "was fed."[63] How should one regard this action? It has been argued that, on occasion, pressing circumstances require analysts to give patients assistance; in this instance it might be assumed that Ernst had missed a meal or more than one and that in offering him food Freud was doing nothing more than extending a courtesy. Thereafter Freud paid close attention to the repercussions, to the fantasies Ernst wove around the meal—more particularly around the herring, which he disliked and left untouched.[64] As for the meal itself, Freud apparently did not reckon it a therapeutic maneuver; apparently he considered it as "outside of technique."[65]

His daughter, when she began working with children, made a similar distinction, that is, designating a variety of interventions as prior to technique. For example: the steps she took with a 6-year-old obsessional girl to turn the "decision for analysis from one taken by others" into the child's own:

> The little girl already knew two children who were being analyzed by me, and she came to her first appointment with her slightly older friend. I said nothing special to her, and merely let her become familiar with the strange surroundings.
>
> The next time, when I had her alone, I made the first approach. I said that she knew quite well why her two friends came to me: one because he could never tell the truth and wanted to give up this habit, the other because she cried so often and was angry with herself for doing so; and I wondered whether she too had been sent to me for some such reason.

Whereupon she said quite straightforwardly, "I have a devil in me. Can it be taken out?"

I was for a moment taken aback at this unexpected answer. Certainly it could, I said, but it would be no light work. And if I were to try with her to do it, she would have to do a lot of things which she would not find at all agreeable. (I meant, of course, that she would have to tell me everything no matter how unpleasant.)

She became quite serious and thoughtful before she replied, "If you tell me that this is the only way to do it, . . . then I shall do it that way." Thereby of her own free will she bound herself to the fundamental analytic rule.

With a 10-year-old boy suffering from "an obscure mixture of . . . anxieties, nervous states, insincerities, and infantile perverse habits," the preliminaries—"winning the boy's confidence by devious methods"—created considerably more trouble:

[F]or a long time I did nothing but follow his moods along all their paths and by-paths. If he came to his appointment in a cheerful mood, I was cheerful too; if he was serious or depressed, I acted seriously. If he preferred to spend the hour under the table, I would treat it as the most natural thing in the world, lift the tablecloth and speak to him under it. If he came with a string in his pocket, and began to show me remarkable knots and tricks, I would let him see that I could make more complicated knots and do more remarkable tricks. If he made faces, I pulled better ones; and if he challenged me to trials of strength, I showed myself incomparably stronger. . . . My first aim was in fact merely to make myself interesting to the boy. . . .

After a time I introduced a second factor. I proved myself useful to him in small ways, wrote letters for him on the typewriter, and was ready to help him with the writing down of daydreams and self-invented stories of which he was proud, and made all sorts of little things for him during his hour with me. . . .

Next came something even more important. I made him realize that being analyzed had great practical advantages; that, for example, punishable deeds have an altogether different and much more fortunate result when they are first told to the analyst, and only through him to those in charge of the child. Thus he became accustomed to relying on analysis as a protection from punishment and to claiming my help for repairing the consequences of rash acts; he let me restore stolen money for him and got me to make all necessary but disagreeable confessions to his parents. . . .

After that . . . there were no more doubts; besides an interesting and useful companion I had become a very powerful person, without whose help he could no longer get along. Thus in these three capacities I had made myself indispensable to him and he had become dependent on me. But I had only waited for this moment to demand of him the most extensive cooperation, though not in words and not all at one stroke: I asked for the surrender ... of all his previously guarded secrets.[66]

Anna Freud herself did not hide her purpose: to establish "a very definite emotional relationship with her patient." She was equally clear that without such an attachment, "real analytic work" could not begin.[67]

*   *   *

"Pathological research," Freud wrote in 1923, "has directed our interest too exclusively to the repressed. We should like to learn," he added, "more about the ego."[68] His point of departure was resistance and his hypothesis that resistance emanated from the ego:

We must ... get rid of the mistaken notion that what we are dealing with in our struggle against resistances is resistance on the part of the *unconscious*. The unconscious—that is to say, the "repressed"—offers no resistance whatever to the efforts of the treatment. Indeed, it itself has no other endeavour than to break through the pressure weighing down on it and force its way either to consciousness or to a discharge through some real action. ... But the fact that ... the resistances themselves are unconscious at first ... is a hint to us that we should correct a shortcoming in our terminology. We shall avoid a lack of clarity if we make our contrast not between the conscious and the unconscious but between the ... *ego* and the *repressed*. It is certain that much of the ego is itself unconscious.[69]

In focusing on the ego Freud leaned heavily on earlier theory and earlier findings. From the beginning of his career his preferred explanation of inner conflict was cast in terms of incompatibility: an incompatibility between certain ideas, which consequently underwent repression, and a mental agency, which applied the repressive force. Freud identified the agency as the ego and always conceived of its repressive activity as unconscious. Not until the 1920s, however, did he describe the ego as "a coherent organization of mental processes."[70] At the same time he made clear that repression was simply a "special method" of defense, with defense itself being "a general designation for all the techniques" the ego employed in conflicts.[71]

As long as hysterics provided the basis for his theorizing, Freud tended to conflate defense and repression. In disentangling the two, he gave obsessional neurotics a more prominent position; he now drew on his work with such patients to articulate key defensive mechanisms:

When we came to study the obsessional neuroses, we found that in that illness pathogenic occurrences are not forgotten. They remain conscious but they are "isolated" in some way that we cannot as yet grasp, so that much the same result is obtained as in hysterical amnesia. . . . Our attention has, moreover, been drawn to . . . a procedure, that may be called magical, of "undoing" what has been done—a procedure about whose defensive purpose there can be no doubt; but which has no longer any resemblance to the process of "repression."[72]

With hysterics occupying pride of place, Freud defined his therapeutic task as providing assistance to the patient's ego, thereby enabling it "to lift its repressions" and "allow the instinctual impulses to run their course."[73] When obsessional neurotics eclipsed hysterics, lifting repression no longer served as a thumbnail sketch of the analyst's assignment. Freud was beginning to appreciate that defenses and defense mechanisms did not lend themselves to being lifted. He was coming to realize that such mechanisms functioned in treatment as resistances not only to making conscious the contents of the id, but also as resistances "against the uncovering of resistance," as "resistances . . . to the analysis as a whole, and thus to recovery."[74]

In making these comments, Freud referred to his daughter's book *The Ego and the Mechanisms of Defense*. It was thanks to her efforts that he recognized the role defense mechanisms played in therapy. For further enlightenment he advised his readers to look to her.

*   *   *

In the 1970s, Anna Freud reflected back on interwar psychoanalytic practice. Then, she said "it was really the task of the patient to free associate."

If a patient says to the analyst, as many now do, "Of course I can't tell you about my sex life, that's much too embarrassing," many analysts would accept it . . . and say to themselves, "perhaps next year." . . . [I]n the past one would have said, "All right, but don't expect me to help you until you tell me about it, because we will not be doing analysis until you do." A patient may say nowadays, "Of course I can't mention money, that's very embarrassing.". . . In the past one would say to the patient, "Well, of course, don't if you don't want to, but then the analytic method that I explained to you won't work because it is built on your saying what is in your mind."

Nowadays, she continued, "for analysts to ask the patient to undertake free association represents an undue interference with his rights as a citizen, with his right to say what he wants to say, and to retain what he does not want to say. But at that time an analyst was entitled to give up a patient if he did not agree to free associate."[75]

In turn it was up to the analyst to watch for resistances. In the first instance, the absence of material announced their presence. Anna Freud was careful to draw a distinction between a patient who simply withheld and a patient who tried to tell something and found it difficult or impossible:

> [I]t is the inability to carry out . . . [a] conscious intent which shows us the resistances. . . . If the intent is not there, we cannot see resistance. . . . Of course, many patients, especially at the beginning of an analysis, say, "There is so much more in my mind than I can say." My answer to that is, "That is quite natural. Never mind it, just take what is uppermost."[76]

Second, a break in the flow of associations—an interruption or an abrupt change of subject—served as a sign. For all Anna Freud's insistence on free association, she mocked beginners in analysis who believed that they must induce "their patients really and invariably to give all their associations without modification or inhibition, i.e., to obey implicitly the fundamental rule. . . . Fortunately for analysis," she added, "such docility" was "in practice impossible. The fundamental rule" could "never be followed beyond a certain point."[77]

At that certain point, Anna Freud focused on something new, something "not generally recognized at the time." The resistance, she argued, signaled the "transference of defense," the bringing into the analytic situation of an ingrained defensive method.[78] Here is the example she included in her 1936 book:

> A young girl came to me to be analyzed on account of states of acute anxiety, which were interfering with her daily life and preventing her regular attendance at school. Although she came because her mother urged her to do so, she showed no unwillingness to tell me about her life both in the past and in the present. Her attitude toward me was friendly and frank, but I noticed that in all her communications she carefully avoided making any allusion to her symptom. She never mentioned anxiety attacks which took place between the analytic sessions. If I myself insisted on bringing her symptom into the analysis or gave interpretations of her anxiety which were based on unmistakable indications in her associations, her friendly attitude changed. On every such occasion the result was a volley of contemptuous . . . remarks. . . . In these repeated outbursts of . . . ridicule the analyst found herself at a loss and the patient was, for the time being, inaccessible to further analysis. As the analysis went deeper, however, we found that these reactions . . . indicated the patient's customary attitude toward herself whenever emotions of tenderness, longing, and anxiety were about to emerge in her affective life. The more powerful the affect forced upon herself, the more vehemently and scathingly did she ridicule herself.[79]

How did Anna Freud convey her understanding to her patient? She gave this account:

> What she [the patient] displays toward the analyst is an attitude toward herself, and it reveals itself in what we might call a form of transference. But if it did not reveal itself in the transference, the analyst would notice after some acquaintance with the patient that this particular attitude appears at inappropriate moments. One could say to the patient, "Why are you so angry with yourself?" Just as later on one could say, "Why are you so angry with me?" Then we could show the patient her way of warding off unwelcome feelings.

In general, Anna Freud continued, she did not see a great difference between the analyst starting with the patient's attitude toward herself and only then showing her that she did the identical thing with the analyst—or going in the reverse order.

> So long as you get hold of it the impression on the patient is very much the same. It does not matter whether you say, "Now I know whenever you are angry with me such and such is really the case," or whether you say, "Whenever you are so self-abusive it is because of so and so."[80]

Only after the patient's method of defending herself against her feelings "by contemptuous disparagement—a process which had become automatic in every department of her life ... had been brought into consciousness and so rendered inoperative,"[81] only then could the next step be taken: an exploration of the feelings behind the defense. The point Anna Freud insisted upon was that the analyst had to take "the whole thing in small steps."[82]

What about the retrieval of the past, so much a feature of analysis in its early years? This Anna Freud considered a "later step"—but, nonetheless, crucial.[83] In the case of the girl with acute anxiety states, she offered this summary statement:

> Historically this mode of defense by means of ridicule and scorn was explained by her identification of herself with her dead father, who used to try to train the little girl in self-control by making mocking remarks when she gave way to some emotional outburst. The method had become stereotyped through her memory of her father, whom she dearly loved.

That was not all. Anna Freud argued that elucidating the origins of a particular defense did more than fill in a "gap in the patient's memory of his instinctual life"; it also filled in "gaps in the history of his ego development."

> The . . . [patient] does not feel . . . [this] kind of transference reaction to be a foreign body, and this is not surprising when we reflect how great a part the ego plays—even though it be the ego of earlier years—in its production. . . . The form in which . . . [these phenomena] emerge in his consciousness is ego syntonic . . . By means of rationalization he easily shuts his eyes to the discrepancies between cause and effect which are so noticeable to the observer and make it evident that the transference has no objective justification.[84]

In these circumstances, a reconstruction, by adding historical depth, could make the analyst's "demonstration" of the patient's defense mechanism more compelling.[85] And in response the patient might be persuaded to open his or her eyes again.

Patients' interest in their past, Anna Freud implicitly reasoned, could well trigger and/or reinforce interest in current functioning—and vice versa. In her mind the two sorts of curiosity were inseparable. And she was intent on encouraging both. She invited patients to turn their attention to a sequence of material—perhaps something that had happened only a moment earlier—as evidence of defenses in operation. Working with her patients in this fashion, she assisted them in analyzing, rather than simply in defying, the resistances they encountered.

Working in this fashion, Anna Freud stopped damning resistances as obstacles. On the contrary, she argued that they "are inevitable in every analytic treatment, are dealt with and dissolved within the analytic process, and . . . prove to be, when interpreted, next to the transference the best and most fruitful material on the way to analytic cures." [86]

Greenson: Forging a working alliance

In concluding his account of Ernst Lanzer, Freud recorded his impression that "he had, as it were, disintegrated into three personalities: into one unconscious personality, . . . and into two preconscious ones between which his consciousness could oscillate. His unconscious comprised those of his impulses which had been suppressed at an early age and which might be described as passionate and evil." In his first preconscious personality, which Freud regarded as his "normal state," Ernst was "kind, cheerful, and sensible—an enlightened and superior . . . person." In his second preconscious personality "he paid homage to superstition and asceticism. Thus he was able to have two different creeds and two different outlooks upon life. This second preconscious personality comprised chiefly the reaction-formations against his repressed wishes, and it was easy to foresee that it would have swallowed up the normal personality if the illness had lasted much longer."[87]

Up until the 1920s, Freud's concept of the ego roughly corresponded to that sensible and enlightened person. His subsequent ego psychology made him think again:

> As is well known, the analytic situation consists in our allying ourselves with the ego of the person under treatment, in order to subdue portions of the id which are uncontrolled—that is to say to include them in the synthesis of the ego. . . . The ego, if we are able to make such a pact with it, must be a normal one. But a normal ego of this sort is, like normality in general, an ideal fiction. . . . Every normal person, in fact, is only normal on the average.[88]

How then could an alliance be forged? Richard Sterba, a Viennese analyst of Anna Freud's generation, offered an initial answer. In his paper "The Fate of the Ego in Analytic Therapy" (1934), he proposed the notion of a "therapeutic ego split" and of a "therapeutic alliance."[89] He thus provided the foundation for all subsequent alliance talk—Greenson's included.[90]

Sterba took as his point of departure the characteristically human ability for reflection, "the sort of thing . . . a man in the street might say amounts to looking hard at oneself,"[91] and quoted Freud's gloss on this ability:

> We wish to make the ego the object of our study, our own ego. But how can that be done? The ego is the subject *par excellence*: how can it become the object? There is no doubt, however, that it can. The ego can take itself as object; it can treat itself like any other object, observe itself, criticize itself, do Heaven knows what besides with itself. In such a case, one part of the ego stands over against the other. The ego can, then, be split; it becomes dissociated during many of its functions, at any rate in passing. The parts can later join up again.[92]

Sterba latched on to the idea of "dissociation" and insisted on using the word, suggestive of serious pathology, for something distinctly non-pathological—indeed essential for psychoanalytic treatment. "The capacity of the ego for dissociation," he claimed, gave "the analyst the chance . . . to effect an alliance with the ego against the . . . forces of instinct and repression and, with the help of one part of it, to try to vanquish the opposing forces."[93]

How did Sterba envision the analyst making use of this capacity? His answer fell into two parts. He granted pride of place to the interpretation of "transference-resistance," by which he meant the transference of defensive measures as well as instinctual impulses:

[T]he interpretation of defensive reactions and instinctual trends become interwoven with one another, for analysis cannot overcome the defense unless the patient comes to recognize his instinctual impulses, nor put him in control of the latter unless the defense has been overthrown. The typical process is as follows: First of all, the analyst gives an interpretation of the defense, making allusion to the instinctual tendencies which he has already divined and against which the defense has been set up. With the patient's recognition that his attitude in the transference is of the nature of a defense, there comes a weakening in that defense. The result is a more powerful onslaught of the instinctual strivings upon the ego. The analyst then has to interpret the infantile meaning and aim of these impulses.

Thanks to this interpretive work, "a *new point of view of intellectual contemplation* . . . emerges in the mind of the patient." This shift in the patient's consciousness—from emotional experience to rational reflection—Sterba considered "the peculiar character of the method used in analysis."[94]

That was not all. Additionally Sterba emphasized the patient's identification with the analyst—an identification deliberately fostered by the analyst:

From the outset the patient is called upon to "co-operate" with the analyst against something in himself. Each separate session gives the analyst various opportunities of employing the term "we," in referring to himself and the part of the patient's ego which is consonant with reality. The use of the word "we" always means that the analyst is trying to draw that part of the ego over to his side and to place it in opposition to the other part which in the transference is . . . influenced from the side of the unconscious.[95]

Note: Sterba's alliance, although requiring continuous preparation on the part of the analyst, was "not a . . . contract, but a happening." It was "a momentary dispassionate identification with the analyst" on the part of the patient at a time of transference resistance. "Thus: no transference resistance, no alliance!"[96]

What, then, was the fate of the ego?

All the instinctual and defensive reactions aroused in the ego in the transference impel the analyst to induce . . . ego-dissociation by means of the interpretations he gives. There is constituted, as it were, a standing relation between that part of the ego which is cathected with instinctual or defensive energy and that part which is focussed on reality and identified with the analyst. . . . Each separate interpretation reduces the instinctual and defensive cathexis of the ego in favour of intellectual contemplation, reflection and correction by the standard of reality.[97]

More than 50 years later, Paul Gray, picking up on Sterba, suggested that "changes in the self-observing ego" should be thought of as more than . . . [an] inevitable byproduct of the analysis"; they should become an explicit goal—at least in the treatment of neurotics.[98]

*   *   *

The term working alliance will be used in preference to the diverse terms others have used. . . . [It] has the advantage of stressing the vital elements: the patient's capacity to work purposefully in the treatment situation. It can be seen at its clearest when a patient [is] in the throes of an intense transference . . . [reaction] and yet can maintain an effective working relationship with the analyst.[99]

Above all Greenson was intent on maintaining a distinction between non-transference and transference relationships.[100] As Sterba had formulated it, the therapeutic alliance was an intermittent occurrence—the consequence of an accurate transference interpretation. Greenson, in contrast, thought of the working alliance as a cause or a precondition: it was "essential in all cases to recognize, acknowledge, clarify, differentiate and even nurture the non-transference or relatively transference-free reactions between patient and analyst"—all this was necessary "to facilitate the full flowering and ultimate resolution of the patient's transference reactions."[101]

A tall order. How was it to be carried out? Here Greenson echoed Sterba: the patient's identification with the analyst played a crucial role.

A young man, Mr Z., came to me for analysis after having spent two and a half years with an analyst in another city in an analysis which had left him completely untouched. He had obtained certain insights, but he had the distinct impression that his former analyst really disapproved of infantile sexuality, even though the young man realized that analysts were not supposed to be contemptuous of it. In the preliminary interviews the young man told me that he had the greatest difficulty talking about masturbation and often consciously withheld this information from his previous analyst. He had informed the latter about the existence of many conscious secrets, but nevertheless stubbornly refused to divulge them. He never wholeheartedly gave himself up to free association, and there were many hours of long silence in which he and his analyst both remained mute. The patient's manner of relating to me, however, his history, and my general clinical impression led me to believe that he was analyzable.[102]

Mr Z., Greenson wrote, was the only child of an unhappy marriage; his parents divorced when he was two, and his mother remarried a couple of years later; in the interval she left him with his wealthy grandparents and traveled around the world; he experienced his father, whom he visited on weekends, as austere, his stepfather as warm-hearted and affectionate:

> The outstanding psychopathology in this patient revolved around his extremely strong . . . attachment to his mother and his homosexual conflict with his stepfather. There was a great deal of material concerning his deep sense of deprivation and abandonment by his mother. . . . [H]e had a constant yearning for closeness, for fusion with her, along with a terribly destructive rage toward her for neglecting him. He . . . was tempted to beg her for crumbs of interest, . . . yet . . . had a deep distrust of her motives [and] despised her values. . . . The mother was the most exciting of women and also a loathsome creature who revulsed [sic] him. . . . [H]e clung tenaciously to the unreliable and rejecting mother because she was a protection against his homosexuality.[103]

Greenson was pleased with how hard Mr Z. worked in the analysis: he "was extremely conscientious in trying free association, in recognizing his resistances, and in attempting to understand the meaning and implications" of interpretations. "He seemed to be very honest and scrupulous in the way he detected his evasiveness, his holding back, and his tendency to appease." In a relatively short time "he seemed to have formed a good working alliance . . . and over the next several years he was able to let himself develop" strong positive and negative oedipal and preoedipal transferences. Nonetheless, after three years of treatment, "which followed the many years of the earlier analysis, there was no significant change in his behavior outside the analytic situation." Greenson "was certain there was a subtle resistance at work." What could it be? He confessed himself stumped:

> One day the patient told me that at a party he had met an attractive young woman and again found himself reacting in his typically neurotic way: he felt hostile to her, had the obsessive thought she was a whore, and became miserably silent and withdrawn. Then he added: "I had no idea why this should have happened." I was struck by this last sentence, since it seemed obvious to me from the way he described the girl, and his reactions to her, that she must have reminded him of his mother. I was amazed that he had no idea of what had happened since we had talked on countless occasions about how he had "oedipalized" his relationship to women. Pursuing his remark "I had no idea why this should have happened," I discovered that he had a strange and specific inhibition in doing analytic work *outside* of the analytic hour. He described to me how he would try to do a piece of self-analysis. When he was upset he would ask himself what upset him. He would usually succeed in recalling, via free association, the event which had triggered his reaction as well as other associatively connected occurrences. Sometimes he could even

recall an interpretation that I had given him about the point in question. But the insight he would arrive at in this way was meaningless; it felt foreign, artificial, and remembered by rote. It was not *his* insight; it was *my* insight and had no living significance for him. He was therefore blank about the meaning of the event which upset him.[104]

Greenson interpreted: as long as Mr Z. could see him "as an external object in the analytic hour," as long as he could thus reassure himself of Greenson's separateness, he could temporarily and partially identify with his analyst. In Greenson's absence, however, Mr Z. "reacted to the identification as a homosexual and aggressive intrusion."

> With this new insight, the patient became eager to overcome this inhib-ition [in identification]. He felt he might do better at this point if he sat up and could face me. I agreed and the patient did this for three weeks. During this time I reviewed with him the situation at the party which had brought his "identification phobia" to our attention. . . . I helped him discover how he could have thought analytically at the party and yet completely in accordance with his own standards and preferences. He was shown that he could utilize analytic insights in his own way and for his own purposes; he could take them or leave them; he could make them his own or let them remain mine. Above all he had a choice just as long as he did not confuse letting himself be receptive to the analytic point of view with letting himself be homosexually intruded upon. As we slowly and repeatedly reviewed the events at the party, the patient gradually grasped the notion of a homosexual-free . . . identification with me.[105]

In reviewing the case from the standpoint of therapeutic process— Mr Z. resumed lying on the couch and thereafter made steady progress in the analysis—Greenson stressed the vicissitudes of the working alliance. Too much transference, not enough working alliance—that was his summary judgment. The working alliance appeared to be effective; actually it was "gravely impaired"—by an intense transference reaction. Transference, so it seemed, was contagious, and the working alliance could not be immunized against it. Still, Greenson insisted on maintaining a sharp distinction between transference and non-transference in the analytic situation.

A second example of his raised even more serious doubts about quarantin-ing transference:

> For about two years a young professional man, who had an intellectual knowledge of psychoanalysis, maintained a positive and reasonable atti-tude to me, his analyst. If his dreams indicated hostility or homosexual-ity, he acknowledged it but claimed that he knew he was supposed to feel such things for his analyst, but he "really" didn't. If he came late or

forgot to pay his bill, he again admitted that it might seem that he did not want to pay his bill, but "actually" it was not so. He had violent anger reactions to other psychiatrists he knew, but insisted that they deserved it and I was different. He became infatuated with another male analyst for a period of time and he "guessed" that he must remind him of me, but he said this playfully.

As Greenson saw it, the patient had developed "a reasonable relationship" to his analyst and would not allow himself "to feel anything irrational, be it sexual, or aggressive, or both." Greenson attempted "to get the patient to recognize his persistent reasonableness as a means of avoiding. . . his deeper . . . impulses." He attempted "to trace the historical origins of this behavior." In vain:

> Since I could not get the patient to work further and consistently with this material, I finally told the patient that we had to face the fact that we were getting nowhere and we ought to consider some other alternative besides continuing psychoanalysis with me. The patient was silent for a few moments and said "frankly" he was disappointed. He sighed and then went on to make a free-associationlike remark. I stopped him and asked him what in the world he was doing. He replied that he "guessed" I sounded somewhat annoyed. I assured him it was no guess. Then slowly he looked at me and asked if he could sit up. I nodded and he did. He was quite shaken, sober, pale, and in obvious distress.
>
> After some moments of silence he said that maybe he would be able to work better if he could look at me. He had to be sure I was not laughing at him, or angry, or getting sexually excited. The last point seemed striking and I asked him about it. He told me that he often fantasied that perhaps I was being sexually excited by his material and hid it from him. This he never brought up before, it was just a fleeting idea. But this "fleeting" idea led quickly to many memories of his father repeatedly and unnecessarily taking his temperature rectally. This then led to a host of fantasies of a homosexual and sadomasochistic nature.[106]

Greenson readily admitted that his behavior in the hour "was not well controlled." Nevertheless it was effective: it prompted "a realization that the patient's working alliance was being used to ward off" intense transference reactions.[107] Greenson was not prepared to consider that his patient's behavior for the previous two years amounted to acting out in the transference. Nor was he prepared to discard a clear-cut distinction between a transference and a non-transference relationship.[108]

Greenson claimed that both of these cases stood as instances of deviant working alliances. What did they deviate from? In the "classical" psychoanalytic patient, he argued, the working alliance developed "almost imperceptibly" and "relatively silently."

> Usually I can see the first signs of the working alliance in about the third to sixth month of analysis. Most frequently the first indications of this development are: the patient becomes silent and then instead of waiting for me to intervene, he himself ventures an opinion that he seems to be avoiding something. Or he interrupts a rather desultory report of some event and comments that he must be running away from something. If I remain silent, he will then spontaneously ask himself what it can be that is making him so evasive and he will let his thoughts drift into free association which he will say aloud.[109]

General remarks of this sort, and the absence of clinical material, would lead one to suspect that Greenson was constructing an ideal type—imaginable in theory, but never encountered in practice.

Why, then, did Greenson insist on his fiction? A third example suggests an answer. The patient, an intelligent middle-aged man, had had six years of analysis in another city. He felt in need of "some additional analysis"— despite certain general conditions in his life having improved—"because he was still unable to get married and . . . was very lonely."

> From the very beginning of the therapy I was struck by the fact that he was absolutely passive about recognizing and working with his own resistances. It turned out that he expected me to point them out as his previous analyst had continued to do throughout that analysis.
>
> Then I was impressed by the fact that the moment I made some intervention he had an immediate response, although often an incomprehensible one. I discovered that he felt it was his duty to reply immediately to every intervention since he believed it would be a sign of resistance and therefore bad, to keep silent for a moment or so and to mull over what I had said. . . . In free association the patient searched actively for things to talk about, and if more than one thing occurred to him he chose what seemed to be the item he thought I was looking for without mentioning the multiple choices he had. When I would request some information from him, he often answered by doing free association so that the result was . . . bizarre. For example, when I asked him what his middle name was he answered: "Raskolnikov," the first name that occurred to him. When I recovered my composure and questioned this, he defended himself by saying that he thought he was to associate freely.[110]

From the above, Greenson gathered that his patient "had never really established a working relationship with his first analyst. . . . He had been lying down . . . , meekly submitting to what he imagined the previous analyst had demanded, namely, constant and instant free association. Patient and analyst had been indulging in a caricature of psychoanalysis."

> Although I recognized that the magnitude of the patient's problems could not be due solely or even mainly to the first analyst's technical shortcomings, I felt the patient ought to be given a fair opportunity to see whether he might be able to work in an analytic situation. . . . Therefore, in the very first months of our working together, I carefully explained to the patient, whenever it seemed appropriate, the different tasks that psychoanalytic therapy requires of the patient. The patient reacted to this information as though it was all new to him and he seemed eager to try to work in the way I described. However it soon became clear that he could not just say what came to mind, he felt compelled to find out what I was looking for. He could not keep silent and mull over what I said; he was afraid of the blank spaces, they signified some awful danger. If he were silent he might think, and if he thought he might disagree with me, and to disagree was tantamount to killing me. . . . In a period of six months it became abundantly clear that this man . . . could not bear the deprivations of . . . psychoanalysis. I therefore helped him to obtain supportive psychotherapy with a woman therapist.[111]

The "lack of a constant working alliance" in this case and in others as well, served Greenson as a diagnostic tool.[112] It allowed him to separate out those patients for whom psychoanalysis was not the treatment of choice—patients who suffered from an ego deficit or defect, who, in ego psychological parlance, suffered from an impaired "capacity for . . . conflict-free ego functioning."[113] Here he came across another obstacle—an obstacle that he regarded as inaccessible to treatment.

*   *   *

Surveying the material covered in this chapter, I want to point to the obvious theoretical landmark: Freud and his daughter's work in conceptualizing the ego's defensive processes. At the same time as he introduced his structural hypothesis of ego, id, and superego, Freud clarified the notion of resistance: it was defensive, and like other defenses, it was put into practice by the ego.

On the technical side, I want to highlight Anna Freud's distinct contribution: her idea of the transference of defense. Focusing on the ego, its resistances and defenses, she paid close attention to how the ego's defense mechanisms were deployed during an analytic session. And in so doing, she carried out the assignment her father had designated as belonging to the analyst: "He contents himself with studying whatever is present for the time being on the surface of the patient's mind, and he employs the art of interpretation mainly for the purpose of recognizing the resistances which appear there, and making them conscious to the patient."[114]

What about Greenson? Over time he became more, rather than less, insistent on distinguishing the working alliance from transference reactions. Was he attempting to sustain the hope that the patient might share his enthusiasm for what was supremely important to him, namely the analytic process? Was he trying to forestall the frustration that comes from disappointed expectations? Was he, in short, demanding too much of the patient? As one commentator remarked:

> Perhaps it would be ... useful ... to regard the patient as having *no* attitude toward analysis as a process, but only an attitude toward his relationship with his analyst, including all that he wants to get from him and all that he suspects the analyst wants from him. In his life the patient wants freedom from the pain of symptoms and the realization of his wishes and fantasies. . . . Any idea that *apart from these desires* the patient wishes to, or should wish to, engage in a process *per se* is supported by neither analytic theory nor commonsense. . . . [I]t is reasonable to ask a psychoanalyst whether he really wants to analyze, but it makes no sense to ask a patient whether he really wants to be analyzed.[115]

Chapter 3

Depression: Negative therapeutic reaction

Freud initially broached the subject of melancholia in the 1890s. He used the term to refer to the range of clinical conditions now covered by depression, with and without psychotic features.[1] Two decades later he remarked that melancholia came in so many forms that grouping them together "into a single unity" seemed doubtful—and his doubts increased when he considered that some of the forms "suggested somatic rather than psychogenic affections." He took care to specify that his theory-building rested on "a small number of cases whose psychogenic nature was indisputable."[2]

It also rested on a comparison between mourning and melancholia, between a temporary state best left alone and a pathological condition requiring medical intervention. The exciting cause was the same: the loss, of a person or of "some abstraction," which had taken a person's place, "such as one's country, liberty, an ideal, and so on." In mourning what had been lost was clear, in melancholia less so; but in both the ego was hard at work, internally that is, obeying little by little the dictates of reality to relinquish its attachment to the lost object. And the general picture of that work bore a striking similarity: mourning typically produced "a painful frame of mind," a lack of "interest in the outside world—in so far as it . . . [did] not recall" the person lost—an unwillingness "to adopt any new love object (which would mean replacing him)," and a "turning away from any activity . . . not connected with thoughts of him"; likewise "the distinguishing features of melancholia" were "a profoundly painful dejection, cessation of interest in the outside world, loss of capacity to love, [and] inhibition of all activity."[3] For all the resemblance, in one respect mourning and melancholia presented a marked contrast:

> In mourning it is the world which has become poor and empty; in melancholia it is the ego itself. . . . The melancholic displays . . . an extraordinary diminution in his self-regard. . . . The patient represents his ego to us as worthless, incapable of any achievement and morally despicable; he reproaches himself, vilifies himself and expects to be cast out and punished. . . . He is not of the opinion that a change has taken place in

him, but extends his self-criticism back over the past; he declares that he was never any better. This picture of a delusion of (mainly moral) inferiority is completed by sleeplessness and refusal to take nourishment, and—what is psychologically very remarkable—an overcoming of the instinct which compels every living thing to cling to life.[4]

Freud was not ready to dismiss the patient's self-reproaches as nonsensical. He took the line that the patient must surely be on to something. So he listened. He paid careful attention to the "melancholic's many and various self-accusations"; before long he began to suspect that "the most violent of them" were "hardly at all applicable to the patient himself, but that with insignificant modifications they ... fit someone else, someone whom the patient ... loved or should love." The self-reproaches were actually "reproaches against a loved object" which had been "shifted away from it on to the patient's own ego."[5]

Here Freud discerned ambivalence: along with love for an object came hate, and the loss of a love object provided "an excellent opportunity for the ambivalence in love-relationships to make itself effective." He also spotted identification, of which he gave the following account:

> An object-choice, an attachment of the libido to a particular person, had at one time existed; then, owing to a real slight or disappointment coming from this loved person, the object-relationship was shattered. The result was not the normal one of a withdrawal of the libido from this object and a displacement of it on to a new one, but something different. . . . [T]he free libido . . . was withdrawn into the ego. There . . . it . . . served to establish an *identification* of the ego with the abandoned object. Thus the shadow of the object fell upon the ego, and the latter could henceforth be judged . . . as though it were an object, the forsaken object.

Ambivalence and identification, taken together, suggested that the melancholic's erotic attachment to his object had "undergone a double vicissitude": part of it had been carried back to the stage of sadism—the same stage Freud claimed created a disposition to obsessional neurosis; and part of it had regressed from choosing an external object to a stage of object love he considered a preliminary to it. Of the two, he regarded the second as responsible for producing melancholia.[6]

In the early 1920s, Karl Abraham, Freud's leading representative in Berlin, took up the project of linking sexual development with specific mental disorders. He postulated two anal stages, a later one of retaining and controlling the object and an earlier one of expelling and destroying it. The later anal stage he linked to obsessional neurosis, the earlier one to melancholia. Abraham further claimed that the libido of the melancholic did not stop its backward movement at the earlier phase of the anal-sadistic stage but continued to the yet more primitive oral level. This level, also, he divided into two: a later, or cannibalistic, oral stage, during which ambivalence entered the scene and an earlier, or sucking, oral stage, which he considered pre-ambivalent. Even with these refinements at his disposal, making the connection between libidinal stages and a particular mental illness remained very much a work in progress.[7]

What about psychoanalytic therapy? Publicly Abraham claimed that he "lacked sufficient experience to make any judgement about the lasting effects of analytic therapy."[8] Privately he sent Freud word of a 3-year-old patient, who "faithfully presented the basic melancholia" and who was analyzed with "good therapeutic results." The person who "skilfully conducted" the treatment was Melanie Klein.[9]

Klein was to continue Freud and Abraham's work on depression, and in so doing, she was to be joined by Joan Riviere. Along with Freud they are the psychoanalysts in this chapter. A word of introduction about the two women is in order.

Born in Vienna in 1881, Melanie Klein, née Reizes, was the youngest of four children.[10] Her father, who was then over 50, had been raised in an orthodox Jewish milieu and had devoted his early adulthood to religious studies with the aim of becoming a rabbi. In his late thirties he broke with his origins and began pursuing a medical career—without much success. As a breadwinner, he proved a poor model—so poor, that Melanie's mother, a woman with a will of iron, was obliged to open a shop. As a man of learning, however, he set a high standard, which was transmitted to Melanie by two of her siblings. Her sister, who died when Melanie was 4, taught her the fundamentals of reading and arithmetic. Her brother, who died when Melanie was 20, coached her in Greek and Latin, thus helping her pass the entrance examination for the gymnasium. She turned to him as "confidant," "friend," and "teacher,"[11] and he expected great things of her. Her own expectations were equally high; she hoped to enter medical school and specialize in psychiatry. In vain: she was not among the few women who matriculated in German-speaking universities at the turn of the century.

By the time Melanie might have fought for admission to higher education, her father was dead, and the family's uncertain finances no doubt hampered her. They also weighed heavily in her decision to marry Arthur Klein. An industrial chemist, he was, in worldly terms, the most suitable of her admirers. They were married in 1903. Almost from the beginning, Melanie's distress and dissatisfaction were evident. She found her life circumstances trying: in their first seven years together, Arthur's profession took him and his family to a series of small towns in Slovakia and Silesia. She found their children—Melitta, born in 1904, and Hans, born in 1907—trying: in those years she frequently fled to cures and to seaside spots. And she found her mother trying: more and more the widowed woman took over the management of the Klein household and the rearing of the children. In 1910 Arthur was transferred to Budapest, and there Melanie freed herself from the depression that threatened to paralyze her.

That liberation was slow in coming. The earliest it can be dated is 1914, the year Melanie's third and last child, Erich, was born, her mother died, and Arthur was called up for military service. During the war Melanie extricated herself unofficially from the marriage—it did not legally end until the mid-1920s. During the same period she became involved with the psychoanalytic movement. She attended the Fifth International Psycho-Analytical Congress in Budapest in 1918 and caught her first glimpse of Freud. The following July she read a paper to the Budapest Psychoanalytic Society and was immediately made a member. Along the way she had an analysis with Sándor Ferenczi.

What went on in that analysis and in her subsequent analysis with Abraham in 1924 and 1925? Klein did not say. Her scant comments about her two analysts stressed their professional guidance rather than their therapeutic impact. These two men, intellectually and temperamentally very different from each other, agreed in encouraging Klein to work with children. It was Ferenczi who drew her attention to her great gift for understanding them and suggested that she devote herself to their analysis.[12] Child patients—or perhaps any patients—were not, however, readily available to her; so she turned to her son Erich. The paper she presented to the Budapest Society derived from work with him—she concealed his identity in subsequent versions under the pseudonym "Fritz."[13] A few years later—political turmoil had forced her to leave Budapest, and in 1921 she had settled in Berlin—it was Abraham who came to her defense during heated discussions in the Berlin Psychoanalytic Society.[14] By then she had become "absolutely firm" on "keeping parental influence . . . apart from analysis" and reducing it to "its minimum." That minimum, Alix Strachey quipped, was "to keep the child from . . . poisoning itself on mushrooms, to keep it reasonably clean, and to teach it its lessons."[15]

It was Alix Strachey who brought Klein to the attention of the British Psycho-Analytical Society. When in the fall of 1924, she arrived in the German capital for an analysis with Abraham, she met Klein. Alix was impressed, and through her, and her husband, James, Klein's proposal to give a series of lectures made its way to Ernest Jones. He took her offer to his colleagues, and James provided Alix with a report of what followed:

> Jones announced at the meeting that he'd had a letter from Frau Klein but that he hadn't answered it, so that he might first discover what the society thought about the matter. He then, very haltingly, read out her letter. When he got through her scenario, or whatever you call it, he muttered to himself "very interesting programme." . . . [H]e himself was very anxious that it should be put through but felt doubtful of what other people would think. Anyhow, after some talk, he said in dubious terms:

"Well, as to the number that are likely to attend . . . I'm afraid it's much too early yet to ask people now if they'll be prepared to come . . . h'm? . . . Well perhaps I might ask . . . h'm? . . . those who think they will hold up their hands." It was a rather unusually small meeting: only 15 or 16 altogether. Without an instant's hesitation every single hand rose in the air. Jones's whole manner instantly changed. He became wreathed in smiles . . . .

There couldn't be any question at all that there was a most unusual amount of interest at the prospect of her visit; quite a stir, in fact. . . . [Y]ou can pile it on as thick as you please.[16]

And so Klein went to London in the summer of 1925. A year later, her position in Berlin having become even more uncomfortable after Abraham's premature death, she was ready to go permanently.

Klein had been "sniffed at" by people in Berlin;[17] she was fussed over in London. Within a year of her arrival, Ferenczi wrote to Freud, after visiting the British capital, of "the prominent influence" Klein exerted over "the entire group."[18] She attended her first meeting in October 1926 and presented her first paper the following month. After she became a member, in 1927, she played an active role in the educational and administrative life of the society; in 1929 she was named a training analyst, started work with her first candidate, and was elected a member of the Training Committee—a position she held for many years.[19] With the publication of *The Psycho-Analysis of Children* in 1932, she reached her highpoint of acceptance by her British colleagues. Edward Glover, for example, had "no hesitation" in stating that her book was "of fundamental importance for the future of psycho-analysis"—indeed that it could be reckoned "a landmark in analytical literature worthy to rank with some of Freud's own classical contributions."[20]

In the mid-1930s misfortune struck. In April 1934 Klein's older son, Hans, fell to his death in a mountain-climbing accident. Her surviving son maintained that his brother's death "was a source of grief to her for the rest of her life." At the time her depression was amply apparent to those around her; it prompted her to see Sylvia Payne professionally, though only briefly, and it also inspired her to write "A Contribution to the Psychogenesis of Manic-Depressive States" (1935) and "Mourning and its Relation to Manic-Depressive States" (1940).[21] In the second of these Klein drew on her own experience, thinly disguised as that of "Mrs A," "to illustrate . . . a normal mourner's" distress. A few weeks after her son's death,

Mrs A went for a walk with her friend through familiar streets, in an attempt to re-establish old bonds. She suddenly realized that the number of people in the street seemed overwhelming, the houses strange and the sunshine artificial and unreal. She had to retreat into a quiet restaurant. But there she felt as if the ceiling were coming down, and the people in the place became vague and blurred. Her own house suddenly seemed the only secure place in the world.[22]

And even "her own house" was no longer safe. In the controversy that erupted after Anna Freud's emigration to Britain in 1938, Klein's daughter, Melitta, and Glover, her analyst, went over to Anna's camp. They were not so much pro-Anna as viciously anti-Melanie, and vicious it was. As one German émigrée noted; "At the meetings I could see something terrible and very un-English happening, and that was a daughter hitting her mother with words and this mother being very composed, quite quiet, never defending herself." A British member concurred: "It was horrible at times, *really* horrible."[23]

Who measured up to the demands for undivided loyalty that Klein now made? Alix and James Strachey drifted away; neither turned out to be abso-lutely steadfast. Nor did Jones for that matter; once the Freuds crossed the English Channel, Klein could no longer count on him. Of the early members of the British Society, Joan Riviere proved the most faithful.

Born in 1883, Joan Riviere, née Verrall, was the oldest of three surviving siblings.[24] The year before, a brother had died a few hours after birth. Joan's father, a solicitor, belonged to a well-established Sussex family, with literary connections stretching back to the eighteenth century. Thanks to his social and intellectual background—her mother's beginnings were more modest—Joan laid claim to high social status. And to some, she appeared pretentious. Jones, in writing to Freud in 1922, commented that "she had a strong com-plex about being a well-born lady (county family) and despises all the rest of us."[25] James Strachey, in an obituary—she died in 1962—put her snobbery in a more charitable light. The two of them, he said, "came out of the same middle-class, professional, cultured, later Victorian box. . . . I suppose that contact is always easier between people out of the same box, however much they may have drifted from it. I still have a vivid visual picture of her standing by the fireplace at an evening party, tall, strikingly handsome, distinguished-looking, and . . . impressive."[26]

Trying to recollect when he first met Joan, Strachey placed it at Cambridge. He was a student at Trinity College, she a frequent visitor at her Uncle Arthur's—A. W. Verrall, a noted classicist.[27] Joan herself never attended uni-versity; indeed her education was somewhat irregular. Sent to a well-known boarding school, she had not flourished; so at the age of 17 she went to Gotha for a year, and it was then that she acquired her knowledge of German. On her return to England, she occupied herself with drawing, designing dresses, and, for a brief period, working as a professional dressmaker. When she was 23, she married Evelyn Riviere, a Chancery barrister and the son of a highly respected painter. Their one child, Diana, was born in 1908.

How did Riviere find her way to psychoanalysis? Strachey speculated that, like him, she may have initially heard of Freud through the Society for Psy-chical Research. Her Cambridge relatives figured prominently in it, and Freud published his "Note on the Unconscious in Psycho-Analysis" (1912) in the Society's *Proceedings*. Her route may actually have been more emotional than intellectual. In 1909 her much-loved father died. In the years following she suffered physically and mentally. She sought the advice of various medical experts, including one specialist whom Leonard Woolf consulted about his wife, Virginia. In neither case did the specialist provide relief. Riviere took rest cures as well, both at home and in a sanatorium. Again to no avail. By the mid-1910s she was ready to try psychoanalytic treatment.

Riviere, in fact, had two analyses. The first, from 1916 to 1921, was with Jones. By 1919 he was referring patients to her. He also set her to work translating Freud's *Introductory Lectures*; subsequently he gave her the job of editing Freud's *Collected Papers*; and he included her, along with the Stracheys, in the so-called Glossary Committee, which took upon itself the assignment of deciding "for all time how the technical terms of psycho-analysis were to be translated."[28] As for the therapy, it did not go smoothly— to say the least[29]—and eventually Jones encouraged Riviere to go to Vienna for further analysis. Freud's response to her request for treatment could not have been more flattering: "It goes without saying that, if you want to enter analysis, you will take precedence over everyone else, as my translator and as an outstanding member of the London group."[30] That second analysis was brief, lasting roughly five months in the spring and autumn of 1922, with another stint of six weeks in 1924.

Over the next several years, Riviere continued translating Freud, bringing to that task "a thorough knowledge of the German language, a highly accomplished literary style, and a penetrating intellect."[31] Well known as Freud's translator, she became even better known for her relationship to Melanie Klein

By the time Klein settled in London in 1926, the two were already acquainted, and a friendship quickly followed. Between "the haughty, genteel Riviere and the plump, unconstrained Klein ... there was a meeting of minds."[32] In 1927 Riviere stood in the forefront of British analysts defending Klein's views on child analysis against the attacks of Anna Freud. In 1936 she took her advocacy of Klein's theory of infant development to the Austrian capital; there she delivered one of four lectures that had been scheduled to make sure that psychoanalysis in London and Vienna developed along similar lines. In vain: the two societies continued to grow apart, and in 1943 and 1944, with the Viennese now in London, the British Society held the so-called Controversial Discussions to examine the differences. Behind the scenes, Riviere did yeoman service organizing Klein's supporters.[33] Then, in the 1950s, the relationship between her and Klein cooled, and, before her death in 1960, Klein turned increasingly to a younger generation to carry on her work.

*   *   *

Both Riviere and Klein were intrigued by what Freud had labeled the negative therapeutic reaction. In *The Ego and the Id* (1923), in discussing the third member of his structural triad, the superego, he provided his most complete description of it:

> There are certain people who behave in a quite peculiar fashion during the work of analysis. When one speaks hopefully to them or expresses satisfaction with the progress of the treatment, they show signs of discontent and their condition invariably becomes worse. . . . [T]hey react inversely to the progress of the treatment. Every partial solution or a temporary suspension of symptoms produces in them for the time being an exacerbation of their illness.

Freud did little more than characterize "this most powerful of all obstacles."[34] As for Klein, she focused initially on the analysis of the superego in children. In the process she transformed the Freudian superego into a world of internal objects. She next turned to depression. Here too a reconceptualization took place: in Klein's hands, depression underwent a sea change, from a psychiatric category to a grouping of anxieties and defenses that are part of the human condition. Only then did Riviere—and later Klein herself—tackle the negative therapeutic reaction.

Freud and his translator

Shortly before Riviere left for Vienna in early 1922, Jones sent Freud these words of caution:

> I thought it might interest you if I told you . . . about your new patient. . . . She came to me in 1916 and was with me until last June, with about a year's interruption from tuberculosis and other causes. Seeing that she was unusually intelligent I hoped to win her for the cause, a mistake I shall never repeat. I underestimated the uncontrollability of her emotional reactions and in the first year made the serious error of lending her my country cottage for a week when I was not there, she having nowhere to go for a holiday. This led to a declaration of love and to the broken-hearted cry that she had never been rejected before (she has been the mistress of a number of men). From that time she devoted herself to torturing me without any intermission and with considerable success and ingenuity, being a fiendish sadist; my two marriages gave her considerable opportunity for this which she exploited to the full.[35]

(In 1917, following a whirlwind courtship, the first of the marriages to which Jones referred took place. In 1918 the young bride died as the result of chloroform poisoning—the chloroform having been administered in an emergency appendectomy. In 1919 Jones wooed, won, and wed all within the space of six weeks. That marriage lasted until his death almost 40 years later.)

A couple of months after his first wife's death, Jones received this communication from Riviere.

> I regard it as absolutely unquestionable that your wife was to you a substitute for me, in the beginning perhaps even to some extent deliberately and consciously so, though I now have some doubts about this— but at the time it was so obvious ("the exact opposite" etc.) that I imagined you saw it quite clearly. It added very much to my pain that you should imagine there could be a substitute for me, much less my exact opposite, but I need not go into that. When under all the very painful circumstances you married and I left London, I had no idea what your feelings for your wife were, and I remained in total ignorance of your relations with her until after I got back, but it had been quite clear that you *expected* to be happy in your marriage, and I with great difficulty constrained myself to resuming the analysis (because it was my only means to a knowledge of psycho-analysis which I felt was bound up with my interest in life) under the expectation that your feeling for me in the future would be simply one of friendly indifference. What was my astonishment when I got back after 6 months to find, not this, but a formality and impersonality in you that amounted to "hardness" quite brutal to *my* then "quivering" and "wounded" state; in the discussion in regard to your marriage which shortly resulted, a refusal on your part to admit anything more than a "blundering" in your treatment of me. . . .[36]

In a paper published shortly before Riviere entered treatment with Jones, Freud had put his colleagues on notice that their patients would fall in love with them. And it was not just a matter of some patients and some doctors: it happened in all cases irrespective of age and gender alike. The analyst, Freud warned, "must not derive any personal advantage" from a patient's passionate attachment.

> I do not mean to say that it is always easy for the doctor to keep within the limits prescribed by ethics and technique. Those who are still young and not yet bound by strong ties may in particular find it a hard task. . . . Again, when a woman sues for love, to reject and refuse is a distressing part for a man to play; and, in spite of neurosis . . . , there is an incomparable fascination in a woman of high principles who confesses her passion.[37]

Jones resisted the temptation; at the same time the anger he aroused made him despair of his technical competence—he considered Riviere's case "the worst failure" he had ever had:

The treatment finally broke down over my inability to master this negative transference, though I tried all the means in my power. The situation was complicated by her position in the society, which gave her certain personal contact with me. Her dissatisfied reproaches were equally great whether I limited this as far as possible, which I usually did, or allowed it, so for two years at least I have seen that the only solution was to get her to go to you and have finally succeeded in this. . . . Naturally she comes to you with a strong positive transference ready, and my only fear is lest there be not time enough to provoke and work through the necessary negative aspect of this.[38]

Jones trusted that Freud's authority—his "position of acknowledged supremacy"—would enable him to get on with his new patient. He trusted that somehow Freud would pass the "severe test" that Riviere's "visit to Vienna" posed.[39]

*   *   *

The exchanges between Jones and Freud about Riviere did not cease with her arrival in the Austrian capital. From the start of her second analysis, Freud questioned Jones's handling of his former patient.

Mrs. Riviere does not appear to me half as black as you had painted. We agree quite nicely so far. May be the difficulties will come later. . . . I am very glad you had no sexual relations with her as your hints made me suspect. To be sure it was a technical error to befriend her before her analysis was brought to a close. No doubt she is very clever and clear-headed.[40]

Jones, thus finding himself on the defensive, countered with technical advice of his own:

I am not surprised that she is showing her best qualities at present, and she certainly has many, but I only hope that she will have an opportunity to bring out and overcome her bad ones. . . . As she will not be with you in the critical ninth month, when she changed with me, it is a question if it might not be possible later on to regard her as an advanced patient, which of course she is in every respect, and provoke the feelings of disappointment?[41]

It was now Freud's turn to feel under attack:

Somehow . . . I guess your opinion of me in this matter. You think that Mrs. R. has put on her sweetest face and moods, has taken me in completely and seduced me to defend her against you in a chivalrous manner, so that now I am a puppet in her hands. . . . I am sure you are wrong and I feel rather sorry there should be a need to point it out to you. But if I have misconstrued your opinion I beg you will pardon me.[42]

Freud soon shifted to the offensive:

The necessities of a "secondary analysis" put me into the unwished for position to criticize and analyze yourself, a task highly undesirable with a friend of whose value you feel sure and whose frailties you are accustomed to forbear. Now what made the case hard for me was the fact that accuracy and plainness is not in the character of your dealings with people. Slight distortions and evasions, lapses of memory, twisted denials, a certain predilection for sidetracks prevail and whenever I had to examine a case between you and her in detail I had to find, that you were to be doubted while that implacable woman overemphasising the importance of the slightest features yet was right and could not be refuted.[43]

Having concluded that Jones had been "too hard in criticising" Riviere, "took her resistance too seriously and could not control her sadism after it came up as it had to do," Freud set his course. And although "she soon became harsh, unpleasant, critical," he made it a rule—and stuck to it—"to be . . . kind to her" and "not to spare concessions."[44] Twice he advanced her interests, both instances concerned translations and both entailed stepping on Jones's toes—which Freud justified on the grounds that Jones owed her compensation for "having aggravated her analysis by inconsequent behaviour."[45] Freud's determination to secure "due recognition" for her meant, as Jones pointed out, introducing into the second analysis the same "intermixture of analytical considerations with external actual ones" that had plagued the first.[46]

Freud's "diplomacy" aimed at making Riviere "open her mind and disclose . . . the deeper layers." What did he learn? Nothing "definite nor complete":

But one important point soon emerged. She [Riviere] cannot tolerate praise, triumph or success, not any better than failure, blame and repudiation. She gets unhappy in both cases, in the second directly, in the first by reaction. So she has arranged for herself what we call "*eine Zwickmühle*" [a dilemma]. . . . Whenever she has got a recognition, a favour or a present, she is sure to become unpleasant and aggressive and to lose respect for the analyst. You know what that means, it is an infallible sign of a deep sense of guilt, of a conflict between Ego and Ideal. . . . To be sure this conflict, which is the cause of her continuous dissatisfaction, is not known to her consciousness; whenever it is revived she projects her self criticism to other people, turns her pangs of conscience into sadistic behaviour, tries to render other people unhappy because she feels so herself.[47]

As Freud prepared to interrupt his work with Riviere for his summer vacation—they resumed for a month in October—he commented to Jones that he could not claim to have "much altered" his patient. She would, in his opinion, "require special care and regards indefinitely." That special care he now assigned to Jones; as for himself, he planned to "drop out of the relation . . . soon."[48] Contrary to Freud's expectations, Jones's initial report on Riviere sounded a distinctly positive note: he detected "some changes in her reactions as the result of her visit to Vienna, and for the better." When she arrived back in London after her sojourn in the fall, Jones wrote with equal enthusiasm: "Mrs. Riviere . . . made an excellent impression on her return and I think we shall work well together." And in 1924, after she had spent another six weeks in the Austrian capital, he sent a similarly glowing account: "she has proved a most valuable and loyal cooperator, has given not the slightest trouble to anyone, and is on the best of terms with myself."[49] If one of Freud's goals for the treatment had been to foster a collegial relationship between Jones and Riviere, for their benefit and for the benefit of the psychoanalytic movement, the outcome could be reckoned as positive. This, however, had not been the reason Riviere had sought a second analysis: she later confided to a supervisee that "she resented Freud's use of her as a translator before she was able to relate to him as a patient in analysis."[50]

*   *   *

During the summer of 1922 Freud continued mulling over Riviere's analysis.[51] His "diplomacy" had been insufficient. Given her inability to "tolerate praise, triumph or success," how could it have been otherwise? Freud had set himself the analytic task of conquering "her incapacity for her enjoying success," but he had not had time to accomplish it. Nor had he the means: both theory and technique came up short. He admitted to Jones that "our theory has not yet mastered the mechanism of these cases" and that the "technical ways" of dealing with them still eluded him.[52] In *The Ego and the Id* Freud made a start toward filling in the gaps.

There Freud gave an account of the superego, something that he had pieced together over the years. Its function—prohibitions and bearer of standards—could be traced back to censorship, which played a crucial role in *The Interpretation of Dreams*, to shame, disgust, and morality, which turned up repeatedly in the *Three Essays*, and to the ego-ideal, which loomed large in "On Narcissism." Its formation harked back to "Mourning and Melancholia." Recall Freud's argument that the melancholic identified with an abandoned object. In identifying with the lost object, the melancholic incorporated or introjected it: he took it into himself, more specifically, he felt he had devoured it. Then, in *The Ego and the Id*, Freud claimed that the establishment of the critical agency itself—the superego—could be explained along similar lines. At the same time he spelled out the relations between the superego and the parents and other authority figures in the child's environment. The superego derived from these figures; it was the incorporated or introjected version of them. And in Freud's view that incorporation took place on a massive scale at a particular moment—with the dissolution of the Oedipus complex. Hence, on numerous occasions, he referred to the superego as "the heir to the Oedipus complex."[53] With this concept at his disposal, Freud turned to patients such as Riviere:

> There is no doubt that there is something in these people that sets itself against recovery, and its approach is dreaded as though it were a danger. ... If we analyze this resistance in the usual way—then, even after allowance has been made for an attitude of defiance towards the physician and fixation to the various forms of gain from illness, the greater part of it is still left over.

As Freud saw it in 1923, he was dealing with "a 'moral' factor, a sense of guilt,' " which was "finding its satisfaction in the illness" and refused "to give up the punishment of suffering."

> But as far as the patient is concerned this sense of guilt is dumb; it does not tell him he is guilty; he does not feel guilty, he feels ill. This sense of guilt expresses itself only as a resistance to recovery which is extremely difficult to overcome. It is also particularly difficult to convince the patient that this motive lies behind his continuing to be ill; he holds fast to the more obvious explanation that treatment by analysis is not the right remedy for his case.[54]

More than a decade would pass before Riviere challenged Freud's pessimism in print. Why, she wondered, should the negative therapeutic reaction be "thought of as more unanalysable" than any other reaction.[55] Her comparative optimism rested on Klein's exploration of the superego and its severity.

Klein: The analysis of the superego

"For many years," Jones wrote Freud in 1927, there has been "a rather special interest taken in the problems of childhood in London." He attributed this interest to the presence of women analysts in the British Society. He might have added that most of the women were nonmedical and might have inferred that where lay female analysts prospered, so too did the analysis of children. He continued:

About three years ago we had a thorough discussion of the question of how far analytic methods can be pushed in childhood, particularly to what extent and to how early an age. . . . The outcome of our discussion was a progressive one. We decided that only experience could prove whether the young child's ego was capable of enduring repressed material in the same way that we know an adult's ego can by the help of analysis, and that this should be more important than any theoretical reason to the contrary. Some time after this Mrs. Klein came to London, first to lecture and then to work. There is general confidence in her method and results, which several of us have been able to test at the closest quarters, and she makes the general impression of a sane, well-balanced, and thoroughly analyzed person. . . . [W]e have come to regard her extension of psycho-analysis into this new field . . . as opening up the most promising avenue to direct investigation of the earliest and deepest problems. Holding such an attitude, we could . . . only regard any attempt made to close this avenue as most unfortunate.[56]

Jones obviously regarded Anna Freud's *Introduction to the Technique of the Analysis of Children* (1927) as just such an attempt and penned this letter to Freud, and several others, following the publication both of Anna's book and the British Society's symposium on child analysis:

[I]n the natural course of things a review of Anna's book was read before the Society. . . . The discussion that followed had to be continued to the next meeting, but it was not in any way organized or influenced. . . . It was certainly noteworthy that people so dissimilar and independent of one another as Edward Glover and Mrs. Klein, Mrs. Riviere and Miss Searl, should agree in deprecating the check that Anna's attitude was felt to impose on the development of early analysis.[57]

Among the participants Freud singled out Riviere for criticism. He found her "theoretical statements . . . disconcerting" and wrote her to that effect—so that she might "appreciate her blunder for herself."[58]

If I assumed that you let yourself be carried away by your partisanship in your contribution to the Symposium, then I was seeking an excuse for you. I know your weakness is a tendency to aggression, as Anna's is toward reserve. For I could not easily believe that you profess views, which so much contradict everything we believe in analysis. I think you have not properly considered the significance of your propositions. I reproached Jones for not having brought this to your attention and restrained you. That sounds intolerant, looks like censorship and tutelage, but what else can one do; within a society like ours, one must be in agreement on basic principles.[59]

Where had Riviere, following Klein, been led astray? Here is the paragraph—the last of her symposium contribution—to which Freud took particular exception:[60]

> Psycho-analysis is Freud's discovery of what goes on in the imagination of a child—and it still provokes great opposition from us all; this "childishness," these unconscious phantasies, are abhorred and dreaded—and unwittingly longed for—by us even yet, and this is why even analysts still hesitate to probe these depths. But analysis has no concern with anything else: it is not concerned with the real world, nor with the child's or adult's adaptation to the real world, nor with virtue or vice. It is concerned simply and solely with the imaginings of this childish mind, the phantasied pleasures and the dreaded retributions. *These* have to be taken at their full value and credited with their true importance.[61]

Riviere's views, Jones claimed, coming to her defense, were not themselves "untrue"; she had merely presented them in a "one-sided" and hence provocative manner. To smooth the troubled waters, he glossed her remarks:

> She insists that the child's unconscious picture of the parents to which it reacts in such manifold ways is far from being a photograph of them, but is throughout coloured by entirely individual contributions from the child's own component instincts, e.g. the idea of the parent may be much more sadistic than the reality, etc. etc. This I should have thought was common ground in psycho-analysis. . . . Naturally Mrs. Riviere would not deny the influence of real attributes to the parents in this compound, and I told her she was making a mistake in dwelling only on what might be called the phantastic half of the picture.[62]

He might have also pointed out—as he did on another occasion—that there was "no serious danger of any analysts neglecting external reality"; it was, however, "always possible for them to under-estimate Freud's doctrine of the importance of psychical reality."[63]

In thus accentuating "the phantastic half," Riviere highlighted what Klein herself regarded as the principal lesson she was learning from her young patients.

*   *   *

When, in 1923, Abraham mentioned Klein to Freud, he referred to her skillful handling of a 3-year-old boy, who presented "the basic melancholia." Over that summer Klein was also analyzing a little girl—"Rita"—aged 2 years and 3 months at the beginning of treatment. The analysis took place in the child's home; she played with her toys, and Klein interpreted her play, just as she had done with her first patient, her son Erich, alias Fritz. (After her experience with Rita, Klein insisted on using her own consulting room for child analysis.) The treatment itself was brief—it lasted only three or four months—but it prompted much reflection on both theory and practice. Klein was still drawing on this case when she wrote "The Oedipus Complex in the Light of Early Anxieties" (1945) more than two decades later.

What did the basic melancholia look like? The child suffered from attacks of moodiness and cried a good deal, apparently without cause. "When asked by her mother why she was crying [she] answered: 'Because I'm so sad.' To the question: 'Why are you so sad?' she replied: 'Because I'm crying.' " The little girl, in turn, asked her mother and asked constantly: "Am I good?" "Do you love me?" At the same time "she alternated between an exaggerated 'goodness' accompanied by feelings of remorse, and states of 'naughtiness' when she attempted to dominate everybody around her."[64] She also suffered from severe anxieties, particularly night terrors, and invented an elaborate bedtime ritual. She had to be tightly tucked up in the bedclothes, otherwise a "mouse or a butty might come through the window and bite off her butty."[65] Her doll had to be tucked up too, and this double ceremonial became more and more drawn out and was performed with every sign of compulsion. Altogether Klein regarded Rita as a very difficult child to manage.

Here are some of the facts of her history, including those Klein considered the most salient:

> Rita shared her parents' bedroom until she was nearly two, and she repeatedly witnessed sexual intercourse between . . . [them]. When she was two years old, her brother was born, and at that time her neurosis broke out in full force. Another contributing circumstance was that her mother was herself neurotic and obviously ambivalent towards Rita.
>
> Her parents told me that Rita was much more fond of her mother than of her father until the end of her first year. At the beginning of her second year she developed a marked preference for her father, together with pronounced jealousy of her mother. At fifteen months Rita repeatedly and unmistakably expressed the wish, when she sat on her father's knee, to be left alone with him in the room. She could already put this into words. At the age of about eighteen months there was a striking change. . . . Her mother once again became the favourite. . . . She clung to her mother so much that she could hardly let her out of sight. This went together with . . . an often unconcealed hatred of her. Concurrently Rita developed an outspoken dislike of her father.[66]

Under the watchful gaze of Rita's mother and aunt, Klein set to work:

> Rita, when left alone with me in her nursery, . . . was anxious and silent and very soon asked to go out into the garden. I agreed and went with her—I may add, . . . her mother and aunt . . . took this as a sign of

failure. . . . From a few things she [Rita] said, and the fact that she was
less frightened when we were in the open, I concluded that she was particularly afraid of something which I might do to her when she was alone
with me in the room. I interpreted this and referring to her night terrors, I
linked her suspicion of me as a hostile stranger with her fear that a bad
woman would attack her when she was by herself at night. When, a few
minutes after this interpretation, I suggested that we should return to the
nursery, she readily agreed.[67]

A start—Rita at least tolerated Klein's presence. But her play remained
stereotyped: "the only thing she could do with her dolls, for instance, was to
wash them and change their clothes in a compulsive way. As soon as she
introduced any imaginative element, she had an outburst of anxiety and
stopped playing."[68] Before too long a shift occurred, though when and how
Klein did not say. Nowhere did she provide a consecutive account of the
treatment. Instead she reported on games Rita played.

In the first, Klein saw allusions to the primal scene. One day Rita told her
analyst that "the dolls had disturbed her in her sleep: they kept on saying to
Hans, the underground train man (a male doll on wheels): 'Just go on driving
your train up and down.' " On another occasion Rita put a triangular block
on one side and said: " 'That's a little woman'; she then took a 'little hammer,' " as she called another rectangular block and hit the box that contained
the blocks "exactly in a place where it was only stuck together with paper,
so that she made a hole in it. She said: 'When the hammer hit hard, the
little woman was *so* frightened.' " Klein interpreted: " 'Your Daddy hit hard
like that inside your Mummy with his little hammer, and you were so
frightened.' "[69]

A second game that Rita played repeatedly pointed to her wish to possess
a penis. She and her teddy-bear went in a train to the "house of a 'good'
woman where she was to be given a 'marvelous treat.' " The journey, however,
did not go smoothly. Rita fought with the trainman: she wanted to drive the
train herself and get rid of the driver. He either refused to go or came back
and threatened her. "An object of contention between her and him was her
Teddy-bear whom she felt to be essential for the success of the journey. Here
the bear represented her father's penis, and her rivalry with her father was
expressed by this fight over the penis. She had robbed her father of it, partly
from feelings of envy, hatred and revenge, [and] partly in order to take his
place with her mother."[70]

A third shed light on Rita's bedtime ritual. On one occasion during her
analytic session, she tucked her doll into bed to go to sleep and then she put
an elephant into the bed as well. The elephant was supposed to keep the
" 'child' from getting up"; otherwise she "would steal" into her "parents'
bedroom and either do them some harm or take something from them."[71] It
now became clear that Rita's insistence on being tucked securely into bed was

designed to prevent her from getting up and carrying out aggressive wishes against her own parents. "Since, however, she expected to be punished for those wishes by a similar attack on herself by her parents, being tucked up also served as a defense against such attacks. . . . In these games she used to punish her doll and then give way to an outburst of rage and fear, thus showing that she was playing both parts herself—that of the powers which inflict punishment and that of the punished child."[72]

Her interpretations, Klein claimed, fit with Rita's "way of thinking and speaking."[73] They also fit with her own theory-in-the-making; they encouraged her to take the steps that ranked as major departures in the 1920s: pushing back in time the first appearance of both the Oedipus complex and the superego.

*   *   *

As I see it, the boy's and girl's sexual and emotional development *from infancy onwards* includes genital sensations and trends, which constitute the first stages of the inverted and positive Oedipus complex; they are experienced under the primacy of oral libido and mingle with urethral and anal desires and phantasies. The libidinal stages overlap from the earliest months of life onwards. The positive and inverted Oedipus tendencies are from their inception in close interaction.[74]

By stressing the ways in which libidinal trends overlapped and coincided with oedipal dramas, Klein took a major step toward reconceptualizing the child's emotional ties to an external object. Where Freud retained two separate developmental lines, libido and object love, whose convergence at a fairly late date produced the Oedipus complex, Klein assumed that so clear a distinction was more misleading than helpful.

One can find in Klein's writings, as in Freud's, four versions, two female and two male, of the Oedipus complex. For the girl the positive course involves carrying over the "*receptive* [instinctual] aim . . . from the oral to the genital position." In so doing she becomes receptive toward the penis and simultaneously turns to her father as love object. In contrast, for the boy the "normal" succession entails a change of instinctual aim but not of object: when he abandons "the oral and anal positions for the genital, he passes on to the aim of *penetration* associated with possession of the penis"—all the while retaining his original love object.[75] From this outline the negatives are easy to infer: in the girl, change of aim and retention of object; in the boy, retention of aim and change of object. Yet rather than taking positive and negative elements and arranging them in a limited number of fixed patterns, Klein was intent on transforming the Oedipus complex into a constantly fluctuating configuration.

In similar fashion Klein argued that the superego took shape in tandem with the Oedipus complex. Both were set in motion when oral sadism was at its height. Both were initially under the sway of the anxiety aroused by that sadism.

> According to my observations, the formation of the super-ego begins at the same time as the child makes its earliest oral introjection of its objects. Since the first imagos it thus forms are endowed with all the attributes of the intense sadism belonging to this stage of its development, and since they will once more be projected on to the objects of the outer world, the small child becomes dominated by the fear of suffering unimaginable cruel attacks, both from its real objects and from its super-ego.[76]

For Klein the superego's punitive harshness, readily apparent in clinical material, posed no problem, whereas for Freud it remained a puzzle. In his work he offered two different, though not mutually exclusive, explanations. As Klein summarized them: "According to one, the severity of the super-ego derived from the severity of the real father. . . . According to the other, . . . its severity . . . [was] an outcome of the destructive impulses of the subject."[77] Klein did more than endorse the second view. She had the right to claim priority in this matter, and Freud—who rarely referred to her writings—granted her a measure of recognition, albeit in a footnote.[78]

How could the Kleinian superego (or the Freudian for that matter) be regarded as an ego ideal? When, in *The Ego and the Id*, Freud had first used the term "super-ego" he had considered it to be synonymous with ego ideal. After close to a decade, during which "ego ideal" failed to reappear in print, he attempted, in the *New Introductory Lectures*, to define it once again. Simply put, the superego had at least two recognizably different tasks: as the agent of prohibition and punishment and as "the advocate of a striving toward perfection" or the "ideal."[79] Two sets of parental images were playing these two roles: parents as terrifying figures who were hated and feared and parents as ideal figures. Though Klein initially stressed the first—the superego's severity—she had no vested interest in regarding the superego as a unitary structure. A 4-year-old boy, she wrote, who "suffered from the pressure of a castrating and cannibalistic superego, in complete contrast to his loving parents," had "certainly not only this one super-ego":

> I discovered in him identifications which corresponded more closely to his real parents, though not by any means identical with them. These figures, who appeared good and helpful and ready to forgive, he called his "fairy papa and mamma," and, when his attitude towards me was positive, he allowed me in the analysis to play the part of the "fairy mamma" to whom everything could be confessed. At other times . . . I played the part of the wicked mamma from whom everything evil that he

phantasied was anticipated. . . . A whole series of [the] most varied identifications, which were in opposition to one another, originated in widely
different strata and periods and differed fundamentally from the real
objects, had in this child resulted in a super-ego which actually gave the
impression of being normal and well developed.[80]

It stood to reason, then, that Klein regarded the "gradual modification" of
a harsh superego as one of the principal aims of treatment.[81] In Rita's case,
she felt that much had been accomplished and also that much remained to be
done. The analysis lasted only 83 sessions and was broken off when her
parents went to live abroad. The child's "depressive symptoms . . . were a
good deal moderated"; her "anxiety was lessened and her obsessive ceremo-
nials disappeared." The changes in Rita brought with them an improvement
in her mother's ambivalent attitude toward her; "even so it remained a severe
handicap in the child's development." Klein concluded that "it would have
been advisable to have continued her analysis. . . . There is no doubt that
if . . . [Rita's] analysis had been carried through to the end . . . , she would
have gained a more effective counterbalance against the neurotic and
neurosis-inducing environment in which she lived.[82]

*   *   *

Did such obvious dependence of the child on external objects rule out transference? Anna Freud's affirmative answer provoked sharp dissent from
Klein's British colleagues. Riviere mounted the most vigorous challenge.
Could Anna Freud actually believe, Riviere wondered, that so long as
the child remained attached to his parents—and the "Oedipus situation"
was "still active in relation to the original objects"—there could be no
transference from them?

> [T]he really important part of this proposition seems to be the way it
> questions and invalidates all that we have hitherto learnt about the true
> nature of the Oedipus complex, i.e. its unconscious character. It is surely
> clear enough from adult analyses that it is not the reality of the patient's
> relations with his parents at any age that is reflected in his neurosis. The
> Oedipus complex and the pregenital phantasies woven into it originate
> and have their existence in the mind—or in the "imagination," as we
> might express it in ordinary everyday speech. . . . These phantasies are
> played out in the *Unconscious*, and the objects of them are not the real
> father and mother at all, but the unconscious imagos of them. The
> unconscious relations with these imagos are then *transferred* to the *real*
> parents and worked off on them (just as they are worked off on the
> analyst in the transference). . . . This is a perfectly commonplace and
> familiar fact to every analyst, but it would nevertheless be fundamentally
> disproved if the statements made by Anna Freud were true.

How could Anna Freud, Riviere asked, have missed the obvious? Riviere placed the blame on her technique, on the mixing of the pedagogical with the analytic:

> She says that since she does not preserve the aloofness of the adult's analyst, cannot be a mere reflection of the unconscious, and has to be an imposing and attractive personality to the child, the imagos are blurred and indistinguishable. It is, of course, true that in such conditions the imagos would be blurred, but it does not follow that no transference . . . has developed, just because it is indistinguishable. In this connection Anna Freud's contentions are not even logical: throughout her book she says analysis cannot be done in the customary way with children because they are not like adults, and here she says that they are not like adults because analysis is not done in the customary way with them.[83]

In light of Klein's work with children, to re-examine transference and its interpretation in adult cases was a reasonable next step. It turned out to be the necessary preparation for grappling with the overlapping issues of depression, the unconscious sense of guilt, and negative therapeutic reactions.

Riviere, Klein, and negative therapeutic reactions

During the Controversial Discussions of the 1940s, Klein remarked that thanks to her work with young children she had arrived at a broader understanding of transference:

> In my experience the transference situation permeates the whole actual life of the patient during the analysis. When the analytic situation has been established, the analyst takes the place of the original objects, and the patient . . . deals again and again with the feelings and conflicts which are being revived, with the very defenses he used in the original situation. While repeating . . . in relation to the analyst some of his early feelings, phantasies and sexual desires, he displaces others from the analyst to different people and situations. . . . In other words, the patient is "acting out" part of his transference feelings in a different setting outside the analysis.[84]

How had stretching the concept of transference affected psychoanalytic technique? Sylvia Payne, also as part of the Controversial Discussions, reflected on the changes she had witnessed:

> When I started my training with James Glover in 1919 I sat in a chair facing him and he wrote down every word I said. . . . Then after he had

had training with Dr Abraham in Berlin he changed his technique and the patient lay on the couch, the analyst sitting behind. Interpretations were given mainly at the end of the session but not exclusively. Transference interpretations were given when transference resistance occurred and there was evidence in the material. The analyst was very passive.

When I worked with Dr [Hanns] Sachs the technique was very much the same except that interpretation was much more systematized. There was more reconstruction and again transference was only interpreted when it was resistance.

In subsequent years . . . I observed that English analysts used transference interpretations very much more actively than Dr Sachs had done and some tended to bring every relationship spoken of by the patient into the transference situation.[85]

Those English analysts—Klein among them[86]—invariably cited James Strachey's paper "The Nature of the Therapeutic Action of Psycho-Analysis" (1934). In it he articulated the rationale for making transference interpretation a central, indeed the central, feature of treatment.

Strachey began by reviewing Freud's technical recommendations. All of them, he noted, had appeared in print in the 1910s, that is, before Freud introduced the structural model of ego, id, and superego. In the 1920s and 1930s he wrote little on technical matters. A couple of items, however, stood out. In his *Inhibitions, Symptoms and Anxiety* (1926) Freud mentioned five sorts of resistance. Strachey fastened on the fifth, the one "coming from the *super-ego*." It was "the most obscure though not always the least powerful one." It seemed "to originate from the sense of guilt or the need for punishment"; and it opposed "every move towards success, including . . . the patient's own recovery through analysis."[87] Strachey also fastened on a passage in Freud's *Group Psychology and the Analysis of the Ego* (1921) and interpreted it as hinting that the analyst could influence the patient through the latter's superego.[88] Taken together, Strachey argued, these two items pointed to "the patient's super-ego as occupying a key position in analytic therapy": it was the part of the patient's mind in which "a favourable alteration would be likely to lead to a general improvement" (Strachey did not specify the particular improvement Freud's remarks suggested—overcoming a guilt-induced opposition to recovery) and it was the "part of the patient's mind" which was "especially subject to the analyst's influence." Strachey then took it upon himself to restate "the principles of therapeutics . . . in super-ego terms."[89]

But in terms of whose superego? The answer is Melanie Klein's. It was her account of "the extreme severity of the super-ego in small children" that Strachey drew on. He stressed how the child constantly introjects and projects the objects of his id-impulses, how the character of the introjected objects depends on "the character of the id-impulses directed towards the external objects," how, for example, when the child is dominated by oral aggression, his feelings towards his external object will be orally aggressive, and how he will then "introject the object, and the introjected object will now act (in the manner of a super-ego) in an orally aggressive way towards the child's ego." This was standard Kleinian fare. So too was the following step, which amounted to a tightening of the screw. "[N]ext . . . will be the projection of this orally aggressive introjected object back on to the external object, which will now in its turn appear to be orally aggressive. The . . . external object being thus felt as dangerous and destructive once more causes the id-impulses to adopt an even more aggressive and destructive attitudes towards the object in self-defense." The neurotic remained trapped: "exposed to the pressure of a savage id on the one hand and a correspondingly savage super-ego on the other."[90] He remained trapped in what Strachey characterized as a vicious circle. The analyst's task, as Strachey saw it, consisted in breaching this circle:

> If . . . the patient could be made less frightened of his super-ego or introjected object, he would project less terrifying imagos on to the outer object and would therefore have less need to feel hostility towards it; the object which he then introjected would in turn be less savage in its pressure upon the id-impulses, which would be able to lose something of their primitive ferocity.

In short, a "*benign* circle would be set up instead of the vicious one," and as in the case of the normal adult, the patient's superego would become "comparatively mild" and his ego would have "a relatively undistorted contact with reality."[91]

How was this to be accomplished? The patient, Strachey argued, tended "to accept the analyst in some way or other as a substitute for his super-ego." He tended "to make the analyst into an 'auxiliary super-ego.'" This new bit of superego operated differently from the old: it operated with neither the archaic harshness nor kindliness of the rest of the superego. Instead its "advice to the ego" was "consistently based upon . . . *contemporary* considerations." The advice, however, did not always register with the patient. Strachey took pains to underline just how uncertain the new dispensation appeared to be.

> The patient is liable at any moment to project his terrifying imago on to the analyst. . . . If this happens, the introjected imago of the analyst will be wholly incorporated into the rest of the patient's harsh super-ego, and the auxiliary super-ego will disappear. And even when the *content* of the auxiliary super-ego's advice is realized as being different from and contrary to that of the original super-ego, very often the *quality* will be

felt as being the same. For instance, the patient may feel that the analyst has said to him: "If you don't say whatever comes into your head, I shall give you a good hiding," or, "If you don't become conscious of this piece of the unconscious I shall turn you out of the room."

Labile and limited though the authority of the analyst as auxiliary superego might be, it put within the analyst's reach "the main weapon" in his "armoury": the "mutative" interpretation.[92]

According to Strachey, a mutative interpretation falls into two phases, which, for descriptive purposes, he treated as sequential. In the first phase, thanks to the permission granted by the analyst as auxiliary superego, a patient allows an aggressive or erotic impulse into consciousness. The patient sees this impulse as being aimed at the analyst. In the second phase the patient recognizes his mistake; he becomes aware that his impulse is "directed towards an archaic phantasy object and not towards a real one." At the critical moment, the patient proves able to distinguish between the two. The patient's sense of reality thus serves as "an essential but ... very feeble ally."[93]

How not to tax or overtax the feeble partner? Other defining attributes of mutative interpretations spoke to this concern. In the first instance, Strachey insisted that a mutative interpretation be immediate: "interpretation must always be directed to the 'point of urgency.'" At any given moment some particular impulse would be active; this was the impulse that was susceptible of mutative interpretation, then and only then. In the second instance, Strachey maintained that "a mutative interpretation must be 'specific'": it must be "detailed and concrete." He acknowledged that specificity was a question of degree. "When the analyst embarks upon a given theme, his interpretations cannot always avoid being vague and general to begin with. ... [M]uch of the ... apparent repetition of interpretations" could "be explained by the need for filling in the details." Finally, Strachey asked: were mutative interpretations also "deep," that is, was the material interpreted "either genetically early and historically distant from the patient's actual experience or ... under an especially heavy weight of repression"? Here safety, not depth, ruled, with safety being understood as a matter of how much anxiety a patient could manage and still hold on to his sense of reality. In certain circumstances—but not all—deep interpretations of urgent material rather than "more superficial interpretations of non-urgent material" might be the safer course.[94]

In Strachey's view, mutative interpretations operated on a small scale; they were "governed by the principle of minimal doses." By the same token, therapeutic change, which resulted from "an immense number of minute steps," each of which corresponded "to a mutative interpretation," was equally gradual.[95] And mutative interpretations were by definition transference interpretations—though not all transference interpretations were mutative. Thanks, then, to the repeated confrontation between a fantasy analyst and the real analyst, the patient's perception of both his inner and outer worlds was altered: the vicious circle slowed down, and a benign circle started up.

A remark by Freud—a footnote in *The Ego and the Id*—had earlier pointed to the analyst assuming the position of auxiliary superego and had cautioned against it. Here is the footnote:

> The battle with the obstacle of an unconscious sense of guilt is not made easy for the analyst. . . . It [the outcome] depends principally on the intensity of the guilt; there is often no counteracting force of a similar order of strength which the treatment can oppose to it. Perhaps it may depend, too, on whether the personality of the analyst allows of the patient putting him in the place of his ego ideal, and this involves a temptation on the part of the analyst to play the part of prophet, saviour and redeemer to the patient.

But adopting the role of prophet was not advisable: "the rules of analysis," Freud emphasized, were "diametrically opposed to the physician's making use of his personality in any such manner."[96] Without referring explicitly to this passage, Strachey took the warning to heart:

> [T]he patient is all the time on the brink of turning the real external object (the analyst) into the archaic one; that is to say, he is on the brink of projecting his primitive introjected imagos on to him. In so far as the patient actually does this, the analyst becomes like anyone else that he meets in real life—a phantasy object. . . . The analyst must [therefore] avoid any real behaviour that is likely to confirm the patient's view of him as a "bad" or a "good" phantasy object. This is perhaps obvious as regards the "bad" object. If, for instance, the analyst were to show that he was really shocked or frightened by one of the patient's id-impulses, the patient would immediately treat him . . . as a dangerous object and introject him into his archaic severe super-ego. . . . But it may be equally unwise for the analyst to act really in such a way as to encourage the patient to project his "good" introjected object on to him. For the patient will then tend to regard him as a good object in an archaic sense and will incorporate him with his archaic "good" imagos and will use him as a protection against his "bad" ones. . . . It is a paradoxical fact that the best way of ensuring that his [the patient's] ego shall be able to distinguish between phantasy and reality is to withhold reality from him as much as possible.[97]

*   *   *

Klein's papers "A Contribution to the Psychogenesis of Manic-Depressive States" and "Mourning and its Relation to Manic-Depressive States" taken together are generally regarded as having marked a new departure. In them she sought to describe the building up of an internal world and to chart the vicissitudes of object relations within that world.

Recall the introjection and projection of both good and bad objects. Initially such objects were not whole objects; they were part objects, and the mother's breast was the prototype. The "badness" of the breast was not simply a function of how the mother presented it to her infant; its "badness" was not merely a consequence of frustration, though frustration certainly played a part. Rather, because the infant projected his own aggression onto the breast, the breast that was introjected or incorporated was bad. And its badness was very bad indeed. In contrast, the breast's "goodness" (which Klein distinguished from a defensive idealization) appeared to be dependent on oral satisfaction. The result was a certain asymmetry: bad objects derived from a child's sadism; good objects from the external world; bad breasts differed fundamentally from the real objects; good breasts more closely approximated actual mothers who had been on hand in early infancy.

It was a development of the "highest importance" when an infant took the step from "a partial object-relation to the relation with a complete object." At this point the good object came into its own. Wholeness heightened the likelihood that the ego would "identify itself more fully with 'good' objects." This last phrase is obscure: "identify" gives trouble. Klein did not mean that the "ego"—infant would be more appropriate here—tried to be like its good external object. Rather she seems to mean that the infant became dependent upon it, and upon its internalized counterpart, with a new force. "From now on preservation of the good object is regarded as synonymous with the survival of the ego."[98]

Thus the infant came to the anxieties that marked the depressive position: the infant felt "constantly menaced" in his "possession of internalized good objects"; he was "full of anxiety lest such objects should die." And these good objects were threatened from all sides. "It is not only the vehemence of the subject's uncontrollable hatred but that of his love too which imperils the object. For at this stage of his development loving an object and devouring it are very closely connected." A little child who believed, when his mother disappeared, that he had "eaten her up and destroyed her (whether from motives of love or of hate) is tormented by anxiety."[99] And not only by anxiety: guilt and remorse were its constant companions.

How could the anguish Klein described be assuaged? Successful reparation was the answer she provided. Early in her career she noted the violence and cruelty with which children dealt with their objects—and the concern and repentance that came after:

> [T]he impression I get of the ways in which even the quite small child fights his unsocial tendencies is rather touching. . . . [A] manifestation of

> primitive tendencies is invariably followed by anxiety and by perform-
> ances which show that the child now tries to make good and atone for
> that which he has done. Sometimes he tries to mend the very same . . .
> [toy figures], trains and so on he has just broken. Sometimes drawing,
> building and so on express the same reactive tendencies.[100]

When Klein formulated the concept of the depressive position, reparation
assumed a leading role.

> When the child's belief in his capacity to love, in his reparative powers
> and in the integration and security of his good inner world increase . . . ,
> manic omnipotence decreases . . . , which means in general that the
> infantile neurosis has passed.[101]

What had happened to the Oedipus complex? What had become of the
"infantile neurosis" par excellence? Did the depressive position oust what
Freud referred to as "the nucleus of the neuroses"? The relation between the
two was more complicated that one of simple substitution. Klein in fact had
no intention of discarding the Oedipus complex. She tried to keep it and the
depressive position working in tandem: both, she argued, appeared at the
same time, roughly midway through the infant's first year. (Initially Klein had
claimed that the Oedipus complex was bound up with the "phase of maximal
sadism," at roughly age one. Subsequently she pushed back that phase to the
first few months of life and joined it to the onset of persecutory—as opposed
to depressive—anxieties.)[102] In linking the two, she made the depressive position fundamental: if the Oedipus complex became a drama of whole object
relations, the depressive position provided its subtext:

> The sorrow and concern about the feared loss of the "good" objects, that
> is to say, the depressive position is, in my experience, the deepest source
> of the painful conflicts of the Oedipus situation, as well as in the child's
> relations to people in general.[103]

*   *   *

In "Mourning and Melancholia" Freud had observed that "the most remarkable characteristic of melancholia . . . is its tendency to change round into
mania—a state which is the opposite to it in its symptoms." Nevertheless, he
added, several psychoanalytic investigators had suggested that "the content
of mania is no different from that of melancholia, that both disorders are
wrestling with the same 'complex,' but that probably in melancholia the ego
has succumbed to the complex whereas in mania it has mastered it or pushed
it aside."[104] In her paper "A Contribution to the Analysis of the Negative
Therapeutic Reaction" (1936), Riviere conceptualized this pushing aside as a
"manic defensive system."

The essential feature of the manic attitude is omnipotence and the *omnipotent denial of psychic reality*. . . . The *denial* relates especially to the ego's object-relations and its *dependence on its objects*, as a result of which *contempt* and depreciation of the value of its objects is a marked feature, together with attempts at inordinate and tyrannical *control and mastery of its objects*.[105]

To turn to the negative therapeutic reaction. The patient who does not get well, the patient who—and here Riviere quoted Freud—"cannot endure any praise or appreciation of progress in the treatment," she saw as desperately trying to preserve the status quo, a state of things that, painful though it might be, was still bearable. The patient "does not intend to . . . change, or to end the analysis, because he does not believe it possible that any change or any lessening of control on his part can bring anything but . . . disaster." So the patient " 'keeps things going,' keeps some belief that 'one day' he will have done with it all, and *postpones* the crash, the day of reckoning and judgement."

One patient had woven this into a lifelong defensive pattern: his death would be exacted yes, but he would see to it that this was postponed until his normal span had elapsed. He had reached a position of success and recognition in his own department of the world's work, so in old age his obituary notices would eventually serve him still as his last and final denials and defenses against his terrible anxieties.[106]

Riviere refused to lose heart. She glossed Freud's account of the negative therapeutic reaction as something that was happening *"for the time being."* It was not immutable. As Riviere saw it, the unconscious sense of guilt—the very reason, according to Freud, for the patient's getting worse instead of better—provided a motive, albeit an unconscious one, for the patient to seek treatment:

The patient's conscious aim in coming to analysis is to get well himself; unconsciously this point is relatively secondary, for other needs come first. Unconsciously his aim is . . . to cure and make well and happy all his loved and hated objects . . . before he thinks of himself. . . . All the injuries he ever did them in thought and deed arose from his "selfishness," from being too greedy, and too envious of them, not generous and willing enough to allow them what they had . . .—from not loving *them* enough, in fact. In his mind every one of these acts and thoughts of selfishness and injury . . . has to be reversed, to be made good, by sacrifices on his own part, before he can even be sure that his own life is secure—much less begin to think about getting well and happy himself. . . . I have to remind you that his unconscious aims are really *unconscious* and that we cannot use them directly as a lever to help on the analysis. We cannot say, "What you really want is to cure and help other people, those you love, and not yourself," because that thought . . . brings up at once . . . all his greatest anxieties. . . . We have to be . . . guarded about directly imputing any altruistic motives to such patients. . . . Nevertheless, when we know the unconscious situation, we know how to watch our steps; and even if we cannot use this lever ourselves for a very long time at least, we know it is there and can bring into play any indications of it there are, in subtle, indirect and gradual ways which do not rouse instant and unmanageable resistances.[107]

Analysis, if successful, would mean unmasking "the internal depressive reality"; it would mean "making real, 'realizing,' . . . [the] despair . . . and *sense of failure.*" It was not difficult to grasp why the patient would want none of it. On the one hand, the patient doubts that "he would eventually use . . . benefits obtained through analysis for the good of his objects; he knows very well . . . [that] he will merely repeat his crimes and now use up the analyst for his own gratification and add him to the list of those he has despoiled and ruined." On the other hand, the patient has an even greater fear that "if he were cured, . . . and . . . at last able to compass the reparation needed by all those he loved and injured, . . . the magnitude of the task would then absorb . . . his whole physical and mental powers . . . , every breath, every heartbeat, drop of blood, every thought, every moment of time, every possession . . .—an extremity of slavery . . . which passes conscious imagination." Yet, "he knows that no one but an analyst ventures to approach even to the fringes of these problems of his; and so he clings to analysis" despite having little faith in it.[108]

As for the analyst, he needed to proceed with caution. He was too likely to see in the patient's attempts to control everything nothing but a negative transference at work, and to interpret accordingly:

This interpretation, so far as it goes, is certainly correct; the patient is extremely hostile; but that is not all. Things are not so simple. The very great importance of analysing aggressive tendencies has perhaps carried some analysts off their feet, and in some quarters is defeating its own ends. . . . Nothing will lead more surely to a negative therapeutic reaction in the patient than failure to recognize anything but the aggression in his material.

It was the positive transference—"a *love* (a craving for absolute bliss in complete union with a perfect object forever and ever), . . . [a] love . . . bound up with an uncontrollable and insupportable fury of disappointment, together with anxiety for all other love-relations"—that Riviere feared would be given short shrift:

[T]hey [patients] know well how to parade a substitute "friendliness," which they declare to be normal and appropriate and claim ought to satisfy us as "not neurotic." They claim that their transference is resolved before it has been broached. We shall be deluded if we accept that.[109]

Was Riviere offering Freud supervision after the fact? Was she pointing out what had not been analyzed in her own case?

*   *   *

In her paper "Envy and Gratitude" (1957), Klein came back to the negative therapeutic reaction—or at least to one aspect of it: the inability of "the patient to accept . . . an interpretation which in some parts of his mind he recognizes as helpful."[110] In her earlier account of the depressive position, she had assumed a capacity for love—and also for hate. Given that capacity, given the infant's ability to "cathect sufficiently the breast or its symbolic representative, the bottle," the mother would be "turned into a loved object." This object would then be introjected; it would "take root in the ego with relative security," thereby laying the basis for "satisfactory development." And it would remain "the foundation for hope, trust, and belief in goodness." What about things going awry? What about those patients who had difficulty taking in and safeguarding "the primal good object"?[111] Here Klein introduced envy. Hers was no small insertion. With her work on envy, she presented the last of her major hypotheses.

Envy, of course, constituted nothing new in psychoanalysis. Freud had reckoned women's envy of the penis the reason for many interminable or stalemated analyses:

At no other point in one's analytic work does one suffer more from an oppressive feeling that one's repeated efforts have been in vain, and from a suspicion that one has been "preaching to the winds," than when one is trying to persuade a woman to abandon her wish for a penis on the ground of its being unrealizable. . . . We often have the impression that with the wish for a penis . . . we have penetrated through all the psychological strata and have reached bedrock, and that thus our activities are at an end.[112]

For Klein, Freudian penis envy had never figured as bedrock. She had given priority—on the part of boys and girls alike—to envy of the mother's body, of "the mother receiving the father's penis, having babies inside her, giving birth to them, and being able to feed them." In her 1957 paper she singled out, as something even more fundamental, "the primary envy of the mother's breast." That the infant hated and envied the breast he felt to be "mean and grudging" fit with notions that deprivation increased destructive impulses.[113] That the infant also envied the satisfactory and satisfying breast ranked as a novel thought. Klein insisted on this point: envy constituted an attack upon the good *because it was good*; it attacked the goodness of the object.

Klein proceeded to clarify her argument in a fashion typical of her, that is, by offering an account of infancy. The ego, she argued, existed in rudimentary form from the beginning of post-natal life, and it had the assignment of defending against the death instinct. (In *Beyond the Pleasure Principle* [1920] Freud had introduced the notion of a death instinct and he continued to subscribe to it for the rest of his life. Alone among his intellectual heirs, Klein followed suit.) She had claimed that the ego deflected the death instinct outward onto external objects and split them into good and bad—and, still more, that splitting took place not only in relation to external objects but to internal ones as well. In a 1946 paper, she went even further. She bluntly stated that the ego was "incapable of splitting the object—internal and external—without a corresponding splitting taking place within the ego" itself.[114]

What figured as crucial was the amount or degree of splitting. If the splitting were just about right, the good object and the bad one were kept apart, and the infant, thereby, gained a "relative and temporary security."

> The presence in the mind of the good ... object enables the ego to maintain at times strong feelings of love and gratification. The good object also affords protection against the ... [bad] object because it is felt to have replaced it (as instanced by wish-fulfilling hallucination). These processes underlie, I think, the observable fact that young infants alternate so swiftly between states of complete gratification and of great distress.[115]

In due course a more integrated ego would develop, capable of mitigating fear of the bad object by trust in the good, capable of bringing the two together, and capable of negotiating the depressive position. If the splitting were too deep or too sharp, it would not be the good and bad object that were separated, but an idealized and an extremely bad one. The idealized object would be unstable and would all too often flip, turning into a persecutor. Thus buffeted about, the infant would be unable to arrive at, let alone work through, the depressive position. The normal amount of splitting Klein attributed to the infant's capacity for love; the pathological amount she attributed to excessive envy.

Klein's comments about the infant's envious spoiling of the object remained speculative; her remarks about "envy in the transference situation" captured what analysts observed in their consulting rooms:

> For instance: the analyst has just given an interpretation which brought the patient relief and produced a change of mood from despair to hope

and trust. With some patients, or with the same patient at other times, this helpful interpretation may soon become the object of destructive criticism. It is then no longer felt to be something good he has received and has experienced as an enrichment. His criticism may attach itself to minor points; the interpretation should have been given earlier; it was too long, and has disturbed the patient's associations; or it was too short, and this implies that he has not been sufficiently understood. The envious patient grudges the analyst the success of his work; and . . . he feels that the analyst and the help he is giving have become spoilt and devalued by his . . . criticism.[116]

To illustrate envy at work Klein reported on a patient who "had suffered from depressive states over a long period." During the early part of the treatment Klein had not fully appreciated the severity of her patient's difficulties. It was "an unexpected success in her professional career" that "brought more to the fore" the patient's intense rivalry with her analyst and a sense that she might in her own field become Klein's equal or even superior. In the wake of her success, the patient felt elated and reported a dream that showed her triumph over the analyst, and underlying this, "the destructive envy" of Klein "standing for her mother."

In the dream she was up in the air on a magic carpet which supported her and was above the top of a tree. She was sufficiently high up to look through a window into a room where a cow was munching something which appeared to be an endless strip of blanket. . . .

The associations to the dream made it clear that being on top of the tree meant having outstripped me, for the cow represented myself, at whom she looked with contempt. Quite early on in her analysis she had had a dream in which I was represented by an apathetic cow-like woman, whereas she was a little girl who made a brilliant . . . speech. My interpretations at that time that she made the analyst into a contemptible person, whereas she gave such a successful performance in spite of being so much younger, had only partly been accepted although she fully realized that the little girl was herself and the cow-woman was the analyst. . . . Ever since, the cow-woman standing for myself, had been a well-established feature in the material, and therefore it was quite clear that in the new dream the cow in the room into which she was looking was the analyst. She associated that the endless strip of blanket represented an endless strip of words, and it occurred to her that these were all the words I had ever said in the analysis and which I now had to swallow. The strip of blanket was a hit at the woolliness and worthlessness of my interpretations. . . . The patient was surprised and shocked at her attitude towards me, which prior to the dream she had for a long time refused to acknowledge in its full impact.[117]

This acknowledgment of her envy—"as the impetus towards damaging and humiliating the analyst, whom in another part of her mind she highly valued"—the patient found well-nigh intolerable. Though she had never appeared "particularly boastful or conceited, . . . by means of a variety of splitting processes and manic defenses she had clung to an idealized picture of herself." Now the idealization broke down; the patient "felt bad and despicable": she felt guilty about "harm done in the past and in the present," which she imagined to be irrevocable.[118]

As the analysis progressed, if it progressed, Klein expected that envy and fear of envy would diminish, "leading to a greater trust in constructive and reparative forces, actually in the capacity for love."

> From the beginning, all emotions attach themselves to the first object. If destructive impulses [and] envy . . . are excessive, the infant grossly distorts and magnifies every frustration from outer sources, and the mother's breast turns externally and internally predominantly into a persecuting object. . . . In . . . the analysis . . . , we enable the patient to revive fundamental situations—a revival which I have often spoken of as "memories in feeling.". . . [I]t [then] becomes possible for the patient to develop a different attitude to his early frustrations. . . . [T]he weakening of projections, and therefore the achieving of greater tolerance, bound up with less resentment, make it possible for the patient to find some features and to revive pleasant memories of the past, even when the early situation was very unfavourable.[119]

Klein ended on a hopeful note: when the patient's initial difficulty in establishing a good object was, to some extent, overcome, she could work through the depressive position. But Klein's was a tempered optimism. At the present state of knowledge, she tended to think that with more seriously disturbed patients success would be limited or would not be achieved at all.[120]

*   *   *

Looking back over the material I have discussed in this chapter, I want to highlight two conceptual advances: the superego and the depressive position. With the first of these, Freud found a home for depression, the unconscious sense of guilt, and the negative therapeutic reaction. With the second, Klein transformed the superego into a world of internal objects, and in so doing provided a much more richly elaborated account of depressive anxiety and/or guilt. At the same time she and Riviere took on what Freud had come to regard as an insurmountable obstacle to psychoanalytic treatment—the negative therapeutic reaction.

Let me begin with the superego. Before its introduction, the negative therapeutic reaction, the unconscious sense of guilt, and depression existed, conceptually, in isolation from one another; afterwards the three came bundled together. In his account of the Wolf Man's treatment, Freud noted that every time a symptom "had been conclusively cleared up," Sergei "attempted to contradict the effect for a short while by an aggravation" of that very symptom, in other words, he produced "transitory 'negative reactions.' "[121] In a short paper on religious practices, Freud wrote that "the sufferer from compulsions and prohibitions" behaved as if "he were dominated by a sense of guilt," albeit an unconscious one.[122] As for depression, Freud emphasized the melancholic's self-criticism, his self-denigration, and concluded that the self-reproaches were really reproaches against a loved object which had been redirected from it to the patient's ego. In formulating the superego, Freud transferred—without fanfare—the ego's reproaches to the superego. The superego now launched attacks against the ego.[123] And the ego did not protest; it admitted its guilt; it submitted to punishment; indeed it found satisfaction in a negative therapeutic reaction.

Klein took off from the superego. In the late 1920s Jones wrote Freud defending the orthodoxy of her claims:

> Many thanks for your recent letter. I should like to return to one sentence in it of extreme importance, namely where you say that you find Melanie Klein's view about the super-ego quite incompatible with your own. I would seem to be suffering from a scotoma, for I do not perceive this at all. The only difference I was aware of is that she dates both the Oedipus conflict and the genesis of the super-ego a year or two earlier than you have. As one of your chief discoveries has been the fact that young children are much more mature than had been generally supposed, both sexually and morally, I had regarded the conclusions reached from Frau Klein's experience as being simply a direct continuation of your own tendencies.[124]

A half-decade later, Klein's ideas had become decidedly more heterodox; by the mid-1930s she had replaced the Freudian superego with a world of internal objects:

> [T]he phenomenon which was recognized by Freud, broadly speaking, as the voices and the influence of actual parents established in the ego is, according to my findings, a complex object-world, which is felt by the individual, in deep layers of the unconscious, to be concretely inside himself, and for which I and some of my colleagues therefore use the term "internalized objects" and an "inner world." This inner world consists of innumerable objects taken into the ego, corresponding . . . to the multitude of varying aspects, good and bad, in which the parents (and other people) appeared to the child's unconscious mind throughout various stages of his development. . . . In addition, all these objects are . . . in an infinitely complex relation both with each other and with the self.[125]

The depressive position, then, constituted an account of those complex relations—of the self's fear for its good objects, of its guilt about destructive impulses toward them, of its desire to repair the damage inflicted on them, and of its grief over failing to do so.

What about the negative therapeutic reaction? With Klein's conceptualization of an inner world, it took on added meanings. For Riviere, it represented a desperate attempt to maintain the status quo—a painful but still bearable state of things. For Klein, it signaled the presence of envy; and although she considered envy, and its degree, a matter of constitution, she did not, on that account, judge it to be unanalyzable. Its modification stood as a necessary step toward what both she and Riviere considered crucial: working through "the depressive situation of failure."[126]

On the technical side, I want to highlight Klein's understanding of transference. In two interconnected respects her work marked an advance over Freud's. Both owed much to her analysis of children. First, Klein saw adults—like children—re-enacting in the consulting room the complex relations of their inner worlds. To interpret—especially feelings and the defenses against them—in terms of those relations or in terms of relations between objects and self, followed. Second, the inner world, though molded by childhood experiences, remained active in the present and could, indeed should, be interpreted in the transference. To explore meticulously unconscious meaning in the here-and-now must come before attempting any reconstruction of the past. No wonder that Klein shared Strachey's view that transference interpretations—at least those that counted as mutative—possessed particular therapeutic power.

I can readily imagine a question being posed: Had Klein so broadened the notion of transference that reality disappeared or suffered a total eclipse? Here, too, Klein and Strachey found themselves in agreement. The patient's appreciation of reality could not be relied upon and should not be overtaxed. Being able to face reality stood, not as a precondition for treatment, but as a consequence of it. And the end of an analysis, with the loss it entailed, always put that ability to a severe test.

In writing of termination, Klein likened it to mourning—and mourning, she claimed, revived the infantile depressive position. So, once more, the patient would have to work through those painful feelings; though that work might begin while he was still in analysis, he would have to finish it on his own. It could be done—but only if "the whole gamut of love and hatred, anxiety, grief and guilt in relation to the primary objects" had been "experienced again and again."[127]

Chapter 4

Paranoia: Abnormal changes in the ego

Mapping the psychoneuroses of defense in the 1890s, Freud included paranoia along with hysteria and obsessional neurosis. Each, he argued, employed a different and distinguishing mode of defense: hysteria he coupled with conversion, obsessional neurosis with substitution, and paranoia with projection.[1] Paranoia itself he initially regarded as a very broad category covering most forms of chronic delusional states. He viewed it more narrowly when, more than a decade later, he came to write about Daniel Paul Schreber; he took care, in line with the German psychiatrist Emil Kraepelin, to separate off paranoia from dementia praecox.[2] Niceties of psychiatric classification, however, did not loom large for Freud. Of far greater interest to him were the peculiarities and particularities of the paranoiac's belief system.

And Schreber's ranked as very peculiar indeed. Born in 1842, the second son of a well-known orthopedist and educational reformer, the younger Schreber had a long and distinguished judicial career, chiefly in Saxony. Then, in October 1884, after an unsuccessful campaign for the Reichstag, he suffered his first breakdown and had to be hospitalized. The following June, having been pronounced cured, he received his discharge. For the next eight years all seemed to go smoothly; he made further professional advances, becoming, in 1893, a presiding judge of Saxony's highest court. The period ended with a second breakdown, after which he was never again considered mentally healthy.

Dr. Weber, the superintendent of the Sonnenstein Asylum, where Schreber was transferred in 1894, described at some length "how out of the stormy tides . . . of acute insanity . . . a sediment was, so to speak, deposited . . . , and gave the illness the picture of paranoia."[3] Those stormy tides stirred up hypochondriacal ideas: Schreber "thought he was dead and rotten, suffering from the plague . . . that all sorts of horrible manipulations were being performed on his body"; they stirred up visual and auditory hallucinations to which at times he responded by "bellowing very loudly at the sun with threats and imprecations"; they caused eating disturbances: "he refused nourishment so that he had to be forcibly fed . . . [and] retained his stool, apparently deliberately"; and they caused sleep disturbances accompanied by such noisy behavior that for a number of months he had to be put in an isolated room. Gradually he became accessible to those around him: he began to be able to control himself for short intervals; he "even answered simple questions about his condition." In the spring of 1897 a more marked change was observed: he "entered into a lively correspondence with his wife and other relatives; and . . . the letters were correctly and deftly written," and hardly showed any derangement. He was, nevertheless, "filled with pathological ideas," which were "woven into a complete system, more or less fixed, and not amenable to correction by objective evidence."[4]

In 1900 Schreber undertook legal steps for his release from tutelage (that is, guardianship by the courts), steps that in 1902 led to his discharge from the Sonnenstein Asylum. (In late 1907 he broke down again and remained in a mental institution until his death three and a half years later.) For the court the decisive issue was not whether he was mentally ill—of that there was no doubt—but whether he was capable of taking care of his own affairs and defending his interests—of that the court seemed equally certain. Schreber's insistence upon publishing a volume of memoirs did not tell against him; in the eyes of the court that wish stood not as proof of incapacity to look out for himself but rather as proof "of the strength of his belief in the truth of the revelations which had been granted him by God."[5] In 1903 his insistence bore fruit: Schreber saw his memoirs in print and "brought to the notice of a wider circle."[6] Freud was a member of that wider circle.

In his preface Schreber explained why publication was so urgent: "I believe that expert examination of my body and observation of my personal fate during my lifetime would be of value both for science and for the knowledge of religious truths." The medical examination that Schreber was eager to undergo would, he claimed, reveal a process of "unmanning" at work—a process "imperiously demanded" by the "Order of Things." In the event of a world catastrophe bringing about the destruction of humankind—and Schreber was convinced that such a catastrophe had occurred—the Order required the survival of a single human being. Schreber was the chosen one. (For a long time he thought that all the others were merely "fleeting-improvised-men.")[7] And once he had been chosen, the rest followed: he would be turned into a woman, impregnated by divine rays, and give birth to a new race of men. It also followed that whether or not he personally liked it, there was no reasonable course open to him but to reconcile himself to this transformation.

The transformation was never finished—despite Schreber's experiencing a penis in retreat, a swelling bosom, and a whole body "filled with nerves of voluptuousness," like that of a adult female. "For several years," he wrote, "I lived in the certain expectation that one day my unmanning . . . would be completed . . . but whether . . . [it] can . . . be . . . I dare not predict. . . . It is therefore possible, indeed probable, that to the end of my days there will be strong indications of femaleness, but that I shall die a man." In the meantime he had "wholeheartedly inscribed the cultivation of femininity" on his "banner."[8]

Freud, for one, was not inclined to ridicule Schreber's account on the grounds that he was insane. "[E]ven thought structures so extraordinary as these and so remote from our common modes of thinking," Freud assumed, sprang from understandable "impulses of the human mind."[9] With this precept to guide him, he brought along Schreber's memoirs, when, in September 1910, he and Sándor Ferenczi set off for Palermo. In the first part of December he put down on paper, in an essay entitled "Psycho-Analytic Notes on an Autobiographical Account of a Case of Paranoia," reflections prompted by the book. His own essay Freud described as "formally imperfect" and then, borrowing from Schreber's vocabulary, as "fleetingly improvised." Still, he thought there were "a few good things in it," more particularly his boldest thrust yet at psychiatry: his theory of paranoia.[10]

Here Freud took up his self-appointed task of connecting a specific mental disorder—paranoia—with sexual development. He focused not on the oral and anal, that is on libidinal organization, but on the unfolding of object love. Writing of Schreber, he posited a narcissistic phase:

> What happens is this. There comes a time in the development of the individual at which he unifies his sexual instincts (which have hitherto been engaged in auto-erotic activities) in order to obtain a love-object; and he begins by taking himself, his own body, as his love-object, and only subsequently proceeds from this to the choice of some person other than himself.

In this "half-way phase," the subject chooses an external object with genitals similar to his own.[11] And in this same half-way phase, Freud located the weak spot, the disposition, to paranoia.

It was a homosexual wishful fantasy, Freud claimed, that lay "at the core of the conflict in cases of paranoia among males." Thanks to a reversal of feeling—I do not love him, I hate him—and to projection—I do not hate him, he hates me—"what should have been felt internally as love" was "perceived externally as hate." And thus the paranoiac imagined himself as being persecuted by someone whom he had once loved. So it had been, Freud argued, with Schreber. Taking a close took at his delusions, Freud detected Schreber's father thinly disguised by the figure of God. In his "phantasy (at first resisted but later accepted) of being transformed into a woman," Freud saw a return to "the feminine attitude towards his father which he had exhibited in the earliest years of his childhood."[12]

Freud's theorizing, more particularly the connection he hypothesized between homosexuality and paranoia, rested on the memoirs of an asylum inmate. It rested on his experience with his erstwhile friend Wilhelm Fliess as well. Fliess had, Freud confided to Carl Gustav Jung, "developed a dreadful case of paranoia after throwing off his affection" for him, "which was undoubtedly considerable."[13] For his own part, in reflecting on Schreber, so he reported to Ferenczi, he had simultaneously been dreaming of Fliess and analyzing anew his homosexual investment in his former friend.[14] As for evidence derived from clinical work, Freud had very little. In the early 1910s he was hopeful that the younger men gathered around him—Jung and Ferenczi, as well as Karl Abraham—would make good his deficiencies. Those hopes were more scientific than therapeutic. "Success," he wrote Ferenczi, was "not possible" in such cases, but they were needed "in order to reach an understanding of all the neuroses."[15] A decade later he sounded even more doubtful: "cases of paranoia" were "not usually amenable to analytic investigation"[16]—let alone analytic treatment.

Thus Freud will not figure in this chapter as a therapist. A former patient of his, Sergei Pankejeff—the Wolf Man—will, however, make an appearance. In 1926 Pankejeff entered treatment with Freud's analysand and pupil Ruth Mack Brunswick. She made the diagnosis of paranoia. And she, along with Wilfred R. Bion and Betty Joseph, are the principal psychoanalysts in this chapter. All three need to be introduced.

Through her brother-in-law, who had had a short analysis with Freud, Ruth Brunswick, then Ruth Blumgart, went to Vienna in 1922 at age 25—"a vigorous, independent spirit, . . . with a fine mind, cultured, vivacious and elegant."[17] The daughter of Judge Julian Mack, noted both as a jurist and as a Jewish philanthropist, she had graduated from Radcliffe, earned a medical degree from Tufts, completed a psychiatry residency, and married Hermann Blumgart, a cardiologist with a distinguished career ahead of him. Ruth planned to remain in Vienna only long enough for analysis and training with Freud—which in those days might be a matter of months; she stayed, apart from a year in the United States, 1928–1929, and summer trips to visit family, until 1938.

Brother-in-law, who shortly became a former brother-in-law, a future husband and his brother—all these family members were in analysis with Freud at one time or another and often at the same time as Ruth. She, in fact, arranged for Mark Brunswick to be analyzed by Freud. When, in 1924, treatment began, he and Ruth were already lovers. After three and a half years, Freud pronounced him cured. Mark terminated the analysis and married his inamorata. Freud attended the ceremony: he acted as a witness, and his son Martin, a lawyer, drew up the necessary legal documents. In late 1933 or early 1934, Mark told Freud that he still had all his symptoms, and Freud, disturbed by the news, took him back into analysis. During the course of this second treatment, which lasted until 1938, Mark had an extra-marital affair, divorced Ruth, then remarried her six months later. This last step displeased Freud. Mark divorced Ruth a second time in 1945, less than a year before her premature death.[18]

As for Ruth, Freud had none of his usual reservations about Americans. She soon became the conduit for patients from the United States, often looking after them while they were in Vienna. She also became his emissary; he trusted her to see that his work was correctly interpreted in American circles. On a more personal level, Ruth helped supervise Freud's health. Their intimacy was such that she was present at his April 1931 operation, alongside Dr. Max Schur.[19] (Ruth also analyzed both Schur and his wife.)[20] Through her father's influence, she managed to bring a Harvard medical professor to Vienna where he fashioned a special prosthesis for Freud's mouth. (Unfortunately the result was not a success.) Freud regarded her, as he wrote a son, as almost a member of his family. In his brief diary he noted: "Ruth birthday, opal necklace." Two days earlier he had jotted down: "Jade necklace for Anna."[21] The year was 1930, and at that time Freud may have been closer to Ruth than to his own daughter.

What of Ruth's analysis? It seemed to have been interminable. In 1937 Freud wrote that "Every analyst should periodically . . . submit himself to analysis once more, without feeling ashamed of taking this step."[22] By then Ruth had had several such re-analyses. As early as 1928, Freud noted that she was "taking on a portion of follow-up analysis."[23] Four years later he complained that she was "a very irregular patient and difficult to grasp owing to organic complications."[24] The following year he complained again of forced interruptions: Ruth was "eternally ill, coughs . . . feverish."[25] In August 1938, after he had been persuaded to leave Vienna and had settled in London, Ruth came from New York for what he referred to as a "bit of after-analysis, which will probably be very good for her." He added, somewhat ruefully: "How incomplete all my earlier analyses were."[26]

One matter that Ruth's analysis seemed not to have touched was her use of painkillers. In the 1930s she suffered from myriad complaints, among them stomach and gallbladder problems, and as a doctor, she could prescribe medications—morphine and sleeping pills—for herself. She did so to the point of becoming addicted. For a while she managed to overcome her dependency on drugs, only to relapse. The worst period occurred after she returned to New York. When Princess Marie Bonaparte visited her in the winter 1945–1946, she was appalled by Ruth's condition, by the toll ill-health, morphine addiction, and depression had taken. On January 23, 1946, though confined to bed, Ruth arranged a small dinner party for Marie. The following morning, probably heavily sedated, she slipped in the bathroom and fell. She died as a consequence of a fractured skull.

Brunswick's death occurred very close in time to the start of Bion's analysis with Melanie Klein. Though they had been born the same year—1897—they belonged to different professional generations and to different intellectual lineages. Life experiences divided them as well.

"Could anyone, outside a public-school culture, believe in the fitness of a boy of nineteen to officer troops in battle?" Bion posed this question in the first volume of his autobiography. In it he painted a graphic and grisly picture of his service during the First World War. According to official records he performed with great distinction: in 1917 he was awarded the Distinguished Service Order for his part in the battle of Cambrai; the next year he was awarded the Legion of Honor and again mentioned in the dispatches. According to his own account, on both occasions he felt that he "might with equal relevance have been recommended for a Court Martial. It depended on the direction which one took when one ran away." As he saw it, he lacked discipline—"either of the kind that is a part of spontaneous maturation," or of the kind that rests "on endless mechanical repetition such as military drill." All he possessed was "the remains of a disintegrated moral system" in which he had been brought up and to which he clung because he had "nothing better to put in its place." Sometimes it felt like grasping at a straw:

> Shells were falling close around. Perhaps the enemy had found the map reference of the blasted hut. . . . I felt like a cornered rat. Clumsy brutes! . . . So simple really. But no; they were too clumsy to finish me off, couldn't solve the problem of how to club me to death. And I couldn't even sit up on my hind quarters and put my little paws together and pray the damned swine to let me off—just once! Just this little once! Oh God! I will never be naughty again—never! The guns were fewer! Well, maybe *once* more. Damn it, they've started again. Oh God! I *swear* I won't. Please, *please* just this once!
>
>   I got out. Sulky, frightened, resentful—God be damned for making a cringing rat of me![27]

Religion—of a Protestant Nonconformist variety—had been the mainstay of Bion's childhood and youth. Born in Muttra, in what were then the United Provinces of India (now Muthara, Uttar Pradesh)—his father was working there as a civil engineer—Bion left India and his family at the age of 8.[28] As was customary for the sons of British government officials, he was sent to England to be educated. For the better part of a decade, he attended Bishop's Stortford College, a well-regarded nonconformist institution. He then joined the army, more precisely the Royal Tank Corps. After the war and after graduating from Oxford with a degree in modern history, he returned to teach at his old school. He did not stay long. The decision to resign, however, was made for him, not by him: he was fired. In the mid-1920s, Bion passed a grim verdict on himself: he was "no good for war" and "no good for peace."[29]

What was to be done? Psychoanalysis seemed to offer a way out, but it took Bion a very long time to make the most of it, both personally and profession-ally. He started by going to University College Hospital for his medical quali-fication. That he accomplished by 1930; not until the end of the decade did he begin an analysis with John Rickman and apply to the British Psycho-Analytical Institute. Then war broke out again, and Bion found himself back in the army. He served from 1940 to 1945, as a psychiatrist, working some of the time alongside Rickman at the Northfield Hospital. Together they wrote a paper which formed the basis of Bion's later studies of groups.[30] Only at the war's end did he resume training at the Institute and enter analysis with Melanie Klein. In 1950, when he was turning 53, he became at last a full member of the British Society

From that point on, Bion prospered professionally. (He also prospered personally. During the war his first wife had died in childbirth, leaving him with an infant daughter. In 1951 he remarried and subsequently fathered two more children.) Each decade, roughly, seemed to mark a shift in his intellectual interests and certainly marked a change in the subjects he wrote about and how he wrote about them. During the 1950s he published a series of papers, replete with acute and sensitive observations, dealing with psychotic processes. During the 1960s he attempted to create a psychoanalytic epistemology and presented his ideas in quasi-mathematical form. In 1968 he announced that he was moving to the United States. He wanted relief from the administrative work he had been doing for the British Society—he held the post of president from 1962 to 1965—and he longed to escape, as he put it, from "being loaded with honours and sunk without a trace."[31] His sojourn in Los Angeles allowed him to indulge what he called his "wild thoughts" and compose a mystical and fantastic trilogy.[32] He intended to remain in California only three or four years; he stayed 11, returning to England in 1979, where he died two months later.

By the time Bion came back to England, Betty Joseph was in the course of gaining recognition. Thanks to her ongoing seminar in technique, her influence was gradually making itself felt. The actual group was small and started meeting in the 1960s; it was still meeting, with a remarkably constant membership, four decades later. It came together once every two weeks and provided its participants with an opportunity to present case material which troubled or puzzled them. Fortunately for those neither in personal contact with Joseph nor with others in the seminar, she published. When it was suggested to her—a suggestion she accepted—that a collection of her papers be brought out, she objected to the plural: in her mind, she had been continuously at work on a single one, with themes and variations, pondered over and carefully elaborated.[33]

Joseph came to psychoanalysis from the mental health field. Born in Birmingham in 1917, she was thus 20 years younger than Bion, almost a decade younger than Herbert A. Rosenfeld, and a contemporary of Hanna Segal, with whom she established a close intellectual and personal relationship. Unlike these three, who figured as Klein's chief lieutenants after the Second World War, she had not trained as a physician. (Klein and she used to joke that someday they would get a medical education.) Nor had she been analyzed by Klein. During the war she had worked first in London and then in the Manchester area. Since she was now a mental health professional—she had set up a child-guidance clinic—she thought it appropriate to get an analysis. Michael Balint, having emigrated from Hungary happened to be in Manchester at that time, and she went into treatment with him. When Balint moved to London, Joseph, who had already been accepted as a candidate by the British Psycho-Analytical Institute, went with him. Her initial affiliation, like that of her analyst, was with the Independent (Middle) Group. Subsequently she had a second analysis with Paula Heimann and switched to the Klein Group. When a number of years later, Heimann broke with Klein, she asked her recent analysand if she wanted to follow suit. Joseph did not. By then she had qualified in adult analysis and soon thereafter she qualified in child analysis as well. She was also on her way to becoming a much respected and sought after training analyst.

When Joseph turned 70, she stopped taking new analytic patients. (She kept seeing patients who, because of circumscribed stays in England, she expected to have in treatment for a relatively short period of time.)[34] She started to visit the United States. There, through discussions of clinical material, usually in a small group setting, she fostered, as she had throughout her career, the oral transmission of psychoanalytic know-how.

*   *   *

Both Bion and Joseph took off from Klein's conceptualization of the paranoid-schizoid position. As with depression, so too with paranoia: Klein began the work of transforming a psychiatric category into a grouping of anxieties and defenses that once again came to be seen as part of the human condition.[35] Bion continued and elaborated. In so doing he—and later Joseph as well—grappled with "abnormal changes in the ego." Freud had used this expression in writing about Schreber; he had regarded such changes as "the distinctive characteristic of psychoses" and as an insurmountable obstacle to treatment.[36] Klein had argued that the ego's abnormality derived from "excessive splitting processes"[37] and had doubted whether "patients with strong paranoid anxieties and schizoid mechanisms" could be successfully analyzed.[38] Bion's grappling leaned toward the theoretical, Joseph's toward the technical. They both, however, operated on the assumption that if they could not make contact with the patient, it was because they had not yet understood what was going on in the transference–countertransference situation.

Freud, Brunswick, and the Wolf Man

In June 1914, on the eve of leaving treatment, Sergei Pankejeff gave Freud a female Egyptian figure. Freud, a lover of archeology, appreciated and accepted the gift; more than that, he had suggested it. According to Sergei:

> In the weeks before the end of my analysis, we often spoke of the danger of the patient's feeling too close a tie to the therapist. If the patient

remains "stuck" in the transference, the success of the treatment is not a lasting one, as it soon becomes evident that the original neurosis has been replaced by another. In this connection, Freud was of the opinion that at the end of treatment a gift from the patient could contribute, as a symbolic act, to lessening his feeling of gratitude and his consequent dependence on the physician. So we agreed that I would give Freud something as a remembrance.[39]

In 1919 Sergei had another stint of analysis, lasting a few months. Thanks to this reanalysis, "a piece of the transference which had not hitherto been overcome was successfully dealt with."[40] In 1926 Sergei went to Brunswick for the first time. Once again "an unresolved remnant of the transference" figured as the chief concern.[41] Obviously the gift of the female Egyptian figure had misfired.

Sergei had begun with Freud in February 1910. As for his presenting symptoms or an exact diagnosis, Freud offered neither; he merely stated that his new patient was "entirely incapacitated and completely dependent upon other people."[42] He had in fact arrived in Vienna accompanied by a medical student and a psychiatrist, who knew something of psychoanalysis and hence sought out Freud's help for his charge. These two attendants remained on hand until late in the year, by which time Sergei was obliged or able to manage minimally on his own.

The 23-year-old Russian came from an enormously wealthy landed family, a number of whose members were seriously disturbed. Sergei remembered and reported to Freud that in his earliest years he and his father had enjoyed a close and affectionate tie; subsequently the two had become estranged, and Sergei's "maturer years were marked by a very unsatisfactory relation to his father, who, after repeated attacks of depression, was no longer able to conceal the pathological features of his character."[43] The ill-health of Sergei's mother had become manifest much sooner, in abdominal pain and hemorrhages and also in hypochondria, all of which had prevented her from having much to do with either her daughter or her son. Her physical condition improved as time went on, and she lived to the age of 87. The daughter, Anna—two and a half years older than her brother—was gifted and tempestuous, and her father's favorite. Sergei himself described her as behaving "less like a little girl than like a naughty boy," and indeed, as a child, he was often told that he ought to have been the girl and Anna the boy.[44] Among her many talents was a knack for tormenting her brother, for exploiting his fears and then delighting in his terror.

According to Freud, Sergei had "broken down in this eighteenth year after a gonorrhoeal infection."[45] Between then and his arrival in Vienna, his sister committed suicide, and his father died, possibly also a suicide. During those same years he tried a variety of remedies. He visited the leading neurologist in St. Petersburg, who labeled him a neurasthenic and prescribed hypnosis. The treatment worked wonders—for one whole day. He was escorted to Munich to be examined by Kraepelin. This preeminent psychiatrist had periodically treated Sergei's father and diagnosed both father and son as manic-depressive. He recommended an extended stay in a sanatorium. There Sergei fell in love with a nurse named Therese. Back and forth he went, pursuing his mistress and fleeing from her, from Germany to Russia and from Russia to Germany. Eventually his psychiatric sampling took him to Berlin and to Theodor Ziehen, then chief of the Charité Hospital. Again the psychiatrist recommended an extended stay in a sanatorium, and again, owing to the vicissitudes of his love life, Sergei decamped.

In contrast to relatives and psychiatrists alike, who had uniformly advised him to sever his ties to Therese, Freud offered no such advice. When Sergei told his new therapist of the turbulent courtship and asked whether he should continue the quest, Freud replied in the affirmative "but with the condition that this would take place only after several months of analysis." According to Sergei, Freud regarded his attachment as "the breakthrough to the woman," and "under certain circumstances" a breakthrough of this sort "could be considered the neurotic's greatest achievement, a sign of his will to live, an active attempt to recover."[46] A year into the treatment, Freud at last consented to Sergei's reunion with Therese. In accordance, however, with his rule that a patient "promise not to take any important decisions affecting his life" during analysis,[47] marriage was postponed until after termination— which coincided with the assassination of the Archduke Franz Ferdinand.

What concerned Freud was his patient's "over-powerful homosexuality." His account of it fell into two parts. First he pointed to the fact—and he regarded it as a fact not a fantasy—that when Sergei was roughly three and a half, at a time when his father was away from home, his sister, remembered in the family as a "forward and sensual little thing," had engaged him in sexual activity. The "seduction," Freud claimed, had forced his patient "into a passive role, and had given him a passive sexual aim." Sergei recalled fantasies dating from this period "of boys being chastized and beaten, and especially being beaten on the penis," and they confirmed, in Freud's mind, the impact the seduction had had on his patient's sexual aim. Second, with regard to his choice of love object, when Sergei's father returned, the boy transferred to him "a passive attitude"—a stance he had initially taken toward his sister and then toward his nurse, both of whom had discouraged him in one way or another. He now sought to have his beating fantasies enacted. Through fits of naughtiness he tried "to force punishments . . . out of his father"; he recalled how, during one of these fits, "he had redoubled his screams as soon as his father" came near. His father, alas, "did not beat him"; Sergei did not obtain the sexual satisfaction he desired.[48]

What made him repress the wish for such masochistic satisfaction? The simple answer was a threat of castration, but not any threat would do. When, after his sister had initiated him, Sergei had attempted to seduce his nurse by playing with his penis in her presence, and she had responded by making a "serious face" and warning him that "children who did that . . . got a 'wound' in the place," he had not been deterred. Until he was 4 years old and had the dream of white wolves sitting in a walnut tree—the most famous dream dreamt by a patient in psychoanalytic literature—he had "no belief" in castration and had "no dread of it." The dream-induced activation of a long-forgotten primal scene changed all that. The boy now reacted "adequately" to the impression he had received at the age of one and a half—the age at which, according to Freud, Sergei had witnessed his parents having intercourse *a tergo*. He now "saw with his own eyes the wound" his nurse had spoken of: " 'If you want to be sexually satisfied by Father,' " Freud imagined him as saying to himself, " 'you must allow yourself to be castrated like Mother; but I won't have that!' "[49] Sergei remained sufficiently enamored of his own genitals to relinquish "his wish to be loved by his father."[50]

Before the dream he had no fear of castration; he also had no fear of wolves. The dream changed that too. There was a particular picture book in which a wolf was portrayed, "standing up and striding along," and the sight of it made him scream that the wolf would eat him up. (His sister took delight in forcing him to look at the picture.) And the fear of the wolf/father did not disappear. Freud considered it the "strongest motive" for Sergei's "falling ill" and claimed that "his ambivalent attitude toward every father-surrogate was the dominating feature of his life as well as of his behaviour during treatment."[51] And Brunswick regarded it as "the source of the new illness"— a "hypochondriacal type of paranoia."[52]

*   *   *

When, in October 1926, Sergei entered Brunswick's consulting room, he complained that his nose had been injured, thanks to a dermatologist's use of electrolysis to treat obstructed sebaceous glands. "According to him, the injury consisted varyingly of a scar, a hole, or a groove in the scar tissue. The contour of the nose was ruined." According to Brunswick, "nothing whatsoever was visible on the small, snub, typically Russian nose of the patient." And Sergei himself, "while insisting that the injury was all too noticeable, nevertheless realized that his reaction to it was abnormal. For this reason, having exhausted all dermatological resources," he had consulted his former analyst. Freud refused to take him into treatment for a third time; instead he referred him to Brunswick.[53] The patient arrived in "a state of despair":

> Having been told that nothing could be done for his nose because nothing was wrong with it, he felt unable to go on living in what he considered his irreparably mutilated state. . . . He neglected his daily life and work because he was so engrossed, to the exclusion of all else, in the state of his nose. . . . [H]e carried a pocket mirror which he took out to look at every few minutes. First he would powder his nose; a moment later he would

inspect it and remove the powder. He would then examine the pores, to
see if they were enlarging, to catch the hole, as it were, in its moment of
growth and development. Then he would again powder his nose, put
away the mirror and a moment later begin the process anew. . . .

The maid who opened the door in my [Brunswick's] apartment was
afraid of him, because, as she said, he always rushed past her like a
lunatic to the long mirror in the poorly-lighted reception hall. He would
not sit down and wait, like the other patients, to be admitted to my office;
he walked incessantly up and down the small hall, taking out his mirror
and examining his nose in this light and that. It was in this condition that
he began his analysis with me.[54]

His hypochondriacal *idée fixe*, notwithstanding, Sergei refused to discuss
his nose or his attitude toward Professor X., his dermatologist. "Beyond the
statement that he had been to X. during his first analysis, that X. had been
recommended by Freud and was a friend of Freud's, and about of an age
with Freud, and obviously, as the patient said at once, a substitute for Freud,
no advance was possible."

And then fate played into my [Brunswick's] hands. A few weeks after
the Wolf-Man began his analysis with me, Professor X. died suddenly
on a Sunday night. In Vienna there is no good morning newspaper
on Monday; the Wolf-Man was due at my office at about the time of
the appearance of the afternoon edition. Thus my first question was:
"Have you seen today's paper?" As I expected, he answered in the negative. I then said: "Professor X. died last night." He sprang from the
couch, clenching his fists and raising his arms with a truly Russian air of
melodrama. "My God," he said, " . . . I can't kill him any more!"

Now with Brunswick's encouragement, Sergei began talking about X. He had
wished X. dead "a thousand times and had tried to think of ways of injuring"
him. But "he had had no definite plans" for murdering him; rather "he had
had ideas of suing him, of suddenly appearing in his office and exposing him,
of litigating with the purpose of obtaining financial recompense for his muti-
lation." The next step, Brunswick expected, should present little difficulty.
She reminded her patient that he "himself had admitted that X. was an
obvious substitute for Freud" and hence his "feelings of enmity toward X.
must have their counterpart in hostility to Freud."[55]

Sergei scoffed at this suggestion. How could he be hostile to Freud, he
asked his analyst, when Freud had given him no cause? On the contrary,
Freud "had always shown him the most tremendous partiality and affection."[56] He was well aware, as Brunswick put it, that "he had served the
theoretical ends of analysis";[57] indeed Freud had presented him a volume
containing his own case history.[58] (He did not know that in 1919 Freud had

made room for him by terminating Helene Deutsch's analysis. She had reluctantly yielded her hour: "I . . . realized that . . . this patient . . . was the source of important discoveries for psychoanalysis. . . . Certainly it would have been irrational for me to expect Freud to give up for my sake the time he needed for his creative work.")[59] Years later Sergei was still insisting on his specialness.

Brunswick launched a full-scale attack. Her "technique . . . consisted in a concentrated attempt to undermine the patient's idea of himself as the favourite son." She "drove home to him his actual position with Freud," the total absence—which she knew to be a fact—"of any social or personal relationship between them." She pointed out that "his was not the only published case. . . . He countered with the statement that no other patient had been analyzed for so long a period." Brunswick contradicted him. He came back with a dream which she interpreted as indicating a wish to be in analysis with Freud once again. He demurred and added that through her "he was really getting all the benefit of Freud's knowledge and experience." He was sure Brunswick discussed all the details of his case with his former analyst, "so as to be advised by him!" This she denied: she claimed that at the beginning of treatment she had asked Freud for an account of his earlier illness and that since then she "had barely mentioned him nor had Freud inquired after him." Her assertion—whose veracity is open to question—"enraged and shocked" her patient:

> He could not believe that Freud could show so little interest in his (famous) case. He had always thought Freud sincerely interested in him. Freud, in sending him to me [Brunswick], had even said—but here his recollection of what had been said became hazy. He left my office in a rage at Freud.[60]

Dreams now served as the royal road to Sergei's death wishes against father/Freud. Brunswick set to work interpreting: a Jewish professor—derived from a dream of the patient's father as a professor with a long, hooked nose; castrated—based on the nose as a symbol of the genital, its Jewishness a reminder of circumcision, and circumcision equivalent to castration; a castrated father, in turn, suggested a dead father; killed by his son for his money—taken from the dream-father's concern about his son's financial speculations. Dreams also paved the way to Sergei's fears of retaliation and/or persecution:

> In a broad street is a wall containing a closed door. To the left of the door is a large, empty wardrobe with straight and crooked drawers. The patient stands before the wardrobe . . . [B]ehind the wall is a pack of grey wolves, crowding toward the door and rushing up and down. Their eyes gleam, and it is evident that they want to rush at the patient. . . . The patient is terrified . . . that they will succeed in breaking through the wall.

Sergei associated to the dream elements:

> The door is the window of the original wolf-dream. The empty ward-
> robe is one which the Bolsheviki emptied: the patient's mother related
> that when it was broken open, the cross was found in it with which
> the patient had been baptized, and which to his sorrow he had lost at
> the age of ten. Also the wardrobe reminds the patient of his fantasies
> about the Czarevitch, in which the latter is shut up in a room (the ward-
> robe) and beaten. In this connection Professor X. occurs to him: during
> the patient's first visit, X. had spoken of Alexander III with great sym-
> pathy, and then made some scornful remarks about his weak successor,
> Nicholas II. This recalls in turn the stories of Peter the Great and his
> son Alexi, whom he killed. So, too, God allowed his son to die. Both
> these sons, Christ and Alexi, were tormented and persecuted by their
> fathers. At the word *persecuted*, the wolves in the dream occur to the
> patient, with the further association of Rome (Romulus and Remus), and
> the persecution of the early Christians. He then connects this dream,
> through the wolves, with his wolf-dream at the age of four, in which the
> wolves sat motionless on the tree, staring fixedly at the child. ... The
> shining eyes of the wolves now remind the patient that for some time
> following the dream at four years he could not bear to be looked at
> fixedly. He would fly into a temper and cry: "Why do you stare at me
> like that?" An observant glance would recall the dream to him, with all
> its nightmare quality.[61]

Wolves, fathers and/or doctors—Freud along with myriad others—were
trying to get at him to destroy him. At this point Sergei's "persecution
mania" dominated the scene. It turned out to be "more diffuse than the
one hypochondriacal symptom" had led Brunswick to expect. And more
alarming:

> During this trying period the patient conducted himself in the most
> abnormal manner. He looked slovenly and harassed, and as if devils were
> at his heels, as he rushed from one shop window to another to inspect his
> nose. During the analytic hour he talked wildly in terms of his fantasies,
> completely cut off from reality. He threatened to shoot both Freud and
> me—now that X. was dead!—and somehow these threats sounded less
> empty than those which one is accustomed to hear. One felt him capable
> of anything because he was in such complete desperation. ... [H]e ...
> seemed plunged into a situation which neither he nor the analysis could
> cope with.[62]

Brunswick was greatly relieved when Sergei related two further dreams.
Here is the first:

> The patient and his mother are together in a room, one corner of whose walls is covered with holy pictures. His mother takes the pictures down and throws them to the floor. The pictures break and fall into bits. The patient wonders at this act of the part of his pious mother.

Brunswick saw in the dream a reversal of the past. Distressed by her son's anxiety, Sergei's mother had taught him, at the age of four and a half, the story of Christ. Thanks to a ceremonial he invented—it "consisted in his going about the room at bedtime, crossing himself and praying, and kissing the holy pictures one after another"—the little boy, who had been suffering from insomnia because of worry about bad dreams, dropped off to sleep at once. Instead of giving Sergei religion, Brunswick, as mother in the dream, destroyed it for him, and along with it his masochistic identification with Christ. Sergei reported the second dream the next day:

> The patient stands looking out of his window at a meadow, beyond which is a wood. The sun shines through the trees, dappling the grass; the stones in the meadow are of a curious mauve shade. The patient regards particularly the branches of a certain tree, admiring the way they are intertwined.

Brunswick compared this landscape to that of the famous wolf dream. There it was night, always a frightening time for Sergei; here the sun was shining. The branches of the tree where the wolves once sat were now empty and "intertwined in a beautiful pattern. (The parents in a sexual embrace.)"[63] A hopeful dream, but unfortunately Sergei's daytime progress was not commensurate with it.

As to how to account for his "final restoration," Brunswick admitted to being at a loss. It happened quite suddenly. "All at once he found he could read and enjoy novels." From that moment on, he was well. "He could paint and plan work and study in his chosen field, and again take the general intelligent interest in life and the arts and literature which naturally was his."[64] Still, Brunswick ended her report on a cautious note: she refused to predict whether or not Sergei would stay healthy.

Her caution turned out to be fully warranted. Sergei's first analysis with Brunswick lasted five months. Two years after its termination, he resumed treatment with her, and it continued intermittently for several more years. In 1938, when his wife committed suicide, a distraught Sergei pursued his therapist to Paris and London for a few weeks of treatment. After the Second World War he was in irregular contact with Muriel Gardiner, herself a former analysand of Brunswick's, and from the mid-1950s on in regular contact with Kurt Eissler, who spent a number of weeks each summer in Vienna.[65] From this history of treatment, it is easy to conclude that Sergei's lifelong involvement with psychoanalysis did not make him an advertisement for it. How he would have fared without it is much more difficult to determine.

One further question. What had happened to Sergei's remnant of transference to Freud? Brunswick thought (was it wishful thinking?) that he had resolved it; she thought that he had "sufficiently lived through his reactions to his father"—and by extension to Freud—"and was therefore able to give them up." Whatever living or working through there may have been, had not occurred in the transference. Early in treatment Brunswick had assumed that it was safer for Sergei to be "analyzed by a woman, because he hereby avoided the homosexual transference which at this point was evidently so strong that it would have become a danger to the cure, rather than an instrument of it." Her own transferential role, she insisted, was "negligible": she acted "purely as a mediator between the patient and Freud.[66] How her relationship to Freud influenced her countertransference, how Freud acted as a mediator between herself and Sergei, she did not say. Transference and countertransference alike were evaded.[67]

*   *   *

In her work with Sergei, Brunswick kept in mind Freud's views on paranoia and on its relation to homosexuality. She assumed that his paranoia resulted from reversal and projection in that order, from turning love of father into hate and then attributing the hate to father. Were defensive processes to be undone, Sergei's "feminine attitude toward his father" could be brought into the open—and repudiated. (Had it been acceptable to him, Brunswick reasoned, had he "been capable of assuming the feminine role and admitting his passivity to the full," he would not have felt compelled to guard against it and would not have produced his illness.)[68] To move from a homosexual to a heterosexual position, from the feminine desire to have father to the masculine wish to be like father, this was the step that both Freud and Brunswick hoped Sergei would take.

Melanie Klein saw the case differently. In her *Psycho-Analysis of Children* (1932) she took as her starting point a child's "oral–sadistic instincts." These, coupled with his desire to introject his father's penis, gave rise to fears of a dangerous animal—with Sergei, it was a devouring wolf—which he equated with father's genital and later with father himself. The boy then pressed into service homosexual components of his libido to defend against this overwhelming anxiety. In Klein's account, oedipal dramas were less stories of a child's incestuous loves than stories of searches for new objects to combat the child's fears of his "terrifying introjected objects."[69]

Bion: Learning from psychotics

"In the course of working out my concept of the infantile depressive position," Klein wrote, "the problems of the phase preceding it"—what she called the paranoid-schizoid position—"forced themselves of my attention."[70] In so doing, she found herself grappling, albeit gingerly, with problems that heretofore she had managed to avoid: problems of structure. Above all, she felt obliged to look hard at the ego. (Up to this point, among Freud's triad, only the superego had figured prominently in her work; as for the id, it never made more than fleeting appearances.)

Once again her interest focused on fantasy, in this instance on Schreber's fantasy of world catastrophe:

> At the climax of his illness, under the influence of visions which were "partly of a terrifying character, but partly, too, of an indescribable grandeur," Schreber became convinced of the imminence of a great catastrophe, of the end of the world. Voices told him that the work of the past 14,000 years had now come to nothing, and that the earth's allotted span was only 212 years more; ... [subsequently he became convinced] that that period had already elapsed. He himself was the "only real man left alive," and the few human shapes that he still saw— the doctor, the attendants, the other patients—he explained as being "miracled up, cursorily improvised men."[71]

Freud and Klein agreed that Schreber's "end of the world" delusion represented "the projection of ... [an] internal catastrophe";[72] she described it in terms of "anxieties and phantasies about inner destruction and ego-disintegration."[73] (Even more than Freud, Klein slid between "ego" as some sort of psychical agency and "ego" as self.) What "abnormal changes in the ego" brought about paranoid hallucinations such as Schreber's—this was the question that intrigued her.

Two ideas emerged as crucial in her paper "Notes on Some Schizoid Mechanisms" (1946): splitting and projective identification, and of the two, splitting ranked as the schizoid mechanism par excellence. On this subject Freud had left behind only a few brief remarks, set down late in life. His emphasis fell on the splitting off of ideas or the disavowing of pieces of reality: the persistence of "two attitudes ... side by side ... without influencing each other" might "rightly be called a splitting of the ego."[74] Elsewhere, "two contrary reactions" to instinctual conflict—the first, continuance of satisfaction, the second, compliance with a prohibition against such a satisfaction—persisted "as the centre-point of a splitting of the ego."[75] Klein's notions were far more concrete. "Splitting the ego," she argued, resulted in the feeling that the ego was "in bits"; it amounted "to a state of disintegration."[76]

When Klein had written of splitting in connection with the depressive position, it had been splitting of the object that she had had in mind. When she turned from object to ego, and advanced the additional claim that the ego was "incapable of splitting the object—internal and external—without a corresponding splitting taking place in the ego itself," she also moved from projection to projective identification. Projection operated on qualities or properties like anger and love; in contrast, projective identification operated on things or bits of things—more specifically, on split off parts of the self:

> [S]plit-off parts of the ego, . . . expelled in hatred, . . . are . . . projected on to the mother, or as I would rather call it, *into* the mother. These . . . bad parts of the self are meant not only to injure but also to control and take possession of the object. . . .
>
> Much of the hatred against parts of the self is now directed towards the mother. This leads to a particular form of identification which establishes the prototype of an aggressive object-relation. I suggest for these processes the term "projective identification."

In this fashion the split-off parts of the self came to be lodged in an external object. Not literally. Klein did not think that the patient literally put things into another's mind or body. Here too it was a question of the patient's fantasy:

> The processes I have described are, of course, bound up with the infant's phantasy-life; and the anxieties which stimulate the mechanism of splitting are also of a phantastic nature. It is in phantasy that the infant splits . . . the self, but the effect of the phantasy is a very real one, because it leads to feelings and relations (and later on, thought-processes) being cut off from one another.[77]

*   *   *

> The abnormal ego, which is unserviceable for our purposes, is unfortunately no fiction. Every normal person, in fact, is only normal on the average. His ego approximates to that of the psychotic in some part or other and to a greater or lesser extent.[78]

At this point in his essay "Analysis Terminable and Interminable" (1937), Freud introduced Anna's work on the mechanisms of defense and then confined himself to the neurotic end of the spectrum. In "Differentiation of the Psychotic from the Non-Psychotic Personalities" (1957), Bion drew on Klein's notions of splitting and projective identification and took up the psychotic and/or schizophrenic end. (His usage seemed to suggest that every psychotic personality was schizophrenic.)

Bion assumed, and made this assumption his point of departure, that the psychotic, or rather the person who became psychotic, was inordinately endowed with destructive impulses, aimed, above all, at reality, external and internal alike. This hatred, moreover, extended to all that made awareness of reality possible. Accordingly, the psychotic, in passing through the paranoid-schizoid phase, attacked his mental apparatus:

> As a result of these ... attacks, ... those features of the personality
> which should one day provide the foundation for intuitive understand-
> ing of himself and others are jeopardized at the outset. ... [T]he func-
> tions which Freud described as being, at a later stage, a developmental
> response to the reality principle, that is to say, consciousness of sense
> impressions, attention, memory, judgement, thought, have brought
> against them, in such inchoate form as they may possess at the outset of
> life, the sadistic splitting eviscerating attacks that lead to their being
> minutely fragmented and then expelled from the personality.[79]

Not surprisingly the psyche of the schizophrenic came to be seriously
depleted. At the same time his or her world became more and more
menacing—thanks to the accumulation of ejected fragments or particles:

> In the patient's phantasy the expelled particles of ego lead an independent
> and uncontrolled existence, either contained by or containing the external
> objects; they continue to exercise their function as if the ordeal to which
> they have been subjected had served only to increase their number and
> provoke their hostility to the psyche that ejected them. In consequence
> the patient feels himself to be surrounded by bizarre objects.[80]

Still, on the basis of his clinical experience, Bion claimed that psychotics
could benefit from analytic treatment. Still more, he argued that "even in the
severe neurotic," there was "a psychotic personality" that had "to be dealt
with ... before success" was "achieved."[81]

*   *   *

Bion was trying to investigate phenomena that seemed to imply a crippling of
the patient's capacity for thought. Nowhere did he provide a more vivid
description than in his paper "On Hallucination" (1958). In it he reported on
sessions from the analysis of a certified schizophrenic, an analysis that had
been underway "for some years" and in which a great deal of work "had
already been done."[82]

Here is the first of the sessions:

> The patient has arrived on time and I have asked him to be called. ... As
> he passes into the room he glances rapidly at me; such frank scrutiny
> has been a development of the past six months and is still a novelty.
> While I close the door he goes to the foot of the couch, facing the head
> pillows and my chair, and stands, shoulders stooping, knees sagging,
> head inclined to the chair, motionless until I have passed him and am
> about to sit down. So closely do his movements seem to be geared with
> mine that the inception of my movements to sit appears to release a
> spring in him. As I lower myself into my seat he turns left about, slowly,

evenly, as if something would be spilled, or perhaps fractured, were he to be betrayed into a precipitate movement. As I sit the turning movement stops as if we were both parts of the same clockwork toy. The patient, now with his back to me, is arrested at a moment when his gaze is directed to the floor near the corner of the room which would be to his right and facing him if he lay on the couch. This pause endures perhaps a second and is closed by a shudder of his head and shoulders which is so slight and so rapid that I might suppose myself mistaken. Yet it marks the end of one phase and the start of the next; the patient seats himself on the couch preparatory to lying down.

He reclines slowly, keeping his eyes on the same corner of the floor, craning his head forward now and then as he falls back on the couch as if anxious not to become unsighted. His scrutiny, as if he feared the consequences of being detected in it, is circumspect.

He is recumbent at last; a few more surreptitious glances and he is still. Then he speaks: "I feel quite empty. Although I have hardly eaten anything, it can't be that. No, it's no use; I shan't be able to do any more today." He then relapses into silence.

Watching these opening moves, Bion recalled how the previous day's session had ended. The patient had been "hostile and afraid that he would murder" his analyst. Bion had interpreted his patient's splitting off of "painful feelings, mostly envy and revenge," forcing them into his analyst, and so getting rid of them. (Had killing his analyst—in whom his own envy and revenge had been lodged—seemed, to the patient, the surest way to protect himself? Bion did not say.) What Bion had now witnessed he saw as an effort by the patient "to remove" from his analyst "those bad aspects of himself before he attempted the main business of the session, the ingestion of cure."

When the patient glanced at me he was taking a part of me into him. It was taken into his eyes, as I later interpreted his thought to him, as if his eyes could suck something out of me. This was then removed from me, before I sat down, and expelled, again through his eyes, so that it was deposited in the right-hand corner of the room where he could keep it under observation while he was lying of the couch. The expulsion took a moment or two. . . . The shudder I have described was the sign that the expulsion was complete. . . .

To turn now to the object supposedly deposited in the corner of the room. . . . Evidently it is an hostile object: its extrusion has emptied the patient: its presence threatens him and makes him fear he will be able to make no further use of the session.

Most of these reflections Bion apparently communicated to his patient, all the while observing him carefully:

[H]e [the patient] made jerky convulsive movements which were confined mostly to the upper part of his body. Each syllable I uttered seemed to be felt by him as a stabbing thrust from me. I pointed this out and said that he felt a very bad thing was being violently intruded into him, partly by me, and partly by himself in spite of the precaution he had taken by hardly eating anything. . . . The convulsive movements stopped and he said, "I have painted a picture." His subsequent silence meant that the material for my next interpretation was already in my possession.

What could it be? Bion looked back over the events of the session up to this point. He had detected one pattern, that of the bad object withdrawn from himself and deposited in the right-hand corner of the room. He assumed another must be lurking:

Before I passed on to a consideration of this pattern, I interpreted an aspect of this situation. . . . It is that the patient is . . . expressing, with an unusual degree of urgency and force, a belief in his capacity to communicate matters, which he feels to be worth while, to a person whom he thinks likely to be receptive to them. But, I was, I said, in addition a part of the picture which he had painted when he made himself and myself into two automata in a reciprocal but lifeless relationship. He replied, "The wireless next door kept me awake last night."
    I knew that strong persecutory feelings were associated by him with all electrical apparatus [sic], and I said he felt attacked by the electricity which he felt was like the life and sex which he had removed from the two objects which he had pushed out of himself when he painted his picture. He said, "Quite right" and then remarked that he did not know what would happen after the session, which in fact ended at this point.[83]

The patient had achieved a degree of integration, and this hour ranked, for analyst and patient alike, as a good one. Bion had noticed, however, "that such sessions were followed with great consistency by 'bad' " ones in which "the patient seemed to return to an . . . uncooperative state of mind and produced material" that Bion "found almost impossible to interpret." And so it was with the next hour:

The patient came in, gave me [Bion] a swift glance, waited till I reached my chair, and then lay down without further ado. He said tonelessly: "I don't know how much I shall be able to do today. As a matter of fact I got on quite well yesterday." At this point I felt his attention began to wander and he faltered in his speech. . . . He went on: "I am definitely anxious. Slightly. Still I suppose it does not matter." Rapidly becoming incoherent, he continued, "I asked for some coffee. She seemed upset. It may have been my voice but it was definitely good coffee too. I don't know why I shouldn't like it. When I passed the mews I thought the walls bulged outwards. I went back later but it was all right." There was more that I cannot attempt to reconstruct. He continued to speak, hesitatingly, with minor pauses, for some five or more minutes.

Bion had a hunch that nothing he could say would reach his patient. Still, he said something:

I pointed out that he was showing me how "much" he could do, but without regard to the quality. He replied that he had placed his gramophone on the seat. . . .

My suspicion was that when he said . . . [this] he was denying me life and independent existence in the analytic chair and treating my interpretations as auditory hallucinations. I did not immediately interpret . . . , but said that it appeared that he was reactivating a state of mind which, we must assume, it had now become important for him to preserve. . . . His response to this was to move his head and eyes as if my words were visible objects which were passing over his head to become impacted on the opposite wall. . . . On previous occasions I had interpreted his behaviour to mean that he saw my words as things and was following them with his eyes. . . . I said that he was again seeing objects passing overhead and reminded him of the previous occasion. This time he became anxious and said, "I feel quite empty. Better to close my eyes." He remained silent and very anxious and then said, somewhat apologetically I thought. "I have to use my ears. I seem to hear things all wrong." . . . My interpretation was being taken in by his ears, but in a way which he felt to be "all wrong"—that is to say, cruelly and destructively. If so, the interpretations were being taken in and transformed by his ears and ejected by his eyes. This seemed so extraordinary that it was a moment or two before the explanation flashed on me. I gave it in the following interpretation: "You," I said to him, "are feeling that your ears are chewing up and destroying all that I say to you. You are so anxious to get rid of it that you at once expel the pieces out of your eyes." I reminded him that when he had wished greedily to take something in, he did so through his eyes, because his eyes could reach a long way to things he could not possibly touch with his mouth. I went on, "You are now using your eyes for the opposite reason, that is to say, to throw the broken up bits of interpretation as far away from yourself as you possibly can." The patient seemed extremely frightened, yet there was relief in his voice when he agreed. I drew his attention to his fear. He replied that he felt too weak to go on, "I am fading out." I suggested that he was afraid of me because he felt he was destroying me as well as my interpretations and also afraid because he could not get enough interpretations to cure him. This interpretation enabled him to go on with his associations. . . .

He said that he had seen a painting in D—. It had a penis in it. He complained that he had ruined a painting by making it pretty instead of ugly. He then said, "All sounds turn into things I see around me." I interpreted that he was again turning my interpretations into sounds and then evacuating them through his eyes, so that he now saw them as objects surrounding him. He replied, "Then everything around me is made by me. This is megalomania." After a pause he said, "I like your interpretation very much." . . .

At this point his associations became less coherent. . . . [They] seemed to consist of parts of sentences, disjointed references to what I assumed to be actual events, and a certain amount of material which had a meaning for me because it had appeared in other sessions. . . . [T]he session came to an end without my being able to formulate any clear idea of what was going on. I said that we did not know why all his analytic intuition and understanding had disappeared. He said "Yes" commiseratingly, and if one word can be made to express "and I think that your intuition must have gone too," then his "Yes" did so on this occasion.[84]

Having got rid of things, including his capacity for judgment, how might Bion's patient take them back and retain them? Or to put it another way: if working through attacks on the ego figured as the crucial therapeutic goal, how did Bion conceptualize its achievement? He did not address this question explicitly in his paper on hallucinations. Elsewhere he wrote of projective identification in reverse. During treatment, he claimed, the patient attempts to bring back "expelled particles of ego, and their accretions," by the route by which they had been expelled. But according to Bion's own reckoning, such attempts were likely to fail. How could it be otherwise? The objects expelled by projective identification became "infinitely worse after expulsion" than they had been when originally expelled. Consequently the patient felt "intruded upon, assaulted, and tortured by this re-entry even if willed by himself."[85] As an account of ego integration, or "reconstitution of the ego," projective identification in reverse came up short.[86]

*   *   *

Bion did not abandon this concept. Instead he extended and elaborated it. Once again he began by taking a cue from Klein. She had written of the ego's excessive projective identification and "expelling into the outer world parts of itself" and how, as a consequence, the ego was deprived of "desired qualities" such as "power, potency, strength, knowledge," all of which were bound up with the less desirable "aggressive component of feelings."[87] Excessive compared to what? To an amount or kind of projective identification that might be regarded as normal? Implicit in Klein's comment was a notion of projective identification as nonpathological. Bion adopted this suggestion and simply declared: "I shall suppose that there is a normal degree of projective identification, without defining the limits within which normality lies."[88]

For both Klein and Bion "normal" carried with it the connotation of developmental. Where Klein wrote of the development of the ego through repeated cycles of projection and introjection, Bion took it further in claiming that these were cycles of projective and introjective identification. A claim about development—which, Bion acknowledged, rested on an adult's analysis:

> When the patient strove to rid himself of fears of death which were felt to be too powerful for his personality to contain he split off his fears and put them into me, the idea apparently being that if they were allowed to repose there long enough they would undergo modification by my psyche and could be safely reintrojected. On the occasion[s] I have in mind the patient had felt . . . that I evacuated them so quickly that the feelings were not modified, but had become more painful. . . .
>
> [W]hat he felt was my refusal to accept parts of his personality. Consequently he strove to force them into me with increased desperation and violence. His behaviour, isolated from the context of the analysis, might have appeared to be an expression of primary aggression. The more violent his phantasies of projective identification, the more frightened he became of me. . . . The analytic situation built up in my mind a sense of witnessing an extremely early scene. I felt that the patient had experienced in infancy a mother who dutifully responded to the infant's emotional displays. The dutiful response had in it an element of impatient "I don't know what's the matter with the child." My deduction was that in order to understand what the child wanted the mother should have treated the infant's cry as more than a demand for her presence. From the infant's point of view she should have taken into her, and thus experienced, the fear that the child was dying. It was this fear that the child could not contain. He strove to split it off together with the part of his personality in which it lay and project it into the mother. An understanding mother is able to experience the feeling of dread, that this baby is striving to deal with by projective identification, and yet retain a balanced outlook. This patient had had to deal with a mother who could not tolerate experiencing such feelings and reacted either by denying them ingress, or alternatively by becoming a prey to the anxiety which resulted from the introjection of the infant's feelings. The latter reaction must, I think, have been rare: denial was dominant.[89]

Note two moves Bion made in this passage. First he shifted from an imagined infant to an imagined mother. Second he slid from nature to nurture, from the infant's innate death instinct and inordinate destructive impulses to the mother's capacity for containing projective identifications or her capacity for reverie—the state of mind the infant required of the mother if she were to take in the infant's feelings and make them bearable. Like Klein's mother as good breast, Bion's mother as container derived from the external world: both approximated an actual mother who had been on hand in early infancy.

Bion elaborated on his "mother," examining the vicissitudes of the containing relationship. Here too he harked back to Klein. In the 1920s, in connection with disturbances in learning and with the intellectual problems of psychotic disorders, she had explored the epistemophilic component of the libido.[90] Then, in the 1930s, her interest in it had waned. Three decades later Bion reintroduced the "impulse of curiosity on which all learning" depended and granted it a status equivalent to that of love and hate.[91] He described the link between the containing mind and its contents as being of three kinds: "L," "H," and "K," standing for a loving, a hating, and a wanting to know about the contents. "Mother" at times loved her infant, hated him, or found herself trying to understand how he was experiencing, feeling, thinking; her linking with her infant in this third way allowed him to introject an understanding object and, in turn, promoted his capacity for thought. Where Klein had written of the introjection of a good object as crucial for ego functioning, Bion wrote of the introjection of an understanding object as crucial for one capacity in particular, that of learning from experience.

How credible is Bion's narrative of infant development? (Or Klein's for that matter?) Not very. For infants and mothers should one read patients and analysts? Yes. Had Bion represented or misrepresented an analytic tale as a story of infancy? Yes again. These answers underline the fact that the consulting room, not the nursery, figured as Bion's laboratory, so to speak. That was the venue for reconstituting the patient's ego—if at all possible. With the concept of container–contained and the relationship(s) between them—as opposed to the notion of projective identification in reverse—that possibility could at least be entertained.

Joseph: Countertransference and its uses

Bion's "just-so" story about "in the beginning" had led him to rethink the analyst's role. Something similar had happened with Michael Balint. From his speculations about primary object love, he had gone on to fashion the "unobtrusive analyst." In the course of this fashioning he had managed both to raise and to finesse the thorny problem of countertransference, with countertransference being broadly construed to cover the full range of the analyst's feelings toward the patient. Others, Balint's contemporaries and those younger, were prepared for a more direct and sustained confrontation.

Among those others, Paula Heimann, working in London, and Heinrich Racker, in Buenos Aires, took the lead in studying countertransference. Both emphasized its potential usefulness as a source of information about the patient. Betty Joseph enlarged on this theme. In so doing she suggested how the gathering of such information might enable the analyst to reduce and/or manage the obstacle Freud had originally associated with paranoia— "abnormal changes in the ego."

*   *   *

In the course of teaching analytic candidates, Heimann wrote, she had been struck by their firm belief that countertransference was nothing but trouble. And they thought they had Freud to back them up. Here Heimann suspected that her students had misunderstood Freud's recommendations, "particularly his comparing the analyst's attitude with that of the surgeon." So preoccupied were they with their fight against themselves, that they "lost sensitivity" to the analytic situation and took "flight into theory or the patient's remote past, ... presenting clever intellectual interpretations."[92] They had failed to notice that along with his well-known worries about countertransference endangering the analyst's objectivity, Freud had also entertained the idea that it might be exploited for purposes of analytic work. He had suggested as much when he had remarked: "[E]veryone possesses in his own unconscious an instrument with which he can interpret the utterances of the unconscious in other people."[93] Heimann picked up on his suggestion: "the analyst's emotional response to his patient within the analytic situation," she insisted, represented one of his most important tools.[94]

What did Heimann offer in the way of instructions for using this tool? She started with Freud, with his admonition to the analyst to obey "a counterpart to the 'fundamental rule' " laid down for the patient, that is, to "maintain the same 'evenly-suspended attention' " in the face of all that he heard.[95] Along with "this freely working attention," Heimann argued, the analyst needed "a freely roused emotional sensibility." He needed to be open to feelings the patient created in him. Then, having noticed the feelings, the analyst should compare them with the understanding he derived from the patient's associations. If the analyst was on track, feelings and understanding would be in accord. And Heimann assumed that there would be "stretches in the analytic work" when this was so and when the analyst's feelings would scarcely be put to use.[96]

The occasions when feelings and understanding were not in harmony clearly posed a challenge. Heimann gave an example from her own practice. "The patient was a man in his forties who ... sought treatment when his marriage broke down. Among his symptoms promiscuity figured prominently." At the beginning of a session, in the third week of the analysis, he told Heimann that "he was going to marry a woman whom he had met only a short time before." If the patient were merely attempting to "short-circuit analysis," an occurrence so frequent "at the beginning of or at a critical point in the treatment," Heimann would have been prepared to handle the obvious resistance without any qualms. Her reaction, "a sense of apprehension and worry," thus surprised her. She surmised that "something more was involved in his situation," which, however, eluded her.[97]

How did Heimann come to fathom that something more? She relied on the interpretation of a dream which the patient reported later in the same session. "[H]e had acquired from abroad a very good second-hand car which was damaged. He wished to repair it, but another person in the dream objected for reasons of caution." The patient, as he put it, had " 'to make him confused' in order that he might go ahead and repair the car." He "spontaneously recognized" that the car—"very good, second-hand, from abroad"—represented his analyst, who had been a refugee from Nazi Germany. "The other person in the dream who tried to stop him," Heimann interpreted as "that part of the patient's ego which aimed at security and happiness." The patient's wish that she, the car, be damaged, his guilt about this sadistic wish, and his compulsion to make reparation, which required "blotting out the voice of reason," and was thus itself masochistic—all this Heimann found in the dream. A "powerful sado-masochistic system," she concluded, fed both his "transference conflicts" and his intention to act them out by marrying his new friend, someone who, like his analyst, had had a "rough passage."[98]

Heimann reviewed what had happened: she "had immediately grasped the seriousness of the situation"—and had felt apprehensive; but her "conscious understanding lagged behind": only later in the session, after more material had come up, could she "decipher the patient's message and appeal for help." In this fashion her "immediate emotional response" served as "a significant pointer to the patient's unconscious processes" and "as a useful criterion for the selection of interpretations."[99] Her response led her to focus on those elements in the patient's material which might account for her feelings— feelings which, she argued, the patient had produced in her. Heimann ended her paper with an important caveat—one that other analysts writing about countertransference took pains to reiterate:

> The approach to the counter-transference which I have presented is not without danger. It does not represent a screen for the analyst's shortcomings. When the analyst in his own analysis has worked through his infantile conflicts and anxieties . . . , so that he can . . . establish contact with his own unconscious, he will not impute to his patient what belongs to himself. . . . At the same time he will find ample stimulus for taking himself to task again and again and for continuing the analysis of his own problems.[100]

* * *

In his discussion of countertransference, Racker took a look at Heimann's experience, that is, the analyst's feeling worried and apprehensive about something happening in the transference. He specified likely anxieties: they might be paranoid, prompted by "an intensification of aggression from the patient himself"; they might be depressive, arising from fear that the analysand might come to harm. As Racker saw it, the analyst should be able "to deduce from each of his countertransference sensations" a particular transference situation.[101] In contrast to Heimann he assumed that the analyst's feelings would serve as a regular, instead of as an occasional, source of information about the patient.

More than that: Racker regarded countertransference as providing the patient with information as well. Not that he advised the analyst to communicate his feelings. Both he and Heimann agreed that "such honesty" would be a burden to the patient and would lead away from the analysis.[102] Rather Racker appreciated, as did Sándor Ferenczi, "that patients have an extremely refined feeling for the wishes, tendencies, moods, likes and dislikes of the analyst."[103] The consequence of the patient's refined feeling, whether conscious or not, seemed clear: real or imagined countertransference situations, Racker claimed, "determined the transference." It followed that "analysis of the patient's fantasies about countertransference" constituted "an essential part of the analysis of transference."[104]

Where did the patient and analyst's inner worlds figure in this account? At the very center. The transference, Racker wrote, echoing James Strachey, arose from the patient's projection onto the analyst of his internal objects—"introjected parents" who frustrated, attacked, threatened, and recriminated and were "at the same time . . . desired, loved, hated and feared."[105] These transferences, in turn, provoked countertransferences: the analyst identified himself either with the analysand's internal object—which Racker labeled a complementary countertransference—or with the patient's ego—which Racker termed a concordant countertransference. And given the reciprocal nature of transference and countertransference, one could readily imagine transference running in reverse, namely, the analyst projecting onto the patient and the patient identifying with those projections. Here was interaction at the intrapsychic level.

Racker presented the following example to illustrate such an interaction—one which kept the patient trapped in what Racker, following Strachey, referred to as a "vicious circle":

> During her first analytic session, a woman patient talked about how hot it was and other matters which to the analyst (a candidate) seemed insignificant. She said to the patient that very likely the patient dared not talk about herself. Although the analysand was indeed talking about herself (even when saying how hot it was), the interpretation was, in essence, correct, for it was directed at the central conflict of the moment, but it was badly formulated.

Racker offered supervision after the fact: the analyst should have sought to understand why the patient "dared not"; and then she might have speculated aloud that "something in the analytic situation (in the relationship between patient and analyst)" made her fearful and "made her thoughts turn aside from what meant much to her to what meant little."

> Later in the same session, the patient, feeling that she was being criticized, censured herself for her habit of speaking rather incoherently. She said her mother often remarked on it, and then criticized her mother for not listening, as a rule, to what she said. The analyst understood that these statements related to the analytic situation and asked her: "Why do you think I'm not listening to you?" The patient replied that she was sure the analyst was listening to her.

"What had happened?" Racker asked. The analyst did not explicitly say to the patient, " 'No, I will listen to you, trust me,' but she suggested it by her question." Again she failed to examine the analytic situation. Once more the patient was exposed to an archaic object, initially experienced as fault finding and punitive and then as seeking to "allay its own anxieties rather than to understand . . . the therapeutic need of the patient." And the patient "submitted," telling the analyst that she trusted her and denying an aspect of her own internal reality. The candidate's botched interventions, Racker argued, stemmed from her "uncontrolled countertransference," from her failure to recognize her "identification with the analysand's internal objects."[106]

Racker gave another example, this time of countertransference successfully utilized to make a breach in the patient's resistance:

> An analysand who suffered chiefly from an intense emotional inhibition began the session by saying that he felt completely disconnected from the analyst. He spoke with difficulty . . . , and always in an unchanging tone of voice which seemed in no way to reflect his . . . feelings. Yet the countertransference response to the content of his associations (or, rather of his narrative, for he exercised a rigid control over his ideas) did change from time to time. At a certain point the analyst felt a slight irritation. This was when the patient, a physician, told him how, in conversation with another physician, he sharply criticized analysts for their passivity (they give little and cure little), for their high fees, and for their tendency to dominate their patients.

The analyst felt annoyed at the patient's "aggression" and attributed his annoyance to an identification with the patient's harsh internal object, an object that demanded "complete submission" and forbade any complaint. What might the patient be experiencing? Having been disloyal and defiant, having protested to his friend, the physician, so the analyst imagined, the patient would expect to be met with anger and would have no recourse but to endure "this punishment." As for what the analyst interpreted—Racker did not report the actual words spoken—he focused on the disconnection that the patient had mentioned at the beginning of the session and pointed out how it kept him, the patient, from feeling uneasy. The patient then recalled that "his conversation with the physician . . . the previous day . . . did indeed cause him anxiety." Momentarily, at least, the analyst's understanding of his patient's fearfulness shook the latter's image of him "as persecutor."[107]

Racker's understanding of the psychoanalytic process, as illustrated by these examples, bore a striking resemblance to that of Strachey—to be sure, his discussion of countertransference as a guide to transference represented a significant addition. By the same token it resonated with Klein's work, particularly with her account of the depressive position. Racker, however, did not draw on her discussion of the ego. In his bibliography he cited Strachey's paper and a number of Klein's as well. Her "Notes on Some Schizoid Mechanisms" was conspicuously absent from the list.

*　　*　　*

This same publication served as Joseph's point of departure. She was intrigued by patients whom she referred to as being "difficult to reach," by which she meant difficult to reach with interpretations and thereby "to give them real emotional understanding."

> In some cases, when . . . progress has been made, insight has been gained, and, for example, . . . more warmth and contact have been established, one finds all further progress blocked by a markedly increased, apparently intractable passivity. The patient seems to become apathetic, to lose . . . interest, and any involvement in the work which we may believe to be going on. He does not appear to be actively uncooperative, just helplessly passive. One often gets the impression following an interpretation that everything has gone dead and flat. . . . This is often true. The patient remains quiet or subsequently comes up with a very superficial remark.[108]

Joseph expanded on patients of this sort in a paper entitled "On Understanding and Not Understanding" (1983). A patient she called S. "would give a long description of the behaviour of his girl friend, . . . which seemed to convey that any sane person in the room would assume that she, the girl friend, was very sadistic."

> If the analyst . . . demonstrates that the patient must realize that he is talking about a girl friend who is deeply disturbed, the patient is likely to react as if the analyst were attacking his girl friend and then be upset, hurt, or offended, and the analyst may find . . . herself urging, almost bullying the patient to see her "point of view"—so a vaguely forcing or near sado-masochistic situation arises, as if the problem has shifted from

the home to the consulting room. I think that in this kind of situation one can see both the projection of apparent sanity into the analyst and the appearance in the patient of naïvety bordering on stupidity—which is apparently innocent but, in fact, is splendidly provocative.[109]

In these patients, part of the ego "needed for understanding" seemed to be unavailable, owing, Joseph surmised, to "splitting and projective mechanisms."

To take an example from B., who came into analysis worried about his relationship with his wife—or, to be more accurate, worried that she was worried that their relationship seemed poor and unsatisfactory to her; he did not see anything particularly wrong with it. He seemed a very decent man, basically honest, immature, and terribly lacking in awareness of himself and his feelings. It soon seemed that he unconsciously wanted an analysis in which things would be explained in relationship to the outside world, not experienced in the transference, and usually when I interpreted he would go quiet, blank, unable to remember what I said, and shift off untouched on to another topic. Or he would repeat what he just said. The impression I got was that he became anxious, . . . stopped being able to listen or hold together what we were discussing. This began to improve. Slowing I gained the feeling that I was supposed to follow him, almost pursue him with interpretations, but he did not seem interested in trying to understand or actively to use the analysis—it was as if it was I who wanted him to use individual interpretations or the analysis in general, just as it was his wife who apparently wanted him to have the analysis and who was worried about the marriage. So we could see that the active, alert, wanting part of the self was split off and apparently projected into me and he remained passive and inert. . . .

B. was anxious but also relieved as he began to feel himself coming more alive sometimes during the sessions. . . . [J]ust before a holiday, . . . [he] became very clear about simple feelings of jealousy and anger linked . . . with his early and current family experiences. He was unusually moved by . . . [a] dream and our work on it, and as the session was coming to an end, said in a happier voice: "I must tell you about my grandiose idea. I think that car manufacturers should build a front passenger seat so that it can turn round and the passenger join in with and face the children sitting in the back, or a child could sit in the front and turn to the others. I should write to the head of BL [British Leyland]."

So I showed him by his tone and the way that he spoke to me, as well as by what he said, . . . that what he had been talking about had brought him into contact with the child in himself, which he was beginning to turn to and face, instead of his usual way of withdrawing, losing contact, and projecting the needing-to-know part of himself into me.

Joseph felt encouraged: some part of her patient wanted to have a look at what was going on. She appreciated the vital importance of his integrating "this part more fully and consciously into his personality": until he did so, he would not be able "to use his mind properly."[110]

*   *   *

What about the countertransference? "Much of our understanding of the transference," Joseph wrote, "comes through our understanding of how our patients . . . try to draw us into their defensive systems; . . . how they convey aspects of their inner worlds built up from infancy—elaborated in childhood and adulthood, experiences often beyond the use of words, which we can only capture through the feelings aroused in us, through our countertransference, used in the broadest sense of the word." In her paper "Transference: The Total Situation" (1985), she elaborated, drawing on "the discussion of a case at a recent postgraduate seminar":

> The analyst brought material from a patient who seemed very difficult to help adequately: schizoid, angry, and unhappy childhood with probably emotionally unavailable parents. The analyst was dissatisfied with the work of a particular session which she brought, and with its results. The patient had brought details of individual people and situations.
>
> The seminar felt that many of the interpretations about this were sensitive and seemed very adequate. Then the seminar started to work very hard to understand more. Different points of view about various aspects were put forward, but no one felt quite happy about their own or other people's ideas. Slowly it dawned on us . . . that our problem in the seminar was reflecting the analyst's problem in the transference, and that what was probably going on in the transference was a projection of the patient's inner world, in which she, the patient, could not understand and, more, could not make sense of what was going on. . . .
>
> I think that the clue to the transference here (assuming that what I am describing is correct) lay in our taking seriously the striking phenomenon in the seminar, of our struggling to understand and our desperate need to understand. . . . Our countertransference . . . enabled us, we thought, to sense a projective identification of a part of the patient's inner world and the distress, of which we got a taste in the seminar.[111]

If, Joseph concluded, the analyst "could really contain"[112] the patient's "experience of living in an incomprehensible world," then the analysis could go on[113]—"as opposed to subtle acting out . . . by both patient and analyst," which most likely would lead to a stalemate or to a repetition of what had gone on in the patient's past.[114] Here countertransference and containment worked together.

*   *   *

In writing about "unreachable patients," in describing her efforts to make more of the ego available, Joseph paid close attention to "the patient's method of communication," the actual way he spoke, and the way he reacted to her interpretations. And she urged her readers to do likewise: "to recognize that these patients, even when . . . quite verbal," were "in fact doing a great deal of acting, sometimes in speech itself."[115] Verbal communications, thus, should be scrutinized not only for their content, but for what was being acted in the transference as well. To illustrate her point, Joseph gave the following account:

> A rather new patient, whom I shall call A., a young professional woman, arrived a few minutes late, explaining that she was very tired and had overslept. Her boss was expecting her to do a great deal of work which should be shared out to other people as well; she was very angry; she was going to discuss it with him. No, no, no, she was not going to do that work. The reason for anger, if genuine, seemed real enough, but the way she talked was rather like a self-consciously naughty little girl. I made a rather general interpretation linking what she was saying with what we had been seeing in previous sessions about her actual annoyance being that I don't let her do my work, so she digs in her heels and rejects what I have to say. She replied. "Yes, I always dig in my heels. I can't let people be over me, just as when I was at the university and people tried to bully me. I . . ."
>
> Now that sounds as if my patient is agreeing with my too general remark that she can't let people be over her (but said very, very easily) but if they, I, am over her then apparently I am like her bullying boss— so one would think she would be right to dig in her heels . . . [I]n so far as I am bullying one would assume that I must be wrong, but she indicates that her behaviour is wrong. So I am quietly placated by her statement of guilt. But this . . . twist takes all the meaning out of our communication and leaves it useless. I show her this. She quickly adds that this must be "because . . . ," so long before anything has been established between us, any understanding, it is explained away— "because . . .". It seems as if there is nothing genuine and sincere going on. I tried to show this point. . . . Immediately she responded that the word that really affected her in what I was saying was about the notion of "no trust"—she again started to explain about the notion of no trust in the abstract "because . . .". But again the meaning has gone, there seems to be no feeling about what I was trying to show her but a quick explaining it away "because . . ."[116]

Joseph had a number of options: she could interpret the contents of the material—for example, how she was "experienced in a persecuting way as her [patient's] bullying boss"; she "could explain something about the fragments of her childhood" that were "brought up after the 'becauses.' " But neither of these interventions would have captured "the thing being acted out in the session": how the patient, disturbed by Joseph's interpretations, by the implication that there might be something she did not know, sought to regain her balance by drawing her analyst into "perpetual agreement." This Joseph linked with another feeling she had, almost constantly, with this patient and which seemed unique to her:

> I find I listen but almost do not believe what she is telling me, as if she were confabulating history, inventing boy friends, or details about boy friends, or stories that she tells me that people have told her. Yet I do not think ... that she is consciously lying. ... My suspicion is—and only time will or may show whether I am right—that this patient as an infant or young child had no real belief in her world, in her emotional surroundings, as if deep sincerity was lacking between her parents and herself and that there was a lack of belief in, and phony idealization of, her parents—whom I suspect at depth ... she saw through. And this ... disbelief ... in ... relationships is what she is living out with me in the transference.[117]

If the analyst managed to accept the pressure that the patient brought to bear on him to feel or do something, to hold onto it, to reflect on the fact of being subjected to it, and then make a limited and precise interpretation of what was happening at the moment—would that be sufficient to overcome the "abnormal changes" in the ego that splitting and projective identification produced? Recall that Klein herself remained skeptical about the possibility of successfully analyzing "patients with strong paranoid anxieties and schizoid mechanisms." She thought of the analytic work—"the painstaking, careful and consistent" effort to show the patient how and why he was "again and again splitting off parts of his self"[118]—as taking place in the transference, with transference understood to include everything the patient brought into the relationship. Joseph thought of it as taking place in the countertransference as well, with countertransference enriched by Bion's notion of containment. Countertransference and containment, even in conjunction, could not guarantee a favorable outcome. The pairing did, however, encourage analysts to press on.

*   *   *

Should "ego weakness" be viewed as a deficit or defect originating in early childhood? Had something happened to the child and/or had something failed to develop in the child, with "ego weakness" figuring as either a lacuna or a developmental arrest? Alternatively, should "ego weakness" be considered a result of processes mobilized to cope with intense anxiety—paranoid anxiety in Klein's parlance? Should the infant be thought of as an active agent, motivated by unconscious fantasies and capable of deploying defense mechanisms, which are themselves intimately related to particular sorts of fantasy? The issue of how to construe "ego weakness"—a term favored by American ego psychologists—has been lurking offstage.

Let me reframe the question in order to highlight its clinical implications: Should a patient's ego strength—like his reality testing—be reckoned a precondition for treatment or as a consequence thereof? Kleinians have leaned toward the latter choice—without, however, going all the way. Here they have found themselves in agreement with Freud:

> The problem of psychoses would be simple and perspicuous if the ego's detachment from reality could be carried through completely. But that seems to happen only rarely or perhaps never. Even in a state so far removed from the reality of the external world as one of hallucinatory confusion, one learns from patients after their recovery that at the time in some corner of their mind (as they put it) there was a normal person hidden who, like a detached spectator, watched the hubbub of illness go past him.[119]

To turn to the substance of this chapter: I want to single out the paranoid-schizoid position as the principal conceptual advance. Even before Klein introduced it in 1946, a number of its elements figured prominently in psychoanalytic writing. *Anxiety*: both Freud and Klein were thinking hard about it in the 1920s. Freud set down, side by side with his earlier view of anxiety as the product of inadequate sexual satisfaction, the notion of "anxiety as a signal announcing a situation of danger."[120] Klein understood that situation as something internal and as something sadistic. In 1932 she adopted Freud's hypothesis of the death instinct to underpin her preoccupation with persecutory or paranoid states. *Internal objects*: Klein brought them into the picture—given her work on the depressive position, there was no chance that she would have left them out. *Splitting of the ego*: Freud bequeathed only scattered remarks. On this point Klein referred to the work of W. R. D. Fairbairn; she insisted that his term schizoid position be understood to cover both persecutory fears and schizoid defenses—later she changed her term to paranoid-schizoid.[121] In thus conceiving of the ego as fissionable, Klein began to flesh out what Freud had simply referred to as "abnormal changes."

Along with splitting, projective identification came onto the psychoanalytic scene. Or should I say into? For many years, "projection onto" had been non-Kleinian usage, while Kleinians had been careful to say projection "into." More recently, some non-Kleinian commentators have indicated that the phrase "into the object" has become acceptable[122]—or should I say digestible? Klein herself described projective identification as one among several defenses against paranoid anxiety and devoted only a few sentences to it in her "Notes on Some Schizoid Mechanisms." In the course of the paper, she made it clear that in theory the infant or patient's fantasies of projecting included what was good as well as what was bad—though in analytic practice, the emphasis has fallen on the bad.

What, then, have been the practical consequences of Klein's theorizing, which, to my mind, would count as progress? The most obvious development has been in the use of countertransference. But its connection to Klein's later work is not straightforward. Klein, for one, took the line that "if the analyst was influenced by what the patient was doing to him it was evidence of something the analyst was not coping with."[123] There is a "classic story" which illustrates her view: "a young analyst . . . told her he felt confused and therefore interpreted to his patient that the patient had projected confusion into him, to which she replied, 'No, dear, *you* are confused.' "[124] She did not approve of Heimann's broad use of the term to cover all the feelings the analyst experienced toward his patient, fearing that such a use "would open the door to claims by analysts that their own deficiencies were caused by their patients."[125] Heimann, for her part, made no reference to the paranoid-schizoid position, ego-splitting, or projective identification in her classic paper. Racker did mention projective identification, but only in passing;[126] it was Klein's earlier work and Strachey's application of it to psychoanalytic technique that had the greatest impact on him. In short, there were a number of roads leading to countertransference, none of which Klein chose to follow.

The course that Joseph charted took off from Bion as well as from Klein. Going beyond Klein, she stressed the way the patient attempted to induce feelings and thoughts in the analyst, and tried, often very subtly and without being aware of it, to "nudge" the analyst into acting in a manner consistent with the projection. Even when she felt herself little affected, a more detailed look at the material would reveal some "nudging." It would also reveal some acting out, however slight, on her side. In line with Bion, Joseph appreciated that it was one thing, by paying close attention to what was being lived—or acted—in the transference–countertransference situation, to grasp the meaning of the patient's projected fragments, and quite another for the patient to take back the projections into himself:

> With . . . [a female] patient it was possible to open up her feelings that I was antagonistic and controlling, that I did not want her to get on in life or in her career. As we looked at her feelings about my motivation it became clear that in her mind I felt deeply threatened by her, and deeply envious of her as a young person with her life ahead of her. I would then wish to explore most carefully her picture of me, this old, supposedly lonely, rather embittered person, . . . and only very slowly and over a long period, hope to explore how much of these ideas might be linked with

actual observations of myself or the way I function, how much projected parts of herself. . . . To assume that all these ideas were projections from the beginning would almost certainly be inaccurate, would numb one's sensitivity . . . to what was going on and prevent one from seeing what else was being talked about and why it came up at that moment.

This slow and careful exploration, she added, was in large measure "what we mean when we talk about 'containing.' "[127]

In writing about psychic change, Joseph urged analysts to search for the part of the ego that was "able moment to moment" to take an interest in understanding, "even though that part" might be "quickly lost again. For long-term . . . change, and for thinking about the ending of an analysis," she regarded "the strengthening of this part of the personality" as crucial[128]— and feasible. Time and again she proved unwilling to join Freud in declaring an "abnormal ego" "unserviceable for our purposes."

Chapter 5

Narcissism: Megalomania

In its brief pre-psychoanalytic history narcissism found itself subsumed under the perversions. "The term," Freud wrote, was "chosen by Paul Näcke in 1899 to denote the attitude of the person who treats his own body in the . . . way . . . the body of a sexual object is ordinarily treated—who looks at it, . . . strokes it and fondles it till he obtains complete satisfaction through these activities." Freud borrowed the name and broadened its range. It struck him that "individual features of the narcissistic attitude" were found in people suffering from other disorders—and indeed in people suffering from no disorder at all.[1] He also opened up space for it between auto-erotism and object love. Then, having fitted narcissism into his reckoning, he tended to blur the distinction between it and auto-erotism and to lose interest in the latter. Narcissism, not auto-erotism, became crucial to his longstanding project of connecting sexual development to mental disorders.

According to Freud, the so-called "narcissistic neuroses" displayed "two fundamental characteristics." First, a "diversion of . . . interest from the external world."

> A patient suffering from hysteria or obsessional neurosis has also, so far as his illness extends, given up his relation to reality. But analysis shows that he has by no means broken off his erotic relations to people and things. He still retains them in phantasy. . . . It is otherwise with the . . . [narcissistic patient]. He seems really to have withdrawn his libido from people and things . . . , without replacing them by others in phantasy.

The question of what happened to the libido pointed to the second characteristic—megalomania:

> The libido that has been withdrawn from the external world has been directed to the ego. . . . This megalomania has no doubt come into being at the expense of object-libido. . . . But the megalomania itself is no new creation; on the contrary, it is, as we know, a magnification and plainer manifestation of a condition which had already existed previously.[2]

Both characteristics suggested that with the onset of the disorder(s), a primary narcissism had been revived.

Both characteristics also represented formidable obstacles to psychoanalytic treatment. Reinforcing one another, they foreclosed the possibility of transference. Of "positively central importance in hysteria, anxiety hysteria [phobia] and obsessional neurosis," it played no role or only a minimal role in the narcissistic neuroses. Patients afflicted with these disorders, Freud claimed, had "no capacity for transference or only insufficient residues of it."

> They reject the doctor, not with hostility but with indifference. . . . [C]onsequently the mechanism of cure which we carry through with other people—the revival of the pathogenic conflict and the overcoming of . . . repression—cannot be operated with them. . . . They . . . are inaccessible to our efforts. . . . They remain as they are.[3]

Given his therapeutic pessimism, it is not surprising that Freud made little effort to distinguish among the so-called narcissistic neuroses. At one time or another he assigned melancholics, paranoiacs, schizophrenics, as well as sufferers from dementia praecox, to that amorphous category.[4] Psychoanalysts, who have generally shown scant interest in nosology, have made an exception for narcissism. And in this, Heinz Kohut and Otto F. Kernberg have been leading figures. They along with Herbert A. Rosenfeld are the protagonists of this chapter. They need to be introduced.

All three derived from German-speaking Jewish backgrounds; all were forced to flee Nazi terror and start afresh as émigrés. Each came to psychoanalysis in his new setting; each encountered a different psychoanalytic tradition and made varying use of that tradition.

Born in 1913, Kohut was the only child of assimilated and financially secure Viennese Jews.[5] At the time of his son's birth, Felix Kohut stood on the verge of a career as a concert pianist. Fifteen months later, the First World War began. Four years of military service, including a stint as a prisoner of war in Italy, left Felix, if not a broken man, a much diminished one: his concert career finished, he went into the paper business; his marriage too was finished—he was never again close to his wife. In 1937 he developed an acute form of leukemia and died within the year. The loss of his father prompted Heinz to seek psychotherapeutic treatment, initially with Walter Marseilles and later with August Aichhorn.

Her husband's absence during the war and his emotional distance after it, left Heinz's mother, Else, in sole charge of her son. Seldom was he let out of her sight. "She vacationed with him often and was particularly fond of taking him to Italy to visit art museums." She refused to allow him to attend school; instead she hired tutors and had him taught at home. She was "thorough in her selection of teachers, and Heinz got the best possible instruction in elementary reading, writing, literature, mathematics, and science." At last, when he was 10, she became involved in a love affair, and he entered a regular classroom. Even then her "grip on her adored son" remained tight.[6]

Else was a Lampl. Her younger brother was Hans Lampl, recurrent suitor of Anna Freud, husband of prominent Freudian loyalist Jeanne Lampl-de Groot. Uncle and nephew had many cultural interests in common and presumably friends and acquaintances as well. The Freuds and psychoanalysis were not among them. Kohut's first encounter with Freud, by way of reading his *Introductory Lectures* as an adolescent, left him unmoved. At that point he was beginning to matriculate in medicine at the University of Vienna. At that point, too, Hitler was coming to power in Germany and finding numerous sympathizers among Austrian Nazis. Kohut's university years turned into a race against time: would he or would he not be able to complete his training before anti-semitism barred him from further study? He managed to receive his medical degree in November 1938, eight months after German troops occupied Vienna and a week before Kristallnacht. The following year mother and son fled Austria, the one to Italy, the other to England.

In early 1940 they were reunited in Chicago, where each was to fashion a new life. A common feature stood out: a repudiation of Jewishness and Judaism. Sometime in the 1940s, Else converted to Catholicism, and when she died in 1972, a priest attended her. For his part, Heinz "began presenting himself ethnically as half-Jewish at most (and not Jewish at all if he thought he could get away with it.)" In terms of belief, he seems to have decided that he was a Christian and proceeded to join a Unitarian church. It also seems that he obscured his ethnic and religious identity from his son. The son— an only child born in 1950—insisted that Kohut was both "militantly non-Jewish" and "Christian in a basic and authentic way."[7]

Heinz's fashioning or refashioning included becoming a psychoanalyst— initially of an orthodox variety. Having settled in Chicago, he completed an internship and then began a residency in neurology at the University of Chicago's Billings Hospital. A couple of years later he decided "to switch his appointment (he had by then been made an instructor) from neurology to neurology and psychiatry." At the same time he moved from the laboratory to the clinic. Even before the switch he had applied to the Chicago Psychoanalytic Institute for training—and had been rejected. Why is unclear. Kohut's biographer suggests that it was his "fluid sexual boundaries" that got him into trouble:[8] as an adolescent he had had a homosexual experience and as an adult he had a friendship with a strong homoerotic undercurrent. He did not let the rejection deter him: he entered psychoanalytic treatment with the well-connected Ruth Eissler and successfully reapplied to the Institute. In 1948 he married and in late 1950 he graduated.

For the next two decades, during which he served a term as president of the American Psychoanalytic Association in 1964–1965, Kohut considered himself to be very much part of mainstream psychoanalysis in the United States.

In those years "mainstream" meant psychoanalytic ego psychology; it meant the trio of Heinz Hartmann, Ernst Kris, and Rudolph M. Loewenstein, with Hartmann generally acknowledged as preeminent in matters theoretical. Kohut's early publications were all written as if he were looking over his shoulder at Hartmann for recognition and approval; he employed the same technical language or jargon and the same ponderous tone. Indeed when Hartmann died in 1970, so John Gedo reported, Kohut telephoned him at 2:30 in the morning:

> With great urgency, he announced that Hartmann was dead. I said I was sorry to hear that, but that I did not understand the reason for the urgent ... call. Kohut replied, half in exasperation, half in despair, "Heinz Hartmann in dead!" I am sure I was supposed to say that, from then on, Kohut would be the premier theoretician of psychoanalysis. In *my* exasperation about being pushed into such a transaction, the idea came to me in the nastiest form imaginable: "The Heinz is dead, long live the Heinz!" ... I refused to indulge Kohut's need for affirmation.[9]

In the last decade of his life—he died in 1980 after a long struggle with cancer—Kohut charted a new course and "to an extraordinary degree ... closed out other thinkers." That decade saw the publication of *The Analysis of the Self* (1971) and *The Restoration of the Self* (1977). (Kohut's third book, *How Does Analysis Cure?*, was published posthumously in 1984.) It saw the crystallization of Kohut's theoretical and technical approach to narcissism; it saw self psychology take shape as a movement outside of and threatening to the American psychoanalytic establishment. Convinced that each generation had "to find its own conceptual voice," Kohut became persuaded that his was "the new voice of psychoanalysis" for his generation, "that he was the new Freud in a new land."[10]

And like Freud he left behind a piece of autobiography. Freud made no secret that many of the dreams reported in *The Interpretation of Dreams* (1900) were his, and, accordingly, psychoanalysts and historians alike have plumbed the work to fathom his intellectual and emotional course during the years he was launching a new discipline.[11] In contrast Kohut hid from his readers the fact that he was the patient discussed in "The Two Analyses of Mr Z" (1979).[12] Written near the end, not the start, of his career, the paper stands as an apologia for his life as well as a justification for his theory.

Kohut had come to the United States after a year-long stay in England. Kernberg arrived after having spent roughly two decades in South America. Born in Vienna in 1928, he and his family settled in Chile in January 1940. His Austrian background left its mark on his accent; his Chilean education and medical training left their mark on his professional concerns. Ironically, it was in Chile that Kernberg became thoroughly familiar with German descriptive psychiatry. His psychiatric residency bequeathed him a keen interest in problems of diagnosis and classification. Coming to the United States, initially on a one-year fellowship in 1959–1960 and then permanently in 1961, he was shocked by his new colleagues' ignorance of the fine discriminations that had been drummed into him.[13]

In Chile Kernberg trained in psychoanalysis as well as in psychiatry, and he did so at a time when Chilean analysts were shifting from an ego psychological to a Kleinian orientation. In the United States he deepened his understanding of a broad theoretical range. After his permanent move, he spent more than a decade at the Menninger Memorial Hospital in Topeka, Kansas and simultaneously served as a training and supervising analyst at the Topeka Institute. The Menninger in the 1950s and 1960s stood as a Mecca for analysts of various persuasions: there Kernberg met Joseph Sandler who introduced him to the work of Edith Jacobson; there too he met John Sutherland who introduced him to the work of British object relations theorists.[14]

Kernberg had worked in psychiatric hospitals in Chile and Kansas; he continued to do so after moving to New York with his wife and three children in 1973. From the mid-1970s on, he held the positions of medical director of the New York Hospital–Cornell Medical Center, Westchester Division and of training and supervising analyst at the Columbia University Center for Psychoanalytic Training and Research. In 1974 he joined the faculty of the New York Psychoanalytic Institute, but cut his formal ties to that bastion of ego psychological orthodoxy in 1981. And finally in the mid-1970s he began bringing together and republishing papers in book form. A decade later Robert Wallerstein wrote of him that there was "probably no psychoanalytic author more widely read or quoted in the world today both within specifically psychoanalytic circles and in the far wider area . . . of mental health professionals."[15]

Institutionally, as well as theoretically, Kernberg tried to build bridges. He was an energetic participant in mainstream academic psychiatry, presenting his findings, often the fruit of collaborative research, in major psychiatric journals; he was actively involved with psychoanalysis on the international scene, serving a four-year term as president of the International Psychoanalytical Association from 1997 to 2001. He never claimed to be offering a new paradigm for psychoanalysis nor to be founding a new school. Here the contrast with Kohut could not be more striking.

Rosenfeld, like Kohut, fled Nazi rule shortly after completing his medical education.[16] Born in 1910 in Nuremberg, he was one of four children, the others all daughters, in a middle-class Jewish family. His father wanted him to join the family business; he chose to study medicine instead. Already intrigued by psychology, he became interested in psychiatry while training in Munich. He graduated in 1934. A year later the infamous Nuremberg laws barred him from treating Aryan patients, so he chose to emigrate to England; fortunately he still had a choice.

Starting afresh turned out to be no simple matter. To practice as a doctor, he had to take all his examinations over again, which he did with little delay. He then encountered British restrictions on foreigners doing general medicine. He could move elsewhere or he could give up his hopes of a general practice. Having just met his future wife (they later had three children), and having learned that there were still openings for foreign psychotherapists, he took the second course. He applied, successfully, for a position at the Tavistock Clinic in London. The date was 1937. Five years later he sought analytic training and entered analysis with Melanie Klein.

Rosenfeld, along with Wilfred R. Bion and Hanna Segal, figured as the three principals—all Klein analysands—endeavoring to extend psycho-analysis to the treatment of psychotics. Even before his own analysis, Rosenfeld had acquired experience with such patients, both hospitalized and ambulatory. Working without pay at the Maudsley Hospital, he started tak-ing histories, asking patients about the circumstances surrounding their breakdowns. Working with pay at the Tavistock, he found that it was possible to make meaningful contact with various types of psychotic patients. His superiors, who were of the opinion that psychological factors played no role in psychosis, insisted that he stop therapy with these patients. He complied, but never again. When during his analytic training, his second control case turned out to be a borderline patient who suffered intense anxiety and developed depersonalized states, his supervisor, Sylvia Payne, initially sug-gested that he terminate treatment. He refused, and she agreed both to let him continue and to count the case toward qualification. She readily admitted that she had little direction to offer; she could listen and did so for three and a half years. By then the patient was able to marry, and because she was leaving for India with her husband, the analysis came to an end. Throughout the rest of his long career—Rosenfeld died in 1986—he always kept a vacancy in his practice for a psychotic patient.[17]

*   *   *

Freud had highlighted two "fundamental characteristics" of those suffering from narcissistic neuroses, which, he claimed, posed insuperable obstacles to treatment. As for the first, their lack of capacity for transference, Kohut and Kernberg, along with Rosenfeld, demurred. Kohut, in particular, offered a careful delineation of transference phenomena—he initially called them narcissistic transferences and later selfobject transferences. As for the second, the narcissistic patient's "megalomania," he regarded it as part of normal development. In contrast, Kernberg viewed the "grandiose self" as patho-logical, as an instance of development gone awry. Both he and Rosenfeld also understood it as defensive. And the complex object relations it obscured or disguised, Rosenfeld argued, could be brought into the transference and there clarified. All three resisted Freud's therapeutic pessimism, which itself stood as a major impediment to treatment.

Kohut and narcissistic transferences

In his "Two Analyses of Mr Z," Kohut described two treatments, each lasting four years, with a break of five and a half years in between—the first beginning in 1954 or 1955 and the second in 1963 or 1964. Kohut's own analysis with Ruth Eissler occurred a decade before Z's supposed first stint. Like Z's, however, it took place under the old dispensation. It also took place before Kohut's mother deteriorated. By the start of the so-called second analysis, she had "undergone a serious personality change; she ... had become increasingly isolated, leaving the house ... rarely, and ... had developed a set of circumscribed paranoid delusions."[18] His mother's worsening condition prompted Kohut to reassess what he had learned from his previous analytic experience.

Narcissistic issues had never been absent. During the first year of the first analysis, Z's "unrealistic, deluded grandiosity and his demands that the psychoanalytic situation should reinstate the position ... of being admired and catered to by a doting mother" figured prominently. It was a trying period:

> He [Z] blew up in rages against me, time after time. ... These attacks arose either in response to my interpretations concerning his narcissistic demands and his arrogant feelings of "entitlement" or because of such unavoidable frustrations as weekend interruptions, occasional irregularities in the schedule, or, especially, my vacations. In the last mentioned instances, ... the patient also reacted with depression accompanied by hypochondriacal preoccupations and fleeting suicidal thoughts. After about a year and a half, he rather abruptly became much calmer.

Thanks to "the cumulative effect of ... working-through processes," Kohut surmised, "the patient was now giving up his narcissistic demands."[19]

The treatment, once past its stormy beginning, proceeded just as "the classical theories of psychoanalysis" suggested it should:

> The centre of the analytic stage was from then on occupied, on the one hand, by transference phenomena and memories concerning his ... pathogenic conflicts in the area of infantile sexuality and aggression—his Oedipus complex, his castration anxiety, his childhood masturbation, his fantasy of the phallic woman, and, especially his preoccupation with the primal scene—and, on the other hand, by his revelation that, beginning at age 11, he had been involved in a homosexual relationship, lasting about two years, with a 30-year-old high school teacher, a senior counsellor and assistant director of the summer camp to which he had been sent by his parents.

In due course Z's father turned up more and more frequently in the material:

The most significant sign in facing what I then believed to be his deepest conflicts was a dream which occurred about half a year before the termination. In this dream—his associations pointed to the time when the father [after a considerable absence] rejoined the family—*he was in a house, at the inner side of a door which was a crack open. Outside was the father, loaded with giftwrapped packages, wanting to enter. The patient was intensely frightened and attempted to close the door in order to keep the father out.* We did a good deal of work on this dream. . . . I stressed in my interpretations and reconstructions . . . his hostility toward the returning father, the castration fear, vis-à-vis the strong, adult man; and in addition, I pointed to his tendency to retreat from competitiveness and male assertiveness either to the old pre-oedipal attachment to his mother or to a defensively taken submissive and passive homosexual attitude toward the father.

To Kohut's "analytic eye, trained to perceive the configurations described by Freud, everything seemed to have fallen into place. . . . It all seemed right, especially in view of the fact that it was accompanied by what appeared to be . . . improvement in all the essential areas of the patient's disturbance."[20]

In retrospect Kohut concluded otherwise: the benefits Z had derived from the first analysis should be reckoned as nothing but a "transference success." Outside the analytic setting, the patient had simply acceded to his analyst's "expectations by suppressing his symptoms . . . and by changing his behaviour" so as to conform to the prevailing psychoanalytic "maturity morality." Within that setting, he had gone along with this analyst's beliefs by "presenting . . . oedipal issues."

Put most concisely: my theoretical convictions, the convictions of a classical analyst who saw the material that the patient presented in terms of infantile drives and conflicts about them, and of agencies of a mental apparatus either clashing or co-operating with each other, had become for the patient a replica of the mother's hidden psychosis, or a distorted outlook on the world to which he had adjusted in childhood, which he had accepted as reality—an attitude of compliance . . . that he had . . . reinstated with regard to me and to the seemingly unshakable convictions that I held.[21]

The second analysis did not produce new material; rather it prompted a reappraisal of the old: material that had earlier failed to claim the attention of analyst and analysand alike was now scrutinized at great length. Z's mother and his relationship to her, especially, came in for reconsideration and reinterpretation. "What had been missing from his reports was the crucial fact that the mother's emotional gifts were bestowed on him under the . . . accompanying condition that he submit to total domination by her, that he must not allow himself any independence." Certain items stood out. After each of Mr Z's bowel movements, his mother insisted on examining what he had produced. When Z was about 6 years old, her interest in excrement ceased, to be replaced by an equally obsessive preoccupation with his skin. "Every Saturday afternoon—the procedure became an unalterable ritual—she examined his face in minutest detail, in particular—and increasingly as he moved toward adolescence—with regard to any developing blackheads she could detect."

> Mr Z's increasing awareness of his mother's psychopathology and his understanding of its pathogenic influence on him could not be maintained without a great deal of emotional toil. The . . . analytic illumination of this material was interrupted time and again by serious resistances in the form of doubts. . . . Which reality was real? His mother's reality? The reality for which the first analysis stood? Or the present one? Over and over, he struggled with these questions. And many times, . . . he turned in his search for certainty to the fact that his mother had now developed a set of delusions which demonstrated without question that her outlook was distorted. And over and over, he remembered his reaction when he had first realized that the mother was mentally ill. . . . His immediate reaction—deeply puzzling to him at the time but now becoming intelligible—had been one of a quietly experienced, intense inner joy. It was the expression of his sense of utter relief about the fact that he now, potentially at least, had witnesses; that he was not alone in knowing that the way the mother saw the world, particularly, of course, the way she had behaved toward him during his childhood was pathological.[22]

His mother's attitude, Kohut claimed, had left Z feeling depressed and hopeless. She did not care about him, only about his feces and blackheads—"with an intensity, a self-righteous certainty . . . that allowed no protest and created almost total submission." As Z freed himself from this enmeshed relationship, "the depressive elements receded, and active yearnings, . . . vigorously expressed demands, an increasingly prominent vitality, buoyancy, and hopefulness" became evident.[23] Simultaneously the content of his communications shifted: he turned his attention, previously focused almost exclusively on his mother, to the camp counselor, who had satisfied the boy's keen wish for a strong and admired paternal figure, and then to the father himself.

Z's father, despite the oedipal emphasis of the first analysis, had remained a shadowy figure. "[N]ow—and with a glow of happiness . . .—Z began to talk about the positive features of his father's personality:

> This was . . . the crucial moment in the treatment—the point at which he may be said to have taken the road toward emotional health. But the road was not an easy one. . . . [T]he unfolding of the principal

theme—the recovery of the strong father—was interrupted by recurrent attacks of severe anxiety, including a number of frightening, quasi-psychotic experiences in which he felt himself to be disintegrating and was beset by intense hypochondriacal concerns.

Z "dwelt particularly on a two-week skiing vacation he had taken with his father at the age of 9."

> Z's father seems . . . to have been a good skier and also something of a man of the world. He had a way with waiters and chambermaids, and was soon surrounded by a circle of followers who were fascinated by his stories and appeared to look up to him. From listening to his telephone conversations and hearing his comments when he read the papers, the patient also got a glimpse of his father's business activities; and he came to admire his resoluteness, perceptiveness, and skill in this area. The psychological essence, however, of this phase of the analysis lay . . . in his [Z's] recovery of the intensely experienced awareness that his father was an independent man who had a life independent from the life of the mother—that his father's personality, whatever its shortcomings, was by no means as distorted as that of the much more powerful mother.

At long last, Kohut insisted, Z "found an image of masculine strength."[24]

With that, ending the analysis became possible. The actual termination phase began by Z recalling the dream that had ushered in the similar phase of the first analysis, "the dream of his father's return, loaded with packages containing gifts for the patient, in which the patient . . . desperately struggled to shut the door against the father's pressure." It was not, Kohut now interpreted, "a portrayal of a child's aggressive impulse against the adult male accompanied by castration fear, but of the mental state of a boy who had been all-too-long without a father; of a boy deprived of the psychological substance from which . . . he would build up, little by little, the core of an independent masculine self." His father's reappearance offered the boy "all the psychological gifts for which he had secretly yearned." At the same time its "overwhelming suddenness" subjected him to a "traumatic state."[25]

Z, Kohut claimed, should not be reckoned a little Oedipus. Nor should he be reckoned another Sergei Pankejeff—the Wolf Man being the patient of Freud's who, most likely, would have come to an informed reader's mind. Z should be counted among those suffering from a narcissistic personality disorder. To understand patients of this sort, Kohut insisted, required rethinking narcissism itself.

*   *   *

I left the reading of your paper . . . for the peace of the Christmas holidays, and I have just finished it to-day. I feel very excited about it since I do not only feel your argumentation very convincing but also I feel it to be one of the most beautiful analytic papers which I have read in recent years. I like the way ... you build on and widen existent knowledge. ... There has been no analytic writing like this, really, for a very long time.[26]

Thus Anna Freud greeted Kohut's paper "Forms and Transformations of Narcissism," first delivered at a plenary session of the American Psychoanalytic Association in December 1965. In July 1980, he wrote his last letter to her:

How are you? Despite the passing years during which we have not seen each other, I feel myself still bound to you. As you perhaps know, my new works have made me a very controversial person. ... But I really don't want to burden you with all that now. I trust in your inner greatness which, in spite of growing questions with respect to my works, will not lead you to see me with the eyes of my contemporaries who treat me in a most unworthy fashion.[27]

In the intervening decade and a half, Kohut had come to regard his own theorizing—especially his sharp differentiation between the pathology of the transference neuroses and that of the narcissistic disorders—as superseding, rather than building on, "existent knowledge."[28] To such provocation, Freud's daughter responded with discreet silence.

At the start of the paper Anna Freud had praised, Kohut made plain his intention: to rescue narcissism from "a negatively toned evaluation," from its condemnation as obnoxious and/or unhealthy. "The altruistic value system of Western civilization" had intruded where it did not belong: as a consequence the contribution of narcissism to "adaptation and achievement" had been overlooked.[29] By furnishing narcissism with a developmental story of its own—in contrast to Freud's account, which pictured narcissism as a way-station on the road to object love—Kohut aimed to make good this neglect.

Kohut's account took off from the notion of primary narcissism, understood as an infantile state in which the "I–you differentiation" had not yet been established. This state, imagined as blissful, became unsettled by failures on the part of the mother. No mother could be perfect; so disruption proved inevitable. The infant then attempted to regain the earlier state by "building up" two "new systems of perfection." One sought to imbue the "rudimentary you, the adult, with absolute perfection and power." Kohut called this system or configuration the "idealized parent-imago." The other aimed at creating a rudimentary self to which "everything pleasant, good, and perfect" belonged.[30] This configuration Kohut dubbed the "narcissistic self"—though to Anna Freud he commented that "exhibitionistic self" or "grandiose-exhibitionistic self" would be closer to his meaning.[31] In the end he opted for grandiose self.[32]

It stood to reason that "the developmental stream of narcissism," be it the idealized parent imago or the grandiose self, could be interfered with "leading to fixations and developmental arrests."[33] How, in specific instances, did Kohut understand such interference? In *The Analysis of the Self*, he used Mr. A. to illustrate the pathogenic disruption of the idealizing system. In his twenties, Mr. A. came for treatment "feeling vaguely depressed, drained of energy, and lacking in zest" and suffering from "a great . . . vulnerability . . . to the absence of praise from the people whom he experienced as his elders or superiors."

> Over and over again, throughout his childhood, the patient . . . had felt abruptly and traumatically disappointed in the power and efficacy of his father just when he had (re)established him as a figure of protective strength and efficiency. . . . The father who, during the patient's early childhood, had been a virile and handsome man had owned a small but flourishing industry. Judging on the basis of many indications and memories, . . . father and son were very close . . ., and . . . the son admired the father greatly. . . . Suddenly the threat that the German armies would overrun the country interrupted their close relationship. At first the father was away a great deal, trying to make arrangements for the transfer of his business to another . . . country. Then, when the patient was six, German armies invaded the country and the family, which was Jewish, fled. Although the father initially reacted with helplessness and panic, he later succeeded in re-establishing his business, though on a much reduced scale; but as a consequence of the German invasion of the country to which they had escaped (the patient was eight at the time), everything was again lost and the family had to flee once more. . . . There is no doubt . . . that later events (his father's failure in the U.S.A.) compounded the damage; and there is similarly no doubt that the child's still earlier experiences—his being subjected to his father's extreme, sudden, and unpredictable mood swings during the preoedipal and oedipal period . . .—had sensitized him.[34]

Still, Kohut insisted that the nub of the matter was his patient's disappointment in and by his father at the beginning of latency.

Kohut was equally confident about reconstructing the pathogenic past that shattered the maturation of the grandiose self. Mr. B. was a case in point. A college instructor in his late twenties, he came to be a supervisee of Kohut's for analysis. "[H]e suffered from a vague and widespread personality disturbance, experienced alternatively as severe states of tension and as a feeling of painful emptiness." In this instance Kohut was certain that "very early . . . fixation points" stemmed from the relationship with the mother. A very domineering woman:

> The patient's mother had ... supervised ... him in a most stringent
> fashion. His exact feeding time, for example, and, in later childhood,
> his eating time, were determined by a mechanical timer which the
> mother used as an extension of her need to control the child's activities.
> ... [S]triving to attain greater autonomy, he would in later childhood
> withdraw to his room, locking the doors, to think his own thoughts
> uninfluenced by her interference. When he had just begun to achieve
> some reliance on this minimum of autonomous functioning, his mother
> had a buzzer installed. ... From then on, she would interrupt his
> attempts ... to be alone; she would summon him to her, more compel-
> lingly (because the mechanical device was experienced as akin to
> an endopsychic communication) than would have been her voice, or
> knocking, against which he would have rebelled.

And a censorious one as well:

> When he would tell her exuberantly about some achievement or experi-
> ence she seemed not only to be cold and inattentive but, instead of
> responding to him and the event that he was describing, would suddenly
> remark critically about a detail of his appearance or current behavior
> ("Don't move your hands while you are talking!" etc.). This reaction
> must have been experienced by him not only as a rejection of the particu-
> lar display for which he had needed a confirming response but also as an
> active destruction of the cohesiveness of his self experience (by shifting
> attention to a *part* of his body) ... just at the most vulnerable moment
> when he was offering his total self for approval.

Add to this "a period of maternal depression"—the death of twin siblings
shortly after birth had left his mother deeply depressed when the patient was
3 years old. And even earlier, even "during the preverbal stage ... his pathological mother—she was addicted to barbiturates"—had shown him little
empathy.[35]

Just as Kohut was on the verge of locating the origins of narcissistic pathology in parental failure, he pulled back: "in the vast majority of even the
most severe narcissistic personality disturbances," it was "the child's reaction
to the parent rather than to gross traumatic events, in the early biography"
that accounted "for the narcissistic fixations."[36] And given two parents, the
child had two chances to react. Mr. A., for example, had experienced his
mother as unempathic and out of tune with him; he had turned to his father
in part to make up for what he had not received from his mother.
Unfortunately this second attempt had proved no more satisfactory than the
first. What other resources did the child have at his disposal?

Sexual activity and/or fantasy offered a kind of relief—albeit one that
produced discontents of its own. Mr. A., for instance, on entering analysis

complained that ever since adolescence he had felt sexually excited by men. He did not engage in overt homosexual practices; instead he masturbated and fantasized. The men he desired "were always of great bodily strength and of perfect physique. . . . In his fantasies he manipulated the situation" in such a fashion that "even though he was weak, he was able to enslave the strong man and to make him feel helpless."[37] He achieved "a feeling of triumph . . . at the thought . . . of thus draining him [the strong man] of his power." But only fleetingly. The masturbatory act "had to be repeated again and again—and the patient was indeed addicted to it."[38] As Kohut saw it, Mr. A.'s sexuality, "including its conflicts and anxieties," functioned as "a remedial stimulant"—in much the same way that a small child's "self-inflicted pain (head banging, for example)" served to maintain "a sense of aliveness."[39]

What about aggression? Mr. B., for one, on coming to treatment told of feeling "threatened by sudden upsurges of intense, tantrumlike rage."[40] Kohut took pains to distinguish between a nondestructive variety of aggression, which went along with the "demands of the rudimentary self" and narcissistic rage, which was provoked by the chronic and traumatic frustration of these demands, particularly the child's phase-appropriate insistence on "the grandiosity and omnipotence of the self."

> Narcissistic rage occurs in many forms; they all share, however, a specific psychological flavor. . . . The need for revenge, for righting a wrong, for undoing a hurt by whatever means, and a deeply anchored, unrelenting compulsion in the pursuit of these aims, which gives no rest to those who have suffered a narcissistic injury—these . . . characteristic features of narcissistic rage . . . set it apart from other kinds of aggression.[41]

Rage figured as the byproduct of an injury; sex, or more precisely, perverse sexuality, figured as an attempt at repair. Both stood as signs of narcissistic disturbance. Neither constituted bedrock. "The deepest level to be reached," Kohut insisted, was "not the drive, but the threat to the organization of the self."[42] Here Kohut broke with American psychoanalytic ego psychology.

*　　*　　*

Analysis, according to Kohut, aimed at the restoration of the self—a phrase he used as the title of a 1977 monograph. What did he mean by self? His definition changed over time. Initially he borrowed Hartmann's distinction between ego and self: the subjective experience of one's self was not the ego; it was merely an ego function.[43] By 1977 the self had become Kohut's central construct: he granted it agency, once the property of the ego; he envisioned it as a "locus of initiative and a recipient of impressions."[44] His was no longer an ego psychology; it was a psychology of the self. And where he had earlier spoken of narcissistic disturbances—disturbances in the "libidinal investment of the self"—he now talked about disorders of the self.[45] Analysis, in his view, might offer the patient another chance of developing a cohesive self—provided that the analyst understood and accommodated himself to the unfolding transferences.

In the case of Miss L., the analyst, a colleague of Kohut's, had not grasped what his patient needed. A "prolonged stalemate" set in at the very start of treatment and prompted the analyst to seek Kohut's advice. Miss L. "presented with a history of severe childhood trauma" and "a severe disturbance of her ability to establish meaningful object relationships." She was "an emotionally shallow, shiftless, and promiscuous woman." Still, she had shown "some warmth toward the analyst and . . . interest in the treatment." So Kohut asked his colleague to give him an account of the first hours of the analysis, "with particular attention to possible activities on his part that the patient might have experienced as a rebuff."

> Among the earliest transference manifestations, several dreams of this Catholic patient had contained the figure of an inspired, idealistic priest. While these . . . dreams had remained uninterpreted, the analyst remembered—clearly against some resistance—that he had subsequently mentioned to the patient that *he* was *not* a Catholic. He had seemingly not given her this information in response to the dreams, but had justified the move by her supposed need to be acquainted with a minimum of the actual situation since in his view the patient's hold on reality was tenuous. This event must have been very significant for the patient. We later understood that, as an initial transference step, she had reinstated an attitude of idealizing religious devotion from the beginning of adolescence, an attitude which in turn appeared to have been the revival of vague awe and admiration which she had experienced in early childhood. . . . The analyst's misguided remark . . . that he was not a Catholic—i.e., not like the priest of her dreams— . . . was taken as a rebuff by the patient and led to the analytic stalemate which the analyst, with the aid of a number of consultations . . . , was later largely able to break.

The analyst had missed the patient's newly minted idealizing transference; he had missed "the revival during psychoanalysis . . . of an early phase of psychic development," one that had been disrupted by "traumatic disappointments in the admired parent."[46]

The analyst's miss may have had less to do with his hold on concepts than with control over his countertransference:

> If the analyst has not come to terms with his own grandiose self, he may respond to the idealization with an intense stimulation of his unconscious grandiose fantasies. These pressures will call forth an intensification of defenses and may, in an elaboration and buttressing of the defenses, bring about the analyst's rejection of the patient's idealizing

transference. If the analyst's defensive attitude becomes chronic, the establishment of a workable idealizing transference is interfered with and the gradual working through processes . . . in the realm of the idealized parent imago are prevented.[47]

With his analysand, Miss F., Kohut himself felt challenged. At age 25, she came to treatment complaining of "diffuse dissatisfaction." Despite being professionally active and having numerous social contacts, "she felt she was different from other people and isolated from them." And despite having "had several love relationships and some serious suitors, she had rejected marriage because she knew that such a step would be a sham." As she saw it, she simply "was not intimate with anyone."

> During extended phases of the analysis, . . . the following progression of events frequently occurred. . . . The patient would come in a friendly mood, would settle down quietly, and begin to communicate her thoughts and feelings about a variety of subjects: interactions at work, with her family, or with the man with whom she was currently on friendly terms; dreams and relevant associations, including tentative but genuine references to the transference; and a variety of insights (arrived at against what seemed like appropriate resistances) concerning the connection between the present and the past, and between transferences upon the analyst and analogous strivings channeled toward others. In brief, in the first part of the analytic sessions during this phase, the process of therapy had the appearance of a well-moving self-analysis. . . .
>
> Unlike the analysand during periods of genuine self-analysis, [how-ever,] Miss F. could not tolerate my silence, nor would she be satisfied with noncommittal remarks; . . . at approximately the midpoint of the sessions, she would suddenly get violently angry at me for being silent and would reproach me for not giving her any support. . . . I gradually learned . . . that she would become immediately calm and content when I, at these moments, simply summarized or repeated what she had in essence already said (such as "You have worked your way through to the understanding that the fantasies about the visiting Englishman are reflections of fantasies about me"). . . . [I]f I went beyond what the patient herself had already said or discovered, even by a single step only (such as: "The fantasies about the visiting foreigner are reflections of fantasies about me and, in addition, I think that they are a revival of the dangerous stimulation to which you felt exposed by your father's fantasy stories about you"), she would again get violently angry (regardless of the fact that what I had added might be known to her, too), and would furiously accuse me, in a tense, high-pitched voice, of undermining her; that with my remark I had destroyed everything she had built up; and that I was wreaking the analysis.

Initially Kohut had only an unclear notion of his patient's psychopathology and had not yet fathomed its origins. In due course he came to appreciate that Miss F.'s mother had been depressed at several times during her daughter's childhood. As a consequence, Miss F. had been "deprived of that optimal maternal acceptance" which would have "transformed crude exhibitionism and grandiosity into adaptably useful self-esteem and self-enjoyment." Now in the treatment setting, Miss F.'s grandiose self became active again and produced what Kohut dubbed a mirror transference. Like the idealizing transference, the mirror transference revived an early phase of development, in this instance, a phase in which "the gleam in the mother's eye" mirrored "the child's exhibitionistic display." In due course he also came to understand his role: "to respond empathically" to Miss F.'s "narcissistic display and to provide her with narcissistic sustenance through approval, mirroring, and echoing."[48]

Not an easy job for the analyst. Kohut found that his "attention would often lag," his thoughts would begin to drift, and that he had to make a deliberate effort to stay "focused on the patient's communications." He soon realized that "specific hindrances" in his own personality were getting in the way:

> There was a residual insistence, related to deep and old fixation points, on seeing myself in the narcissistic center of the stage; and although I had of course for a long time struggled with the relevant childhood delusions and thought that I had, on the whole, achieved dominance over them, I was temporarily unable to cope with the cognitive task posed by the confrontation with the reactivated grandiose self of my patient. Thus I refused to entertain the possibility that I was not an object for the patient, . . . but only, as I reluctantly came to see, an impersonal function, without significance except insofar as it related to the kingdom of her own remobilized narcissistic grandeur and exhibitionism.[49]

What "impersonal function" did the analyst serve? He allowed himself to be used as a selfobject and thus fulfilled the selfobject needs of the patient. The needs themselves dated from infancy. For Kohut, the nascent infantile self was amorphous. It required the participation of others to provide a sense of cohesion and constancy. Those others, who from the infant's point of view were indistinguishable from the self, Kohut termed selfobjects. Through the empathic responsiveness of caregivers or analysts, needs for merger with an idealized selfobject and/or for mirroring by an affirming selfobject diminished; they matured; they did not disappear.

How, then, as Kohut asked in the title of a posthumously published book, did analysis cure? ("Transmuting internalization," a codeword, much criticized for its vagueness,[50] has stood as the short self-psychological answer.) "The analyst's protracted and consistent" efforts "to understand his patient,"

Kohut wrote, would lead to an outcome analogous to that "of normal child-hood development," that is, his, the analyst's "occasional failures, constitut-ing optimal frustrations," would "lead to the building up" of psychic structure. By optimal frustration, he meant the countless misses that were minor and benign rather than major and malignant. By psychic structure, he meant the ability to carry out certain functions previously performed by a selfobject. The analyst's efforts would, additionally, produce a further result: the patient would increasingly realize that "contrary to his experiences in childhood, the sustaining echo of empathic resonance" was "indeed available in this world."[51]

*   *   *

Kohut insisted that a capacity for so-called selfobject transferences counted as a crucial requirement for psychoanalytic treatment. Had he taken a cue from Melanie Klein, had he claimed that object relations began at birth, he would not have needed to create a new and arbitrary category.[52] Transference itself would have proved elastic enough to serve his purposes: it would have permitted him to capture both the narcissistic phenomena that emerged in the psychoanalytic process and the analyst's response to them; it would have permitted him to make his signal contribution—encouraging analysts to treat narcissistic patients. It would not, however, have permitted him to see himself as founding a new psychology of the self.

Kernberg and pathological narcissism

Near the end of his life, Kohut, together with Ernest Wolf, tried to map his nosology onto current psychiatric categories. He distinguished between primary and secondary "disorders of the self," that is, between patients with a damaged and those with an undamaged self structure. The primary dis-turbances he then divided into several subgroups: the psychoses, borderline states, narcissistic behavior disorders, and narcissistic personality disorders. Of these four, only patients falling under the last two rubrics did he consider "capable of tolerating the frustrations of reactivated narcissistic needs"; of these four, only the last two were analyzable.[53]

For Kernberg, addressing the problem Freud had referred to as "choice of neurosis" did not rank as an afterthought to a life of theorizing; its central importance he considered a given. Beyond that, he took up unfinished busi-ness: Freud had not attempted—perhaps because of waning interest in attracting a psychiatric audience—to match his narrative of regression and fixation with his structural triad of ego, id, and superego. Here Kernberg turned to the work of Margaret Mahler and Edith Jacobson. He latched on to Mahler's developmental stages: the autistic, the symbiotic, and separ-ation–individuation. According to Mahler, the double process of separation and individuation began at about four or five months of age and comprised four overlapping subphases: differentiation, practicing, rapprochement, and on the way to object constancy.[54] Kernberg also adopted Jacobson's account of structure formation.[55] He furnished this summary of her claims:

> Intrapsychic life starts out as a primary psychophysiological self within which the ego and the id are not yet differentiated, and within which aggressive and libidinal drives are undifferentiated as well. The first intrapsychic structure is a fused self-object representation which evolves gradually under the impact of the relationship between the mother and infant. . . .
>
> [This] . . . phase of development comes to an end with a gradual differentiation between the self-representation and the object representation. . . . [There is a further] differentiation of painful experiences into aggressively invested self- and object representations, . . . so that at a certain point, the intrapsychic world of object relations is reflected in "good" and "bad" self-representations and similarly, "good" and "bad" object representations. . . .
>
> The next stage of development consists in the gradual, more realistic integration of good and bad self-representations into real self-representations, and the good and bad object representations into real object representations. . . . The completion of the separation–individuation phase and the establishment of object constancy marks, precisely, the accomplishment of this developmental task.[56]

As Kernberg saw it, the borderline patient—the primary focus of his diagnostic project—regressed to or was fixated at the rapprochement subphase.[57] And being stuck at that subphase, the borderline patient kept the "libidinally invested and aggressively invested self- and object-representations" apart—and to that end used splitting to the fullest.[58] Neither interpersonally nor intrapsychically had the borderline made it to object constancy.

Where did the narcissistic patient fit in? Should he or should he not be grouped with the borderline? Yes and no. Kernberg thought that narcissistic personalities were "both strikingly similar and specifically different" from borderlines. The similarity consisted in "the overriding influence of pre-genital (especially oral) aggression."

> These patients present a pathologically augmented development of oral aggression and it is hard to evaluate to what extent this development represents a constitutionally determined strong aggressive drive, a constitutionally determined lack of anxiety tolerance in regard to aggressive impulses, or severe frustration in their first years of life.

The similarity also showed itself "in the predominance of mechanisms of splitting and primitive dissociation," and, additionally, "primitive forms of projection, . . . primitive and pathological idealization, omnipotent control, narcissistic withdrawal and devaluation."[59]

As for the differences between the two types of patient, Kernberg pointed to a "grandiose self": it was present in the narcissist, absent in the borderline. It reflected a "condensation of some aspects of the real self (the 'specialness' of the child reinforced by early experience), the ideal self (the fantasies and self images of power, wealth, omniscience, and beauty which compensated the small child for the experience of severe oral frustration, rage and envy), and the ideal object (the fantasy of an ever-giving, ever-loving and accepting parent, in contrast to the child's experience in reality; a replacement for the devalued real parental object)."

> In their fantasies, these patients identify themselves with their own ideal self images in order to deny normal dependency on external objects and on the internalized representations of the external objects. It is as if they were saying, "I do not need to fear that I will be rejected for not living up to the ideal of myself which alone makes it possible for me to be loved by the ideal person I imagine would love me. That ideal person and my ideal image . . . and my real self are all one, and better than the ideal person whom I wanted to love me, so that I do not need anybody else any more. . . . At the same time, the remnants of unacceptable self images are repressed and projected onto external objects, which are devaluated.[60]

Not all narcissists were alike, and Kernberg took care to discriminate among them. At this point matters of psychic structure took a back seat to more obvious signs of psychological functioning. At the highest level:

> We find patients without neurotic symptoms, with good surface adaptation, and with very little awareness of any emotional illness except for a chronic sense of emptiness or boredom, an inordinate need for tribute from others and for personal success, and a remarkable incapacity for intuitive understanding, empathy, and emotional investment in others.

At the middle range of the spectrum:

> Narcissistic personalities tend to be inordinately envious of other people, to idealize some people, from whom they expect narcissistic supplies, and to deprecate and treat with contempt those from whom they do not expect anything (often their former idols). Their relations with others are frequently exploitative and parasitic. Beneath a surface that is often charming and engaging, one senses coldness and ruthlessness. They typically feel restless and bored when no new sources feed their self-regard. Because of their great need for tribute and adoration from others, they

are often considered to be excessively dependent. But they are, in fact, unable to depend on anyone because of a deep underlying distrust and devaluation of others and an unconscious "spoiling" of what they receive.

At the severest level:

> We find patients who . . . present overt borderline features—that is, lack of impulse control, lack of anxiety tolerance, severe crippling of their sublimatory capacities, and a disposition to explosive or chronic rage reactions or severely paranoid distortions.[61]

Of these three groups, Kernberg regarded the lowest as unsuitable for psychoanalysis. Many of these patients, he claimed, responded "well to modified expressive psychotherapy"—a kind of treatment he also regarded as appropriate for borderline patients.[62] As for the highest group, he thought it unlikely that they would seek treatment. Patients belonging to the middle group, then, figured as the prime candidates for psychoanalysis. So too, of course, did neurotics. If Kernberg had any difficulty distinguishing narcissist from neurotic, he expected "the characteristic development of a narcissistic transference" would clear it up.[63] In this he found himself agreeing with Kohut. Such consensus was rare, and Kernberg, for one, had no wish to minimize the points at issue.

*   *   *

Recall the key role Kernberg assigned to aggression, attributing to its pregenital variety an "overriding influence" in borderline and narcissistic personalities alike. In his mind, here lay his most serious difference with Kohut. To make his point, he glossed Kohut's account of Miss F.:

> At one point, the patient [Miss F.] was able to "establish connexions between the rage which she experienced against me when I did not understand her demands and the feelings she had experienced in . . . reaction to the narcissistic frustration which she had suffered as a child." [*Analysis of the Self*, p. 293] Kohut states: "I was finally able to tell her that her anger at me was based on . . . a transference confusion with a depressed mother who had deflected the child's narcissistic needs on to herself. These interpretations were followed by the recall of clusters of analogous memories concerning her mother's entering a phase of depressive self-preoccupation during later periods of the patient's life" [ibid., p. 292]. . . . I [Kernberg] would raise the question . . . , in making this interpretation, was the analyst implicitly blaming the patient's mother for having caused the patient's anger and protecting the patient from full examination of the complex origins of her own rage?[64]

Kernberg thought that the answer was an emphatic yes.

Recall, too, that Kernberg discerned in the narcissist—but not in the borderline—the presence of a grandiose self. He acknowledged that the term "grandiose self" had been coined by Kohut; he adopted it without subscribing to Kohut's definition. The "basic disagreement" was this: whether the grandiose self reflected "the fixation of an archaic 'normal' primitive self (Kohut's view)," or whether it reflected a "structure clearly different from normal infantile narcissism" (Kernberg's view). For Kohut, the grandiose self figured as a developmental arrest; for Kernberg, it figured as a pathological formation:

> I agree with Kohut that the psychoanalytic treatment of narcissistic personalities centers on the activation of the grandiose self and the need for helping the patient achieve full awareness of it in the neutral analytic situation, but I think that focusing exclusively on narcissistic resistances from the viewpoint of libidinal conflicts with an almost total disregard of the vicissitudes of aggression . . . interferes with [its] systematic interpretation. . . . In my view, . . . the patient needs to become aware, . . . in a noncritical atmosphere, of his need to devalue and depreciate the analyst as an independent object, in order to protect himself from the reactivation of underlying oral rage and envy and the related fear of retaliation.[65]

Kernberg concluded, and it was a damning conclusion indeed, that Kohut's was a supportive, re-educative, rather than an analytic approach to narcissistic patients. The outcome of therapy of this kind was bound to be less than optimum:

> [T]here are cases in which the narcissistic resistances cannot be worked through. . . . This is particularly true for patients with relatively effective social adaptation, who consult because of a symptom which improves in the course of the analysis before working through their basic narcissistic resistances; and for cases in which secondary gains, particularly important narcissistic gratifications linked to their pathological character structure, militate against the painful nature of analytic work. . . . In . . . cases of this kind, the treatment may have to shift at some point, into a supportive tolerance of the narcissistic constellation in combination with preparation for termination of the treatment.[66]

Among those who underwent psychoanalytic therapy in which narcissistic structures were not systematically analyzed, Kernberg singled out former psychoanalytic candidates (graduated or not) for comment:

> A composite of traits one particularly finds among this group are: a gradual disappointment with intensive psychotherapeutic work with

patients, a feeling of boredom when considering . . . intensive work with a patient over a period of months or years, and rationalizations of this loss of interest in clinical work in terms of theoretical criticisms of psychoanalytic theory or technique. Frequently these former candidates—or analysts—eagerly explore new treatment methods, particularly those which promise to bring about an immediate activation of emotional reactions. . . . They feel more comfortable with methods which permit "instant intimacy" of a nondifferentiated nature rather than the lengthy, complex build-up of personal relationships in depth. . . . It is interesting to observe how in the postanalytic stage [such] patients . . . continue to idealize their analyst for a time, and then gradually shift into a basic indifference. Their retrospective evaluation of analysis is that while it was a very helpful experience, they did not learn anything really new about themselves.[67]

Pathological narcissism left unresolved had "ominous long-range prognostic implications." Young patients might be temporarily spared. In adolescence and early adulthood, they could expect narcissistic gratifications to come their way. But at some point they would be faced with conflicts "around aging, chronic illness, physical and mental limitations, above all, separations, loss, and loneliness." Eventually the grandiose self would be confronted with "the frail, limited and transitory nature of human life."[68] Psychoanalytic treatment, if thorough enough, Kernberg maintained, held out the hope of radically changing narcissistic structures and thus promised to benefit the patient enormously in the second half of his life.

*   *   *

Mr. T. A professional in the field of social rehabilitation, an unmarried man in his mid-thirties, consulted because of difficulties in his relations with women and in his work with clients, a severely limited capacity for empathy, and a general sense of dissatisfaction expressed in experiences of boredom, irritability, and uncertainty over the meaning life held for him. He suffered from a narcissistic personality without overt borderline or antisocial features.[69]

Mr. T himself had a markedly ambivalent attitude toward entering treatment. On the one hand he considered Kernberg to be a very desirable analyst "in the relatively small local professional community" where Kernberg was then working. On the other hand he thought psychoanalysis "a rather old-fashioned and passé technique, and he regarded what he experienced" as his analyst's "rigid maintenance of a psychoanalytic stance" to be "pompous and pedestrian."[70]

During the first two years of the analysis, Mr. T talked at length about his difficulties with the latest of his many girlfriends; together he and Kernberg traced them back to "his relation with his mother, a locally prominent social-ite who dominated his father and whom he had experienced as . . . intrusive, dishonest, and manipulative." At the same time Mr. T accused his analyst of feigning interest in him, or pretending to listen to him, whereas in fact he was engaged in his own activities, such as balancing his checkbook. Mr. T, in short, likened Kernberg to his mother: "sly, exploitative, and guilt provoking."

> In the third year of his psychoanalysis, I realized that Mr. T's relation to me in the transference had basically not changed since the beginning of treatment. Nor had his discovery of childhood experiences with his mother (which explained, apparently, his current relations to his girl-friends and to me) resulted in any change of his consciously held convic-tions about his present or past. I also noticed in his continuing suspicion and anger toward me an easy activation of fantasies of stopping the treatment. Although he never actually stopped, I did not have the feeling of certainty about his engagement in analysis that I had with other patients who might miss occasional sessions when acting out negative transference reactions but without shaking my conviction that they would return. With this man, I sensed both a fragility in our relation and a definite lack of deepening of it.[71]

Given this fragility, Kernberg wondered what use, if any, his patient was making of the analysis. He focused on Mr. T's responses to his interpret-ations. Mr. T listened "eagerly enough"; then he either "agreed with them, with the implication that he had earlier reached those very conclusions him-self, disagreed with them immediately, or attempted to argue . . . about them." These responses Kernberg saw as efforts on the part of his patient to avoid acknowledging that he, the analyst, had anything to offer. "Over a period of time, Mr. T began to understand that he was torn between his views" of Kernberg "as someone who might be instrumental in helping him to over-come his difficulties with women, someone he would therefore feel extremely envious of, which was intolerable, and someone he did not have to envy at all, which would reconfirm his conviction that nothing was to be expected from psychoanalysis." The immediate effect of this understanding, however, was to make matters worse. Mr. T felt that if what Kernberg was pointing out was accurate, the very accuracy amounted to a showing off on his analyst's part and "a grandiose triumph over him."

> In this context, in the fourth year of his psychoanalysis, the following rather protracted episode took place. Mr. T became increasingly alert to whatever he could experience of my shortcomings, both inside and outside the sessions. Unbeknown to me, he developed a network of information about me that extended through various related groups in

the small town where we both lived and culminated in his establishing contact with a group of disaffected members of the local psychiatric community who deeply resented the institution I was in and my role in it. Mr. T began to extract from one person who felt especially hostile to me information that the patient considered damaging to me, while feeding his contact information about my shortcomings as an analyst. When this information, amplified, came back to my patient through a third person, he became alarmed and "confessed" the whole process to me.[72]

Kernberg's immediate emotional reaction was a mix of intense hurt and anger. He felt controlled by his patient—and helpless. It took several sessions before he came to appreciate that Mr. T's relationship with his mother, long the dominant theme in the transference, remained active still; the roles had simply been reversed: he was identifying with Mr. T "as the victim of his mother's manipulations," and Mr. T "was now identifying himself with the aggressor." That his behavior resembled his description of his mother's treatment of him: this was an interpretation Mr. T could now accept. He told Kernberg that all along he felt that he had been "transgressing" an "essential understanding about open communication," risking, as he saw it, the continuation of their relationship, "but also experiencing a sense of freedom and power that was exciting, even intoxicating."[73]

After the fact, Kernberg discerned a pattern—and it fit with Heinrich Racker's discussion of countertransference. During the early years of the analysis, Kernberg sensed that he had had to function as if he were "a dominant mother or else remain impotently in the background"—and indeed every time he interpreted aggressive aspects of Mr. T's behavior, Mr. T likened Kernberg to that guilt-inducing woman. Functioning like a dominant mother suggested a complementary identification, an identification with the patient's internal object. Then Kernberg's hurt and angry reaction in the wake of Mr. T's hostile acting out signaled, in addition to his own "countertransference potential," the activation within him of his patient's self-image "as the helpless, attacked, and hurt little boy faced with an overpowering mother."[74] This ranked as a clear example of a concordant identification, an identification with the patient's ego.

What of the grandiose self? Again and again Kernberg claimed that underneath the pathological grandiose self, there existed primitive object relations.[75] These could be analyzed, and so they eventually were in the case of Mr. T. His grandiose self thus turned out to be a cover for a complex world of object relations—a world that Melanie Klein's British followers were in the course of teasing apart.

*   *   *

Kernberg spent considerable energy distancing himself from and disputing with Kohut. He questioned the very premise of Kohut's project: he was adamant that narcissism and object relations were not two separate developmental lines, that they went hand in hand. And though he agreed with Klein that the concept of primary narcissism was without warrant, he did not admit to having taken a cue from her.[76] "For some years," an astute observer remarked, "it seemed that the work of Klein had been declared an un-American activity!"[77]

Rosenfeld and narcissistic object relations

Recall Betty Joseph's account of patients who were difficult to reach:

> In the treatment of such cases I believe we can observe a splitting of the personality, so that one part of the ego is kept at a distance from the analyst and the analytic work. Sometimes this is difficult to see since the patient may appear to be working and cooperating with the analyst, but the part of the personality that is available is actually keeping another more needy or potentially responsive part split off. Sometimes the split takes the form of one part of the ego standing aside as if observing all that is going on between the analyst and the other part of the patient and destructively preventing real contact being made, using various methods of avoidance and evasion.

In these cases, she added, what looked, at least early in the treatment, like a therapeutic alliance turned out to be "inimical to a real alliance," what looked like cooperation turned out to be "a pseudo-cooperation aimed at keeping the analyst away from the really unknown and more needy infantile parts of the self."[78] Here Joseph cited a paper by Rosenfeld. In that paper, "On the Psychopathology of Narcissism: A Clinical Approach" (1964), Rosenfeld discussed case material "from a patient who showed a marked narcissistic transference," by which he meant, following Freud, a patient who seemed to have little or no capacity for transference at all.

> He is the son of fairly wealthy parents, and he has two sisters. He had apparently always managed superficially to get on quite well with people, and was successful at school because of his high intelligence. When he started treatment he had just married and he had some difficulties with his wife. . . . When I first saw the patient he appeared slightly withdrawn from reality and other people, and had a vaguely superior and patronizing attitude which he tried to disguise. . . . He was very interested in being analyzed in spite of the fact that he did not feel that he really needed analysis. He pictured himself almost immediately as the perfect patient who made enormous progress. . . . He did not

resent interpretations, ... on the contrary took them up quickly and talked about them in his own way, feeling very self-satisfied with his knowledge since he did not feel that the analyst had made any contribution. ... He enjoyed interpreting his own dreams in detail and explaining his thoughts and feelings, but any conflict, anxiety, or depression which emerged was so quickly discharged that it could barely be experienced.

No wonder Rosenfeld felt up against a stone wall and found it "extremely difficult to effect any change" in his patient's personality:

[V]ery slowly ... he [the patient] began to notice that he constantly lost contact with everything which had been discussed during the sessions. This was painful to him, but the pain was again quickly eliminated, despite the fact that it meant the expulsion of the good experience with the analyst which had led to the painful insight. ... We discovered that whenever the patient acknowledged any real understanding about himself and tried not to project his feelings, he became anxious and depressed. At that moment ... he heard himself saying, "This is dangerous," in response to which he expelled the anxiety, depression, and insight. I then showed him that what was endangered in such a situation was not his sane or good self but his omnipotent mad self.[79]

A needy, dependent, or libidinal self and an omnipotent self: these structural notions served to orient Rosenfeld as he explored "the many clinically observable conditions," which resembled "Freud's description of primary narcissism," but which were in fact "primitive object relations."[80]

*   *   *

What "primitive object relations" did Rosenfeld discern? In his paper, "A Clinical Approach to the Psychoanalytic Theory of the Life and Death Instincts: An Investigation Into the Aggressive Aspects of Narcissism" (1971), he offered the following clinical material:

The patient is an unmarried business man of 37, who has been in treatment for several years. He came to analysis because of character problems and was consciously very determined to have analysis and to cooperate in it. However there was a chronic resistance to the analysis, which was very elusive and repetitive. The patient had to leave London occasionally for short business trips and he often returned too late on Mondays and ... missed either part or the whole of his session. He frequently met women during these trips and brought to the analysis many of the problems which arose with them.

From the beginning Rosenfeld surmised that "some acting out was taking place." As for its meaning, only after the patient told of "murderous activities" in dreams he dreamt upon returning from his weekend jaunts, did Rosenfeld come to appreciate that "violently destructive attacks against the analysis and the analyst were hidden in the acting out behaviour." And so he interpreted to the patient. Though reluctant to confirm the interpretation, the patient gradually "changed his behaviour and the analysis became more effective and he reported considerable improvement in some of his personal relationships and his business activities."

> At the same time he began to complain that his sleep was frequently disturbed and that he woke up during the night with violent palpitations which kept him awake for several hours. During these anxiety attacks he felt that his hands did not belong to him; they seemed violently destructive as if they wanted to destroy something by tearing it up, and were too powerful for him to control so that he had to give in to them. He then dreamt of a very powerful arrogant man who was nine feet tall and who insisted that he had to be absolutely obeyed. His associations made it clear that this man stood for a part of himself and related to the destructive overpowering feelings in his hands which he could not resist.

Rosenfeld interpreted: the patient "regarded the omnipotent destructive part of himself as a superman who was nine feet tall and much too powerful for him to disobey. He had disowned this omnipotent self, which explained the estrangement of his hands during the nightly attacks." The patient reacted with both surprise and relief and "reported after some days that he felt more able to control his hands at night. Gradually he became aware that "the destructive impulses at night had some connection with the analysis because they increased after any success that could be attributed to it."

> Simultaneously the aggressive narcissistic impulses which had been split off became more conscious during analytic sessions and he sneered saying: "Here you have to sit all day wasting your time." He felt that he was the important person and he should be free to do anything he wanted to do, however cruel and hurting this might be to others and himself. . . . He then reported a dream, that he was running a long-distance race and he was working very hard at it. However, there was a young woman who did not believe in anything that he was doing. She was unprincipled, nasty and did everything to interfere and mislead him. There was a reference to the woman's brother, who was called "Mundy." He was much more aggressive than his sister and he appeared in the dream snarling like a wild beast, even at her. . . . The patient thought that the name "Mundy" referred to his frequent missing of the Monday sessions a year ago. He realized that the violent uncontrolled aggressiveness related to himself

but he felt that the young woman was also himself. During the last year
he had often insisted ... that he felt he was a woman, and was very
contemptuous of and superior to the analyst.

Rosenfeld summed up: in the dream the patient admitted "that the aggressive
omnipotent part of himself, represented as male, which had dominated the
acting out until a year ago, had now become quite conscious." That was not
all. The dream also served as a warning: the patient "would continue his
aggressive acting out in the analysis by asserting ... that he could present
himself omnipotently as a grown-up woman."[81]

What did Rosenfeld make of this increasingly complex drama? He
characterized the object relations that were coming into the transference
as omnipotent and narcissistic. Both terms require comment. The notion of
omnipotence, or more precisely omnipotence of thought, derived from the
omnipotence Freud's obsessional patient Ernst Lanzer (a.k.a. Rat Man)
"ascribed to his thoughts and feelings, and to his wishes, whether good or
evil."[82] As Rosenfeld used it, omnipotence stood in opposition to reality: to
treat an object omnipotently meant to treat it as one's own possession, to
deny the reality of its separate existence. Similarly, the adjective narcissistic
pointed to processes at work, to introjective and projective identifications,
which served to deny "the separateness of self and other."

> In the case of introjection the object becomes part of the self to such a
> degree that any ... boundary between self and object is felt not to exist.
> In the case of projective identification parts of the self become so much
> part of the object ... that the patient has the idea that he possesses all the
> desirable qualities of the object—in fact that he is the object in these
> respects.[83]

For all the idealization, violence was never far away. And should the idealization be dented, it would come to the fore. No wonder, then, that Rosenfeld
insisted on the aggressive or destructive aspects of narcissism: in writing of
his businessman patient, he alternately referred to an "omnipotent destructive part" and an "aggressive omnipotent part." Above all he stressed the
organized nature of destructive narcissism—"as if one were dealing with a
powerful gang dominated by a leader, who controls all the members of the
gang to see that they support one another in making the criminal ... work
more effective and powerful."

> The main aim seems to be to prevent the weakening of the organization
> and to control the members of the gang so that they will not desert the
> destructive organization and join the positive parts of the self or betray
> the secrets of the gang to the police, ... standing for the helpful analyst,
> who might be able to save the patient. Frequently when a patient of this

kind makes progress in the analysis and wants to change he dreams of being attacked by members of the Mafia or adolescent delinquents. . . . To change, to receive help, implies weakness and is experienced as wrong or as a failure by the destructive narcissistic organization which provides the patient with his sense of superiority.[84]

In cases of this kind, Rosenfeld added, "only the very detailed exposure of the system" enabled "analysis to make some progress."[85] His businessman patient had proved to be such a case.

*   *   *

Could the patient's internal situation have been represented as one "where a healthy, sane, but weak part of the self" was "in the grip of a Mafia-like organization" which the patient was "powerless to resist"?[86] Rosenfeld suggested that such a simplification might be more misleading than helpful. John Steiner, acknowledging his debt to Rosenfeld and building on his work,[87] spoke directly to this question.

Rosenfeld had mentioned "the idealization of the omnipotent destructive parts of the self"; he had remarked upon a "most confusing element": the "successful disguise of the omnipotent structure . . . as benevolent."[88] And in treating a patient he called Eric, he had noted that Eric "had developed a pleasurable identification with the ugly rejecting object and seemed to feel caught up in a masochistic and sadistic object relation. This investment in a destructive object relation gave him greater security than good object relations."[89] The interaction between the libidinal self and the omnipotent destructive part of the self was turning out to be anything but straightforward.

In his paper "Perverse Relationships Between Parts of the Self: A Clinical Illustration" (1982),[90] Steiner presented case material from the analysis of Mr. F, a 40-year-old doctor: "Although reasonably successful professionally, he felt obliged to give up clinical work for research and was painfully aware that he led a restricted life, unable to maintain personal relationships."

> He was a tall, very thin, awkward but attractive-looking man who set great store on health and sometimes jogged to his sessions. A striking feature was that his anxiety, while quite evident as he came into the room, would disappear as he gave me a formal nod of greeting and lay down. It seemed as though the couch represented a haven where he could feel protected from anxiety. . . . Although . . . talking in a superior way which appeared to give him much pleasure, he also conveyed an experience of great suffering. He often referred to the way life was passing him by and to his fear that unless I could help him to emerge from his present state his life would never have any meaning for him. Very occasionally he did let me see a needy, dependent part of himself—for example, when he

described with feeling how as a small boy he forgot to get off the bus near his home and had to walk up a steep hill alone and miserable. Mostly, however, his dependent needs could only be hinted at in part, it seemed, because of a great fear of being mocked.[91]

About 15 months after the beginning of the analysis, Mr. F "described how one of his many exciting platonic relationships had come to an end when the girl in question told him she had another man."

> He then reported a dream in which he broke into her flat, knowing where the key was kept, and got into her bed while she was out. When she returned with her boy-friend, he called out to warn her of his presence and the boy-friend walked into the bedroom. The dream ended as he realized that he would soon be asked to leave.

Steiner "interpreted in terms of a small boy with a desire for warmth and comfort" who "was persuaded to get into the bed by a part of him that claimed to look after him. . . . However, all the time he knew very well" that a humiliating outcome awaited him.[92]

> In a further dream, . . . he [Mr. F] was a tourist in Nepal, and was shown a boy who had swollen eyes and was weeping. A Nepalese doctor was called but the treatment consisted of putting the boy out of his misery. The boy was asked if he wanted to die and he said that he did. The doctor tried to kill him with blows on his head, but when this failed he began sawing through the neck in a very painful way. The patient wondered why as a tourist he was watching all this and he felt quite powerless to intervene, but when he tried to turn away he was unable to stop himself watching.[93]

If Mr. F admitted, Steiner interpreted, that "he was an ill, weeping boy he was convinced . . . that he would receive Nepalese medicine of the kind shown by the doctor in the dream." And that same conviction found its way into Steiner's consulting room: to acknowledge his dependent needs was so mortifying for Mr. F that "he experienced the analysis as a cruelty which nevertheless he agreed to by coming to his session each day." That Mr. F felt imprisoned "by a cruel, destructive part of himself which professed to be his friend"—so much seemed perfectly clear.[94]

Here Steiner urged caution. The dependent self as innocent victim, held captive by a narcissistic organization and helpless to escape or alter the situation, was not the whole story:

> On closer inspection many good elements are discernible in the narcissistic organization, which does attempt to protect and look after the child but fails to master the cruelty. And, perhaps more important, perverse

elements are to be found in the needy . . . self which often asks for and accepts [this] . . . protection and exploitation.

Mr. F "knew that his superior devaluing of things he actually admired" served to block progress; he also knew "that he was allowing this to happen." On occasion, "he saw that constructive work was possible" in the analysis; yet he could not stop attacking it—and getting perverse "gratification from the excited attempts at destruction."[95]

This perverse gratification, Steiner compared to an addiction, and the very word signaled how difficult it would be for the patient to free himself from it. What was to be done? Like Rosenfeld, Steiner urged a "detailed exposure of the system," with the added injunction: to unmask the collusion between the libidinal self and the narcissistic organization.[96]

*   *   *

Recall Joan Riviere's discussion of a manic defensive system. Following in the wake of Klein's 1935 paper on manic-depressive states, she stressed how such a system operated as a "disguise to conceal . . . a more or less depressive condition in the patient."[97] Rosenfeld and Steiner, influenced by Klein's 1946 paper on schizoid mechanisms, stressed defenses against anxieties of the paranoid-schizoid position as well. All three appreciated the desperate quality of the anxiety which threatened the patient if the defensive system broke down.

At the same time the very notion of defensive system suggested a strategy for tackling a recognized obstacle to psychoanalytic treatment—in this instance, the "megalomania" Freud attributed to narcissistic patients. Rosenfeld might write of narcissistic organizations, Steiner might prefer pathological to narcissistic; despite these terminological differences, both were intent on transforming an obstacle not into an ally—that was out of the question—but into a complex organization that linked object relations and defense mechanisms. Once conceptualized in this fashion, the prospects for therapy brightened: the organization would perforce come into the transference and be subject to analytic scrutiny.

What about psychoanalytic practice? Did changes in technique follow from rethinking megalomania? Just as the idea of pathological organization had a Kleinian pedigree, so too the way Rosenfeld and Steiner practiced—as evidenced by their clinical vignettes—bore witness to their descent from Klein. Descent with modification: Rosenfeld could be reckoned a second-generation Kleinian; Steiner belonged to a third and was not personally connected to Klein. Both shared an emphasis on painstaking work in the transference–countertransference situation, with transference understood to involve "repeated projections and introjections" and, in turn, sensitivity to the "containing function of the analyst."[98]

A very demanding task. For his part, Rosenfeld stated his guiding principle: "even the most disturbed and tricky patients, whose pathology may cause them time and time again to defend themselves against anxiety by distorting and undermining the analytic process, not only seek to communicate their predicament but also have a . . . capacity for co-operating with the therapeutic endeavour, if the analyst can recognize it."[99]

*   *   *

This chapter has been organized differently from its predecessors. In the earlier discussions, the two protagonists, who followed upon Freud, were linked to one another, intellectually and/or personally. Here Freud made only the briefest appearance, just long enough to locate the principal obstacles that psychoanalysts encountered in attempting to treat narcissistic patients. Thereupon the three protagonists entered the scene, all of whom could be reckoned descendants of Freud, but who, nonetheless, figured more as rivals than as collaborators. Some comparisons are in order.

A preliminary comment: consider Freud's legacy as consisting of multiple components. Kohut latched on to one—narcissism—and bracketed or ignored much of the rest. Over time his chosen item loomed larger and larger until, in his eyes at least, other conceptual components sank into insignificance. Kernberg sought to be inclusive, to bring together psychoanalytic ego psychology and object relations theory of both American and British varieties. Unlike Kohut, who claimed to be a progenitor in his own right, Kernberg applied the label Freudian as widely as possible. Ironically, these two contrasting approaches to theory building served a similar purpose: they broke the stranglehold that psychoanalytic ego psychology had exercised over psychoanalysis in the United States.

When it came to transference, Kohut, Kernberg, and Rosenfeld thought along similar lines. They all dissented from Freud's categorical assertion that narcissistic patients had "no capacity for transference or only insufficient residues of it."[100] Still more, they stretched the notion of transference. Rosenfeld, following Klein, used the term to refer to the totality of the patient's relation to the analyst. As for Kohut, given his view that thwarted developmental needs came alive in analyzing narcissistic patients, it stood to reason that for long periods of the treatment, selfobject transferences would include everything in the patient–analyst relationship. And as for Kernberg, without explicitly subscribing to a broad construction of transference, he implicitly moved away from a narrow one: his insistence on the reactivation of internalized object relations within the transference–countertransference situation, did not fit with a notion of transference as displacement—possibly distorted—from an earlier object to the person of the analyst.

When it came to megalomania—Freud's term—or the grandiose self—Kohut and Kernberg's term—or the omnipotent self—Rosenfeld's term—there was disagreement. The contrast between Kohut and Rosenfeld stood out most sharply: Kohut started from Freud's notion of primary narcissism and postulated a developmental line distinct from that of object relations;

Rosenfeld started from Klein's hypothesis of object relations beginning at birth, then used her idea of projective identification to conceptualize narcissistic object relations. Developmental arrest or pathological formation? That he sided with Rosenfeld, Kernberg made abundantly clear.

Conclusion

When I was growing up in the late 1950s and early 1960s, Freud ranked as a cultural icon without peer. "To us," as to W. H. Auden, he was "no more a person . . . but a climate of opinion." Auden sensed—I think correctly—that, for better or worse, we were all Freudians. More than 60 years on, it is still the case. Freud "has fundamentally altered the way we think. He has changed our intellectual manners, often without our being aware of it."[1] As everyone knows, "his influence extends . . . beyond the realm of thought, finding its way into . . . child rearing, educational practices, social work."[2] And into the mental health professions as well. Freud himself considered it far from "desirable for psycho-analysis to be swallowed up by medicine and to find its last resting-place in a textbook of psychiatry under the heading 'Methods of Treatment.' "[3] (Psychiatry has both swallowed and disgorged psychoanalysis, and may be nibbling at it again.) Yet it has been in working with patients and in finding obstacles to that work that the discipline has evolved

Have the obstacles encountered been transformed into allies? At this point it may be helpful to review what has been a to and fro between the technical and the theoretical—with the personal playing a part as well—and to do so in words that appeared earlier in the text. The score should then be clear.

*   *   *

Let's start with transference. A theoretical shift was underway before my story began. Freud had already moved beyond his dream-inspired model—transference as displacement of feeling from one idea to another—and had started to think of it in oedipal terms—transference as bringing to light that critical childhood conflict. For Freud, repetition figured as crucial to bending transference to therapeutic purposes: thanks to repetition in the transference, to the patient's repeating repressed material as a contemporary drama in which the analyst was assigned a role, the "relics of antiquity," as he put it, could become conscious and more manageable.[4] For Ferenczi, his efforts to promote repetition in the transference were aimed at making certain that it was accompanied by the "throb of experience."[5] That throb ranked as key to getting the patient to accept the reality of what had been repressed.

"Experience," however, might get out of hand; it might overwhelm the patient. Ferenczi knew this full well. He was not on that account prepared to abandon his experiments in technique. Instead he held himself responsible: something in him was acting as a hindrance in the treatment. In his mind countertransference stood as a second great obstacle—and neither it nor transference was fully mastered.

What about Balint's contribution? Transference, repetition, acting out, regression—all these concepts appeared in his work; he saw them as overlapping and frequently spoke of a "regressed transference." Balint's notion of a benign, as opposed to a malignant, regression opened up the prospect of the patient enjoying a new relationship, in the present, with the analyst. The relationship itself promised to be therapeutic; it promised to be a new beginning. It ran the risk of promising too much.

Let's continue with resistance. Resistance did not have a comfortable place in Freud's topography of Conscious–Preconscious–Unconscious. Within the structural model of ego–id–superego, it fit nicely: it could be reckoned an ego function—and a defensive one to boot. Here Anna Freud made her chief technical contribution: her idea of the transference of defense. Focusing on the ego, its resistances and defenses, she paid close attention to how the ego's defense mechanisms were deployed during an analytic session. And in so doing, she carried out the assignment her father had designated as belonging to the analyst: "He contents himself with studying whatever is present for the time being on the surface of the patient's mind, and he employs the art of interpretation mainly for the purpose of recognizing the resistances which appear there, and making them conscious to the patient."[6] Resistance would dog the analytic process from first to last.

Resistance, understood as that "which . . . brings the [analytic] work to a halt,"[7] was a broad notion indeed. Defense soon became equally broad: even the working alliance could be used defensively and serve as resistance in treatment. Greenson thought otherwise. Over time he became more, rather than less, insistent on an ideal typical working alliance, without fully appreciating its fictional quality. Was he attempting to sustain the hope that the patient might share his enthusiasm for what was supremely important to him, namely the analysis itself? Was he trying to forestall the frustration that comes from disappointed expectations? He was in danger of demanding too much from the patient.

As for the negative therapeutic reaction, before the introduction of the superego, it and depression, as well as the unconscious sense of guilt, existed, conceptually, in isolation from one another; afterwards the three came bundled together. Freud had initially emphasized the melancholic's self-criticism, his self-denigration, and concluded that the self-reproaches were really reproaches against a loved object which had been redirected from it to the patient's ego. In formulating the superego, Freud transferred—without fanfare—the ego's reproaches to the superego. The superego now launched attacks against the ego. And the ego did not protest; it admitted its guilt; it submitted to punishment; indeed it found satisfaction in a negative therapeutic reaction.

Klein took off from the superego. By the mid-1930s she had replaced the Freudian structure with a world of internal objects:

> [T]he phenomenon which was recognized by Freud, broadly speaking, as the voices and the influence of actual parents established in the ego is, according to my findings, a complex object-world, which is felt by the individual, in deep layers of the unconscious, to be concretely inside himself, and for which I and some of my colleagues therefore use the term "internalized objects" and an "inner world." This inner world consists of innumerable objects taken into the ego, corresponding . . . to the multitude of varying aspects, good and bad, in which the parents (and other people) appeared to the child's unconscious mind throughout various stages of his development. . . . In addition, all these objects are . . . in an infinitely complex relation both with each other and with the self.[8]

The depressive position, in turn, brought into sharp relief the self's fear for its good objects, its guilt about destructive impulses toward them, its desire to repair the damage inflicted on them, and its grief over failing to do so.

On the technical side, Klein's understanding of transference—which owed much to her analysis of children—marked an advance over Freud's. With her child patients, she conceived of transference not as pointing to unconscious fantasies from a long-gone past, but from the immediate present, active right here and now in the relationships played out in her consulting room. With adults, she thought of transference as conveying aspects of an inner world built up from infancy, elaborated in childhood and adulthood, and, again, currently active. How to detect it? "For many years," Klein wrote, "transference was understood in terms of direct references to the analyst in the patient's material." As she saw it, all the material, not just some, provided clues: "For instance, reports of patients about their everyday life, relations, and activities . . . reveal—if we explore their unconscious content—the defenses against anxieties stirred up in the transference."[9] To explore meticulously unconscious meaning in the here and now must come before attempting any reconstruction of the past. No wonder that Klein shared Strachey's view that transference interpretations—at least those that counted as mutative—possessed particular therapeutic power.

To return to the negative therapeutic reaction. For Riviere, it represented a desperate attempt to maintain the status quo—a painful but still bearable state of things. For Klein, it signaled the presence of envy; and although she considered envy, and its degree, a matter of constitution, she did not, on that account, judge it to be unanalyzable. Its modification stood as a necessary step toward what both she and Riviere considered crucial: working through "the depressive situation of failure."[10]

What about "abnormal changes in the ego"? Let's start with Klein's conception of the paranoid-schizoid position. Even before she introduced it in 1946, a number of its elements figured prominently in psychoanalytic writing. Anxiety: both Freud and Klein were thinking hard about it in the 1920s. Freud set down, side by side with his earlier view of anxiety as the product of inadequate sexual satisfaction, the notion of "anxiety as a signal announcing a situation of danger."[11] Klein understood that situation as something internal and as something sadistic. In 1932 she adopted Freud's hypothesis of the death instinct to underpin her preoccupation with persecutory or paranoid states. Internal objects: Klein brought them into the picture—given her work on the depressive position, there was no chance that she would have left them out. Splitting of the ego: Freud bequeathed only scattered remarks. On this point Klein referred to the work of W. R. D. Fairbairn; she insisted that his term schizoid position be understood to cover both persecutory fears and schizoid defenses. (Later she opted for "paranoid-schizoid.") In thus conceiving of the ego as fissionable, Klein began to flesh out what Freud had simply referred to as "abnormal changes."

What, then, have been the practical consequences of Klein's formulation of the paranoid-schizoid position and, along with it, projective identification? The most obvious development has been in the use of countertransference. "Much of our understanding of the transference," Joseph wrote, "comes through our understanding of how our patients . . . unconsciously act out with us . . . , trying to get us to act out with them"—sometimes by the very way they speak—"which we can often only capture through the feelings aroused in us, through our countertransference, used in the broad sense of the word."[12] She stressed the way the patient attempted to induce feelings and thoughts in the analyst, and tried, often very subtly and without being aware of it, to "nudge" the analyst into acting in a manner consistent with the projection.

In line with Bion, Joseph appreciated that it was one thing, by paying close attention to what was being lived—or acted—in the transference–countertransference situation, to serve as a container for the patient's projected fragments, and quite another for the patient to take back the projections into himself. She urged analysts to search for the part of the ego that was "able moment to moment" to take an interest in understanding, "even though that part" might be "quickly lost again. For long-term . . . change, and for thinking about the ending of an analysis," she regarded "the strengthening of this part of the personality" as crucial[13]—and feasible. Time and again she proved unwilling to join Freud in declaring an "abnormal ego" "unserviceable for our purposes."

Let's move on the narcissism. Kohut, Kernberg, and Rosenfeld all thought that narcissistic patients were susceptible to analytic treatment. They all dissented from Freud's categorical assertion that such patients had "no capacity for transference or only insufficient residues of it."[14] Rosenfeld, following Klein, used the term to refer to the totality of the patient's relation to the analyst. As for Kohut, given his view that thwarted developmental needs came alive in analyzing narcissistic patients, it stood to reason that for long periods of the treatment, selfobject transferences would include everything in the patient–analyst relationship. And as for Kernberg, without explicitly subscribing to a broad construction of transference, he implicitly moved away form a narrow one: his insistence on the reactivation of internalized object relations within the transference–countertransference situation, did not fit with a notion of transference as displacement—possibly distorted—from an earlier object to the person of the analyst.

When it came to megalomania—Freud's term—or the grandiose self—Kohut and Kernberg's term—or the omnipotent self—Rosenfeld's term—there was disagreement. The contrast between Kohut and Rosenfeld stood out most sharply: Kohut started from Freud's notion of primary narcissism and postulated a developmental line distinct from that of object relations; Rosenfeld started from Klein's hypothesis of object relations beginning at birth, then used her idea of projective identification to conceptualize narcissistic object relations. Developmental arrest or pathological formation? That he sided with Rosenfeld, Kernberg made abundantly clear.

*   *   *

To tally up the score. Transference and countertransference now rank as powerful allies—though both remain obstacles as well. None of the others has been similarly transformed. Instead they have become foci of analytic investigation and interpretation, sources of recurring puzzlement. Nor is the story over. In due course, additional obstacles have made their appearance. After all, the evolution of psychoanalysis is by no means finished—and the impetus to that evolution provided by clinical difficulties by no means at an end. As Joan Riviere put it:

> I feel that analysts . . . are not always incapable of shutting their eyes to a fact . . . , namely, that when a patient . . . [is refractory], the onus still remains with the analyst: to discover the cause of his reaction.[15]

Notes

Introduction

1 Freud, "Notes upon a Case of Obsessional Neurosis" (1909), in *SE* 10: 207–208*n*.
2 Freud, "Fragment of an Analysis of a Case of Hysteria" (1905), in *SE* 7: 109.
3 Ibid., pp. 116, 118, 117.
4 Freud, "Analysis of a Phobia in a Five-Year-Old Boy" (1909), in *SE* 10: 142.
5 Freud, "Fragment of an Analysis," p. 19.
6 See Judith M. Hughes, *From Freud's Consulting Room: The Unconscious in a Scientific Age* (Cambridge, MA: Harvard University Press, 1994).
7 Freud to Fliess, December 22, 1897, *The Complete Letters of Sigmund Freud to Wilhelm Fliess 1887–1904*, trans. and ed. Jeffrey Moussaieff Masson (Cambridge, MA: Harvard University Press, 1985), p. 289.
8 Freud, *The Ego and the Id* (1923), in *SE* 19: 49.
9 Ralph R. Greenson and Milton Wexler, "The Non-Transference Relationship in the Psychoanalytic Situation," *IJP* 50 (1969): 29.
10 Freud, "Psycho-Analytic Notes on an Autobiographical Account of a Case of Paranoia (Dementia Paranoides)" (1911), in *SE* 12: 75.
11 Stephen Jay Gould, *The Mismeasure of Man*, rev. ed. (New York: Norton, 1996), p. 188.
12 See Freud, "The Infantile Genital Organization (An Interpolation into the Theory of Sexuality)" (1923), in *SE* 19: 141–145.
13 See Freud, "Psycho-Analytic Notes on . . . a Case of Paranoia," pp. 60–61.
14 Freud, "On the History of the Psycho-Analytic Movement" (1914), in *SE* 14: 29.
15 Freud, *Introductory Lectures on Psycho-Analysis* (1916–1917), in *SE* 16: 340, 341.
16 Ralph R. Greenson, *The Technique and Practice of Psycho-Analysis*, vol. 1 (New York: International Universities Press, 1967), p. 53.
17 Ian Hacking, *The Social Construction of What?* (Cambridge, MA: Harvard University Press, 1999), pp. 105, 104, 123.
18 Janet Malcolm, *Psychoanalysis: The Impossible Profession* (New York: Knopf, 1981), pp. 5, 110, 139.
19 Sándor Ferenczi, "Child-Analysis in the Analysis of Adults" (1931), in Sándor Ferenczi, *Final Contributions to the Problems and Methods of Psycho-Analysis*, ed. Michael Balint, trans. Eric Mosbacher (London: Hogarth Press, 1955; reprint, London: Karnac, Maresfield Library, 1980), p. 128.
20 See Josef Breuer and Sigmund Freud, *Studies on Hysteria* (1895), in Freud, *SE* 2: 305.
21 Melanie Klein, "On the Criteria for the Termination of a Psycho-Analysis" (1950), in *The Writings of Melanie Klein*, vol. 3, *Envy and Gratitude and Other*

Works 1946–1963, under the general editorship of Roger Money-Kyrle, in collaboration with Betty Joseph, Edna O'Shaughnessy, and Hanna Segal (London: Hogarth Press, 1975), p. 46.

1 Hysteria: Transference

1 Josef Breuer and Sigmund Freud, *Studies on Hysteria* (1893–1895), in *SE* 2: 22–23.

2 Ibid., p. 7.

3 Sándor Ferenczi, *The Clinical Diary of Sándor Ferenczi*, ed. Judith Dupont, trans. Michael Balint and Nicola Zorday Jackson (Cambridge, MA: Harvard University Press, 1988), January 10, 1932, p. 4. For an extremely helpful review of the vast literature on hysteria as a medical disease and a cultural metaphor, see Mark S. Micale, *Approaching Hysteria: Disease and its Interpretations* (Princeton, NJ: Princeton University Press, 1995).

4 Freud to Fliess, June 22, 1897, *The Complete Letters of Sigmund Freud to Wilhelm Fliess 1887–1904*, trans. and ed. Jeffrey Moussaieff Masson (Cambridge, MA: Harvard University Press, 1985) p. 254; July 7, 1897, ibid., p. 255; August 14, 1897, ibid., p. 261.

5 See Ernest Jones, *The Life and Work of Sigmund Freud*, vol. 1, *The Formative Years and the Great Discoveries 1856–1900* (New York: Basic Books, 1953), pp. 304–305.

6 Ferenczi to Freud, December 26, 1912, *F/Fer Correspondence* 1: 454.

7 For biographical information on Ferenczi, see: Sandor Lorand, "Sándor Ferenczi 1873–1933: Pioneer of Pioneers," in Franz Alexander, Samuel Eisenstein, and Martin Grotjahn, eds., *Psychoanalytic Pioneers* (New York: Basic Books, 1966), pp. 14–35; Ilse Barande, *Sándor Ferenczi* (Paris: Payot, 1972); Claude Lorin, *Le jeune Ferenczi: Premiers écrits 1899–1906* (Paris: Aubier Montaigne, 1983); Pierre Sabourin, *Ferenczi: Paladin et Grand Vizir secret* (Paris: Éditions Universitaires, 1985); André E. Haynal, *The Technique at Issue: Controversies in Psychoanalysis From Freud and Ferenczi to Michael Balint*, trans. Elizabeth Holder (London: Karnac, 1988); William Boyce Lum, "Sándor Ferenczi (1873–1933)—The Father of the Empathic–Interpersonal Approach, Part One: Introduction and Early Analytic Years," *Journal of the American Academy of Psychoanalysis* 16 (1988): 131–153; Martin Stanton, *Sándor Ferenczi: Reconsidering Active Intervention* (London: Free Association Books, 1990); Lewis Aron and Adrienne Harris, eds., *The Legacy of Sándor Ferenczi* (Hillsdale, NJ: Analytic Press, 1993); Claude Lorin, *Sándor Ferenczi: De la médecine à la psychose* (Paris: Presses Universitaires de France, 1993); Peter L. Rudnytsky, Antal Bókay, and Patrizia Giampieri-Deutsch, eds., *Ferenczi's Turn in Psychoanalysis* (New York: New York University Press, 1996); Carlo Bonomi, "Flight into Sanity: Jones's Allegations of Ferenczi's Mental Deterioration Reconsidered," *IJP* 80 (1999): 507–542; Peter T. Hoffer and Axel Hoffer, "Ferenczi's Fatal Illness in Historical Context," *JAPA* 47 (1999): 1257–1268.

8 Ferenczi to Groddeck. December 25, 1921, *The Sándor Ferenczi–Georg Groddeck Correspondence 1921–1933*, ed. Christopher Fortune, trans. Jeannie Cohen, Elisabeth Petersdorff, Norbert Ruebsaat (London: Open Gate, 2002), p. 8.

9 Freud to Ferenczi, February 7, 1909, *F/Fer Correspondence* 1: 42–43.

10 Freud, "Sándor Ferenczi" (1933), in *SE* 22: 227–229.

11 See Phyllis Grosskurth, *The Secret Ring: Freud's Inner Circle and the Politics of Psychoanalysis* (Reading, MA: Addison-Wesley, 1991).

12 Freud, "On the History of the Psycho-Analytic Movement" (1914), in *SE* 14: 33.

13 On psychoanalysis in Hungary, see Paul Harmat, *Freud, Ferenczi und die ungar-ische Psychoanalyse* (Tübingen: Edition Diskord, 1988).

14 Helen Swick Perry, *Psychiatrist of America: The Life of Harry Stack Sullivan* (Cambridge, MA: Harvard University Press, 1982), pp. 202, 227–230; see also Clara M. Thompson, *Interpersonal Psychoanalysis: The Selected Papers of Clara M. Thompson*, ed. Maurice R. Green (New York: Basic Books, 1964), Part II.

15 Freud to Ferenczi, September 19, 1926, *F/Fer Correspondence* 3: 278.

16 Freud, "Sándor Ferenczi," p. 229.

17 Michael Balint, *The Basic Fault: Therapeutic Aspects of Regression* (London: Tavistock Publications, 1968; reprint, London and New York: Tavistock Publications, 1979), pp. 152–153.

18 Freud, "Sándor Ferenczi," p. 229. On Ernest Jones's misrepresentation and vilifi-cation of his former analyst, see: Paul Roazen, *Freud and His Followers* (New York: Knopf, 1975), Part VII, chs. 6 and 7.

19 At Ferenczi's death, his widow asked Balint to represent her late husband's liter-ary estate. "That Ferenczi has been rediscovered in the past 10 or 15 years is mostly a consequence of Balint's efforts": Judith Dupont, "Michael Balint: Analysand, Pupil, Friend, and Successor to Sándor Ferenczi," in Aron and Har-ris, eds., *The Legacy of Sándor Ferenczi*, p. 146. For biographical information on Balint, see Haynal, *The Technique at Issue*, and Harold Stewart, *Michael Balint: Object Relations Pure and Applied* (London and New York: Routledge, 1996).

20 Michael Balint, *Primary Love and Pycho-Analytic Technique* (London: Hogarth Press, 1952; reprint, London: Karnac, Maresfield Library, 1985), pp. 5, 6.

21 Michael Balint, "La genèse de mes idées," *Gazette Médicale de France* 77 (1970): 458, quoted in Haynal, *The Technique at Issue*, pp. 109–110.

22 Dupont, "Michael Balint," p. 146.

23 Balint was loyal to Freud as well. As he saw it, "the two most prominent psycho-analysts" had failed "to understand and properly evaluate each other's clinical findings," and *ad hominem* explanations for that failure—for example, that Fer-enczi's neurotic difficulties blinded him to such an extent that even Freud's warn-ings produced no effect or perhaps were even counter-productive—he found inadequate or inappropriate. Balint, *The Basic Fault*, p. 153.

24 Freud to Stefan Zweig, June 2, 1932, *Letters of Sigmund Freud*, ed. Ernst L. Freud, trans. Tania and James Stern (New York: Basic Books, 1960), p. 413.

25 Jones, *The Formative Years*, pp. 224–225.

26 Freud, "Five Lectures on Psycho-Analysis" (1910), in *SE* 11: 47 (emphasis in the original).

27 See J. O. Wisdom, "A Methodological Approach to the Problem of Hysteria," *IJP* 42 (1961): 224–237; Barbara Ruth Easser and Stanley R. Lesser, "Hysterical Personality: A Re-evaluation," *The Psychoanalytic Quarterly* 34 (1965): 390–405; Jean Laplanche, "Panel on 'Hysteria Today,' " *IJP* 55 (1974): 459–469; Alan Krohn, *Hysteria: The Elusive Neurosis*, Psychological Issues, Monograph 45/46 (New York: International Universities Press, 1978).

28 Freud, "The Disposition to Obsessional Neurosis: A Contribution to the Prob-lem of Choice of Neurosis" (1913), in *SE* 12: 325.

29 Freud, *Introductory Lectures on Psycho-Analysis* (1916–1917), in *SE* 16: 324.

30 Breuer and Freud, *Studies on Hysteria*, pp. 302, 301.

31 Freud, *Introductory Lectures*, p. 442.

32 Peter Gay, *Freud: A Life for Our Time* (New York: Norton, 1988), p. 407.

33 Ferenczi to Groddeck, December 25, 1921, *Ferenczi–Groddeck Correspondence*, pp. 8–9 (emphasis in the original). See also Ferenczi to Freud, May 27, 1911, *F/Fer Correspondence* 1:282, and Ferenczi to Freud, January 17, 1930, *F/Fer Correspondence* 3: 383.

34 Ferenczi to Freud, September 28, 1910, *F/Fer Correspondence* 1: 214, and Ferenczi to Freud, October 3, 1910, ibid., pp. 217–218, 220 (emphasis in the original). On the correspondence between Freud and Ferenczi and the insight it provides into their relationship, see André Haynal, "What Correspondence between Freud and Ferenczi?", in Patrick Mahony, Carlo Bonomi, and Jan Stensson, eds., *Behind the Scenes: Freud in Correspondence* (Oslo: Scandinavian University Press, 1997), pp. 111–122, and Michael Schröter, "The Beginnings of a Troubled Friendship: Freud and Ferenczi 1908–1914," in ibid., pp. 123–154.

35 Freud, "Five Lectures," p. 51.

36 Freud to Jung, September 24, 1910, *The Freud/Jung Letters: The Correspondence between Sigmund Freud and C. G. Jung*, ed. William McGuire, trans. Ralph Manheim and R. F. C. Hull (Princeton, NJ: Princeton University Press, 1971), p. 353. A week later Freud wrote to Ferenczi that he had wished the younger man would have torn himself "away from the infantile role" and would have taken his place "as a companion with equal rights": Freud to Ferenczi, October 2, 1910, *F/Fer Correspondence* 1: 215.

37 Freud to Ferenczi, October 6, 1910, *F/Fer Correspondence* 1: 221.

38 Ferenczi to Groddeck, December 25, 1921, *Ferenczi–Groddeck Correspondence*, p. 9.

39 See Frédéric Kovàcs to Vilma Kovàcs, January 8, 1829, included in ibid., p. 120.

40 See Ferenczi to Freud, January 3, 1911, *F/Fer Correspondence* 1: 248; Ferenczi to Freud, February 7, 1911, ibid., p. 253; Freud to Ferenczi, February 8, 1911, ibid., pp. 253–254.

41 Freud to Ferenczi, July 20, 1911, ibid., p. 196; Ferenczi to Freud, December 3, 1911, ibid., p. 318; Freud to Ferenczi, December 5, 1911, ibid., pp. 318–319.

42 Ferenczi to Freud, December 30, 1911, ibid., p. 323; Ferenczi to Freud, January 1, 1912, ibid., pp. 323–324 (emphasis in the original); Ferenczi to Freud, January 3, 1912, ibid., p. 325.

43 Freud to Ferenczi, January 13, 1912, ibid., p. 326; Freud to Ferenczi, March 13, 1912, ibid., pp. 356–357; Freud to Ferenczi, March 18, 1912, ibid., p. 360; Freud to Ferenczi, March 24, 1912, ibid., p. 362. On Freud's analysis of Elma, see Agustín Genovés Candioti and Luis J. Martín Cabré, "The Brunhilde Fantasy and Freud's Countertransference in the Analysis of Elma," in Mahony et.al., eds., *Behind the Scenes*, pp. 203–223.

44 Ferenczi to Freud, May 27, 1912, *F/Fer Correspondence* 1: 375; Ferenczi to Freud, August 8, 1912, ibid., p. 402 (emphasis in the original); Freud to Ferenczi, August 12, 1912, ibid., p. 403 ("In case of doubt, abstain.")

45 Freud to Gizella Pálos, December 17, 1911, ibid., pp. 319–320, and Freud to Ferenczi, November 20, 1917, *F/Fer Correspondence* 2: 176.

46 Freud, "From the History of an Infantile Neurosis" (1918), in *SE* 17: 118; see also Judith M. Hughes, *From Freud's Consulting Room: The Unconscious in a Scientific Age* (Cambridge, MA: Harvard University Press, 1994), pp. 99–108.

47 In response to yet another report by Ferenczi of his physical symptoms, particularly his "disturbed nasal breathing," Freud commented: "One must be able to decide whether one loves a woman or not even with stuffed nostrils." Shortly following the second part of Ferenczi's analysis, Freud wrote to Gizella: "After containing myself for years with regard to our friend, I have finally come forward with advice, because I . . . have arrived at the conviction that there is no other possibility, and because I am in general disposed to believe in the imminent end of all things—youth among them." Six months later he wrote again telling her of his "urgent wish" that she and Ferenczi be united: "I have worked on the realization of this wish with the most varied means, directly and indirectly, in friendly

intercourse and through analysis, carefully, so that my preambles would not produce recalcitrance in him, and with blunt demands, in order to bring my influence
to bear." Ferenczi to Freud, March 6, 1916, *F/Fer Correspondence*, 2: 118; Freud
to Ferenczi, March 12, 1916, ibid., p. 119; Freud to Gizella Pálos, July 31, 1916,
ibid., pp. 136–137; Freud to Gizella Pálos, January 23, 1917, ibid., p. 176.

48 Freud to Ferenczi, January 3, 1912, *F/Fer Correspondence* 1: 325.

49 Ferenczi to Freud, December 26, 1912, ibid., pp. 450, 455 (emphasis in the
original).

50 Freud to Ferenczi, December 30, 1912, ibid., p. 457.

51 See Judith Dupont, "Freud's Analysis of Ferenczi as Revealed by Their
Correspondence," *IJP* 75 (1994): 301–320.

52 Freud to Ferenczi, October 24, 1916, *F/Fer Correspondence* 2: 149, and Freud to
Ferenczi, November 16, 1916, ibid., p. 153.

53 Ferenczi to Groddeck, February 27, 1922, *Ferenczi–Groddeck Correspondence*,
p. 19 (emphasis in the original).

54 Ferenczi to Freud, January 17, 1930, *F/Fer Correspondence* 3: 382–383 (emphasis
in the original).

55 Freud to Ferenczi, January 20, 1930, ibid., pp. 385–386; see also Ferenczi to
Freud, February 14, 1930, ibid., pp. 387–388. Seven years later, that is, four years
after Ferenczi's death, Freud went public with his self-justification: see Freud,
"Analysis Terminable and Interminable" (1937), in *SE* 23: 221–222.

56 Freud, "Remembering, Repeating and Working-Through (Further Recommendations on the Technique of Psycho-Analysis II)" (1914), in *SE* 12: 148.

57 Freud, *Beyond the Pleasure Principle* (1920), in *SE* 18: 18–19 (emphasis in the
original).

58 Freud, "Fragment of an Analysis," p. 12. See also Breuer and Freud, *Studies on
Hysteria*, p. 139; Freud, "The Aetiology of Hysteria" (1896), in *SE* 3:192; Freud,
"Delusions and Dreams in Jensen's *Gradiva*" (1907), in *SE* 9: 40; Freud, "Notes
upon a Case of Obsessional Neurosis" (1909), in *SE* 10: 77; Freud, "Construc-
tions in Analysis" (1937), in *SE* 23: 259–260.

59 Sándor Ferenczi, "Child-Analysis in the Analysis of Adults" (1931), in Sándor
Ferenczi, *Final Contributions to the Problems and Methods of Psycho-Analysis*,
ed. Michael Balint, trans. Eric Mosbacher (London: Hogarth Press, 1955;
reprint, London: Karnac, Maresfield Library, 1980), p. 128.

60 Sándor Ferenczi, "Technical Difficulties in the Analysis of a Case of Hysteria"
(1919), in Sándor Ferenczi, *Further Contributions to the Theory and Technique of
Psycho-Analysis*, ed. John Rickman, trans. Jane Isabel Suttie (London: Hogarth
Press, 1951; reprint, London: Karnac, Maresfield Library, 1980), pp. 190, 196,
191, 192. Ferenczi wrote to Freud about this case: see Ferenczi to Freud, October
17, 1916, *F/Fer Correspondence* 2: 146–147.

61 Freud, "Lines of Advance in Psycho-Analytic Therapy" (1919), in *SE* 17: 163.

62 Fantasy will be spelled with an *f*, despite the fact that in psychoanalytic literature
it has been the practice—although it is now gradually eroding—to spell it with a
ph.

63 Sándor Ferenczi, "On Forced Fantasies" (1924), in *Further Contributions*,
pp. 74–75.

64 Ibid., p. 75.

65 Sándor Ferenczi and Otto Rank, *The Development of Psycho-Analysis*, trans.
Caroline Newton (New York: Nervous and Mental Disease Pub. Co., 1925;
reprint, Madison, CT: International Universities Press, 1986), p. 4 (emphasis in
the original); see also Sándor Ferenczi, "Contra-indications to the 'Active'
Psycho-Analytical Technique" (1925), in *Further Contributions*, pp. 216–217. For

contrasting assessments of the Ferenczi and Rank volume, see Franz Alexander, review of *Entwicklungsziele der Psychanalyse*, by Sándor Ferenczi and Otto Rank, *IJP* 6 (1925): 484–496, and Gerald I. Fogel, "A Transitional Phase in Our Understanding of the Psychoanalytic Process: A New Look at Ferenczi and Rank," *JAPA* 41 (1993): 585–602. On Alexander's appraisal, see Ferenczi to Freud, Easter Sunday, 1925, *F/Fer Correspondence* 3: 211.

66 Freud to Ferenczi, February 4, 1924, *F/Fer Correspondence* 3:122; see also Ilse Grubich-Simitis, "Six Letters of Sigmund Freud and Sándor Ferenczi on the Interrelationship of Psychoanalytic Theory and Psychoanalytic Technique," *The International Review of Psycho-Analysis* 13 (1986): 267.

67 Ferenczi, "Contra-indications to the 'Active' . . . Technique," p. 220. Freud himself wrote of applying analytic influence to induce agoraphobic patients to "go into the street and . . . struggle with their anxiety": see Freud., "Lines of Advance in Psycho-Analytic Therapy," p. 166.

68 Ferenczi to Freud, October 10, 1931, *F/Fer Correspondence* 3: 419.

69 Sándor Ferenczi, "The Elasticity of Psycho-Analytic Technique" (1928), in *Final Contributions*, p. 95.

70 Ferenczi to Freud, January 15, 1928, *F/Fer Correspondence* 3: 334.

71 On Ferenczi's experimentation in the late 1920s, see: Franz Alexander, "On Ferenczi's Relaxation Principle," *IJP* 14 (1933): 182–192; Izette de Forest, "The Therapeutic Technique of Sándor Ferenczi," *IJP* 23 (1942): 120–139 and de Forest, *The Leaven of Love: A Development of the Psychoanalytic Theory and Technique of Sándor Ferenczi* (Hamden, CT: Archon Books, 1965); Clara M. Thompson, " 'The Therapeutic Technique of Sándor Ferenczi': A Comment," *IJP* 24 (1943): 64–66 and Thompson, *Interpersonal Psychoanalysis*, pp. 65–82; Michael Balint, "Sándor Ferenczi's Technical Experiments," in Benjamin Wolman, ed., *Psychoanalytic Techniques* (New York: Basic Books, 1967), pp. 147–167; Axel Hoffer, "The Freud–Ferenczi Controversy—A Living Legacy," *The International Review of Psycho-Analysis* 18 (1991): 465–472; André Haynal, *Disappearing and Reviving: Sándor Ferenczi in the History of Psychoanalysis* (London: Karnac, 2002).

72 Sándor Ferenczi, "The Principle of Relaxation and Neocatharsis" (1929), in *Final Contributions*, p. 114.

73 Ferenczi, *Clinical Diary*, June 20, 1932, p. 132, and January 7, 1932, p. 2.

74 Freud to Ferenczi, December 13, 1931, *F/Fer Correspondence* 3: 422 (emphasis in the original). Compare Ferenczi to Freud, December 19/20, 1917, *F/Fer Correspondence* 2: 252–254. See also Jeffrey Moussaieff Masson, *The Assault on Truth: Freud's Suppression of the Seduction Theory* (New York: Farrar, Straus and Giroux, 1984), pp. 159–160, and Maria Torok, "La correspondance Freud–Ferenczi: La vie de la lettre dans l'histoire de la psychanalyse," *Confrontations* 12 (1984): 97.

75 Ferenczi, "The Principle of Relaxation", pp. 118–119 (emphasis in the original).

76 Freud to Ferenczi, October 2, 1931, *F/Fer Correspondence* 3: 445. See also Freud to Anna Freud, September 3, 1932, quoted in Gay, *Freud*, p. 584.

77 "Confusion of Tongues between Adults and the Child" has produced a great deal of commentary. See: "The Wise Baby Reconsidered," in John Gedo and George H. Pollock, eds., *Freud: The Fusion of Science and Humanism: The Intellectual History of Psychoanalysis*, Psychological Issues, Monograph 34/35 (New York: International Universities Press, 1976), pp. 357–378; Béla Grunberger, "From the 'Active Technique' to the 'Confusion of Tongues': On Ferenczi's Deviation," in Serge Lebovici and Daniel Widlöcher, eds. *Psychoanalysis in France* (New York: International Universities Press, 1980), pp. 127–150; Johannes Cremerius, " 'Die

Sprache der Zärtlichkeit und der Leidenschaft': Reflexionen zu Sándor Ferenczis Wiesbadener Vortrag von 1932," *Psyche* 37 (1983): 998–1015; Judith Dupont, "Ferenczi's Madness," *Contemporary Psychoanalysis* 24 (1988): 250–261; Harold P. Blum, "The Confusion of Tongues and Psychic Trauma," *IJP* 71 (1994): 871–882; Nicholas Rand and Maria Torok, *Questions for Freud: The Secret History of Psychoanalysis* (Cambridge, MA: Harvard University Press, 1997), pp. 115–135.

78 I have used Masson's more recent translation of Ferenczi, "Confusion of Tongues," in his *Assault on Truth*, pp. 288–289.

79 Ferenczi, *Clinical Diary*, January 7, 1932, p. 3.

80 Ferenczi, "Confusion of Tongues," in Masson, *Assault on Truth*, p. 289.

81 Christopher Fortune, "The Case of 'RN': Sándor Ferenczi's Radical Experiment in Psychoanalysis," in Aron and Harris, eds., *The Legacy of Sándor Ferenczi*, pp. 101–120, and Christopher Fortune, "Mutual Analysis: A Logical Outcome of Sándor Ferenczi's Experiments in Psychoanalysis," in Rudnytsky, Bókay, and Giampieri-Deutsch, eds., *Ferenczi's Turn in Psychoanalysis*, pp. 170–186. In addition, see: Benjamin Wolstein, "Ferenczi, Freud, and the Origins of American Interpersonal Relations," *Contemporary Psychoanalysis* 25 (1989): 672–685. Elizabeth Severn herself wrote on psychology: *Psycho-Therapy: Its Doctrine and Practice* (London: Rider, 1913); *The Psychology of Behaviour: A Study of Human Personality and Conduct with Special Reference to Methods of Development* (New York: Dodd, Mead, 1917); *The Discovery of the Self: A Study in Psychological Cure* (London, Rider, 1933).

82 Ferenczi, *Clinical Diary*, January 12, 1932, p. 88.

83 Balint, *The Basic Fault*, p. 145.

84 Micale, *Approaching Hysteria*, p. 173.

85 Ferenczi, *Clinical Diary*, May 5, 1932, p. 98, and January 12, 1932, pp. 8–10.

86 Ibid., January 24, 1932, p. 18, and March 22, 1932, p. 68.

87 Ibid., May 5, 1932, pp. 97–99.

88 Ibid., March 29, 1932, pp. 71–72 (emphasis in the original).

89 Ibid., May 5, 1932, p. 99.

90 Ibid., May 5, 1932, p. 99.

91 Ibid., October 2, 1932, p. 213, and June 3, 1932, p. 115.

92 See ibid., October 2, 1932, p. 214.

93 In late February 1933 Severn left Budapest to join her daughter in Paris. Although she arrived, so her daughter subsequently reported, in a state of "mental and physical collapse," within a few months she was sufficiently recovered to resume her psychotherapy practice. Fortune, "The Case of R. N.," p. 112.

94 Ferenczi, *Clinical Diary*, March 17, 1932, p. 62.

95 Freud, "The Disposition to Obsessional Neurosis: A Contribution to the Problem of Choice of Neurosis" (1913), in *SE* 12: 320.

96 Ferenczi, "Confusion of Tongues," in Masson, *The Assault on Truth*, p. 285 (emphasis in the original).

97 Michael Balint, "Strength of the Ego and Its Education" (1938), in Balint, *Primary Love*, p. 209.

98 Michael Balint, "Changing Therapeutical Aims and Techniques in Psycho-Analysis" (1949), in Balint, *Primary Love*, p. 227 (emphasis in the original).

99 Michael Balint and Sidney Tarachow, "General Concepts and Theory of Psychoanalytic Therapy," *The Annual Survey of Psychoanalysis* 1 (1950): 233–234.

100 Freud, "Fragment of an Analysis," pp. 23, 28 (emphasis in the original).

101 Michael Balint, "Trauma and Object Relationship," *IJP* 50 (1969): 431.

102 Balint, *The Basic Fault*, pp. 135–136.

103 Ferenczi, *Clinical Diary*, April 3, 1932, p. 79.

104 Michael Balint, "Critical Notes on the Theory of Pregenital Organisations of the Libido" (1935), in Balint, *Primary Love*, pp. 71–72.
105 Balint, *Basic Fault*, p. 59.
106 Michael Balint, "The Doctor, His Patient and The Illness" (1955), in Michael Balint, *Problems of Human Pleasure and Behaviour* (London: Hogarth Press, 1957; reprint, London: Karnac, Maresfield Library, 1987), p. 189 (emphasis in the original).
107 Freud, *Introductory Lectures on Psycho-Analysis*, p. 449.
108 Michael Balint [with Alice Balint], "On Transference and Countertransference" (1939), in Balint, *Primary Love*, pp. 214–216.
109 Balint, "Changing Therapeutical Aims and Techniques," pp. 233–234 (emphasis in the original).
110 See Freud, "The Future Prospects of Psycho-Analytic Therapy" (1910), in *SE* 11: 145.
111 Freud, "Recommendations to Physicians Practicing Psycho-Analysis" (1912), in *SE* 12: 116.
112 See Freud, "On Beginning the Treatment (Further Recommendations on the Technique of Psycho-Analysis I)" (1913), in *SE* 12: 126.
113 Freud, "Analysis Terminable and Interminable," p. 249.
114 Balint, "On Transference and Counter-transference," p. 220.
115 Freud, "Observations on Transference–Love (Further Recommendations on the Technique of Psycho-Analysis III)" (1915), in *SE* 12: 164.
116 Balint, *Basic Fault*, p. 13.
117 Ibid., pp. 13–14.
118 Ibid., pp. 15, 16, 21. For commentary, see Stephen J. Morse, "Structure and Reconstruction: A Critical Comparison of Michael Balint and D. W. Winnicott," *IJP* 53 (1972): 487–500.
119 Balint, *Basic Fault*, p. 150; see also Freud, "An Autobiographical Study" (1925), in *SE* 20: 27.
120 Balint, *Basic Fault*, pp. 146, 142, 141, 149, 151, 152.
121 Ibid., pp. 140, 144, 142, 145.
122 Ibid., pp. 179, 182, 183.
123 Michael Balint, "The Final Goal of Psycho-analytic Treatment" (1934), in *Primary Love*, p. 191.
124 Balint, *Basic Fault*, p. 166.
125 Ibid., p. 132. For commentary on Balint's technical recommendations, see M. Masud R. Khan, "On the Clinical Provision of Frustrations, Recognitions, and Failures in the Analytic Situation: An Essay on Dr Michael Balint's Researches on the Theory of Psychoanalytic Technique," *IJP* 50 (1969): 237–248, and Harold Stewart, *Psychic Equilibrium and Problems of Technique* (London and New York: Tavistock/Routledge, 1992), ch. 8.
126 Freud, "Fragment of an Analysis," p. 12.
127 Ferenczi, "Contra-indications to the 'Active' . . . Technique," p. 220.
128 Michael Balint, "On the Termination of Analysis" (1949), in Balint, *Primary Love*, p. 238.

2 Obsessional neurosis: Resistance

1 Freud, "Notes upon a Case of Obsessional Neurosis" (1909), in *SE* 10: 157, 155, 187.
2 Ibid., pp. 238, 239, 237.
3 See Freud, "The Dynamics of Transference" (1912), in *SE* 12: 106n.

4 Freud, "The Disposition to Obsessional Neurosis: A Contribution to the Problem of Choice of Neurosis" (1913), in *SE* 12: 321, 322.
5 Freud, "Lines of Advance in Psycho-Analytic Therapy" (1919), in *SE* 17:166.
6 Freud, *The Interpretation of Dreams* (1900), in *SE* 4: 106n.
7 See Elisabeth Young-Bruehl, *Anna Freud: A Biography* (New York: Summit Books, 1988), pp. 15, 120. For biographical information on Anna Freud, in addition to Young-Breuhl, see Raymond Dyer, *Her Father's Daughter: The Work of Anna Freud* (New York: Jason Aronson, 1983); Uwe Henrik Peters, *Anna Freud: A Life Dedicated to Children* (New York: Schocken Books, 1985); Robert Coles, *Anna Freud: The Dream of Psychoanalysis* (Reading, MA: Addison-Wesley, 1991); Lisa Appignanesi and John Forrester, *Freud's Women* (New York: Basic Books, 1992), ch. 9. See also Michael John Burlingham, *The Last Tiffany: A Biography of Dorothy Tiffany Burlingham* (New York: Atheneum, 1989). As for published memoirs and correspondence, see Peter Heller, *A Child Analysis with Anna Freud* (Madison, CT: International Universities Press, 1990), and Peter Heller, *Anna Freud's Letters to Eva Rosenfeld*, trans. Mary Weigand (Madison, CT: International Universities Press, 1992).
8 Freud to Ferenczi, October 20, 1918, *F/Fer Correspondence* 2: 302.
9 Freud to Eitingon, December 2, 1919, *Letters of Sigmund Freud*, ed. Ernst L. Freud, trans. Tania and James Stern (New York: Basic Books, 1960), p. 325.
10 See Young-Bruehl, *Anna Freud*, p. 103.
11 Anna Freud, "Beating Fantasies and Daydreams" (1922), in *The Writings of Anna Freud*, vol. 1, *Introduction to Psychoanalysis: Lectures for Child Analysts and Teachers 1922–1935* (New York: International Universities Press, 1965), pp. 144, 145, 146, 154, 156. Freud also drew on Anna's treatment: see Freud, " 'A Child Is Being Beaten': A Contribution to the Study of the Origin of Sexual Perversions," in *SE* 17: 182–183, 190.
12 Freud to Eitingon, May 19, 1922, quoted in Young-Bruehl, *Anna Freud*, p. 108.
13 Young-Bruehl, *Anna Freud*, pp. 111–112. See also Daria A. Rothe, "Letters of Two Remarkable Women: The Anna Freud–Lou Andreas-Salomé Correspondence," in Patrick Mahony, Carlo Bonomi, and Jan Stennson, eds., *Behind the Scenes: Freud in Correspondence* (Oslo: Scandinavian University Press, 1997), pp. 311–334.
14 Anna Freud to Kubie, January 1, 1955, quoted in Young-Bruehl, *Anna Freud*, pp. 161–162. She insisted, however, that "we lose too much if we leave out the topographical view altogether": Joseph Sandler with Anna Freud, *The Analysis of Defense: "The Ego and the Mechanisms of Defense" Revisited* (New York: International Universities Press, 1985), p. 244. For reflections on grappling with Freud's theoretical innovations of the 1920s, see Richard F. Sterba, *Reminiscences of a Viennese Psychoanalyst* (Detroit: Wayne State University Press, 1982).
15 Ernst Kris, review of *The Ego and the Mechanisms of Defense*, by Anna Freud, *IJP* 19 (1938): 143. Reprinted in Ernst Kris, *Selected Papers of Ernst Kris* (New Haven: Yale University Press, 1975.), pp. 343–356. In the same issue of *IJP*, Anna Freud's book was also reviewed by Ernest Jones and Otto Fenichel.
16 See Jones to Freud, May 11, 1927, *The Complete Correspondence of Sigmund Freud and Ernest Jones 1908–1939*, ed. R. Andrew Paskauskas (Cambridge, MA: Harvard University Press, 1993), pp. 617–618 (emphasis in the original), and Freud to Jones, May 31, 1927, ibid., p. 619.
17 Freud to Jones, September 23, 1927, ibid., p. 624.
18 Anna Freud, "Personal Memories of Ernest Jones" (1979), in *The Writings of Anna Freud*, vol. 8, *Psychoanalytic Psychology and Normal Development 1970–1980* (New York: International Universities Press, 1981), p. 350.

19 Pearl H. M. King, "The Life and Work of Melanie Klein in the British Psycho-Analytical Society," *IJP* 64 (1983): 255–256. On the Controversial Discussions, see Riccardo Steiner, "Some Thoughts about Tradition and Change Arising from an Examination of the British Psychoanalytical Society's Controversial Discussions (1943–1944)," *The International Review of Psycho-Analysis* 12 (1985): 27–71, and Pearl King and Riccardo Steiner, eds., *The Freud–Klein Controversies 1941–1945* (London: Routledge, 1991).

20 Anna Freud, typescript of speech sent for Greenson memorial, January 1980, quoted in Young-Bruehl, *Anna Freud*, p. 440; see also ibid., pp. 373, 380.

21 For biographical information on Greenson, see Donald Spoto, *Marilyn Monroe: The Biography* (New York: HarperCollins, 1993), pp. 421–427, and Douglas Kirsner, *Unfree Associations: Inside Psychoanalytic Institutes* (London: Process Press, 2000), pp. 148–151.

22 Ralph R. Greenson, *Explorations in Psychoanalysis* (New York: International Universities Press, 1978) p. vii.

23 Interview, Ralph R. Greenson, December 2, 1962, pp. 1–2, Los Angeles Psycho-analytic Society and Institute Archives, quoted in Nathan G. Hale, Jr., *Freud in America*, vol. 2, *The Rise and Crisis of Psychoanalysis in the United States: Freud and the Americans, 1917–1985* (New York: Oxford University Press, 1995), p. 146.

24 Greenson, *Explorations in Psychoanalysis*, p. viii. See also Ralph R. Greenson, "Otto Fenichel 1898–1946: The Encyclopedia of Psychoanalysis," in Franz Alexander, Samuel Eisenstein, and Martin Grotjahn, eds., *Psychoanalytic Pioneers* (New York: Basic Books, 1966), pp. 439–449.

25 See Robert J. Stoller, "Ralph R. Greenson," *IJP* 61 (1980): 559.

26 Leo Rosten, *Captain Newman* (New York: Harper, 1956), pp. 23, 29, quoted in Hale, *The Rise and Crisis of Psychoanalysis in the United States*, p. 290.

27 Barbara Leming, *Marilyn Monroe* (New York: Crown, 1998), p. 342.

28 Ibid., p. 397.

29 Mandel interview with Kirsner, 1992, quoted in Kirsner, *Unfree Associations*, p. 168, and Grotstein interview with Kirsner, 1992, quoted in ibid., p. 188. For an account of the infighting in the Los Angeles Psychoanalytic Society and Institute, see ibid., ch. 4.

30 Daniel P. Greenson, preface to Alan Sugarman, Robert A. Nemiroff, and Daniel P. Greenson, eds., *The Technique and Practice of Psychoanalysis*, vol. 2, *A Memorial Volume to Ralph R. Greenson* (Madison, CT: International Universities Press, 1992), p. xiii.

31 Freud, *The Interpretation of Dreams* p. 517 (emphasis in the original).

32 Freud, "The Future Prospects of Psycho-Analytic Therapy" (1910), in *SE* 11: 144.

33 Freud, "The Psychogenesis of a Case of Homosexuality in a Woman" (1920), in *SE* 18: 163–164.

34 Freud, "The Disposition to Obsessional Neurosis," pp. 319–320.

35 Freud to Ferenczi, June 23, 1912, *F/Fer Correspondence* 1: 386.

36 Freud to Jung, November 8, 1908, *The Freud/Jung Letters: The Correspondence between Sigmund Freud and C. G. Jung*, ed. William McGuire, trans. Ralph Manheim and R. F. C. Hull (Princeton, NJ: Princeton University Press, 1974), p. 175.

37 Freud to Ferenczi, February 25, 1910, *F/Fer Correspondence* 1: 146n4.

38 On Elfriede Hirschfeld, see Ernst Falzeder, "My Grand-Patient, My Chief Tormentor: A Hitherto Unnoticed Case of Freud's and the Consequences," *The Psychoanalytic Quarterly* 63 (1994): 297–331.

39 Freud, "Two Lies Told by Children" (1913), in *SE* 12: 308.

40 Freud, "Psycho-Analysis and Telepathy" (1941), in *SE* 18: 186.

41 Ibid., pp. 186–187.

42 Ibid., p. 187.

43 Freud, *New Introductory Lectures on Psycho-Analysis* (1933), in *SE* 22: 41.

44 Freud, "The Disposition to Obsessional Neurosis," p. 320.

45 Freud to Jung, April 17, 1911, *F/J Letters*, p. 417.

46 Freud to Ferenczi, February 25, 1910, *F/Fer Correspondence* 1:146.

47 Freud to Jung, December 17, 1911, *F/J Letters*, pp. 473–474; see also Freud to Jung, May 12, 1911, ibid., p. 423.

48 Freud to Pfister, February 9, 1912, Freud Archives, Library of Congress, quoted in Falzeder, "My Grand-Patient," p. 308.

49 Freud to Jung, January 10, 1912, *F/J Letters*, p. 479. See also Ilse Grubrich-Simitis, *Back to Freud's Texts: Making Silent Documents Speak* (New Haven: Yale University Press, 1996), p. 209, and Jung to Freud, January 12, 1912, *F/J Letters*, pp. 476–477.

50 Freud to Pfister, February 9, 1912, Freud Archives, Library of Congress, quoted in Falzeder, "My Grand-Patient," p. 308; see also Freud to Pfister, July 4, 1912, Freud Archives, Library of Congress, quoted in ibid., p. 309.

51 Freud, *Inhibitions, Symptoms and Anxiety* (1926), in *SE* 20: 121.

52 Freud, "On Beginning the Treatment (Further Recommendations on the Technique of Psycho-Analysis I)" (1913), in *SE* 12: 134–135 (emphasis in the original).

53 Freud, "Notes upon a Case of Obsessional Neurosis," p. 166 (emphasis in the original).

54 Ibid., pp. 166, 184 (emphasis in the original).

55 Freud, "Remembering, Repeating and Working-Through (Further Recommendations on the Technique of Psycho-Analysis II)" (1914), in *SE* 12: 155 (emphasis in the original). For a useful discussion of Freud's attack on a patient's resistance, see Roy Schafer, *Retelling a Life: Narration and Dialogue in Psychoanalysis* (New York: Basic Books, 1992), pp. 219–233.

56 Freud to Binswanger, April 24, 1915, *The Sigmund Freud–Ludwig Binswanger Correspondence 1908–1938*, ed. Gerhard Fichtner, trans. Arnold J. Pomerans (New York: Other Press, 2003), p. 132.

57 Freud to Jung, November 29, 1908, *F/J Letters*, pp. 183–184.

58 Freud, "Lines of Advance in Psycho-Analytic Therapy," p. 166.

59 Freud, "From the History of an Infantile Neurosis" (1918), in *SE* 17: 11.

60 Freud, "Analysis Terminable and Interminable" (1937), in *SE* 23: 218–219.

61 Freud, "Remembering, Repeating and Working-Through," pp. 155–156.

62 Freud, "Analysis Terminable and Interminable," p. 218.

63 Freud, "Notes upon a Case of Obsessional Neurosis," p. 303.

64 See ibid., pp. 307, 308, 310, 311, 313, 314.

65 Samuel D. Lipton, "The Advantages of Freud's Technique as Shown in His Analysis of the Rat Man," *IJP* 58 (1977): 259; see also Elizabeth R. Zetzel, "An Obsessional Neurotic: Freud's Rat Man" (1966), in Elizabeth R. Zetzel, *The Capacity for Emotional Growth* (New York: International Universities Press, 1970), pp. 216–228.

66 A. Freud, "Four Lectures on Child Analysis" (1927), in *Introduction to Psychoanalysis: Lectures for Child Analysts and Teachers 1922–1945*, pp. 7, 8–9, 11, 12–14.

67 Ibid., pp. 51, 7.

68 Freud, *The Ego and the Id* (1923), in *SE* 19: 19.

69 Freud, *Beyond the Pleasure Principle* (1920), in *SE* 18: 19 (emphasis in the original).

70 Freud, *The Ego and the Id*, p. 17.

71 Freud, *Inhibitions, Symptoms and Anxiety*, p. 163.
72 Ibid., pp. 163–164.
73 Ibid., p. 154.
74 Freud, "Analysis Terminable and Interminable," p. 239. For interesting commentary on Freud's remarks, see Paul Gray, *The Ego and Analysis of Defense* (Northvale, NJ: Jason Aronson, 1994), pp. 45–46.
75 Sandler, *The Analysis of Defense*, pp. 8, 9–10. For useful commentary on Anna Freud's psychoanalytic treatment of adult patients, see Clifford Yorke, "Anna Freud and the Psychoanalytic Study and Treatment of Adults," *IJP* 64 (1983): 391–400; Robert S. Wallerstein, "Anna Freud: Radical Innovator and Staunch Conservative," *The Psychoanalytic Study of the Child* 39 (1984): 65–80; Arthur S. Couch, "Anna Freud's Adult Psychoanalytic Technique: A Defense of Classical Analysis," *IJP* 76 (1995): 153–171.
76 Ibid., p. 14.
77 Anna Freud, *The Ego and the Mechanisms of Defense* (1936), in *The Writings of Anna Freud*, vol. 2, *The Ego and the Mechanisms of Defense*, rev. ed. (New York: International Universities Press, 1966), p. 13.
78 Sandler, *The Analysis of Defense*, p. 41.
79 A. Freud, *The Ego and the Mechanisms of Defense*, pp. 35–36.
80 Sandler, *The Analysis of Defense*, pp. 95, 96.
81 A. Freud, *The Ego and the Mechanisms of Defense*, p. 37.
82 Sandler, *The Analysis of Defense*, p. 99.
83 Ibid., p. 99.
84 A. Freud, *The Ego and the Mechanisms of Defense*, pp. 37, 21.
85 See Sandler, *The Analysis of Defense*, p. 72.
86 Anna Freud, "Difficulties in the Path of Psychoanalysis: A Confrontation of Past and Present Viewpoints" (1969), in *The Writings of Anna Freud*, vol. 7, *Problems of Psychoanalytic Training, Diagnosis, and the Technique of Therapy 1966–1970* (New York: International Universities Press, 1971), p. 136.
87 Freud, "Notes upon a Case of Obsessional Neurosis," pp. 248–249.
88 Freud, "Analysis Terminable and Interminable," p. 235.
89 Sterba, *Reminiscences of a Viennese Psychoanalyst*, p. 69.
90 See Elizabeth R. Zetzel, "Current Concepts of Transference" (1956), in Zetzel, *The Capacity for Emotional Growth*, pp. 168–181.
91 Lawrence Friedman, "How and Why Do Patients Become More Objective? Sterba Compared with Strachey," *The Psychoanalytic Quarterly* 61 (1992): 3.
92 Freud, *New Introductory Lectures on Psychoanalysis*, quoted in Richard Sterba, "The Fate of the Ego in Analytic Therapy," *IJP* 15 (1934): 120n2 (emphasis in the original). The translation in the *Standard Edition* is slightly different. The penultimate sentence of the quotation reads: "So the ego can be split; it splits itself during a number of functions—temporarily at least." *New Introductory Lectures*, p. 58.
93 Sterba, "The Fate of the Ego," p. 120.
94 Ibid., pp. 123, 121 (emphasis in the original).
95 Ibid., p. 121.
96 Friedman, "How and Why Do Patients Become More Objective?" pp. 2, 8. See also Richard Sterba, "The Dynamics of the Dissolution of the Transference Resistance" (1929), *The Psychoanalytic Quarterly* 9 (1940): 363–379.
97 Sterba, "The Fate of the Ego," p. 122.
98 Gray, *The Ego and the Analysis of Defense*, p. 85.
99 Ralph R. Greenson, *The Technique and Practice of Psychoanalysis*, vol. 1 (New York: International Universities Press, 1967), p. 192.

100 See, for example, Ralph R. Greenson, "Transference: Freud or Klein" (1974), in Greenson, *Explorations in Psychoanalysis*, pp. 519–539.
101 Ralph R. Greenson and Milton Wexler, "The Non-Transference Relationship in the Psychoanalytic Situation," *IJP* 50 (1969): 27.
102 Greenson, *Technique and Practice of Psychoanalysis*, p. 199.
103 Ralph R. Greenson, "The Problem of Working Through" (1965), in Greenson, *Explorations in Psychoanalysis*, pp. 256–257.
104 Ibid., pp. 255–256, 259–260 (emphasis in the original).
105 Ibid., p. 261.
106 Greenson, *Technique and Practice of Psychoanalysis*, pp. 201, 202.
107 Ibid., pp. 202–203.
108 For criticism of this position from American ego psychologists, see Charles Brenner, "Working Alliance, Therapeutic Alliance, and Transference," *JAPA* 27 (Suppl.) (1979): 137–157; Homer C. Curtis, "The Concept of the Therapeutic Alliance: Implications for the 'Widening Scope,' " *JAPA* 27 (Suppl.) (1979): 159–192; Martin H. Stein, "The Unobjectionable Part of the Transference," *JAPA* 29 (1981): 869–892. For a recent discussion, see Steven T. Levy, ed., *The Therapeutic Alliance* (Madison, CT: International Universities Press, 2000).
109 Greenson, *Technique and Practice of Psychoanalysis*, p. 203.
110 Ibid., pp. 195–196.
111 Ibid., pp. 196–197.
112 Ibid., p. 196.
113 Greenson and Wexler, "The Non-Transference Relationship," p. 29.
114 Freud, "Remembering, Repeating and Working-Through," p. 147.
115 Lawrence Friedman, "The Therapeutic Alliance," *IJP* 50 (1969): 152 (emphasis in the original).

3 Depression: Negative therapeutic reaction

1 See Freud, "On the Grounds for Detaching a Particular Syndrome from Neurasthenia Under the Description 'Anxiety Neurosis' " (1895), in *SE* 3: 90; see also Freud, "Draft G. Melancholia" (undated; ? January 7, 1895), in *The Complete Letters of Sigmund Freud to Wilhelm Fliess 1887–1904*, trans. and ed. Jeffrey Moussaieff Masson (Cambridge, MA: Harvard University Press, 1985), pp. 98–105, and Freud, "Draft N" (undated; ? May 31, 1897), in ibid., pp. 250–252.
2 Freud, "Mourning and Melancholia" (1917), in *SE* 14: 243.
3 Ibid., pp. 243, 244.
4 Ibid., p. 246.
5 Ibid., p. 248.
6 Ibid., pp. 250–251, 248–249, 258 (emphasis in the original).
7 Karl Abraham, "A Short History of the Development of the Libido, Viewed in the Light of Mental Disorders" (1924), in *Selected Papers of Karl Abraham*, trans. Douglas Bryan and Alix Strachey (London: Hogarth Press, 1927; reprint, London: Karnac, Maresfield Library, 1979), pp. 418–501.
8 Abraham did mention a "private communication" from Freud reporting success with two melancholic cases. In one of them, there had been "no relapse . . . for over ten years": ibid., p. 479.
9 Abraham to Freud, October 7, 1923, *The Complete Correspondence of Sigmund Freud and Karl Abraham 1907–1925*, ed. Ernst Falzeder, trans. Caroline Schwarzacher (London: Karnac, 2002), p. 471.
10 For biographical information I have drawn on Phyllis Grosskurth, *Melanie Klein: Her World and Her Work* (New York: Knopf, 1986).

11 Melanie Klein, "Autobiography," quoted in Grosskurth, *Melanie Klein*, p. 16.

12 See *The Writings of Melanie Klein*, under the general editorship of Roger Money-Kyrle, in collaboration with Betty Joseph, Edna O'Shaughnessy, and Hanna Segal (London: Hogarth Press, 1975), vol. 2, *The Psycho-Analysis of Children*, trans. Alix Strachey, pp. x–xi. For Ferenczi's appraisal of Klein, see Ferenczi to Freud, June 29, 1919, *F/Fer Correspondence* 2: 361.

13 See Jean-Michel Petot, *Melanie Klein*, vol. 1, *First Discoveries and First System 1919–1932*, trans. Christine Trollope (Madison, CT: International Universities Press, 1990), pp. 14–22.

14 See Alix to James Strachey, December 14, 1924, *Bloomsbury/Freud: The Letters of James and Alix Strachey 1924–1925*, ed. Perry Meisel and Walter Kendrick (New York: Basic Books, 1985), p. 145. For Klein's acknowledgment of Abraham's help, see Klein, *The Psycho-Analysis of Children*, p. xi.

15 Alix to James Strachey, February 11, 1925, *Bloomsbury/Freud*, p. 201.

16 James to Alix Strachey, May 7, 1925, ibid., pp. 258–259.

17 Alix to James Strachey, January 12, 1925, ibid., p. 182.

18 Ferenczi to Freud, June 30, 1927, *F/Fer Correspondence* 3: 313. See also Jones to Freud, September 30, 1927, *The Complete Correspondence of Sigmund Freud and Ernest Jones 1908–1939*, ed. R. Andrew Paskauskas (Cambridge, MA: Harvard University Press, 1993), pp. 627–628.

19 See Pearl H. M. King, "The Life and Work of Melanie Klein in the British Psycho-Analytical Society," *IJP* 64 (1983): 252.

20 Edward Glover, review of *The Psycho-Analysis of Children*, by Melanie Klein, *IJP* 14 (1933): 119. See also Joseph Aguayo, "Patronage in the Dispute over Child Analysis between Melanie Klein and Anna Freud—1927–1932," *IJP* 81 (2000): 733–752.

21 Grosskurth, *Melanie Klein*, pp. 215, 219.

22 Melanie Klein, "Mourning and its Relation to Manic-Depressive States" (1940), in *The Writings of Melanie Klein*, vol. 1, *Love, Guilt and Reparation and Other Works 1921–1945*, pp. 355, 361.

23 Eva Rosenfeld, interview with Pearl King, 1974, and Dr. William Gillespie, interview with Grosskurth, September 24, 1981, both quoted in Grosskurth, *Melanie Klein*, pp. 214, 242 (emphasis in the original). For Melitta's account, see Melitta Schmideberg, "A Contribution to the History of the Psycho-Analytic Movement in Britain," *British Journal of Psychiatry* 118 (1971): 61–68.

24 For biographical information on Riviere, see James Strachey, Paula Heimann, and Lois Munro, "Joan Riviere (1883–1962)," *IJP* 44 (1963): 228–235; Athol Hughes, "Joan Riviere: Her Life and Work," in Joan Riviere, *The Inner World and Joan Riviere: Collected Papers 1920–1958*, ed. Athol Hughes (London: Karnac Books, 1991), pp. 1–43; Athol Hughes, "Letters from Sigmund Freud to Joan Riviere (1921–1939)," *The International Review of Psycho-Analysis* 19 (1992): 265–284; Lisa Appignanesi and John Forrester, *Freud's Women* (New York: Basic Books, 1992), pp. 353–365; Athol Hughes, "Personal Experiences–Professional Interests: Joan Riviere and Femininity," *IJP* 78 (1997): 899–911; Janet Sayers, *Kleinians: Psychoanalysis Inside and Out* (Oxford: Polity Press, 2000), pp. 49–67.

25 Jones to Freud, January 22, 1922, *Freud/Jones Correspondence*, p. 454.

26 Strachey, "Joan Riviere," p. 228.

27 For Strachey's relations with A. W. Verrall, see Brooke to Strachey, January 1 or 2, 1909, *Friends and Apostles: The Correspondence of Rupert Brooke and James Strachey 1905–1914*, ed. Keith Hale (New Haven: Yale University Press, 1998), pp. 54 and 54n2.

28 Strachey, "Joan Riviere," p. 229. On the project of translating Freud into English, see Riccardo Steiner, "A World Wide International Trade Mark of Genuineness? Some Observations on the History of the English Translation of the Work of Sigmund Freud, Focusing Mainly on His Technical Terms," *The International Review of Psycho-Analysis* 14 (1987): 33–102, and Riccardo Steiner, " 'To Explain Our Point of View to English Readers in English Words,' " *The International Review of Psycho-Analysis* 18 (1991): 351–392.

29 See Jones to Freud, January 22, 1922, *Freud/Jones Correspondence*, p. 453.

30 Freud to Riviere, August 12, 1921, in A. Hughes, "Letters from Freud to Riviere," p. 268.

31 Strachey, "Joan Riviere," p. 229.

32 Appignanesi and Forrester, *Freud's Women*, p. 358.

33 See Pearl King and Riccardo Steiner, eds., *The Freud–Klein Controversies 1941–45* (London: Routledge, 1991), pp. 43, 261*n*.

34 Freud, *The Ego and the Id* (1923), in *SE* 19: 49; see also Freud, "Remembering, Repeating and Working-Through (Further Recommendations on the Technique of Psycho-Analysis II)" (1914), in *SE* 12: 152, and Freud, "From the History of an Infantile Neurosis" (1918), in *SE* 17: 69. In 1937, Freud took the line that the negative therapeutic reaction was evidence that wishes and/or pleasure did not govern mental life or did not do so exclusively. He saw it as an unmistakable indication "of the presence of a power in mental life which we call the instinct of aggression or of destruction . . . , which we trace back to the original death instinct of living matter": Freud, "Analysis Terminable and Interminable" (1937), in *SE* 23: 243. For discussions of the negative therapeutic reaction, see Karen Horney, "The Problem of the Negative Therapeutic Reaction," *The Psychoanalytic Quarterly* 5 (1936): 29–45; Stanley L. Olinik, "The Negative Therapeutic Reaction," *IJP* 45 (1964): 540–548; Hans W. Loewald, "Freud's Conception of the Negative Therapeutic Reaction, with Comments on Instinct Theory" (1972), in Hans Loewald, *Papers on Psychoanalysis* (New Haven: Yale University Press, 1980), ch. 14; Stuart S. Asch, "Varieties of Negative Therapeutic Reaction and Problems of Technique," *JAPA* 24 (1976): 383–407; Herbert Rosenfeld, *Impasse and Interpretation: Therapeutic and Anti-Therapeutic Factors in the Psychoanalytic Treatment of Psychotic, Borderline, and Neurotic Patients* (London: Tavistock Publications, 1987), pp. 85–104.

35 Jones to Freud, January 22, 1922, *Freud/Jones Correspondence*, pp. 453–454.

36 Riviere to Jones, October 30, 1918, quoted in Victor Brome, *Ernest Jones: Freud's Alter Ego* (New York: Norton, 1983), p. 16 (emphasis in the original). This letter is not among those from Riviere to Jones in the Jones Papers, Institute of Psycho-Analysis, London.

37 Freud, "Observations on Transference-Love (Further Recommendations on the Technique of Psycho-Analysis III)" (1915), in *SE* 12: 169–170.

38 Jones to Freud, January 22, 1922, *Freud/Jones Correspondence*, pp. 453–454.

39 Jones to Freud, May 22, 1922, ibid., p. 479.

40 Freud to Jones, March 23, 1922, ibid., p. 464. On Freud's analysis of Riviere, see Anton O. Kris, "Freud's Treatment of a Narcissistic Patient," *IJP* 75 (1994): 649–664.

41 Jones to Freud, April 1, 1922, *Freud/Jones Correspondence*, p. 466.

42 Freud to Jones, June 4, 1922, ibid., p. 483.

43 Freud to Jones, June 25, 1922, ibid., p. 491.

44 Freud to Jones, May 11, 1922, ibid., p. 475.

45 Freud to Jones, April 22, 1922, ibid., p. 468.

46 Jones to Freud, May 22, 1922, ibid., p. 478.

47 Freud to Jones, May 11, 1922, ibid., p. 475, and June 4, 1922, ibid., p. 484.

48 Freud to Jones, June 25, 1922, ibid., p. 491.

49 Jones to Freud, July 19, 1922, ibid., p. 494; December 22, 1922, p. 506; February 9, 1924, p. 538.

50 A. Hughes, "Joan Riviere: Her Life and Work," p. 15.

51 It has been argued that Riviere served as "a prime model" for Freud's "second topography of the mind: the id, ego and super-ego": Appignanesi and Forrester, *Freud's Women*, p. 358. See also A. Kris, "Freud's Treatment of a Narcissistic Patient," p. 658*n*12. In fact Freud was eager to have Riviere translate *The Ego and the Id*: see Freud to Riviere, March 24, 1924, in A. Hughes, "Letters from Freud to Riviere," p. 276.

52 Freud to Jones, June 4, 1922, *Freud/Jones Correspondence*, pp. 485, 484, and June 25, 1922, p. 491.

53 Freud, *The Ego and the Id*, pp. 36, 48; Freud, "The Economic Problem of Masochism" (1924), in *SE* 19: 167; Freud, "An Autobiographical Study" (1925), in *SE* 20: 59; Freud, *The Question of Lay Analysis: Conversations with an Impartial Person* (1926), in *SE* 20: 223; Freud, *New Introductory Lectures on Psycho-Analysis* (1933), in *SE* 22: 64; Freud, *An Outline of Psycho-Analysis* (1940), in *SE* 23: 205.

54 Freud, *The Ego and the Id*, pp. 49–50.

55 Joan Riviere, "A Contribution to the Analysis of the Negative Therapeutic Reaction" (1936), in *The Inner World and Joan Riviere*, p. 135.

56 Jones to Freud, September 30, 1927, *Freud/Jones Correspondence*, pp. 627–628.

57 Jones to Freud, September 30, 1927, ibid., p. 629.

58 Freud to Jones, October 9, 1927, ibid., p. 633.

59 Freud to Riviere, October 9, 1927, in A. Hughes, "Letters from Freud to Riviere," p. 280.

60 See Freud to Jones, October 22, 1927, *Freud/Jones Correspondence*, p. 635.

61 Joan Riviere, "Symposium on Child Analysis" (1927), in *The Inner World and Joan Riviere*, p. 87 (emphasis in the original).

62 Jones to Freud, October 18, 1927, *Freud/Jones Correspondence*, p. 634.

63 Ernest Jones, "Early Female Sexuality" (1935), in Ernest Jones, *Papers on Psycho-Analysis*, 5th ed. (London: Baillière, Tindall and Cox, 1948; reprint, London: Karnac, Maresfield Library, 1977), p. 495.

64 Melanie Klein. "The Oedipus Complex in the Light of Early Anxieties" (1945), in *Love, Guilt and Reparation*, pp. 397–398. For commentary on what Klein learned from Rita's case, see Claudia Frank, "The Discovery of the Child as an Object *Sui Generis* of Cure and Research by Melanie Klein as Reflected in the Notes of Her First Child Analysis in Berlin 1921–1926," *Psychoanalysis and History* 1 (1999): 155–174.

65 Melanie Klein, "The Psychological Principles of Early Analysis" (1926), in *Love, Guilt and Reparation*, p. 132.

66 Klein, "Oedipus Complex in the Light of Early Anxieties," pp. 398–399.

67 Melanie Klein, "The Psycho-Analytic Play Technique: Its History and Significance" (1955), in *The Writings of Melanie Klein*, vol. 3, *Envy and Gratitude and Other Works 1946–1963*, p. 124.

68 Klein, "Oedipus Complex in the Light of Early Anxieties," p. 398.

69 Klein, *The Psycho-Analysis of Children*, p. 32 (emphasis in the original).

70 Klein, "Oedipus Complex in the Light of Early Anxieties," p. 401.

71 Melanie Klein, "Personification in the Play of Children" (1929), in *Love, Guilt and Reparation*, pp. 201–202.

72 Klein, *The Psycho-Analysis of Children*, p. 7.

73 Ibid., p. 32.

74 Klein, "Oedipus Complex in the Light of Early Anxieties," p. 416 (emphasis in the original).

75 Melanie Klein, "Early Stages of the Oedipus Conflict" (1928), in *Love, Guilt and Reparation*, p. 186 (emphasis in the original).

76 Melanie Klein, "The Early Development of Conscience in the Child" (1933), in *Love, Guilt and Reparation*, p. 251.

77 Klein, *The Psycho-Analysis of Children*, p. 138.

78 See Freud, *Civilization and Its Discontents* (1930), in *SE* 21: 130n.

79 Freud, *New Introductory Lectures*, p. 67.

80 Melanie Klein, "Symposium on Child-Analysis" (1927), in *Love, Guilt and Reparation*, pp. 157–158.

81 Klein, "Personification in the Play of Children," p. 208.

82 Klein, *The Psycho-Analysis of Children*, p. 3n2. Seven years after the end of Rita's analysis, Klein added, she heard from the girl's mother that Rita was developing satisfactorily.

83 Riviere, "Symposium on Child-Analysis," pp. 83–84, 82–83 (emphasis in the original).

84 Melanie Klein, "Memorandum on Her Technique" October 25, 1943, in King and Steiner, eds., *The Freud–Klein Controversies*, pp. 635–636.

85 Sylvia M. Payne, "Memorandum on Her Technique" November 24, 1943, in King and Steiner, eds., *The Freud–Klein Controversies*, p. 650.

86 See Klein, "Memorandum on Her Technique," p. 638n1.

87 Freud, *Inhibitions, Symptoms and Anxiety* (1926), in *SE* 20: 160 (emphasis in the original).

88 See Freud, *Group Psychology and the Analysis of the Ego* (1921), in *SE* 18: 113–114.

89 James Strachey, "The Nature of the Therapeutic Action of Psycho-Analysis," *IJP* 15 (1934): 134, 133; see also James Strachey, "The Theory of the Therapeutic Results of Psycho-Analysis," *IJP* 18 (1937): 139–145. For helpful commentary on Strachey's 1934 paper, see Herbert Rosenfeld, "A Critical Appreciation of James Strachey's Paper on the Nature of the Therapeutic Action of Psycho-analysis," *IJP* 53 (1972): 455–461; R. Horacio Etchegoyen, "Fifty Years after the Mutative Interpretation," *IJP* 64 (1983): 445–459; Arnold M. Cooper, "Our Changing Views of the Therapeutic Action of Psychoanalysis: Comparing Strachey and Loewald," *The Psychoanalytic Quarterly* 57 (1988): 15–27; Moss L. Rawn, "Classics Revisited: Some Thoughts on Strachey's 'The Nature of the Therapeutic Action of Psycho-Analysis,' " *IJP* 69 (1988): 507–520; Lawrence Friedman, "How and Why Do Patients Become More Objective? Sterba Compared with Strachey," *The Psychoanalytic Quarterly* 61 (1992): 1–17; Robert Caper, "On the Difficulty of Making a Mutative Interpretation," *IJP* 76 (1995): 91–101. Compare Franz Alexander, "A Metapsychological Description of the Process of Cure," *IJP* 6 (1925): 13–34; Sándor Rádo, "The Economic Principle in Psycho-Analytic Technique," *IJP* 6 (1925): 35–44; Hanns Sachs, "Metapsychological Points of View in Technique and Theory," *IJP* 6 (1925): 5–12.

90 Strachey, "The Nature of the Therapeutic Action," p. 137.

91 Ibid., p. 138 (emphasis in the original).

92 Ibid., pp. 138, 140–141 (emphasis in the original).

93 Ibid., pp. 145, 146.

94 Ibid., pp.150, 151 (emphasis in the original).

95 Ibid., p. 144.

96 Freud, *The Ego and the Id*, p. 50n1.

97   Strachey, "The Nature of the Therapeutic Action," pp. 146–147.
98   Klein, "Psychogenesis of Manic-Depressive States," p. 264. Subsequently Klein softened the distinction between relations to part objects and to whole objects: see Melanie Klein, "On the Theory of Anxiety and Guilt" (1946), in *Envy and Gratitude*, pp. 35–36, and Melanie Klein, "Some Theoretical Conclusions Regarding the Emotional Life of the Infant" (1952), in *Envy and Gratitude*, p. 66n.
99   Klein, "Psychogenesis of Manic-Depressive States," p. 266.
100 Melanie Klein, "Criminal Tendencies in Normal Children" (1927), in *Love, Guilt and Reparation*, pp. 176, 175.
101 Klein, "Mourning and its Relation to Manic-Depressive States," p. 353.
102 Klein, *The Psycho-Analysis of Children*, p. xiii.
103 Klein, "Mourning and its Relation to Manic-Depressive States," p. 345.
104 Freud, "Mourning and Melancholia," pp. 253–254.
105 Riviere, "Negative Therapeutic Reaction," pp. 152, 139 (emphasis in the original).
106 Ibid., pp. 152, 139, 135, 144, 145–146 (emphasis in the original).
107 Ibid., pp. 147–148 (emphasis in the original).
108 Ibid., pp. 152, 149–150, 146 (emphasis in the original).
109 Ibid. pp. 142, 151 (emphasis in the original).
110 Melanie Klein, "Envy and Gratitude" (1957), in *Envy and Gratitude*, p. 222.
111 Ibid., pp. 179, 178, 180. For useful commentary, see Meira Likierman, "Primitive Object Love in Melanie Klein's Thinking: Early Theoretical Influences," *IJP* 74 (1993): 241–253, and Meira Likierman, *Melanie Klein: Her Work in Context* (London and New York: Continuum, 2001), ch. 6.
112 Freud, "Analysis Terminable and Interminable," p. 252.
113 Klein, "Envy and Gratitude," p. 183.
114 Melanie Klein, "Notes on Some Schizoid Mechanisms" (1946), in *Envy and Gratitude*, p. 6.
115 Klein, "Some Theoretical Conclusions Regarding the Emotional Life of the Infant," pp. 70–71.
116 Klein, "Envy and Gratitude," pp. 183–184.
117 Ibid., pp. 206, 207–208.
118 Ibid., pp. 208, 209.
119 Ibid., pp. 232, 234.
120 See ibid., p. 232.
121 Freud, "History of an Infantile Neurosis," p. 69.
122 Freud, "Obsessive Actions and Religious Practices" (1907), in *SE* 9: 123.
123 See Freud, "Neurosis and Psychosis" (1924), in *SE* 19: 152; see also Freud, *New Introductory Lectures*, pp. 60–61.
124 Jones to Freud, June 30, 1927, *Freud/Jones Correspondence*, pp. 619–620.
125 Klein, "Mourning and its Relation to Manic-Depressive States," pp. 362–363.
126 Riviere, "Negative Therapeutic Reaction," p. 152.
127 Melanie Klein, "On the Criteria for the Termination of a Psycho-Analysis" (1950), in *Envy and Gratitude*, p. 46.

4 Paranoia: Abnormal changes in the ego

1   See Freud, "Further Remarks on the Neuro-Psychoses of Defense" (1896), in *SE* 3: 175; see also Freud, "Draft H. Paranoia" (enclosed with letter of January 24, 1895), in *The Complete Letters of Sigmund Freud to Wilhelm Fliess 1887–1904*, trans. and ed. Jeffrey Moussaieff Masson (Cambridge, MA: Harvard University Press, 1985), pp. 107–112, and Freud, "Draft K. The Neuroses of Defense

(A Christmas Fairy Tale)" (enclosed with letter of January 1, 1896), in ibid., pp. 162–169.

2 See Freud, "Psycho-Analytic Notes on an Autobiographical Account of a Case of Paranoia (Dementia Paranoides)" (1911), in *SE* 12: 75–76. See also Daniel Paul Schreber, *Memoirs of My Nervous Illness*, trans. and ed. Ida Macalpine and Richard A. Hunter (Cambridge, MA: Harvard University Press, 1988). For biographical information on Schreber, see Franz Baumeyer, "The Schreber Case," *IJP* 37 (1956): 61–74; William G. Niederland, *The Schreber Case: Psychoanalytic Profile of a Paranoid Personality* (New York: Quadrangle/New York Times, 1974); Han Israëls, *Schreber: Father and Son*, trans. H. S. Lake (Madison, CT: International Universities Press, 1989).

3 Dr. Weber, "Asylum and District Medical Officer's Report" (November 28, 1900), in Schreber, *Memoirs*, p. 278.

4 Dr. Weber, "Medical Expert's Report to the Court" (December 9, 1899), in ibid., pp. 267, 268, 269, 270, 271.

5 "Judgment of the Royal Superior Country Court Dresden of 14th July 1902," in ibid., p. 354.

6 Daniel Paul Schreber, "Grounds of Appeal" (July 23, 1901), in ibid., p. 307.

7 Schreber, *Memoirs*, pp. 31, 148, 85.

8 Ibid., pp. 204, 149, 212.

9 Freud, "Psycho-Analytic Notes on . . . a Case of Paranoia," p. 18.

10 Freud to Jung, April 22, 1910, *The Freud/Jung Letters: Correspondence between Sigmund Freud and C. G. Jung*, ed. William McGuire, trans. Ralph Manheim and R. F. C. Hull (Princeton, NJ: Princeton University Press, 1974), p. 311, and Freud to Jung, December 18, 1910, ibid., pp. 379–380.

11 Freud, "Psycho-Analytic Notes on . . . a Case of Paranoia," pp. 60–61. Freud had earlier linked paranoia with a return to an auto-erotic state: see Freud to Fliess, December 9, 1899, *Complete Letters of Freud to Fliess*, p. 390.

12 Freud, "Psycho-Analytic Notes on . . . a Case of Paranoia," pp. 62, 66, 56.

13 Freud to Jung, February 17, 1908, *Freud/Jung Letters*, p. 121.

14 See Freud to Ferenczi, October 6, 1910, *F/Fer Correspondence* 1: 221–222.

15 Freud to Ferenczi, March 25, 1908, ibid., p. 7.

16 Freud, "Some Neurotic Mechanisms in Jealousy, Paranoia and Homosexuality" (1922), in *SE* 18: 225.

17 Lisa Appignanesi and John Forrester, *Freud's Women* (New York: Basic Books, 1992), p. 373. For biographical information on Brunswick, see ibid., pp. 373–376, and Paul Roazen, *Freud and His Followers* (New York: Knopf, 1975), pp. 426–436. See also Paul Roazen, "Freud's Patients: First Hand Accounts," in Toby Gelfand and John Kerr, eds. *Freud and the History of Psychoanalysis* (Hillsdale, NJ: Analytic Press, 1992), pp. 289–305.

18 For Freud's analyses of Mark Brunswick and his brother David, see Paul Roazen, *How Freud Worked: First-Hand Accounts of His Patients* (Northvale, NJ: Jason Aronson, 1995), pp. 31–88.

19 See Sigmund Freud, *The Diary of Sigmund Freud 1929–1939: A Record of the Final Decade*, trans., annotated, with an introduction by Michael Molnar (London: Hogarth Press, 1992), April 24 [23], 1931, p. 97.

20 Roazen, *Freud and His Followers*, pp. 430–431.

21 Freud, *Diary*, February 16, 1930 and February 14, 1930, p. 58. See also ibid., July 31, 1931, p. 102; August 1, 1931, p. 103; August 10, 1931, p. 103.

22 Freud, "Analysis Terminable and Interminable" (1937), in *SE* 23: 249.

23 Freud to Lampl-de Groot, August 22, 1928, quoted in Appignanesi and Forrester, *Freud's Women*, p. 373.

24 Freud to Lampl-de Groot, October 23, 1932, quoted in Freud, *Diary*, p. 140.

25 Freud to Lampl-de Groot, April 15, 1933, quoted in Freud, *Diary*, 152.

26 Freud to Lampl-de Groot, August 22, 1938, quoted in Freud, *Diary*, p. 247.

27 Wilfred R. Bion, *The Long Week-End 1897–1919: Part of a Life*, ed. Francesca Bion (Abingdon: Fleetwood Press, 1982), pp. 133, 278, 194, 267, 209 (emphasis in the original). See also Wilfred R. Bion, *All My Sins Remembered: Another Part of a Life and the Other Side of Genius: Family Letters*, ed. Francesca Bion (Abingdon: Fleetwood Press, 1985), and Wilfred R. Bion, *War Memoirs 1917–1919*, ed. Francesca Bion (London: Karnac, 1997).

28 For additional biographical information on Bion, see Oliver Lyth, "Wilfred Ruprecht Bion (1897–1979)," *IJP* 61 (1980): 269–273; Francesca Bion, Hanna Segal, Isabel Menzies Lyth, and Donald Meltzer, "Memorial Meeting for Dr. Wilfred Bion," *The International Review of Psycho-Analysis* 8 (1981): 3–14; Gérard Bléandonu, *Wilfred Bion: His Life and Works 1897–1979*, trans. Claire Pajaczkowska (London: Free Association Books, 1994); Janet Sayers, *Kleinians: Psychoanalysis Inside and Out* (Oxford: Polity Press, 2000), pp. 113–133.

29 Bion, *All My Sins Remembered*, p. 16.

30 See Wilfred R. Bion, *Experience in Groups and Other Papers* (London: Tavistock Publications, 1961).

31 Quoted by Lyth in "Bion," p. 271.

32 Quoted in Francesca Bion, foreword to Bion, *The Long Week-End*, p. 7.

33 Betty Joseph, interview with the author, June 20, 2001.

34 Ibid.

35 For a useful review of theorizing about paranoia, see W. W. Meissner, *The Paranoid Process* (New York: Jason Aronson, 1978); see also Arnold M. Cooper, "Paranoia: A Part of Most Analyses," *JAPA* 41 (1993): 423–442.

36 Freud, "Psycho-Analytic Notes on . . . a Case of Paranoia," p. 75.

37 Melanie Klein, "Notes on Some Schizoid Mechanisms" (1946), in *The Writings of Melanie Klein*, under the general editorship of Roger Money-Kyrle, in collaboration with Betty Joseph, Edna O'Shaughnessy, and Hanna Segal (London: Hogarth Press, 1975), vol. 3, *Envy and Gratitude and Other Works 1946–1963*, p. 23.

38 Melanie Klein, "Envy and Gratitude" (1957), in *Envy and Gratitude*, p. 232.

39 Wolf-Man, "My Recollections of Sigmund Freud," trans. Muriel Gardiner, in Muriel Gardiner, ed., *The Wolf-Man by the Wolf-Man* (New York: Basic Books, 1971), pp. 149–150.

40 Freud, "From the History of an Infantile Neurosis" (1918), in *SE* 17: 121n1.

41 Ruth Mack Brunswick, "A Supplement to Freud's 'History of an Infantile Neurosis' "(1928), in Gardiner, ed., *The Wolf-Man by the Wolf-Man*, p. 265; see also ibid., p. 304.

42 Freud, "History of an Infantile Neurosis," p. 7; see also p. 8.

43 Ibid., p. 17.

44 "The Memoirs of the Wolf-Man," trans. Muriel Gardiner, in Gardiner, ed., *The Wolf-Man by the Wolf-Man*, p. 7. I have relied on these memoirs for biographical information as well as on Patrick J. Mahony, *Cries of the Wolf Man* (New York: International Universities Press, 1984).

45 Freud, "History of an Infantile Neurosis," p. 7. For a discussion of conflicting statements about Pankejeff's age at the time of the infection, see Mahony, *The Wolf Man.*, p. 20n.

46 "The Memoirs of the Wolf-Man," pp. 83, 138.

47 Freud, "Remembering, Repeating and Working-Through (Further Recommendations on the Technique of Psycho-Analysis II)" (1914), in *SE* 12: 153.

48 Freud, "History of an Infantile Neurosis," pp. 70, 21, 27, 26, 28.
49 Ibid., pp. 24, 25, 45n, 46, 47.
50 Freud, *Inhibitions, Symptoms and Anxiety* (1926), in *SE* 20: 108.
51 Freud, "History of an Infantile Neurosis," pp. 16, 32.
52 Brunswick, "Supplement," pp. 265, 297.
53 Ibid., p. 264.
54 Ibid., p. 265.
55 Ibid., pp. 264, 283, 284 (emphasis in the original).
56 Ibid., p. 284. In 1919 Freud—and later Brunswick as well— treated Pankejeff without charge and Freud collected a sum of money for him for the following six years.
57 Ibid., p. 266.
58 See Muriel Gardiner, "The Wolf-Man in Later Life," in Gardiner, ed., *The Wolf-Man by the Wolf-Man*, p. 364.
59 Helene Deutsch, *Confrontations with Myself: An Epilogue* (New York: Norton, 1973), p. 133.
60 Brunswick, "Supplement," pp. 284–285.
61 Ibid., pp. 288–289 (emphasis in the original).
62 Ibid., p. 290.
63 Ibid., p. 291.
64 Ibid., p. 296.
65 For Pankejeff's later career, see Gardiner, "The Wolf-Man in Later Life," pp. 311–366, and Karin Obholzer, *The Wolf-Man Sixty Years Later: Conversations with Freud's Controversial Patient*, trans. Michael Shaw (London: Routledge and Kegan Paul, 1982); see also Muriel Gardiner, *Code Name "Mary": Memoirs of an American Woman in the Austrian Underground* (New Haven: Yale University Press, 1983), pp. 120–122.
66 Brunswick, "Supplement," pp. 306, 280. The publication of Brunswick's account sparked a discussion of whether or not Pankejeff had recovered any new childhood material during his analysis with her: see J. Hárnik, "Kritisches über Mack Brunswicks Nachtrag zu Freuds 'Geschichte einer infantilen Neurose,' " *Internationale Zeitschrift für Psychoanalyse* 16 (1930): 123–127; Ruth Mack Brunswick, "Entgegnung auf Hániks Bemerkungen," *Internationale Zeitschrift für Psychoanalyse* 16 (1930): 128–129; J. Hárnik, "Erwiderung auf Mack Brunswicks Entgegnung," *Internationale Zeitschrift für Psychoanalyse* 17 (1931): 400–402; Ruth Mack Brunswick, "Schlusswort," *Internationale Zeitschrift für Psychoanalyse* 17(1931): 402.
67 Brunswick wrote short and incomplete accounts of further periods of analysis Pankejeff had with her in the early 1930s. In these brief stints, she discovered remnants of transference to herself as well as new material concerning his childhood nurse. See Ruth Mack Brunswick Research Materials, Muriel Gardiner Papers, Freud Collection, Library of Congress.
68 Brunswick, "Supplement," p. 292.
69 *The Writings of Melanie Klein*, vol. 2, *The Psycho-Analysis of Children*, trans. Alix Strachey (London: Hogarth Press, 1975), pp. 159, 179. When, in her 1946 paper, Klein returned to the subject of paranoid anxieties, she mentioned their connection with homosexuality only in a footnote: see Klein, "Notes on Some Schizoid Mechanisms," p. 12n1.
70 Klein, "Notes on Some Schizoid Mechanisms," p. 1.
71 Freud, "Psycho-Analytic Notes on . . . a Case of Paranoia," p. 68.
72 Ibid., p. 70.
73 Klein, "Notes on Some Schizoid Mechanisms," p. 23.

74 Freud, *An Outline of Psycho-Analysis* (1940), in *SE* 23: 203.

75 Freud, "Splitting of the Ego in the Process of Defense" (1940), in *SE* 23: 276.

76 Klein, "Notes on Some Schizoid Mechanisms," pp. 6, 10.

77 Ibid., pp. 6, 8, 10 (emphasis in the original).

78 Freud, "Analysis Terminable and Interminable," p. 235.

79 W. R. Bion, "Differentiation of the Psychotic from the Non-Psychotic Personalities" (1957), in W. R. Bion, *Second Thoughts: Selected Papers on Psycho-Analysis* (London: Heinemann, 1967; reprint, London, Karnac, Maresfield Library, 1984), p. 47.

80 Ibid. p. 47.

81 W. R. Bion, "Development of Schizophrenic Thought" (1956), in *Second Thoughts*, p. 42.

82 W. R. Bion, "On Hallucination" (1958), in *Second Thoughts*, p. 65. For helpful commentary, see Donald Meltzer, *The Kleinian Development: Part III, The Clinical Significance of the Work of Bion* (Perthshire: Clunie Press, 1978); see also Rafael E. López-Corvo, *The Dictionary of the Work of W. R. Bion* (London: Karnac, 2003).

83 Bion, "On Hallucination," pp. 65–66, 68, 71, 72.

84 Ibid., pp. 72,73, 74–77.

85 Bion, "Differentiation of the Psychotic from the Non-Psychotic Personalities," pp. 61, 62–63.

86 W. R. Bion, "On Arrogance" (1958), in *Second Thoughts*, p. 88.

87 Klein, "Notes on Some Schizoid Mechanisms," p. 8.

88 W. R. Bion, "Attacks on Linking" (1959), in *Second Thoughts*, p. 103.

89 Ibid., pp. 103–104.

90 See Melanie Klein, "The Rôle of the School in the Libidinal Development of the Child" (1923), in *The Writings of Melanie Klein*, vol. 1, *Love, Guilt and Reparation and Other Works 1921–1945* (London: Hogarth Press, 1975), pp. 59–76; Melanie Klein, "The Importance of Symbol-Formation in the Development of the Ego" (1930), in ibid., pp. 219–232; Melanie Klein, "The Psychotherapy of the Psychoses" (1930), in ibid., pp. 233–235; Melanie Klein, "A Contribution to the Theory of Intellectual Inhibition" (1931), in ibid., pp. 236–247.

91 Bion, "Attacks on Linking," p. 108.

92 Paula Heimann, "Counter-transference" (1960), in Paula Heimann, *About Children and Children No-Longer: Collected Papers 1942–1980*, ed. Margaret Tonnesmann (London and New York: Tavistock/Routledge, 1989), p. 151.

93 Freud, "The Disposition to Obsessional Neurosis: A Contribution to the Problem of Choice of Neurosis" (1913), in *SE* 12: 320.

94 Paula Heimann, "On Counter-transference" (1950), in Heimann, *About Children and Children No-Longer*, p. 74.

95 Freud, "Recommendations to Physicians Practicing Psycho-Analysis" (1912), in *SE* 12, 111–112; see also Freud, "Two Encyclopaedia Articles" (1923), in *SE* 18: 239.

96 Heimann, "On Counter-transference," p. 75.

97 Ibid., pp. 75, 76.

98 Ibid., pp. 76, 77.

99 Ibid., p. 77.

100 Ibid., pp. 77–78.

101 Heinrich Racker, *Transference and Countertransference* (London: Hogarth Press, 1969; reprint, London: Maresfield Library, 1985), pp. 161, 164. See Kevin V. Kelly, "Classics Revisited: Heinrich Racker's *Transference and Countertransference*," *JAPA* 45 (1997): 1253–1259.

102 Heimann, "On Counter-transference," p. 78.

103 Sándor Ferenczi, "Confusion of Tongues between Adults and the Child (The Language of Tenderness and the Language of [Sexual] Passion)," trans. Jeffrey M. Masson and Marianne Loring, in Jeffrey Moussaieff Masson, *The Assault on Truth: Freud's Suppression of the Seduction Theory* (New York: Farrar, Straus and Giroux, 1984), p. 285.

104 Racker, *Transference and Countertransference*, pp. 165, 131.

105 Ibid., p. 72.

106 Ibid., pp.152–154.

107 Ibid., pp. 154, 155, 156, 158.

108 Betty Joseph, "The Patient Who Is Difficult to Reach" (1975), in Betty Joseph, *Psychic Equilibrium and Psychic Change: Selected Papers of Betty Joseph*, ed. Michael Feldman and Elizabeth Bott Spillius (London and New York: Routledge, 1989), pp. 75, 82.

109 Betty Joseph, "On Understanding and Not Understanding: Some Technical Issues" (1983), in *Psychic Equilibrium*, pp. 146–147.

110 Ibid., pp. 145–146.

111 Betty Joseph, "Transference: The Total Situation" (1985), in *Psychic Equilibrium*, pp. 157–158.

112 Joseph, "On Understanding and Not Understanding," p. 147.

113 Joseph, "Transference: The Total Situation," p. 158.

114 Joseph, "On Understanding and Not Understanding," p. 147.

115 Joseph, "The Patient Who Is Difficult to Reach," p. 76.

116 Joseph, "On Understanding and Not Understanding," pp. 142–143.

117 Ibid., pp. 143, 144.

118 Klein, "Envy and Gratitude," pp. 232, 226.

119 Freud, *An Outline of Psycho-Analysis*, pp. 201–202.

120 Freud, *New Introductory Lectures on Psycho-Analysis* (1933), in *SE* 22: 85.

121 See Klein, "Notes on Some Schizoid Mechanisms," pp. 2n1, 3–4. For an account of Fairbairn's work, see Judith M. Hughes, *Reshaping the Psychoanalytic Domain: The Work of Melanie Klein, W. R. D. Fairbairn, and D. W. Winnicott* (Berkeley: University of California Press, 1989), ch. 4.

122 See, for example, Joseph Sandler, "The Concept of Projective Identification," in Joseph Sandler, ed., *Projection, Identification, Projective Identification* (Madison, CT: International Universities Press, 1987), p. 20.

123 Elizabeth Bott Spillius, "Clinical Experiences of Projective Identification," in Robin Anderson, ed., *Clinical Lectures on Klein and Bion* (London and New York: Tavistock/Routledge, 1992), p. 61.

124 Elizabeth Bott Spillius, "General Introduction," in Elizabeth Bott Spillius, ed., *Melanie Klein Today: Developments in Theory and Practice*, vol. 2, *Mainly Practice* (London and New York: Routledge, 1988), p. 10 (emphasis in the original).

125 Spillius, "Clinical Experiences of Projective Identification," p. 61.

126 See Racker, *Transference and Countertransference*, pp. 65–66.

127 Joseph, "On Understanding and Not Understanding," p. 148.

128 Betty Joseph, "Psychic Change and the Psychoanalytic Process" (1989), in *Psychic Equilibrium*, p. 198.

5 Narcissism: Megalomania

  1 Freud, "On Narcissism: An Introduction" (1914), in *SE* 14: 73. For helpful commentary, see Sydney E. Pulver, "Narcissism: The Term and the Concept," *JAPA* 18 (1970): 319–340, and David L. Smith, "Freud's Developmental Approach to Narcissism: A Concise Review," *IJP* 66 (1985): 489–497.

2 Freud, "On Narcissism," pp. 74, 75.

3 Freud, *Introductory Lectures On Psycho-Analysis* (1916–1917), in *SE* 16: 445, 447.

4 See, for example, ibid., p. 438.

5 For biographical information on Kohut, see Charles B. Strozier, *Heinz Kohut: The Making of a Psychoanalyst* (New York: Farrar, Straus and Giroux, 2001). See also Douglas Kirsner, "Self Psychology and the Psychoanalytic Movement: An Interview with Dr. Heinz Kohut," *Psychoanalysis and Contemporary Thought* 5 (1982): 483–495.

6 Strozier, *Heinz Kohut*, pp. 21, 22.

7 Ibid., pp. 75, 115.

8 Ibid., pp. 82, 80.

9 John E. Gedo, *Spleen and Nostalgia: A Life and Work in Psychoanalysis* (Northvale, NJ: Jason Aronson, 1997), p. 152 (emphasis in the original).

10 Strozier, *Heinz Kohut*, pp. 243, 266.

11 See, for example, Judith M. Hughes, *From Freud's Consulting Room: The Unconscious in a Scientific Age* (Cambridge, MA: Harvard University Press, 1994), pp. 127–146.

12 For a discussion of Kohut as Mr Z, see editor's introduction to Heinz Kohut, *The Curve of Life: The Correspondence of Heinz Kohut 1923–1981*, ed. Geoffrey Cocks (Chicago: University of Chicago Press, 1994), pp. 4–6, and Strozier, *Heinz Kohut*, pp. 308–316.

13 Otto Kernberg, interview with the author, December 20, 2001.

14 Ibid., and John Sutherland, interview with the author, March 31, 1981.

15 Robert S. Wallerstein, review of *Severe Personality Disorders: Psychotherapeutic Strategies*, by Otto F. Kernberg, *JAPA* 34 (1986): 711; see also Salman Akhtar, "Kernberg and Kohut: A Critical Comparison," in Douglas W. Detrick and Susan P. Detrick, eds., *Self Psychology: Comparisons and Contrasts* (Hillsdale, NJ: Analytic Press, 1989), pp. 329–362.

16 For biographical information on Rosenfeld, see Herbert Rosenfeld, *Impasse and Interpretation: Therapeutic and Anti-Therapeutic Factors in the Psychoanalytic Treatment of Psychotic, Borderline, and Neurotic Patients* (London and New York: Tavistock Publications, 1987), pp. 4–27; see also Hanna Segal and Riccardo Steiner, "Obituary: H. A. Rosenfeld (1910–1986)," *IJP* 68 (1987): 415–419, and Janet Sayers, *Kleinians: Psychoanalysis Inside Out* (Oxford: Polity Press, 2000), pp. 91–110.

17 Herbert A. Rosenfeld, interview with the author, October 15, 1985. Using clinical material from his control case, Rosenfeld published his first psychoanalytic paper: "Analysis of a Schizophrenic State with Depersonalization" (1947), in Herbert A. Rosenfeld, *Psychotic States: A Psycho-Analytical Approach* (London: Hogarth Press, 1965; reprint, London: Karnac, Maresfield Library, 1982), pp. 13–33.

18 Heinz Kohut, "The Two Analyses of Mr Z," *IJP* 60 (1979): 10. This paper has been reprinted in Heinz Kohut, *The Search for the Self*, vol. 4, *Selected Writings of Heinz Kohut: 1978–1981*, ed. Paul H. Ornstein (Madison, CT: International Universities Press, 1991), pp. 395–446. Kohut's biographer noted that between 1965 and 1970, Kohut's mother "was becoming a special burden; her mental state raised questions whether she could . . . continue to live alone; in the end, it was only her failing health and a stroke that allowed Kohut to have her committed" to a nursing home: Strozier, *Heinz Kohut*, p. 160.

19 Kohut, "The Two Analyses of Mr Z," p. 5.

20 Ibid., pp. 5, 8–9 (emphasis in the original).

21 Ibid., pp. 15–16.

22 Ibid., pp. 13, 14, 15, 16.

23 Ibid., pp. 15, 18.

24 Ibid., pp. 19, 20, 21, 22.

25 Ibid., pp. 22, 23.

26 Anna Freud to Kohut, January 4, 1966, *Curve of Life*, p. 133.

27 Kohut to Anna Freud, July 9, 1980, ibid., pp. 409–410.

28 I have found the following accounts of Kohut's work particularly helpful: Allen M. Siegel, *Heinz Kohut and the Psychology of the Self* (London and New York: Routledge, 1996), and Phil Mollon, *Releasing the Self: The Healing Legacy of Heinz Kohut* (London: Whurr, 2001).

29 Heinz Kohut, "Forms and Transformations of Narcissism," *JAPA* 14 (1966): 243–244. This paper has been reprinted in Heinz Kohut, *The Search for the Self*, vol., 1, *Selected Writings of Heinz Kohut: 1950–1978*, ed. Paul H. Ornstein (New York: International Universities Press, 1978), pp. 427–460.

30 Kohut, "Forms and Transformations of Narcissism," p. 246.

31 Kohut to Anna Freud, January 4, 1966, *Curve of Life*, p. 175.

32 See Heinz Kohut, *The Analysis of the Self: A Systematic Approach to the Psychoanalytic Treatment of Narcissistic Personality Disorders* (New York: International Universities Press, 1971), p. 26.

33 Kohut to Anna Freud, September 27, 1967, *Curve of Life*, p. 178.

34 Kohut, *Analysis of the Self*, pp. 57–61.

35 Ibid., pp. 126, 81–82, 121, 85 (emphasis in the original).

36 Ibid., p. 82. Kohut distinguished between a genetic and an etiological approach, the first relating to the "subjective psychological experiences," and the second to "objectively ascertainable factors." His work addressed the first, not the second: ibid., p. 254*n*3.

37 Ibid., p. 70.

38 Heinz Kohut, *The Restoration of the Self* (New York: International Universities Press, 1977), pp. 126–127.

39 Heinz Kohut, "Thoughts on Narcissism and Narcissistic Rage," *The Psychoanalytic Study of the Child* 27 (1972): 370. This paper has been reprinted in Heinz Kohut, *The Search for the Self*, vol. 2, *Selected Writings of Heinz Kohut: 1950–1978*, ed. Paul H. Ornstein (New York: International Universities Press, 1978), pp. 615–658.

40 Kohut, *Analysis of the Self*, p. 127.

41 Kohut, "Thoughts on Narcissism and Narcissistic Rage," pp. 386, 380.

42 Kohut, *Restoration of the Self*, p. 123.

43 See Heinz Hartmann, "Comments on the Psychoanalytic Theory of the Ego" (1950), in Heinz Hartmann, *Essays on Ego Psychology: Selected Problems in Psychoanalytic Theory* (New York: International Universities Press, 1964), p. 127.

44 Kohut, *The Restoration of the Self*, p. 99.

45 Kohut, "Forms and Transformations of Narcissism," p. 243.

46 Kohut, *Analysis of the Self*, pp. 260, 261–262, 37, 27 (emphasis in the original).

47 Ibid., p. 267.

48 Ibid., pp. 283, 284–286, 116, 287.

49 Ibid., pp. 285, 287, 288.

50 See Morris N. Eagle, *Recent Developments in Psychoanalysis: A Critical Evaluation* (New York: McGraw Hill, 1984), p. 70.

51 Heinz Kohut, *How Does Analysis Cure?* ed. Arnold Goldberg (Chicago: University of Chicago Press, 1984), pp. 77–78.

52 In his last book, Kohut added the twinship or alter ego transference to the category of selfobject transferences. He characterized it as the search for "a

selfobject that will make itself available for the reassuring experience of essential likeness": ibid., p. 193.

53 Heinz Kohut and Ernest S. Wolf, "The Disorders of the Self and Their Treatment: An Outline," *IJP* 59 (1978): 416. This paper has been reprinted in Heinz Kohut, *The Search for the Self*, vol. 3, *Selected Writings of Heinz Kohut: 1978–1981*, ed. Paul H. Ornstein (Madison, CT: International Universities Press, 1990), pp. 359–385.

54 For a summary of Mahler's work, see Margaret S. Mahler, Fred Pine, and Anni Bergman, *The Psychological Birth of the Human Infant: Symbiosis and Individuation* (New York: Basic Books, 1975). For Kernberg's account of Mahler's work, see Otto F. Kernberg, *Internal World and External Reality: Object Relations Theory Applied* (New York: Jason Aronson, 1980), ch. 6.

55 For reviews of Kernberg's enterprise, see Victor Calef and Edward R. Weinshel, "The New Psychoanalysis and Psychoanalytic Revisionism—Book Review Essay on *Borderline Conditions and Pathological Narcissism*," *The Psychoanalytic Quarterly* 48 (1979): 470–491; Nathan P. Segel, review of *Borderline Conditions and Pathological Narcissism*, by Otto F. Kernberg, *JAPA* 29 (1981): 221–236; Milton Klein and David Tribich, "Kernberg's Object-Relations Theory: A Critical Evaluation," *IJP* 62 (1981): 27–43; Wallerstein, review of *Severe Personality Disorders: Psychotherapeutic Strategies*, by Otto Kernberg, pp. 711–722. See also Michael Robbins, "Current Controversy in Object Relations Theory as Outgrowth of Schism Between Klein and Fairbairn," *IJP* 61 (1980): 477–492.

56 Otto F. Kernberg, "The Contributions of Edith Jacobson: An Overview," *JAPA* 27 (1979): 804–806; see also Kernberg, *Internal World and External Reality*, ch. 2. For Jacobson herself, see Edith Jacobson, *The Self and the Object World* (New York: International Universities Press, 1964). This monograph was an expansion of an earlier paper: "The Self and the Object World—Vicissitudes of their Infantile Cathexes and their Influence on Ideational and Affective Development," *The Psychoanalytic Study of the Child* 9 (1954): 75–127.

57 See Otto F. Kernberg, *Object Relations Theory and Clinical Psychoanalysis* (New York: Jason Aronson, 1976), ch. 2.

58 Kernberg, *Object Relations Theory and Clinical Psychoanalysis*, p. 67.

59 Otto F. Kernberg, *Borderline Conditions and Pathological Narcissism* (New York: Jason Aronson, 1975), pp. 331, 265, 234.

60 Ibid., pp. 265–266, 231–232.

61 Otto Kernberg, *Severe Personality Disorders: Psychotherapeutic Strategies* (New Haven: Yale University Press, 1984), pp. 193, 194.

62 Ibid., p. 194.

63 Kernberg, *Borderline Conditions and Pathological Narcissism*, p. 269.

64 Ibid., p. 299.

65 Ibid., pp. 332, 266, 286.

66 Ibid., pp. 289–290.

67 Ibid., p. 291.

68 Ibid., pp. 310, 311.

69 Kernberg, *Severe Personality Disorders*, p. 212 (emphasis in the original).

70 Ibid., p. 212.

71 Ibid., pp. 212, 213.

72 Ibid., p. 214.

73 Ibid., p. 215.

74 Ibid., p. 217.

75 See Kernberg, *Borderline Conditions and Pathological Narcissism*, p. 304.

76 See Kernberg, *Internal World and External Reality*, p. 107.

77 John D. Sutherland, "Object-Relations Theory and the Conceptual Model of Psychoanalysis," *British Journal of Medical Psychology* 86 (1963): 109.

78 Betty Joseph, "The Patient Who Is Difficult to Reach" (1975), in Betty Joseph, *Psychic Equilibrium and Psychic Change: Selected Papers of Betty Joseph*, ed. Michael Feldman and Elizabeth Bott Spillius (London and New York: Routledge, 1989), pp. 75, 76. Contrast Kernberg's remarks about the therapeutic alliance: "It is important to keep in mind that, except in the most severe cases of narcissistic personality, there are certain normal ego functions which are maintained and certain realistic aspects of the self-concept which continue in existence, side-by-side with the grandiose self. These, of course, constitute the basis for the establishment of a therapeutic alliance, and the related capacity to really listen to the analyst and to identify with him in thinking psychologically about himself." Kernberg, *Borderline Conditions and Pathological Narcissism*, p. 289.

79 Herbert A. Rosenfeld, "On the Psychology of Narcissism: A Clinical Approach" (1964), in *Psychotic States*, pp. 172–173, 178.

80 Ibid., p. 170.

81 Herbert Rosenfeld, "A Clinical Approach to the Psychoanalytic Theory of the Life and Death Instincts: An Investigation Into the Aggressive Aspects of Narcissism," *IJP* 52 (1971): 176–177.

82 Freud, "Notes upon a Case of Obsessional Neurosis" (1909), in *SE* 10: 233.

83 Rosenfeld, *Impasse and Interpretation*, pp. 20–21.

84 Ibid., p. 174.

85 Ibid., p. 174.

86 John Steiner, *Psychic Retreats: Pathological Organizations in Psychotic, Neurotic and Borderline Patients* (London and New York: Routledge, 1993), pp. 103–104.

87 John Steiner, interview with the author, June 25, 2001. See also John Steiner, "The Psychoanalytic Contribution of Herbert Rosenfeld," *IJP* 70 (1989): 611–617.

88 Rosenfeld, "A Clinical Approach to the Psychoanalytic Theory of the Life and Death Instincts," p. 173.

89 Rosenfeld, *Impasse and Interpretation*, pp. 88, 148.

90 See John Steiner, "Perverse Relationships Between Parts of the Self: A Clinical Illustration," *IJP* 63 (1982): 241–251. Steiner used this paper as the basis for Chapter 9 of his book, *Psychic Retreats*.

91 Steiner, *Psychic Retreats*, pp. 105, 106.

92 Ibid., p. 107 (emphasis in the original).

93 Steiner, "Perverse Relationships Between Parts of the Self," p. 246 (emphasis in the original).

94 Steiner, *Psychic Retreats*, p. 109.

95 Ibid., p. 112.

96 See ibid., p. 115.

97 Joan Riviere, "A Contribution to the Analysis of the Negative Therapeutic Reaction" (1936), in Joan Riviere, *The Inner World and Joan Riviere: Collected Papers 1920–1958*, ed. Athol Hughes (London: Karnac, 1991), p. 138.

98 John Steiner, "Some Reflections on the Analysis of Transference: A Kleinian View," *Psychoanalytic Inquiry* 4 (1984): 459. See also David Tuckett, "A Brief View of Herbert Rosenfeld's Contribution to the Theory of Psychoanalytical Technique," *IJP* 70 (1989): 619–625, and Roy Schafer, "The Contemporary Kleinians of London," *The Psychoanalytic Quarterly* 63 (1994): 409–432.

99 Rosenfeld, *Impasse and Interpretation*, p. 32.

100 Freud, *Introductory Lectures*, p. 447.

Conclusion

1 Paul Robinson, *Freud and His Critics* (Berkeley: University of California Press, 1993), p. 270.
2 Paul Robinson, *Opera, Sex, and Other Vital Matters* (Chicago: University of Chicago Press, 2002), p. 245.
3 Freud, *The Question of Lay Analysis: Conversations with an Impartial Person* (1926), in *SE* 20: 248.
4 Freud, "Fragment of an Analysis of a Case of Hysteria" (1905), in *SE* 7: 12.
5 Sándor Ferenczi, "Contra-indications to the 'Active' Psycho-Analytical Technique" (1925), in Sándor Ferenczi, *Further Contributions to the Theory and Technique of Psycho-Analysis*, ed. John Rickman, trans. Jane Isabel Suttie (London: Hogarth Press, 1951; reprint, London: Karnac, Maresfield Library, 1980), p. 220.
6 Freud, "Remembering, Repeating and Working-Through (Further Recommendations on the Technique of Psycho-Analysis II)" (1914), in *SE* 12: 147.
7 Freud to Fliess, October 27, 1897, *The Complete Letters of Sigmund Freud to Wilhelm Fliess 1887–1904*, trans. and ed. Jeffrey Moussaieff Masson (Cambridge, MA: Harvard University Press, 1985), p. 274.
8 Klein, "Mourning and its Relation to Manic-Depressive States" (1940), in *The Writings of Melanie Klein*, vol. 1, *Love, Guilt and Reparation and Other Works 1921–1945*, under the general editorship of Roger Money-Kyrle, in collaboration with Betty Joseph, Edna O'Shaughnessy, and Hanna Segal (London: Hogarth Press, 1975), pp. 362–363.
9 Melanie Klein, "The Origins of Transference" (1952), in *The Writings of Melanie Klein*, vol. 3, *Envy and Gratitude and Other Works 1946–1963* (London: Hogarth Press, 1975), p. 55.
10 Joan Riviere, "A Contribution to the Analysis of the Negative Therapeutic Reaction" (1936), in Joan Riviere, *The Inner World and Joan Riviere: Collected Papers 1920–1958*, ed. Athol Hughes (London: Karnac, 1991), p. 152.
11 Freud, *New Introductory Lectures on Psycho-Analysis* (1933), in *SE* 22: 85.
12 Betty Joseph, "Transference: The Total Situation" (1985), in Betty Joseph, *Psychic Equilibrium and Psychic Change: Selected Papers of Betty Joseph*, ed. Michael Feldman and Elizabeth Bott Spillius (London and New York: Routledge, 1989), p. 157.
13 Betty Joseph, "Psychic Change and the Psychoanalytic Process" (1989), in *Psychic Equilibrium*, p. 198.
14 Freud, *Introductory Lectures on Psycho-Analysis* (1916–1917), in *SE* 16: 447.
15 Riviere, "Negative Therapeutic Reaction," p. 137.

Selected bibliography

Abraham, Nicolas, and Maria Torok. *The Wolf Man's Magic Word: A Cryptonymy.* Translated by Nicholas Rand. Minneapolis: University of Minnesota Press, 1986.

Abraham, Karl. *Selected Papers of Karl Abraham.* Translated by Douglas Bryan and Alix Strachey. London: Hogarth Press, 1927. Reprint, London: Karnac, Maresfield Library, 1979.

Aguayo, Joseph. "Patronage and the Dispute over Child Analysis between Melanie Klein and Anna Freud–1927–1932." *IJP* 81 (2000): 733–752.

Alexander, Franz. "A Metapsychological Description of the Process of Cure." *IJP* 6 (1925): 13–34.

——. Review of *Entwicklungsziele der Psychanalyse*, by Sándor Ferenczi and Otto Rank. *IJP* 6 (1925): 484–496.

——. "On Ferenczi's Relaxation Principle." *IJP* 14 (1933): 182–192.

Alexander, Franz, Samuel Eisenstein, and Martin Grotjahn, eds. *Psychoanalytic Pioneers.* New York: Basic Books, 1966.

Anderson, Robin, ed. *Clinical Lectures on Klein and Bion.* London and New York: Tavistock/Routledge, 1992.

Andersson, Ola. *Studies in the Prehistory of Psychoanalysis: The Etiology of Psychoneuroses and Some Related Themes in Sigmund Freud's Scientific Writings and Letters 1886–1896.* Norstedts: Svenska Bokförlaget, 1962.

——. "A Supplement to Freud's Case of 'Frau Emmy von N.' in Studies on Hysteria 1895." *Scandinavian Psychoanalytic Review* 2 (1979): 5–16.

Andreas-Salomé, Lou. *The Freud Journal of Lou Andreas-Salomé.* Translated by Stanley A. Leavy. New York: Basic Books, 1964.

Anzieu, Didier. "Comment devient-on Melanie Klein?" *Nouvelle Revue de Psychanalyse* 26 (1982): 235–251.

——. *Freud's Self-Analysis.* Translated by Peter Graham. London: Hogarth Press, 1986.

Apfelbaum, Bernard. "On Ego Psychology: A Critique of the Structural Approach to Psycho-Analytic Theory." *IJP* 47 (1966): 451–475.

Appignanesi, Lisa, and John Forrester. *Freud's Women.* New York: Basic Books, 1992.

Arlow, Jacob A. "Discussion of Paper by Mark Kanzer: The Therapeutic and Working Alliances." *International Journal of Psychoanalytic Psychotherapy* 4 (1975): 69–73.

Arlow, Jacob A., and Charles Brenner. *Psychoanalytic Concepts and the Structural Theory*. New York: International Universities Press, 1964.

Aron, Lewis. "From Ferenczi to Searles and Contemporary Relational Approaches." *Psychoanalytic Dialogues* 2 (1992): 181–190.

Aron, Lewis, and Adrienne Harris, eds. *The Legacy of Sándor Ferenczi*. Hillsdale, NJ: Analytic Press, 1993.

Asch, Stuart S. "Varieties of Negative Therapeutic Reaction and Problems of Technqiue." *JAPA* 24 (1976): 383–407.

Bacal, Howard A., and Kenneth M. Newman. *Theories of Object Relations: Bridges to Self Psychology*. New York: Columbia University Press, 1990.

Balint, Michael. *Primary Love and Psycho-Analytic Technique*. London: Hogarth, 1952. Reprint, London: Karnac, Maresfield Library, 1985.

——. *Problems of Human Pleasure and Behaviour*. London: Hogarth Press, 1957. Reprint, London: Karnac, Maresfield Library, 1987.

——. *Thrills and Regressions*. London: Hogarth Press; New York: International Universities Press, 1959.

——. "The Regressed Patient and His Analyst." *Psychiatry* 23 (1960): 231–243.

——. *The Doctor, His Patient and the Illness*. 2nd ed. London: Pitman Medical Publishing, 1964. Reprint, Edinburgh: Churchill Livingstone, 1986.

——. *The Basic Fault: Therapeutic Aspects of Regression*. London: Tavistock Publications, 1968. Reprint, London and New York: Tavistock Publications, 1979.

——. "Trauma and Object Relationship." *IJP* 50 (1969): 429–435.

Balint, Michael, Enid Balint, Robert Gosling, and Peter Hildebrand. *A Study of Doctors: Mutual Selection and the Evaluation of the Results in a Training Programme for Family Doctors*. London: Tavistock Publications, 1966.

Balint, Michael, John Hunt, Dick Joyce, Marshall Marinker, and Jasper Woodcock. *Treatment or Diagnosis: A Study of Repeat Prescriptions in General Practice*. London: Tavistock Publications, 1970.

Balint, Michael, and Sidney Tarachow. "General Concepts and Theory of Psychoanalytic Therapy." *The Annual Survey of Psychoanalysis* 1 (1950): 227–240.

Balter, Leon, and James H. Spencer, Jr. "Observation and Theory in Psychoanalysis: The Self Psychology of Heinz Kohut." *The Psychoanalytic Quarterly* 60 (1991): 361–395.

Barande, Ilse. *Sándor Ferenczi*. Paris: Payot, 1972.

Baumeyer, Franz. "The Schreber Case." *IJP* 37 (1956): 61–74.

Beigler, Jerome S. "A Commentary on Freud's Treatment of the Rat Man." *Annual of Psychoanalysis* 3 (1975): 271–285.

Bergmann, Martin S., and Frank R. Hartman. *The Evolution of Psychoanalytic Technique*. New York: Basic Books, 1976.

Bernheimer, Charles, and Claire Kahane, eds. *In Dora's Case: Freud–Hysteria–Feminism*. New York: Columbia University Press, 1985.

Berrios, German A. *The History of Mental Symptoms: Descriptive Psychopathology since the Nineteenth Century*. Cambridge: Cambridge University Press, 1996.

Bertin, Celia. *Marie Bonaparte: A Life*. New York: Harcourt Brace Jovanovich, 1982.

Bettelheim, Bruno. *Freud and Man's Soul*. New York: Knopf, 1982.

Bion, Francesca, Hanna Segal, Isabel Menzies Lyth, and Donald Meltzer. "Memorial Meeting for Dr. Wilfred Bion." *The International Review of Psycho-Analysis* 8 (1981): 3–14.

Bion, Wilfred R. *Experience in Groups and Other Papers*. London: Tavistock Publications, 1961.

——. *Learning from Experience*. London: Heinemann, 1962. Reprint, London: Karnac, Maresfield Library, 1984.

——. *Elements of Psycho-Analysis*. London: Heinemann, 1963. Reprint, London: Karnac, Maresfield Library, 1984.

——. *Transformations*. London: Heinemann, 1965. Reprint, London: Karnac, Maresfield Library, 1984.

——. *Second Thoughts: Selected Papers on Psycho-Analysis*. London: Heinemann, 1967. Reprint, London: Karnac, Maresfield Library, 1984.

——. *Attention and Interpretation*. London: Tavistock Publications, 1970. Reprint, London: Karnac, Maresfield Library, 1984.

——. *The Long Week-End 1897–1919: Part of a Life*. Edited by Francesca Bion. Abingdon: Fleetwood Press, 1982.

——. *All My Sins Remembered: Another Part of a Life and the Other Side of Genius: Family Letters*. Edited by Francesca Bion. Abingdon: Fleetwood Press, 1985.

——. *Taming Wild Thoughts*. Edited by Francesca Bion. London: Karnac, 1997.

——. *War Memoirs 1917–1919*. Edited by Francesca Bion. London: Karnac, 1997.

Bird, Brian. "Notes on Transference: Universal Phenomenon and Hardest Part of Analysis." *JAPA* 20 (1972): 267–301.

Blacker, K. H., and Ruth Abraham. "The Rat Man Revisited: Comments on Maternal Influences." *The International Journal of Psychoanalytic Psychotherapy* 9 (1982): 705–727.

Blanton, Smiley. *Diary of My Analysis with Sigmund Freud*. New York: Hawthorn, 1971.

Bléandonu, Gérard. *Wilfred Bion: His Life and Works 1897–1979*. Translated by Claire Pajaczkowska. London: Free Association Books, 1994.

Blum, Harold P. "On the Conception and Development of the Transference Neurosis." *JAPA* 19 (1971): 41–53.

——. "Theories of Self and Psychoanalytic Concepts: Discussion." *JAPA* 30 (1982): 959–978.

——. "The Position and Value of Extratransference Interpretations." *JAPA* 31 (1983): 587–617.

——. "The Confusion of Tongues and Psychic Trauma." *IJP* (1994): 871–882.

Bollas, Christopher. *Hysteria*. London and New York: Routledge, 2000.

Bonomi, Carlo. "Flight into Sanity: Jones's Allegations of Ferenczi's Mental Deterioration Reconsidered." *IJP* 80 (1999): 507–542.

Boor, Clemens de, and Emma Moersch. "Emmy von N.—eine Hysterie?" *Psyche* 34 (1980): 265–279.

Borch-Jacobsen, Mikkel. *The Freudian Subject*. Translated by Catherine Porter. Stanford, CA: Stanford University Press, 1988.

Bornstein, Berta. "The Analysis of a Phobic Child—Some Problems of Theory and Technique in Child Analysis." *The Psychoanalytic Study of the Child* 3 (1949): 181–226.

Brenner, Charles. "Working Alliance, Therapeutic Alliance, and Transference." *JAPA* 27 (Suppl.) (1979): 137–157.

——. *The Mind in Conflict*. New York: International Universities Press, 1982.

Breuer, Josef, and Sigmund Freud. *Studies on Hysteria* (1895). In *SE*, vol. 2.

Brierley, Marjorie. *Trends in Psycho-Analysis*. London: Hogarth Press, 1951.

Britton, Ronald. *Belief and Imagination: Explorations in Psychoanalysis*. London and New York: Routledge, 1988.

Britton, Ronald, Michael Feldman, and Edna O'Shaughnessy. *The Oedipus Complex Today: Clinical Implications*. London: Karnac, 1989.

Brome, Vincent. *Freud and His Early Circle: The Struggles of Psycho-Analysis*. London: Heinemann, 1967.

——. *Ernest Jones: Freud's Alter Ego*. New York: Norton, 1983.

Brooks, Peter. *Reading for the Plot: Design and Intention in Narrative*. New York: Knopf, 1984.

——. *Psychoanalysis and Storytelling*. Oxford: Blackwell, 1994.

Brunswick, Ruth Mack. "A Supplement to Freud's 'History of an Infantile Neurosis' " (1928). In *The Wolf-Man by the Wolf-Man*, edited by Muriel Gardiner. New York: Basic Books, 1971.

——. "Entgegnung auf Hárniks Bemerkungen." *Internationale Zeitschrift für Psychoanalyse* 16 (1930): 128–129.

——. "Schlusswort." *Internationale Zeitschrift für Psychoanalyse* 17 (1931): 402.

——. "The Preoedipal Phase of the Libido Development" (1940). In *The Psycho-analytic Reader: An Anthology of Essential Papers with Critical Introductions*, edited by Robert Fliess. New York: International Universities Press, 1948.

——. Research Materials. Muriel Gardiner Papers, Freud Collection, Library of Congress.

Buckley, Peter. "Fifty Years After Freud: Dora, The Rat Man, and the Wolf Man." *American Journal of Psychiatry* 146 (1989): 1394–1403.

Burlingham, Michael John. *The Last Tiffany: A Biography of Dorothy Tiffany Burlingham*. New York: Atheneum, 1989.

Calef, Victor, and Edward R. Weinshel. "The New Psychoanalysis and Psychoanalytic Revisionism–Book Review Essay on *Borderline Conditions and Pathological Narcissism*." *The Psychoanalytic Quarterly* 48 (1979): 470–491.

Caper, Robert. *Immaterial Facts: Freud's Discovery of Psychic Reality and Klein's Development of His Work*. Northvale, NJ: Jason Aronson, 1988.

——. "On the Difficulty of Making a Mutative Interpretation." *IJP* 76 (1995): 91–101.

Carotenuto, Aldo. *A Secret Symmetry: Sabina Spielrein Between Jung and Freud*. Translated by Arno Pomerans, John Shipley, and Krishna Winston. New York: Pantheon, 1982.

Cavell, Marcia. *The Psychoanalytic Mind: From Freud to Philosophy*. Cambridge, MA: Harvard University Press, 1993.

Chabot, C. Barry. *Freud on Schreber: Psychoanalytic Theory and Critical Act*. Amherst, MA: University of Massachusetts Press, 1982.

Clark, Ronald W. *Freud: The Man and the Cause*. London: Jonathan Cape and Weidenfeld and Nicolson; New York: Random House, 1980.

Coles, Robert. *Anna Freud: The Dream of Psychoanalysis*. Reading, MA: Addison-Wesley, 1991.

Compton, Allan. "On the Psychoanalytic Theory of Instinctual Drives. I: The Beginnings of Freud's Drive Theory." *The Psychoanalytic Quarterly* 50 (1981): 190–218.

——. "On the Psychoanalytic Theory of Instinctual Drives. II: The Sexual Drives and the Ego Drives." *The Psychoanalytic Quarterly* 50 (1981): 219–237.

——. "On the Psychoanalytic Theory of Instinctual Drives. III: The Complications of Libido and Narcissism." *The Psychoanalytic Quarterly* 50 (1981): 345–362.

——. "On the Psychoanalytic Theory of Instinctual Drives. IV: Instinctual Drives and the Ego-Id-Superego Model." *The Psychoanalytic Quarterly* 50 (1981): 363–392.

Cooper, Arnold M. "The Transference Neurosis: A Concept Ready for Retirement." *Psychoanalytic Inquiry* 7 (1987): 569–585.

——. "Our Changing Views of the Therapeutic Action of Psychoanalysis: Comparing Strachey and Loewald." *The Psychoanalytic Quarterly* 57 (1988): 15–27.

——. "Paranoia: A Part of Most Analyses." *JAPA* 41 (1993): 423–442.

Couch, Arthur S. "Anna Freud's Adult Psychoanalytic Technique: A Defense of Classical Analysis." *IJP* 76 (1995): 153–171.

Covello, Adèle. "Lettres de Freud: Du scénario de Jones au diagnostic sur Ferenczi." *Cahiers Confrontation* 12 (1984): 63–78.

Cremerius, Johannes. " 'Die Sprache der Zärtlichkeit und der Leidenschaft': Reflexionen zu Sándor Ferenczis Wiesbadener Vortrag von 1932." *Psyche* 37 (1983): 998–1015.

Curtis, Homer C. "The Concept of the Therapeutic Alliance: Implications for the 'Widening Scope.' " *JAPA* 27 (Suppl.): 159–192.

D'Andrade, Roy. "The Psychoanalyst as Quasi-Experimentalist." Unpublished paper, 1995.

David-Ménard, Monique. *Hysteria from Freud to Lacan: Body and Language in Psychoanalysis*. Translated by Catherine Porter. Ithaca, NY: Cornell University Press, 1989.

Decker, Hannah S. *Freud in Germany: Revolution and Reaction in Science, 1893–1907*. Psychological Issues, Monograph 41. New York: International Universities Press, 1977.

——. *Freud, Dora, and Vienna 1900*. New York: Free Press, 1991.

Detrick, Douglas W., and Susan P. Detrick. *Self Psychology: Comparisons and Contrasts*. Hillsdale, NJ: Analytic Press, 1987.

Deutsch, Helene. *Confrontations with Myself: An Epilogue*. New York: Norton, 1973.

Dewald, Paul A. *The Psychoanalytic Process: A Case Illustration*. New York: Basic Books, 1972.

Dupont, Judith. "Entre Freud and Ferenczi: Groddeck." *Cahiers Confrontation* 12 (1984): 33–42.

——. "Ferenczi's Madness." *Contemporary Psychoanalysis* 24 (1988): 250–261.

——. "Freud's Analysis of Ferenczi as Revealed by their Correspondence." *IJP* 75 (1994): 301–320.

——. "The Story of a Transgression." *JAPA* 43 (1995): 823–834.

Dyer, Raymond. *Her Father's Daughter: The Work of Anna Freud*. New York: Jason Aronson, 1983.

Eagle, Morris N. *Recent Developments in Psychoanalysis: A Critical Evaluation*. New York: McGraw Hill, 1984.

Easser, Barbara Ruth, and Stanley R. Lesser. "Hysterical Personality: A Re-evaluation." *The Psychoanalytic Quarterly* 34 (1965): 390–405.

Edelson, Marshall. *Hypothesis and Evidence in Psychoanalysis*. Chicago: University of Chicago Press, 1984.

——. *Psychoanalysis: A Theory in Crisis*. Chicago: University of Chicago Press, 1988.

Eissler, Kurt. R. "The Effect of the Structure of the Ego on Psychoanalytic Technique." *JAPA* 1 (1953): 104–143.

Ellenberger, Henri. *The Discovery of the Unconscious: The History and Evolution of Dynamic Psychiatry*. New York: Basic Books, 1970.

——. "The Story of 'Anna O': A Critical Review with New Data." *Journal of the History of the Behavioral Sciences* 8 (1972): 267–279.

——. "L'histoire d'Emmy von N." *Evolution psychiatrique* 42 (1977): 519–540.

Ellman, Steven. J. *Freud's Technique Papers: A Contemporary Perspective*. Northvale, NJ: Jason Aronson, 1991.

Etchegoyen, R. Horacio. "Fifty Years after the Mutative Interpretation." *IJP* 64 (1983): 445–459.

——. *The Fundamentals of Psychoanalytic Technique*. Translated by Patricia Pitchon. London: Karnac, 1991.

Ezriel, Henry. "The Scientific Testing of Psycho-Analytic Findings and Theory." *The British Journal of Medical Psychology* 24 (1951): 30–34.

Fairbairn, W. Ronald D. *Psychoanalytic Studies of the Personality*. London: Tavistock Publications and Routledge and Kegan Paul, 1952.

——. *From Instinct to Self: Selected Papers of W. R. D. Fairbairn*. Vol. 1, *Clinical and Theoretical Papers*. Edited by David E. Scharff and Ellinor Fairbairn Birtles. Vol. 2, *Applications and Early Contributions*. Edited by Ellinor Fairbairn Birtles and David E. Scharff. Northvale, NJ: Jason Aronson, 1994.

Falzeder, Ernst. "My Grand-Patient, My Chief Tormentor: A Hitherto Unnoticed Case of Freud's and the Consequences." *The Psychoanalytic Quarterly* 63 (1994): 297–331.

Federn, Paul. "Narcissism in the Structure of the Ego." *IJP* 9 (1928): 401–419.

Feldman, Michael. "Aspects of Reality and the Focus of Interpretation." *Psychoanalytic Inquiry* 13 (1993): 274–295.

——. "Projective Identification in Phantasy and Enactment." *Psychoanalytic Inquiry* 14 (1994): 423–440.

Fenichel, Otto. *Problems of Psychoanalytic Technique*. Translated by David Brunswick. New York: The Psychoanalytic Quarterly, 1941.

——. *The Psychoanalytic Theory of Neurosis*. New York: Norton, 1945.

Ferenczi, Sándor. *Hysterie und Pathneurosen*. Leipzig and Vienna: Internationaler Psychoanalytischer Verlag, 1919.

——. *Thalassa: A Theory of Genitality* (1924). Translated by Henry Alden Bunker. London: Karnac, Maresfield Library, 1989.

——. Review of *Technik der Psychoanalyse: I. Die analytische Situation*, by Otto Rank. *IJP* 8 (1927): 93–100.

——. *First Contributions to Psycho-Analysis*. Translated by Ernest Jones. London: Hogarth 1952. Reprint, London: Karnac, Maresfield Library, 1980. (American ed., *Sex in Psychoanalysis*. New York: Basic Books, 1950.)

——. *Further Contributions to Psycho-Analysis*. 2nd ed. Edited by John Rickman. Translated by Jane Isabel Suttie. London: Hogarth, 1950. Reprint, London: Karnac, Maresfield Library, 1980.

——. *Final Contributions to the Problems and Methods of Psycho-Analysis*. Edited by Michael Balint. Translated by Eric Mosbacher. London: Hogarth Press, 1955. Reprint, London: Karnac, Maresfield Library, 1980.

——. *The Clinical Diary of Sándor Ferenczi*. Edited by Judith Dupont. Translated by Michael Balint and Nicola Zarday Jackson. Cambridge, MA: Harvard University Press, 1988.

——. *The Sándor Ferenczi–Georg Groddeck Correspondence 1921–1933*. Edited by Christopher Fortune. Translated by Jeannie Cohen, Elisabeth Petersdorff, Norbert Ruebssat. London: Open Gate, 2002.

Ferenczi, Sándor, Karl Abraham, Ernst Simmel, and Ernest Jones. *Psycho-Analysis and the War Neuroses*. London, Vienna, and New York: International Psycho-Analytical Press, 1921.

Ferenczi, Sándor, and Otto Rank. *The Development of Psychoanalysis*. Translated by Caroline Newton. New York: Nervous and Mental Disease Publishing Co., 1935. Reprint, Madison, CT: International Universities Press, 1986.

Fichtner, Gerhard, and Albrecht Hirschmüller. "Freuds 'Katharina'—Hintergrund, Entstehungsgeschichte und Bedeutung einer frühen psychoanalytischen Krankengeschichte." *Psyche* 39 (1985): 220–240.

Fogel, Gerald I. "A Transitional Phase in Our Understanding of the Psychoanalytic Process: A New Look at Ferenczi and Rank." *JAPA* 41 (1993): 585–602.

Forest, Izette de. "The Therapeutic Technique of Sándor Ferenczi." *IJP* 23 (1942): 182–192.

——. *The Leaven of Love: A Development of the Psychoanalytic Theory and Technique of Sándor Ferenczi*. Hamden, CT: Archon Books, 1965.

Forrester, John. *The Seductions of Psychoanalysis: Freud, Lacan and Derrida*. Cambridge: Cambridge University Press, 1990.

——. *Dispatches from the Freud Wars: Psychoanalysis and Its Passions*. Cambridge, MA: Harvard University Press, 1997.

——. *Truth Games: Lies, Money, and Psychoanalysis*. Cambridge, MA: Harvard University Press, 1997.

Frank, Claudia. "The Discovery of the Child as an Object *Sui Generis* of Cure and Research by Melanie Klein as Reflected in the Notes of Her First Child Analysis in Berlin 1921–1926." *Psychoanalysis and History* 1 (1999): 155–174.

Frank, Claudia, and Heinz Weiß. "The Origins of Disquieting Discoveries by Melanie Klein: The Possible Significance of the Case of 'Erna.' " *IJP* 77 (1996): 1101–1126.

Frankiel, Rita V. "A Note on Freud's Inattention to the Negative Oedipal in Little Hans." *The International Review of Psycho-Analysis* 18 (1991): 181–184.

——. "Analysed and Unanalysed Themes in the Treatment of Little Hans." *The International Review of Psycho-Analysis* 19 (1992): 323–333.

Freeman, Lucy. *The Story of Anna O*. New York: Walker, 1972.

Freud, Anna. *The Writings of Anna Freud*. 8 vols. New York: International Universities Press, 1965–1981.

Freud, Sigmund. *Gesammelte Werke, Chronologisch Geordnet*. Edited by Anna Freud, Edward Bibring, Willi Hoffer, Ernst Kris, and Otto Isakower. Vols. 1–17. London: Imago Publishing Co., 1940–1952. Vol. 18. Frankfurt: S. Fischer, 1968.

——. *The Standard Edition of the Complete Psychological Works of Sigmund Freud*. 24 vols. Translated from the German under the General Editorship of James Strachey. London: Hogarth Press, 1953–1974.

——. *Letters of Sigmund Freud 1873–1939*. Edited by Ernst L. Freud. Translated by Tania Stern and James Stern. London: Hogarth Press, 1960.

——. *Psychoanalysis and Faith: The Letters of Sigmund Freud and Oskar Pfister*. Edited by Heinrich Meng and Ernst L. Freud. Translated by Eric Mosbacher. New York: Basic Books, 1963.

——. *The Letters of Sigmund Freud and Arnold Zweig*. Edited by Ernst L. Freud. Translated by Elaine and William Robson-Scott. New York: New York University Press, 1970.

——. *Sigmund Freud and Lou Andreas-Salomé: Letters*. Edited by Ernst Pfeiffer. Translated by Elaine and William Robson-Scott. London: Hogarth Press, 1970.

——. *The Freud/Jung Letters: The Correspondence between Sigmund Freud and C. G. Jung*. Edited by William McGuire. Translated by Ralph Manheim and R. F. C. Hull. Princeton, NJ: Princeton University Press, 1974.

——. *L'Homme aux rats: Journal d'une analyse*. Translated by Elza Riberio Hawalka. Paris: Presses Universitaires de France, 1974.

——. *The Complete Letters of Sigmund Freud to Wilhelm Fliess 1887–1904*. Translated and edited by Jeffrey Moussaiff Masson. Cambridge, MA: Harvard University Press, 1985.

——. *A Phylogenetic Fantasy: An Overview of the Transference Neuroses*. Edited by Ilse Grubrich-Simitis. Translated by Axel Hoffer and Peter T. Hoffer. Cambridge, MA: Harvard University Press, 1987.

——. *The Letters of Sigmund Freud to Eduard Silberstein 1871–1881*. Edited by Walter Boehlich. Translated by Arnold J. Pomerans. Cambridge, MA: Harvard University Press, 1990.

——. *The Diary of Sigmund Freud 1929–1939: A Record of the Final Decade*. Translated, annotated, with an introduction by Michael Molnar. London: Hogarth Press, 1992.

——. *The Correspondence of Sigmund Freud and Sándor Ferenczi*. Vol. 1, *1908–1914*. Edited by Eva Brabant, Ernst Falzeder, and Patrizia Giampieri-Deutsch. Translated by Peter T. Hoffer. Vol. 2, *1914–1919*. Edited by Ernst Falzeder and Eva Brabant, with the collaboration of Patrizia Giampieri-Deutsch. Translated by Peter T. Hoffer. Vol. 3, *1920–1933*. Edited by Ernst Falzeder and Eva Brabant, with the collaboration of Patrizia Giampieri-Deutsch. Translated by Peter T. Hoffer. Cambridge, MA: Harvard University Press, 1993–2000.

——. *The Complete Correspondence of Sigmund Freud and Ernest Jones 1908–1939*. Edited by R. Andrew Paskauskas. Cambridge, MA: Harvard University Press, 1993.

——. *The Complete Correspondence of Sigmund Freud and Karl Abraham 1907–1925*. Edited by Ernst Falzeder. Translated by Caroline Schwarzacher. London: Karnac, 2002.

——. *The Sigmund Freud–Ludwig Binswanger Correspondence 1908–1938*. Edited by Gerhard Fichtner. Translated by Arnold J. Pomerans. New York: Other Press, 2003.

Friedman, Lawrence. "The Therapeutic Alliance." *IJP* 50 (1969): 139–153.

——. "Trends in the Psychoanalytic Theory of Treatment." *The Psychoanalytic Quarterly* 47 (1978): 524–567.

——. *The Anatomy of Psychotherapy*. Hillsdale, NJ: Analytic Press, 1988.

——. "How and Why Patients Become More Objective? Sterba Compared with Strachey." *The Psychoanalytic Quarterly* 61 (1992): 1–17.

——. "Ferrum, Ignis, and Medicina: Return to the Crucible." *JAPA* 45 (1997): 21–36.

Gardiner, Muriel. *Code Name "Mary": Memoirs of an American Woman in the Austrian Underground*. New Haven: Yale University Press, 1983.

——. "The Wolf Man's Last Years." *JAPA* 31 (1983): 867–897.

——, ed. *The Wolf-Man by the Wolf-Man*. New York: Basic Books, 1971.

Gardiner, Sebastian. *Irrationality and the Philosophy of Psychoanalysis*. Cambridge: Cambridge University Press, 1993.

Garrison, Marsha. "A New Look at Little Hans." *Psychoanalytic Review* 65 (1978): 523–532.

Gay, Peter. *Freud: A Life for Our Time*. New York: Norton, 1988.

Gedo, John E. "Forms of Idealization in the Analytic Transference." *JAPA* 23 (1975): 458–505.

——. *Beyond Interpretation: Toward a Revised Theory for Psychoanalysis*. New York: International Universities Press, 1979.

——. *Conceptual Issues in Psychoanalysis: Essays in History and Method*. Hillsdale, NJ: Analytic Press, 1986.

——. *Spleen and Nostalgia: A Life and Work in Psychoanalysis*. Northvale, NJ: Jason Aronson, 1997.

——. *The Evolution of Psychoanalysis: Contemporary Theory and Practice*. New York: Other Press, 1999.

Gedo, John E., and Arnold Goldberg. *Models of the Mind: A Psychoanalytic Theory*. Chicago: University of Chicago Press, 1973.

Gedo, John E., and George H. Pollock, eds. *Freud: The Fusion of Science and Humanism: The Intellectual History of Psychoanalysis*. Psychological Issues, Monograph 34/35. New York: International Universities Press, 1976.

Geha, Richard E. "Freud as Fictionalist: The Imaginary Worlds of Psychoanalysis." In *Freud Appraisals and Reappraisals: Contributions to Freud Studies*, edited by Paul E. Stepansky, vol. 2. Hillsdale, NJ: Analytic Press, 1988.

Gill, Merton M. *Topography and Systems in Psychoanalytic Theory*. Psychological Issues, Monograph 10. New York: International Universities Press, 1963.

——. "The Analysis of the Transference." *JAPA* 27 (Suppl.) (1979): 263–288.

——. *Analysis of Transference*. Vol. 1, *Theory and Technique*. Psychological Issues, Monograph 53. New York: International Universities Press, 1982.

——. *Psychoanalysis in Transition: A Personal View*. Hillsdale, NJ: Analytic Press, 1994.

Gill, Merton M., and Irwin Z. Hoffman. *Analysis of Transference*. Vol. 2, *Studies of Nine Audio-Recorded Psychoanalytic Sessions*. Psychological Issues, Monograph 54. New York: International Universities Press, 1982.

Gillespie, William H. "Ernest Jones: The Bonny Fighter." *IJP* 60 (1979): 273–279.

Ginzburg, Carlo. "Morelli, Freud and Sherlock Holmes." *History Workshop* 9 (1980): 5–36.

Giovacchini, Peter L., ed. *Tactics and Techniques in Psychoanalytic Therapy*. New York: Science House, 1972.

Giovacchini, Peter L., and L. Bryce Boyer, eds. *Technical Factors in the Treatment of Severely Disturbed Patients*. New York: Jason Aronson, 1982.

Glenn, Jules. "Freud, Dora, and the Maid—A Study of Countertransference." *JAPA* 34 (1986): 591–606.

Glover, Edward. "The Therapeutic Effect of Inexact Interpretation: A Contribution to the Theory of Suggestion." *IJP* 12 (1931): 397–411.

——. Review of *The Psychoanalysis of Children*, by Melanie Klein. *IJP* 14 (1933): 119–129.

——. "Examination of the Klein System of Child Psychology." *The Psychoanalytic Study of the Child* 1 (1945): 75–118.

——. "The Position of Psycho-Analysis in Britain." *British Medical Bulletin* 6 (1949): 27–31. (Also published in Edward Glover. *On the Early Development of Mind*, 352–363. London: Imago Publishing Co., 1956.)

——. *The Technique of Psycho-Analysis*. London: Baillière, Tindall and Cox; New York: International Universities Press, 1955.

Glover, Edward, Otto Fenichel, James Strachey, Edmund Bergler, Herman Nunberg, and Edward Bibring. "Symposium on the Theory of the Therapeutic Results of Psycho-Analysis." *IJP* 18 (1937): 125–195.

Goldberg, Arnold, ed. *The Psychology of the Self: A Casebook*. New York: International Universities Press, 1978.

——, ed. *Progress in Self Psychology*. Vol. 1. New York: Guilford Press, 1985.

Gould, Stephen Jay. *Ever Since Darwin*. New York: Norton, 1977.

——. *Ontogeny and Phylogeny*. Cambridge, MA: Harvard University Press, 1977.

——. *The Mismeasure of Man*. Rev. ed. New York: Norton, 1996.

Graf, Max. "Reminiscences of Professor Freud." *The Psychoanalytic Quarterly* 11 (1942): 465–476.

Gray, Paul. *The Ego and the Analysis of Defense*. Northvale, NJ: Jason Aronson, 1994.

Green, André. *On Private Madness*. London: Hogarth Press, 1986.

Greenberg, Jay R., and Stephen A. Mitchell. *Object Relations in Psychoanalytic Theory*. Cambridge, MA: Harvard University Press, 1983.

Greenson, Ralph R. *The Technique and Practice of Psychoanalysis*. Vol. 1. New York: International Universities Press, 1967.

——. *Explorations in Psychoanalysis*. New York: International Universities Press, 1978.

Greenson, Ralph R., and Milton Wexler. "The Non-Transference Relationship in the Psychoanalytic Situation." *IJP* 50 (1969): 27–39.

Grinberg, Léon, Darío Sor, and Elizabeth Tabak de Bianchedi. *New Introduction to the Work of Bion*. Northvale, NJ: Jason Aronson, 1971.

Groddeck, Georg W. *The Book of the It*. Translated by V. M. E. Collins. London: Vision Press, 1949.

Gross, Alan G. *The Rhetoric of Science*. Cambridge, MA: Harvard University Press, 1990.

Grosskurth, Phyllis. *Melanie Klein: Her World and Her Work*. New York: Knopf, 1986.

——. *The Secret Ring: Freud's Inner Circle and the Politics of Psychoanalysis*. Reading, MA: Addison-Wesley, 1991.

Grotstein, James S. *Splitting and Projective Identification*. New York: Jason Aronson, 1981.

——. "The Significance of Kleinian Contributions to Psychoanalysis I. Kleinian Instinct Theory." *International Journal of Psychoanalytic Psychotherapy* 8 (1980–1981): 375–392.

——. "The Significance of Kleinian Contributions to Psychoanalysis II. Freudian and Kleinian Conceptions of Early Mental Development." *International Journal of Psychoanalytic Psychotherapy*. 8 (1980–1981): 393–428.

——. "The Significance of Kleinian Contributions to Psychoanalysis III. The Kleinian Theory of Ego Psychology and Object Relations." *International Journal of Psychoanalytic Psychotherapy* 9 (1982–1983): 487–510.

——. "The Significance of Kleinian Contributions to Psychoanalysis IV. Critiques of Klein." *International Journal of Psychoanalytic Psychotherapy* 9 (1982–1983): 511–535.

——, ed. *Do I Dare Disturb the Universe? A Memorial to Wilfred R. Bion.* Beverly Hills, CA: Caesura Press, 1981. Reprint, London: Karnac, Maresfield Library, 1983.

Grotstein, James, and Donald B. Rinsley, eds. *Fairbairn and the Origins of Object Relations.* New York: Guilford Press, 1994.

Grubich-Simitis, Ilse. "Six Letters of Sigmund Freud and Sándor Ferenczi on the Interrelationship of Psychoanalytic Theory and Technique." *The International Review of Psycho-analysis* 13 (1986): 259–277.

——. *Back to Freud's Texts: Making Silent Documents Speak.* New Haven: Yale University Press, 1996.

Grünbaum, Adolf. *The Foundations of Psychoanalysis: A Philosophical Critique.* Berkeley and Los Angeles: University of California Press, 1984.

Grunberger, Béla. "Some Reflections on the Rat Man." *IJP* 47 (1966): 160–167.

——. "From the 'Active Technique' to the 'Confusion of Tongues': On Ferenczi's Deviation." In *Psychoanalysis in France*, edited by Serge Lebovici and Daniel Widlöcher. New York: International Universities Press, 1980.

Guntrip, Harry. *Personality Structure and Human Interaction: The Developing Synthesis of Psychodynamic Theory.* London: Hogarth Press, 1961.

——. *Schizoid Phenomena, Object-Relations and the Self.* London: Hogarth Press; New York: International Universities Press, 1968.

——. *Psychoanalytic Theory, Therapy, and the Self.* New York: Basic Books, 1971. Reprint, London: Karnac, Maresfield Library, 1977.

Hacking, Ian. *Representing and Intervening: Introductory Topics in the Philosophy of Science.* Cambridge: Cambridge University Press, 1983.

——. *Rewriting the Soul: Multiple Personality and the Sciences of Memory.* Princeton, NJ: Princeton University Press, 1995.

——. *Mad Travelers: Reflections on the Reality of Transient Mental Illnesses.* Charlottesville, VA: University of Virginia Press, 1998.

——. *The Social Construction of What?* Cambridge, MA: Harvard University Press, 1999.

Hale, Keith, ed. *Friends and Apostles: The Correspondence of Rupert Brooke and James Strachey 1905–1914.* New Haven: Yale University Press, 1998.

Hale, Nathan G. Jr. *Freud in America.* Vol. 1, *Freud and the Americans: The Beginnings of Psychoanalysis in the United States, 1876–1917.* Vol. 2, *The Rise and Crisis of Psychoanalysis in the United States: Freud and the Americans, 1917–1985.* New York: Oxford University Press, 1971–1995.

——, ed. *James Jackson Putnam and Psychoanalysis: Letters between Putnam and Sigmund Freud, Ernest Jones, William James, Sándor Ferenczi, and Morton Prince, 1877–1917.* Cambridge, MA: Harvard University Press, 1971.

Harmat, Paul. *Freud, Ferenczi und die ungarische Psychoanalyse.* Tübingen: Edition Diskord, 1988.

Hárnik, J. "Kritisches über Mack Brunswicks Nachtrag zu Freuds 'Geschichte einer infantilen Neurose.'" *Internationale Zeitschrift für Psychoanalyse* 16 (1930): 123–127.

——. "Erwiderung auf Mack Brunswicks Entgegnung." *Internationale Zeitschrift für Psychoanalyse* 17 (1931): 400–402.

Hartmann, Heinz. *Ego Psychology and the Problem of Adaptation* (1939). Translated by David Rapaport. New York: International Universities, Press, 1958.

——. *Essays on Ego Psychology: Selected Problems in Psychoanalytic Theory.* New York: International Universities Press, 1964.

Haynal, André. *The Technique at Issue: Controversies in Psychoanalysis from Freud and Ferenczi to Michael Balint.* Translated by Elizabeth Holder. London: Karnac, 1988.

——. *Disappearing and Reviving: Sándor Ferenczi in the History of Psychoanalysis.* London: Karnac, 2002.

Heath, Stephen. "Joan Riviere and the Masquerade." In *Formations of Fantasy*, edited by Victor Burgin, James Donald, and Cora Kaplan. London: Methuen, 1986.

Heimann, Paula. *About Children and Children No-Longer.* Edited by Margaret Tonnesmann. London and New York: Tavistock/Routledge, 1989.

Heller, Peter. *A Child Analysis with Anna Freud.* Madison, CT: International Universities Press, 1990.

——. *Anna Freud's Letters to Eva Rosenfeld.* Translated by Mary Weigand. Madison, CT: International Universities Press, 1992.

Hinshelwood, R. D. "Little Hans's Transference." *Journal of Child Psychotherapy* 15 (1989): 63–78.

——. *A Dictionary of Kleinian Thought.* London: Free Association Books, 1991.

——. *Clinical Klein.* Free Association Books. 1994.

——. "The Elusive Concept of 'Internal Objects' (1934–1943): Its Role in the Formation of the Klein Group." *IJP* 78 (1997): 877–897.

——. "Countertransference." *IJP* 80 (1999): 797–818.

Hoffer, Axel. "The Freud–Ferenczi Controversy: A Living Legacy." *The International Review of Psycho-Analysis* 18 (1991): 465–472.

——. Review of *The Clinical Diary of Sándor Ferenczi*, edited by Judith Dupont. *IJP* 71 (1990): 723–727.

Hoffer, Peter T., and Axel Hoffer. "Ferenczi's Fatal Illness in Historical Context." *JAPA* 47 (1999): 1257–1268.

Hoffman, Irwin Z. "The Patient as Interpreter of the Analyst's Experience." *Contemporary Psychoanalysis* 19 (1983): 389–423.

Holland, Norman N. "An Identity for the Rat Man." *The International Review of Psycho-Analysis* 2 (1975): 157–169.

Hollender, Marc H. "The Case of Anna O.: A Reformulation." *American Journal of Psychiatry* 137 (1980): 797–800.

Horney, Karen. "The Problem of the Negative Therapeutic Reaction." *The Psychoanalytic Quarterly* 5 (1936): 29–45.

Hughes, Athol. "Letters of Sigmund Freud to Joan Riviere (1921–1939)." *The International Review of Psycho-Analysis* 19 (1992): 265–284.

——. "Personal Experiences—Professional Interests: Joan Riviere and Femininity." *IJP* 78 (1997): 899–911.

Hughes, Judith M. *Reshaping the Psychoanalytic Domain: The Work of Melanie Klein,*

W. R. D. Fairbairn, and D. W. Winnicott. Berkeley: University of California Press, 1989.

——. "Psychoanalysis as a General Psychology, Revisited." *Free Associations* No. 23 (1991): 357–370.

——. *From Freud's Consulting Room: The Unconscious in a Scientific Age.* Cambridge, MA: Harvard University Press, 1994.

——. "Another Impossible Profession?" *The Psychohistory Review* 25 (1997): 119–126.

——. *Freudian Analysts/Feminist Issues.* New Haven: Yale University Press, 1999.

Hunter, Dianne. "Hysteria, Psychoanalysis, and Feminism: The Case of Anna O." *Feminist Studies* 9 (1983): 465–488.

Hurst, Lindsay C. "What Was Wrong with Anna O.?" *Journal of the Royal Society of Medicine* 75 (1982): 129–131.

——. "Freud and the Great Neurosis: Discussion Paper." *Journal of the Royal Society of Medicine* 76 (1983): 57–61.

Israëls, Han. *Schreber: Father and Son.* Translated by H. S. Lake. Madison, CT: International Universities Press, 1989.

Jackson, Stanley W. *Melancholia and Depression: From Hippocratic Times to Modern Times.* New Haven: Yale University Press, 1986.

Jacobs, Theodore. *The Use of the Self: Countertransference and Communication in the Analytic Situation.* Madison, CT: International Universities Press, 1991.

Jacobson, Edith. *The Self and the Object World.* New York: International Universities Press, 1964.

Jacobsen, P. B., and Steele, R. S. "From Present to Past: Freudian Archaeology." *The International Review of Psycho-Analysis* 6 (1979): 349–362.

James, Martin. Review of *The Analysis of the Self: A Systematic Approach to the Psychological Treatment of Narcissistic Personality Disorders*, by Heinz Kohut. *IJP* 54 (1973): 363–368.

Jennings, Jerry L. "The Revival of 'Dora': Advances in Psychoanalytic Theory and Technique." *JAPA* 34 (1986): 607–635.

Jensen, Ellen. "Anna O.: A Study of Her Later Life." *The Psychoanalytic Quarterly* 39 (1970): 269–293.

Joffe, Walter. "A Critical Review of the Status of the Envy Concept." *IJP* 50 (1969): 533–545.

Jones, Ernest. "The Origin and Structure of the Super-Ego." *IJP* 7 (1926): 303–311.

——. Introductory Memoir to *Selected Papers of Karl Abraham*. Translated by Douglas Bryan and Alix Strachey. London: Hogarth Press, 1927. Reprint, London: Karnac, Maresfield Library, 1979.

——. "The Future of Psycho-Analysis." *IJP* 17 (1936): 269–277.

——. "A Valedictory Address." *IJP* 27 (1946): 7–12.

——. *Papers on Psycho-Analysis*, 5th ed. London: Baillière, Tindall and Cox, 1948. Reprint, London: Karnac, Maresfield Library, 1977.

——. *The Life and Work of Sigmund Freud.* Vol. 1, *The Formative Years and the Great Discoveries 1856–1900*. Vol. 2, *Years of Maturity 1901–1919*. Vol. 3, *The Last Phase 1919–1939*. New York: Basic Books, 1953–1957.

——. *Free Associations: Memories of a Psycho-Analyst.* New York: Basic Books 1959.

Jones, Katherine. "A Sketch of E. J.'s Personality." *IJP* 60 (1979): 271–273.

Joseph, Betty. "Persecutory Anxiety in a Four-year-old Boy." *IJP* 47 (1966): 184–188.

——. *Psychic Equilibrium and Psychic Change: Selected Papers of Betty Joseph.* Edited by Michael Feldman and Elizabeth Bott Spillius. London and New York: Routledge, 1989.

Kanzer, Mark. Review of *The Wolf-Man by the Wolf-Man*, edited by Muriel Gardiner. *IJP* 53 (1972): 419–422.

——. "The Therapeutic and Working Alliances." *International Journal of Psychoanalytic Psychotherapy* 4 (1975): 48–68.

Kanzer, Mark, and Jules Glenn, eds. *Freud and His Self-Analysis.* New York: Jason Aronson, 1979.

——, eds. *Freud and His Patients.* New York: Jason Aronson, 1980.

Kardiner, Abram. *My Analysis with Freud: Reminiscences.* New York: Norton, 1977.

Keill, Norman. *Freud without Hindsight: Reviews of His Work (1893–1939) By His Contemporaries.* Madison, CT: International Universities Press, 1988.

Kelly, Kevin V. "Classics Revisited: Heinrich Racker's *Transference and Countertransference.*" *JAPA* 45 (1997): 1253–1259.

Kernberg, Paulina. "The Course of the Analysis of a Narcissistic Personality with Hysterical and Compulsive Features." *JAPA* 19 (1971): 451–471.

Kernberg, Otto. "Structural Derivatives of Object Relationships." *IJP* 47 (1966): 236–253.

——. "Early Ego Integration and Object Relations." *Annals of the New York Academy of Sciences* 193 (1972): 233–247.

——. *Borderline Conditions and Pathological Narcissism.* New York: Jason Aronson, 1975.

——. *Object Relations Theory and Clinical Psychoanalysis.* New York: Jason Aronson, 1976.

——. "The Contributions of Edith Jacobson: An Overview." *JAPA* 27 (1979): 793–819.

——. "Some Implications of Object Relations Theory for Psychoanalytic Technique." *JAPA* 27 (Suppl.) (1979): 207–239.

——. *Internal World and External Reality: Object Relations Theory Applied.* New York: Jason Aronson, 1980.

——. *Severe Personality Disorders: Psychotherapeutic Strategies.* New Haven: Yale University Press, 1984.

——. "Identification and Its Vicissitudes as Observed in Psychosis." *IJP* 67 (1986): 147–159.

——. "An Ego Psychology-Object Relations Theory Approach to the Transference." *The Psychoanalytic Quarterly* 56 (1987): 197–221.

——. "Object Relations Theory in Clinical Practice." *The Psychoanalytic Quarterly* 57 (1988): 481–504.

——. *Aggression in Personality Disorders and Perversions.* New Haven: Yale University Press, 1992.

——. "Convergences and Divergences in Contemporary Psychoanalytic Technique." *IJP* 74 (1993): 659–673.

——. *Love Relations: Normality and Pathology.* New Haven: Yale University Press, 1995.

Kerr, John. *A Most Dangerous Method: The Story of Jung, Freud, and Sabina Spielrein.* New York: Knopf, 1993.

Khan, M. Masud R. "On the Clinical Provision of Frustrations, Recognitions, and Failures in the Analytic Situation: An Essay on Dr Michael Balint's Researches on the Theory Psychoanalytic Technique." *IJP* 50 (1969): 237–248.

——. *Privacy of the Self: Papers on Psychoanalytic Theory and Technique.* London: Hogarth Press; New York: International Universities Press, 1974.

——. *Alienation in Perversions.* London: Hogarth Press, 1979.

——. *Hidden Selves: Between Theory and Practice in Psychoanalysis.* London: Hogarth Press, 1983.

King, Pearl H. M. "The Contributions of Ernest Jones to the British Psycho-Analytical Society." *IJP* 60 (1979): 280–284.

——. "The Education of a Psycho-Analyst." *Scientific Bulletin, The British Psycho-Analytical Society* (February 1981): 1–20.

——. "Identity Crises: Splits or Compromises–Adaptive or Maladaptive." In *The Identity of the Psychoanalyst*, edited by Edward D. Joseph and Daniel Widlöcher. International Psycho-Analytical Association Monographs, no. 2. New York: International Universities Press, 1983.

——. "The Life and Work of Melanie Klein in the British Psycho-Analytical Society." *IJP* 64 (1983): 251–260.

King, Pearl H. M., and Riccardo Steiner, eds. *The Freud–Klein Controversies 1941–45.* London: Routledge, 1991.

Kirsner, Douglas. "Self Psychology and the Psychoanalytic Movement: An Interview with Dr. Heinz Kohut." *Psychoanalysis and Contemporary Thought* 5 (1982): 483–495.

——. *Unfree Associations: Inside Psychoanalytic Institutes.* London: Process Press, 2000.

Klein, George S. *Psychoanalytic Theory: An Exploration of Essentials.* New York: International Universities Press, 1976.

Klein, Melanie. *The Writings of Melanie Klein.* Vol. 1, *Love, Guilt and Reparation and Other Works 1921–1945.* Vol. 2, *The Psycho-Analysis of Children.* Vol. 3, *Envy and Gratitude and Other Works 1946–1963.* Vol. 4, *Narrative of a Child Analysis: The Conduct of the Psycho-analysis of Children as Seen in the Treatment of a Ten-year-old Boy.* Under the general editorship of Roger Money-Kyrle, in collaboration with Betty Joseph, Edna O'Shaughnessy, and Hanna Segal. London: Hogarth Press, 1975.

Klein, Melanie, Paula Heimann, Susan Isaacs, and Joan Riviere. *Developments in Psycho-Analysis.* London: Hogarth Press, 1952.

Klein, Melanie, Paula Heimann, and R. E. Money-Kyrle, eds. *New Directions in Psycho-Analysis: The Significance of Infant Conflict in the Pattern of Adult Behaviour.* London: Tavistock Publications, 1955. Reprint, London: Karnac, Maresfield Library, 1977.

Klein, Melanie, Joan Riviere, M. N. Searl, Ella F. Sharpe, Edward Glover, and Ernest Jones. "Symposium on Child-Analysis." *IJP* 8 (1927): 331–391.

Klein, Milton, and David Tribich. "Kernberg's Object-Relations Theory: A Critical Evaluation." *IJP* 62 (1981): 27–43.

Kohon, Gregorio, ed. *The British School of Psychoanalysis: The Independent Tradition.* London: Free Association Books, 1986.

Kohut, Heinz. *The Analysis of the Self: A Systematic Approach to the Psychoanalytic Treatment of Narcissistic Personality Disorders.* New York: International Universities Press, 1971.

——. *The Restoration of the Self.* New York: International Universities Press, 1977.

——. *How Does Analysis Cure?* Edited by Arnold Goldberg. Chicago: University of Chicago Press, 1984.

——. *The Search for the Self: Selected Writings of Heinz Kohut 1950–1981.* 4 vols. Edited by Paul H. Ornstein. New York and Madison, CT: International Universities Press, 1978–1990.

——. *The Curve of Life: The Correspondence of Heinz Kohut 1923–1981.* Edited by Geoffrey Cocks. Chicago: University of Chicago Press, 1994.

——. *The Chicago Institute Lectures.* Edited by Paul Tolpin and Marian Tolpin. Hillsdale, NJ: Analytic Press, 1996.

Kravis, Nathan M. "The 'Prehistory' of the Idea of Transference." *The International Review of Psycho-Analysis* 19 (1992): 9–22.

Kris, Anton O. "Helping Patients by Analyzing Self-Criticism." *JAPA* 38 (1990): 605–636.

——. "Freud's Treatment of a Narcissistic Patient." *IJP* 75 (1994): 649–664.

Kris, Ernst. *Selected Papers of Ernst Kris.* New Haven: Yale University Press, 1975.

Krohn, Alan. *Hysteria: The Elusive Neurosis.* Psychological Issues, Monograph 45/46. New York: International Universities Press, 1978.

Laplanche, Jean. "Panel on 'Hysteria Today.'" *IJP* 55 (1974): 459–469.

——. *New Foundations for Psychoanalysis.* Translated by David Macey. Oxford: Basil Blackwell, 1989.

Laplanche, Jean, and J.-B. Pontalis. "Fantasy and the Origins of Sexuality." *IJP* 49 (1968): 1–18.

——. *The Language of Psycho-Analysis.* Translated by Donald Nicholson-Smith. London: Hogarth Press, 1980.

Lear, Jonathan. *Open Minded: Working Out the Logic of the Soul.* Cambridge, MA: Harvard University Press, 1998.

Leavitt, Harry C. "A Biological and Teleological Study of 'Irma's Injection' Dream." *Psychoanalytic Review* 43 (1956): 440–447.

Leming, Barbara. *Marilyn Monroe.* New York: Crown, 1998.

Levin, Kenneth. "Freud's Paper 'On Male Hysteria' and the Conflict between Anatomical and Physiological Models." *Bulletin of the History of Medicine* 48 (1974): 377–397.

——. *Freud's Early Psychology of the Neuroses: A Historical Perspective.* Pittsburgh: University of Pittsburgh Press, 1978.

Levy, Stephen T., ed. *The Therapeutic Alliance.* Madison, CT: International Universities Press, 2000.

Lewin, Karl K. "Dora Revisited." *Psychoanalytic Review* 60 (1974): 519–532.

Leys, Ruth. *Trauma: A Genealogy.* Chicago: University of Chicago Press, 2000.

Libbrecht, Katrien. *Hysterical Psychosis.* New Brunswick, NJ: Transaction Publishers, 1995.

Lieberman, E. James. *Acts of Will: The Life and Work of Otto Rank.* New York: Free Press, 1985.

Likierman, Meira. "Primitive Object Love in Melanie Klein's Thinking: Early Theoretical Influences." *IJP* 74 (1993): 241–253.

——. *Melanie Klein: Her Work in Context*. London and New York: Continuum, 2001.

Lipton, Samuel D. "The Advantages of Freud's Technique as Shown in His Analysis of the Rat Man." *IJP* 58 (1977): 255–273.

——. "An Addendum to 'The Advantages of Freud's Technique as Shown in His Analysis of the Rat Man.' " *IJP* 60 (1979): 215–216.

Little, Margaret S. *Transference Neurosis and Transference Psychosis: Toward Basic Unity*. New York: Jason Aronson, 1981.

Loewald, Hans. *Papers on Psychoanalysis*. New Haven: Yale University Press, 1980.

Loewenstein, Rudolph M. *Practice and Precept in Psychoanalytic Technique: Selected Papers of Rudolph M. Loewenstein*. New Haven: Yale University Press, 1982.

Lohser, Beate, and Peter M. Newton. *Unorthodox Freud: The View from the Couch*. New York: Guilford Press, 1996.

López-Corvo, Rafael E. *The Dictionary of the Work of W. R. Bion*. London: Karnac, 2003.

Lorin, Claude. *Le jeune Ferenczi: Premiers écrits 1899–1906*. Paris: Aubier Montaigne, 1983.

——. *Sándor Ferenczi: De la médicine à la psychose*. Paris: Presses Universitaires de France, 1993.

Lothane, Zvi. *In Defense of Schreber: Soul Murder and Psychiatry*. Hillsdale, NJ: Analytic Press, 1992.

Lum, William Boyce. "Sándor Ferenczi (1873–1933)—The Father of the Empathic–Interpersonal Approach, Part One: Introduction and Early Analytic Years." *Journal of the American Academy of Psychoanalysis* 16 (1988): 131–153.

Lyth, Oliver. "Wilfred Ruprecht Bion (1897–1979)." *IJP* 61 (1980): 269–273.

Macalpine, Ida. "The Development of the Transference." *The Psychoanalytic Quarterly* 19 (1950): 501–539.

McCaffrey, Phillip. *Freud and Dora: The Artful Dream*. New Brunswick, NJ: Rutgers University Press, 1984.

McDougall, Joyce. *Plea for a Measure of Abnormality*. New York: International Universities Press, 1978.

——. *Theaters of the Mind: Illusion and Truth on the Psychoanalytic Stage*. New York: Basic Books, 1985.

——. *Theatres of the Body: A Psychoanalytic Approach to Psychosomatic Illness*. London: Free Association Books. 1989.

McGrath, William J. *Freud's Discovery of Psychoanalysis: The Politics of Hysteria*. Ithaca, NY: Cornell University Press, 1986.

McGuire, Michael T. *Reconstructions in Psychoanalysis*. New York: Appleton, Century, Crofts, 1971.

McIntosh, Donald. "The Ego and the Self in the Thought of Sigmund Freud." *IJP* 67 (1986): 429–449.

MacKay, Nigel. "Melanie Klein's Metapsychology: Phenomenological and Mechanistic Perspective." *IJP* 62 (1981): 187–198.

——. *Motivation and Explanation: An Essay on Freud's Philosophy of Science*. Madison, CT: International Universities Press, 1989.

Macmillan, Malcolm B. "Freud's Expectations and the Childhood Seduction Theory." *Australian Journal of Psychology* 29 (1977): 223–236.

——. "Delboeuf and Janet as Influences in Freud's Treatment of Emmy von N." *Journal of the History of the Behavioral Sciences* 15 (1979): 299–309.

——. "Freud and Janet on Organic and Hysterical Paralyses: A Mystery Solved?" *The International Review of Psycho-Analysis* 17 (1990): 189–203.

Madison, Peter. *Freud's Concept of Repression and Defense, Its Theoretical and Observational Language*. Minneapolis: University of Minnesota Press, 1961.

Mahler, Margaret, Fred Pine, and Anni Bergman. *The Psychological Birth of the Human Infant: Symbiosis and Individuation*. New York: Basic Books, 1975.

Mahony, Patrick J. *Cries of the Wolf-Man*. New York: International Universities Press, 1984.

——. *Freud and the Rat Man*. New Haven: Yale University Press, 1986.

——. *Freud as a Writer*. Expanded ed. New Haven: Yale University Press, 1987.

——. *On Defining Freud's Discourse*. New Haven: Yale University Press, 1989.

——. *Freud's Dora: A Psychoanalytic, Historical, and Textual Study*. New Haven: Yale University Press, 1996.

Mahony, Patrick, Carlo Bonomi, and Jan Stenson, eds. *Behind the Scenes: Freud in Correspondence*. Oslo: Scandinavian University Press, 1997.

Malcolm, Janet. *Psychoanalysis: The Impossible Profession*. New York: Knopf, 1981.

Marcus, Steven. *Freud and the Culture of Psychoanalysis: Studies in the Transition from Victorian Humanism to Modernity*. New York: Norton, 1984.

Marty, Pierre, Michel Fain, Michel de M'Uzan, and Christian David. "Der Fall Dora und der psychosomatische Gesichtspunkt." *Psyche* 33 (1979): 888–925.

Masson, Jeffrey Moussaieff. Review of *Gespräche mit dem Wolfsmann: Eine Psychanalyse und die Folgen*, by Karin Obholzer. *The International Review of Psycho-Analysis* 9 (1982): 116–119.

——. *The Assault on Truth: Freud's Suppression of the Seduction Theory*. New York: Farrar, Straus and Giroux, 1984.

Meisel, Perry, and Walter Kendrick, eds. *Bloomsbury/Freud: The Letters of James and Alix Strachey 1924–1925*. New York: Basic Books, 1985.

Meissner, W. W. *The Paranoid Process*. New York: Jason Aronson, 1978.

——. "Studies on Hysteria—Katharina." *The Psychoanalytic Quarterly* 48 (1979): 587–600.

——. "A Study on Hysteria: Anna O. Rediviva." *Annual of Psychoanalysis* 7 (1979): 17–52.

——. "Studies on Hysteria—Frau von N." *Bulletin of the Menninger Clinic* 45 (1981): 1–19.

——. *What is Effective in Psychoanalytic Therapy: The Move from Interpretation to Relation*. Northvale, NJ: Jason Aronson, 1991.

——. "The Concept of the Therapeutic Alliance." *JAPA* 40 (1992): 1059–1087.

Meltzer, Donald. *The Psycho-Analytical Process*. Perthshire: Clunie Press, 1967.

——. *Sexual States of Mind*. Perthshire: Clunie Press, 1973.

——. *The Kleinian Development: Part I, Freud's Clinical Development (Method–Data–Therapy). Part II. Richard Week-by-Week. Part III. The Clinical Significance of the Work of Bion*. Perthshire: Clunie Press, 1978.

——. *Dream-Life: A Re-examination of the Psycho-Analytical Theory and Technique*. Perthshire: Clunie Press, 1984.

——. *Studies in Extended Metapsychology: Clinical Applications of Bion's Ideas*. Perthshire: Clunie Press, 1986.

Meltzer, Françoise, ed. *The Trial(s) of Psychoanalysis*. Chicago: University of Chicago Press, 1988.

Mendez, Anita M., and Harold J. Fine, with comments by Harry Guntrip, "A Short History of the British School of Object Relations and Ego Psychology." *Bulletin of the Menninger Clinic* 40 (1976): 357–382.

Micale, Mark S. *Approaching Hysteria: Disease and Its Interpretations*. Princeton, NJ: Princeton University Press, 1995.

Milner, Marion. *The Suppressed Madness of Sane Men: Forty-Four Years of Exploring Psychoanalysis*. London and New York: Tavistock Publications, 1987.

Minutes of the Vienna Psychoanalytic Society. 4 vols. Edited by Herman Nunberg and Ernst Federn. Translated by M. Nunberg. New York: International Universities Press, 1962–1975.

Mitchell, Stephen A. "The Origin and Nature of the 'Object' in the Theories of Klein and Fairbairn." *Contemporary Psychoanalysis* 17 (1981): 374–398.

——. *Relational Concepts in Psychoanalysis: An Integration*. Cambridge, MA: Harvard University Press, 1988.

Modell, Arnold H. *Object Love and Reality: An Introduction to a Psychoanalytic Theory of Object Relations*. New York: International Universities Press, 1968.

——. "The Ego and the Id: Fifty Years Later." *IJP* 56 (1975): 57–68.

——. *Other Times, Other Realities: Toward a Theory of Psychoanalytic Treatment*. Cambridge, MA: Harvard University Press, 1990.

Mollon, Phil. *Releasing the Self: The Healing Legacy of Heinz Kohut*. London: Whurr, 2001.

Momigliano, Luciana Nissim. "A Spell in Vienna—But Was Freud a Freudian? An Investigation into Freud's Technique between 1920 and 1938. Based on the Published Testimony of Former Analysands." *The International Review of Psycho-Analysis* 14 (1987): 373–389.

Money-Kyrle, Roger. *The Collected Papers of Roger Money-Kyrle*. Edited by Donald Meltzer. Perthshire: Clunie Press, 1978.

Morse, Stephen J. "Structure and Reconstruction: A Critical Comparison of Michael Balint and D. W. Winnicott." *IJP* 53 (1972): 487–500.

Muslin, Hyman L. "Transference in the Rat Man Case: The Transference in Transition." *JAPA* 27 (1979): 561–578.

Muslin, Hyman, and Merton Gill. "Transference in the Dora Case." *JAPA* 26 (1978): 311–328.

Nash, Christopher, ed. *Narrative in Culture: The Uses of Storytelling in the Sciences, Philosophy, and Literature*. London and New York: Routledge, 1990.

Nemes, Livia. "Freud and Ferenczi: A Possible Interpretation of Their Relationship." *Contemporary Psychoanalysis* 24 (1985): 240–249.

Niederland, William G. *The Schreber Case: Psychoanalytic Profile of a Paranoid Personality*. New York: Quadrangle/New York Times, 1974.

Novey, Samuel. *The Second Look: The Reconstruction of Personal History in Psychiatry and Psychoanalysis*. Baltimore: Johns Hopkins University Press, 1968.

Nunberg, Herman. "The Synthetic Function of the Ego." *IJP* 12 (1931): 1123–140.

O'Shaughnessy, Edna. "Enclaves and Excursions." *IJP* 73 (1992): 603–611.

Obholzer, Karin. *The Wolf-Man Sixty Years Later: Conversations with Freud's Controversial Patient*. Translated by Michael Shaw. London: Routledge and Kegan Paul, 1982.

Ogden, Thomas H. *Projective Identification and Psychotherapeutic Technique*. New York: Jason Aronson, 1982.

——. *The Matrix of the Mind: Object Relations and the Psychoanalytic Dialogue.* Northvale, NJ: Jason Aronson, 1986.

Olinik, Stanley L. "The Negative Therapeutic Reaction and Problems of Technique." *IJP* 45 (1964): 540–548.

Ornston, Darius Gray Jr. "Strachey's Influence: A Preliminary Report." *IJP* 63 (1982): 409–426.

——. "Freud's Conception is Different from Strachey's." *JAPA* 33 (1985): 379–412.

——. "The Invention of 'Cathexis' and Strachey's Strategy." *The International Review of Psycho-Analysis* 12 (1985): 391–399.

——. "How Standard is the 'Standard Edition'?" In *Freud in Exile: Psychoanalysis and Its Vicissitudes*, edited by Edward Timms and Naomi Segal. New Haven: Yale University Press, 1988.

Orr, Douglas W. "Transference and Countertransference: A Historical Survey." *JAPA* 2 (1954): 621–669.

Orr-Andrawes, Alison. "The Case of Anna O.: A Neuropsychiatric Perspective." *JAPA* 35 (1987): 387–419.

Pankejeff, Sergei. "Letters Pertaining to Freud's 'History of an Infantile Neurosis.' " *The Psychoanalytic Quarterly* 26 (1957): 449–460.

Pappenheim, Else. "Freud and Gilles de la Tourette: Diagnostic Speculations on 'Frau Emmy von N.' " *The International Review of Psycho-Analysis* 7 (1980): 265–277.

——. "More on the Case of Anna O." *American Journal of Psychiatry* 137 (1980): 1625–1626.

Perry, Helen Swick. *Psychiatrist of America: The Life of Harry Stack Sullivan.* Cambridge, MA: Harvard University Press, 1982.

Person, Ethel Spector, Aiban Hagelin, and Peter Fonagy, eds. *On Freud's "Observations on Transference Love."* New Haven: Yale University Press, 1993.

Peters, Uwe Henrik. *Anna Freud: A Life Dedicated to Children.* New York: Schocken Books, 1985.

Petot, Jean-Michel. *Melanie Klein.* Vol. 1, *First Discoveries and First System 1919–1932.* Vol. 2, *The Ego and the Good Object 1932–1960.* Translated by Christine Trollope. Madison, CT: International Universities Press, 1990–1991.

Pine, Fred. *Diversity and Direction in Psychoanalytic Technique.* New Haven: Yale University Press, 1998.

Pollock, George H. "The Possible Significance of Childhood Object Loss in the Josef Breuer–Bertha Pappenheim (Anna O.)–Sigmund Freud Relationship. I. Josef Breuer." *JAPA* 16 (1968): 711–739.

——. "Bertha Pappenheim's Pathological Mourning: Possible Effects of Childhood Sibling Loss." *JAPA* 20 (1972): 476–493.

Pulver, Sydney E. "Narcissism: The Term and the Concept." *Journal of the American Psychoanalytic Association* 18 (1970): 319–340.

Rachman, Arnold Wm. *Sándor Ferenczi: The Psychotherapist of Tenderness and Passion.* Northvale, NJ: Jason Aronson, 1997.

Racker, H. *Transference and Countertransference.* London: Hogarth Press, 1968. Reprint, London: Karnac, Maresfield Library, 1985.

Rádo, Sándor. "The Economic Principle in Psycho-Analytic Technique." *IJP* 6 (1925): 35–44.

——. "In Memoriam—Sándor Ferenczi, M.D. 1873–1933." *The Psychoanalytic Quarterly* 2 (1933): 356–358.

Rand, Nicholas, and Maria Torok. *Questions for Freud: The Secret History of Psychoanalysis*. Cambridge, MA: Harvard University Press, 1997.

Rapaport, David. *The Structure of Psychoanalytic Theory*. Psychological Issues, Monograph 6. New York: International Universities Press, 1960.

Rawn, Moss L. "Classics Revisited: Some Thoughts on Strachey's 'The Nature of the Therapeutic Action of Psycho-Analysis.'" *IJP* 69 (1988): 507–520.

——. "The Working Alliance: Current Concepts and Controversies." *Psychoanalytic Review* 78 (1991): 379–389.

Reeves, Christopher. "Breuer, Freud and the Case of Anna O.: A Reexamination." *Journal of Child Psychotherapy* 8 (1982): 203–214.

Renik, Owen. "Analytic Interaction: Conceptualizing Technique in Light of the Analyst's Irreducible Subjectivity." *The Psychoanalytic Quarterly* 62 (1993): 553–571.

Richards, Arnold D. "The Superordinate Self in Psychoanalytic Theory and in the Self Psychologies." *JAPA* 30 (1982): 939–957.

Rickman, John. *Selected Contributions to Psycho-Analysis*. Edited by W. Clifford M. Scott. London: Hogarth Press, 1957.

Ricoeur, Paul. *Freud and Philosophy: An Essay on Interpretation*. Translated by Denis Savage. New Haven: Yale University Press, 1970.

Rieff, Philip. *Freud: The Mind of the Moralist*. New York: Viking Press, 1959.

——. Introduction to *Dora: An Analysis of a Case of Hysteria*, by Sigmund Freud. New York: Collier, 1963.

Riesenberg-Malcolm, Ruth. *On Bearing Unbearable States of Mind*. London and New York: Routledge, 1999.

Riviere, Joan. *The Inner World and Joan Riviere: Collected Papers 1920–1958*. Edited by Athol Hughes. London: Karnac, 1991.

Rizzuto, Ana-Maria. "Freud's Theoretical and Technical Models in *Studies on Hysteria*." *The International Review of Psycho-Analysis* 19 (1992): 169–177.

Roazen, Paul. *Freud and His Followers*. New York: Knopf, 1975.

——. "Freud's Patients: First Person Accounts." In *Freud and the History of Psychoanalysis*, edited by Toby Gelfand and John Kerr. Hillsdale, NJ: Analytic Press, 1992.

——. *How Freud Worked: First Hand-Accounts of His Patients*. Northvale, NJ: Jason Aronson, 1995.

Robbins, Michael. "Current Controversy in Object Relations Theory as Outgrowth of a Schism Between Klein and Fairbairn." *IJP* 61 (1980): 477–492.

Robinson, Paul. *Freud and His Critics*. Berkeley: University of California Press, 1993.

——. *Opera, Sex, and Other Vital Matters*. Chicago: University of Chicago Press, 2002.

Rogow, Arnold A. "A Further Footnote to Freud's 'Fragment of an Analysis of a Case of Hysteria.'" *JAPA* 26 (1978): 330–356.

Rosenbaum, Max, and Melvin Muroff, eds. *Anna O.: Fourteen Contemporary Reinterpretations*. New York: Free Press, 1984.

Rosenblatt, Allan D. "Epilogue: Transference Neurosis: Phenomenon in Search of a Referent." *Psychoanalytic Inquiry* 7 (1987): 599–603.

Rosenfeld, Herbert A. "Contributions to the Discussion on Variations in Classical Technique." *IJP* 39 (1958): 238–239.

——. "Discussion on Ego Distortion." *IJP* 39 (1958): 274–275.

——. "An Investigation into the Psycho-Analytic Theory of Depression." *IJP* 40 (1959): 105–129.

——. *Psychotic States: A Psychoanalytical Approach.* London: Hogarth Press, 1965. Reprint, London: Karnac, Maresfield Library, 1982.

——. "On the Treatment of Psychotic States by Psychoanalysis: An Historical Approach." *IJP* 50 (1969): 615–631.

——. "A Clinical Approach to the Psychoanalytic Theory of the Life and Death Instincts: An Investigation Into the Aggressive Aspects of Narcissism." *IJP* 52 (1971): 169–178.

——. "A Critical Appreciation of James Strachey's Paper on the Nature of the Therapeutic Action of Psychoanalysis." *IJP* 53 (1972): 455–461.

——. "A Discussion of the Paper by Ralph R. Greenson on 'Transference: Freud or Klein.' " *IJP* 55 (1974): 49–51.

——. "Negative Therapeutic Reaction." In *Tactics and Techniques in Psychoanalytic Therapy.* Vol. 2, *Countertransference,* edited by Peter L. Giovacchini. New York: Jason Aronson, 1975.

——. "Notes on the Psychopathology and Psychoanalytic Treatment of Some Borderline Patients." *IJP* 59 (1978): 215–221.

——. "Some Therapeutic Factors in Psychoanalysis." *The International Journal of Psycho-Analysis and Psycho-Therapy* 7 (1978): 152–164.

——. "Primitive Object Relations and Mechanisms." *IJP* 64 (1983): 261–267.

——. *Impasse and Interpretation: Therapeutic and Anti-Therapeutic Factors in the Psychoanalytic Treatment of Psychotic, Borderline, and Neurotic Patients.* London: Tavistock Publications, 1987.

——. *Herbert Rosenfeld at Work: The Italian Seminars.* Edited by Franco De Masi. London: Karnac, 2001.

Rosenzweig, Saul. *Freud, Jung, and Hall the King-Maker: The Historic Expedition to America (1909).* Seattle: Hogrefe and Huber, 1992.

Rothstein, Arnold. "The Implications of Early Psychopathology for the Analyzability of Narcissistic Personality Disorders." *IJP* 63 (1982): 177–187.

——. *The Structural Hypothesis: An Evolutionary Perspective.* New York: International Universities Press, 1983.

Rubens, Richard L. "The Meaning of Structure in Fairbairn." *The International Review of Psycho-Analysis* 11 (1984): 429–440.

Rubenstein, Benjamin. "Freud's Early Theories of Hysteria." In *Physics, Philosophy and Psychoanalysis: Essays in Honor of Adolf Grünbaum.* Boston Studies in the Philosophy of Science No. 76, edited by R. S. Cohen. Dordrecht, Holland: D. Reidl Publishing Co., 1983.

Rubovits-Seitz, Philip F. D., in collaboration with Heinz Kohut. *Kohut's Freudian Vision.* Hillsdale, NJ: Analytic Press, 1999.

Rudnytsky, Peter, Antal Bókay, and Patrizia Giampieri-Deutsch, eds. *Ferenczi's Turn in Psychoanalysis.* New York: New York University Press, 1996.

Rustin, Michael. "The Social Organization of Secrets: Towards a Sociology of Psychoanalysis." *The International Review of Psycho-Analysis* 12 (1985): 143–159.

Sabourin, Pierre. *Ferenczi: Paladin et Grand Vizier secret.* Paris: Éditions Universitaires, 1985.

Sachs, Hanns. "Metapsychological Points of View in Technique and Theory." *IJP* 6 (1925): 5–12.

Sandler, Joseph. "Countertransference and Role Responsiveness." *The International Review of Psycho-Analysis* 3 (1976): 43–47.

——. "Reflections on Some Relations Between Psychoanalytic Concepts and Psychoanalytic Practice." *IJP* 64 (1983): 35–45.

Sandler, Joseph, with Anna Freud. *The Analysis of Defense: "The Ego and the Mechanisms of Defense" Revisited*. New York: International Universities Press, 1985.

Sandler, Joseph, ed. *Projection, Identification, Projective Identification*. Madison, CT: International Universities Press, 1987.

Sandler, Joseph, Christopher Dare, and Alex Holder. *The Patient and the Analyst: The Basis of the Psychoanalytic Process*. London: George Allen and Unwin. 1973.

Sandler, Joseph, and Anna Ursula Dreher. *What Do Psychoanalysts Want? The Problem of Aims in Psychoanalytic Therapy*. London and New York: Routledge, 1996.

Sandler, Joseph, Alex Holder, and Dale Meers. "The Ego Ideal and the Ideal Self." *The Psychoanalytic Study of the Child* 18 (1963): 139–158.

Sandler, Joseph, Hansi Kennedy, and Robert L. Tyson. *The Technique of Child Analysis: Discussions with Anna Freud*. Cambridge, MA: Harvard University Press, 1980.

Sandler, Joseph, and Humberto Nagera. "Aspects of the Metapsychology of Fantasy." *The Psychoanalytic Study of the Child* 18 (1963): 159–194.

Sandler, Joseph, Ethel Spector Person, and Peter Fonagy, eds. *Freud's "On Narcissism: An Introduction."* New Haven: Yale University Press, 1991.

Sandler, Joseph, and Bernard Rosenblatt. "The Concept of the Representational World." *The Psychoanalytic Study of the Child* 17 (1962): 128–145.

Sandler, Joseph, and Anne-Marie Sandler. "On the Development of Object Relationships and Affects." *IJP* 59 (1978): 285–296.

——. "The 'Second-Censorship', the 'Three Box Model' and Some Technical Implications." *IJP* 64 (1983): 413–424.

——. "The Past Unconscious, the Present Unconscious, and Interpretation of the Transference." *Psychoanalytic Inquiry* 4 (1984): 367–399.

Sayers, Janet. *Mothers of Psychoanalysis: Helene Deutsch, Karen Horney, Anna Freud, Melanie Klein*. New York: Norton, 1991.

——. *Kleinians: Psychoanalysis Inside and Out*. Oxford: Polity Press, 2000.

Schafer, Roy. *Aspects of Internalization*. New York: International Universities Press, 1968.

——. "The Mechanisms of Defence." *IJP* (1968): 49–62.

——. *A New Language for Psychoanalysis*. New Haven: Yale University Press, 1976.

——. *The Analytic Attitude*. New York: Basic Books, 1983.

——. *Retelling a Life*. New York: Basic Books, 1992.

——. "The Contemporary Kleinians of London." *The Psychoanalytic Quarterly* 63 (1994): 409–432.

——, ed. *Contemporary Kleinians of London*. Madison, CT: International Universities Press, 1997.

Schatzman, Morton. *Soul Murder: Persecution in the Family*. New York: Random House, 1973.

Schimek, Jean G. "Fact and Fantasy in the Seduction Theory: A Historical Review." *JAPA* 35 (1987): 937–966.

Schmideberg. Melitta. "A Contribution to the History of the Psycho-Analytic Movement in Britain." *British Journal of Psychiatry* 118 (1971): 61–68.

Schneiderman, Stuart. *Rat Man*. New York: New York University Press, 1986.

Schreber, Daniel Paul. *Memoirs of My Nervous Illness*. Edited and translated by Ida Macalpine and Richard A. Hunter. Cambridge, MA: Harvard University Press, 1988.

Schur, Max. *Freud: Living and Dying*. New York: International Universities Press, 1972.

Searles, Harold F. *Collected Papers on Schizophrenia and Related Subjects*. New York: International Universities Press, 1965.

——. *Countertransference and Related Subjects: Selected Papers*. New York: International Universities Press, 1979.

——. *My Work with Borderline Patients*. Northvale, NJ: Jason Aronson, 1986.

Segal, Hanna. *Introduction to the Work of Melanie Klein*. Enl. ed. London: Hogarth Press, 1978.

——. *Melanie Klein*. New York: Viking Press, 1980.

——. *The Work of Hanna Segal: A Kleinian Approach to Clinical Practice*. New York: Jason Aronson, 1981.

——. *Dream, Phantasy and Art*. London and New York: Routledge, 1991.

——. *Psychoanalysis, Literature and War: Papers 1972–1995*. Edited by John Steiner. London and New York: Routledge, 1997.

Segal, Hanna, and Riccardo Steiner. "Obituary: H. A. Rosenfeld (1910–1986)." *IJP* 68 (1987): 415–419.

Segel, Nathan P. Review of *Borderline Conditions and Pathological Narcissism*, by Otto F. Kernberg. *JAPA* 29 (1981): 221–236.

Severn, Elizabeth. *Psycho-Therapy: Its Doctrine and Practice*. London: Rider, 1913.

——. *The Psychology of Behaviour: A Study of Human Personality and Conduct with Special Reference to Methods of Development* New York: Dodd, Mead, 1917.

——. *The Discovery of the Self: A Study in Psychological Cure*. London: Rider, 1933.

Shapiro, David. *Neurotic Styles*. New York: Basic Books, 1965.

Sharpe, Ella Freeman. *Dream Analysis: A Practical Handbook for Psycho-Analysts*. London: Hogarth Press, 1937.

——. *Collected Papers on Psycho-Analysis*. London: Hogarth Press, 1950.

Shengold, Leonard. *Soul Murder: The Effects of Childhood Abuse and Deprivation*. New Haven: Yale University Press, 1989.

Sherwood, Michael. *The Logic of Explanation in Psychoanalysis*. New York: Academic Press, 1969.

Shorter, Edward. *From Paralysis to Fatigue: A History of Psychosomatic Illness in the Modern Era*. New York: Free Press, 1992.

Showalter, Elaine. *The Female Malady: Women, Madness, and English Culture, 1830–1980*. New York: Pantheon, 1985.

Siegel, Allen M. *Heinz Kohut and the Psychology of the Self*. London and New York: Routledge, 1996.

Silverstein, Barry. "Freud's Psychology and Its Organic Foundation: Sexuality and Mind–Body Interactionism." *Psychoanalytic Review* 72 (1985): 203–228.

——. "Oedipal Politics and Scientific Creativity—Freud's 1915 Phylogenetic Fantasy." *Psychoanalytic Review* 76 (1989): 403–424.

Slipp, Samuel. "Interpersonal Factors in Hysteria: Freud's Seduction Theory and the Case of Dora." *Journal of the American Academy of Psychoanalysis* 5 (1977): 359–376.

Smith, David L. "Freud's Developmental Approach to Narcissism: A Concise Review." *IJP* 66 (1985): 489–497.

Spence, Donald P. *Narrative Truth and Historical Truth: Meaning and Interpretation in Psychoanalysis.* New York: Norton, 1982.

——. *The Freudian Metaphor: Toward Paradigm Change in Psychoanalysis.* New York: Norton, 1987.

——. *The Rhetorical Voice of Psychoanalysis: Displacement of Evidence by Theory.* Cambridge, MA: Harvard University Press, 1994.

Spillius, Elizabeth Bott. "Some Developments from the Work of Melanie Klein." *IJP* 64 (1983): 321–332.

——. "Developments in Kleinian Thought: Overview and Personal View." *Psychoanalytic Inquiry* 14 (1994): 324–364.

——, ed. *Melanie Klein Today: Developments in Theory and Practice.* Vol. 1, *Mainly Theory.* Vol. 2, *Mainly Practice.* London and New York: Routledge, 1988.

Spoto, Donald. *Marilyn Monroe: The Biography.* New York: HarperCollins, 1993.

Stanton, Martin. *Sándor Ferenczi: Reconsidering Active Intervention.* London: Free Association Books, 1990.

Stein, Martin. Review of *The Restoration of the Self*, by Heinz Kohut. *JAPA* 27 (1979): 665–680.

——. "The Unobjectionable Part of the Transference." *JAPA* 29 (1981): 869–892.

Steiner, John. "The Border between the Paranoid-Schizoid and the Depressive Positions in the Borderline Patient." *British Journal of Medical Psychology* 52 (1979): 385–391.

——. "Perverse Relationships Between Parts of the Self: A Clinical Illustration." *IJP* 63 (1982): 241–252.

——. "Some Reflections on the Analysis of Transference: A Kleinian View." *Psychoanalytic Inquiry* 4 (1984): 443–463.

——. "Interplay between Pathological Organizations and the Paranoid-Schizoid and Depressive Positions." *IJP* 68 (1987): 69–80.

——. "The Psychoanalytic Contribution of Herbert Rosenfeld." *IJP* 70 (1989): 611–617.

——. "Pathological Organizations as Obstacles to Mourning: The Role of Unbearable Guilt." *IJP* 71 (1990): 87–94

——. *Psychic Retreats: Pathological Organizations in Psychotic, Neurotic and Borderline Patients.* London and New York: Routledge, 1993.

Steiner, Riccardo. "Some Thoughts about Tradition and Change Arising from an Examination of the British Psychoanalytical Society's Controversial Discussions (1943–1944)." *The International Review of Psycho-Analysis* 12 (1985): 27–71.

——. "A World Wide International Trade Mark of Genuineness? Some Observations on the History of the English Translation of the Work of Sigmund Freud, Focusing Mainly on His Technical Terms." *The International Review of Psycho-Analysis* 14 (1987): 33–102.

——. " 'To Explain Our Point of View to English Readers in English Words.' " *The International Review of Psycho-Analysis* 18 (1991): 351–392.

Stepansky, Paul E., and Arnold Goldberg, eds. *Kohut's Legacy: Contributions to Self Psychology*. Hillsdale, NJ: Analytic Press, 1984.

Sterba, Richard. "The Dynamics of the Dissolution of the Transference Resistance" (1929). *The Psychoanalytic Quarterly* 9 (1940): 363–379.

——. "The Fate of the Ego in Analytic Therapy." *IJP* 15 (1934): 117–126.

——. "Clinical and Therapeutic Aspects of Character Resistance." *The Psychoanalytic Quarterly* 22 (1953): 1–20.

——. *Reminiscences of a Viennese Psychoanalyst*. Detroit: Wayne State University Press, 1982.

Stewart, Harold. *Psychic Equilibrium and Problems of Technique*. London and New York: Tavistock/Routledge, 1992.

——. *Michael Balint: Object Relations Pure and Applied*. London and New York: Routledge, 1996.

Stewart, Walter A. *Psychoanalysis: The First Ten Years 1888–1898*. New York: Macmillan, 1967.

Stoller, Robert J. "Ralph R. Greenson." *IJP* 61 (1980): 559–560.

Stone, Leo. *The Psychoanalytic Situation: An Examination of Its Development and Essential Nature*. New York: International Universities Press, 1961.

Strachey, Alix. "A Note on the Use of the Word 'Internal.' " *IJP* 22 (1941): 37–43.

Strachey, James. "The Nature of the Therapeutic Action of Psycho-Analysis." *IJP* 15 (1934): 127–159.

——. "Opening Remarks at a Practical Seminary" (1941). *Scientific Bulletin, The British Psycho-Analytical Society* (July 1988): pp. 15–24. Mimeo.

Strachey, James, Paula Heimann, and Lois Munro. "Joan Riviere (1883–1962)." *IJP* 44 (1963): 228–235.

Strozier, Charles B. *Heinz Kohut: The Making of a Psychoanalyst*. New York: Farrar, Straus and Giroux, 2001.

Sugarman, Alan, Robert A. Nemiroff, and Daniel P. Greenson, eds. *The Technique and Practice of Psychoanalysis*. Vol. 2, *A Memorial Volume to Ralph R. Greenson*. Madison, CT: International Universities Press, 1992.

Sulloway, Frank J. *Freud, Biologist of the Mind: Beyond the Psychoanalytic Legend*. New York: Basic Books, 1979.

——. "Reassessing Freud's Case Histories: The Social Construction of Psychoanalysis." *ISIS* 82 (1991): 245–275.

Sutherland, John D. "Object-Relations Theory and the Conceptual Model of Psychoanalysis." *The British Journal of Medical Psychology* 36 (1963): 109–124.

——. "Michael Balint (1896–1970)." *IJP* 52 (1971): 331–333.

——. "The British Object Relations Theorists: Balint, Winnicott, Fairbairn, Guntrip." *JAPA* 28 (1980): 829–860.

——. *Fairbairn's Journey into the Interior*. London: Free Associations Books, 1989.

Sylwan, Barbro. "An untoward event: Ou la guerre du trauma, de Breuer á Freud, de Jones á Ferenczi. *Cahiers Confrontation* 12 (1984): 101–115.

Symington, Joan and Neville. *The Clinical Thinking of Wilfred Bion*. London and New York: Routledge, 1996.

Thompson, Clara M. " 'The Therapeutic Technique of Sándor Ferenczi': A Comment." *IJP* 24 (1942): 64–66.

———. *Interpersonal Psychoanalysis: The Selected Papers of Clara M. Thompson.* Edited by Maurice R. Green. New York: Basic Books, 1964.

Timpanaro, Sebastiano. *The Freudian Slip: Psychoanalysis and Textual Criticism.* Translated by Kate Soper. London: Verso, 1985.

Toews, John E. "Historicizing Psychoanalysis: Freud in His Time and for Our Time." *Journal of Modern History* 63 (1991): 504–545.

Torok, Maria. "La correspondence Freud–Ferenczi: La vie de la lettre dans l'histoire de la psychanalyse." *Cahiers Confrontation* 12 (1984): 79–99.

Tower, Lucia E. "Countertransference." *JAPA* 4 (1956): 224–255.

Tuckett, David. "A Brief View of Herbert Rosenfeld's Contribution to the Theory of Psychoanalytical Technique." *IJP* 70 (1989): 619–625.

Turner, Stephen. *The Social Theory of Practice: Tradition, Tacit Knowledge, and Presuppositions.* Chicago: University of Chicago Press, 1994.

Tyson, Robert L. "Countertransference Evolution in Theory and Practice." *JAPA* 34 (1986): 251–274.

Veith, Ilza. *Hysteria: The History of a Disease.* Chicago: University of Chicago Press, 1965.

Vida, Judith E. "Sándor Ferenczi on Female Sexuality." *Journal of the American Academy of Psychoanalysis* 19 (1991): 271–282.

Vogel, L. Z. "The Case of Elise Gomperz." *American Journal of Psychoanalysis* 46 (1986): 230–238.

Waelder, Robert. "The Principle of Multiple Function: Observations on Over-Determination." *The Psychoanalytic Quarterly* 5 (1936): 45–62.

———. "The Problem of the Genesis of Psychical Conflict in Earliest Infancy: Remarks on a Paper by Joan Riviere." *IJP* 18 (1937): 406–473.

———. "Robert Waelder on Psychoanalytic Technique: Five Lectures." Edited by Samuel A. Guttmann. *The Psychoanalytic Quarterly* 56 (1987): 1–67.

Wallerstein, Robert S. "The Bipolar Self: Discussion of Alternative Perspectives." *JAPA* 29 (1981): 377–394.

———. "Defenses, Defense Mechanisms, and the Structure of the Mind." *JAPA* (Suppl.) (1983): 201–226

———. "Self Psychology and 'Classical' Psychoanalytic Psychology: The Nature of Their Relationship." *Psychoanalysis and Contemporary Thought* 6 (1983): 553–595.

———. "Anna Freud: Radical Innovator and Staunch Conservative." *The Psychoanalytic Study of the Child* 39 (1984): 65–80.

———. "How Does Self Psychology Differ in Practice?" *IJP* 66 (1985): 391–404.

———. *Forty-Two Lives in Treatment: A Study of Psychoanalysis and Psychotherapy.* New York: Guilford Press, 1986.

———. Review of *Severe Personality Disorders: Psychotherapeutic Strategies*, by Otto F. Kernberg. *JAPA* 34 (1986): 711–722.

———. *The Talking Cures: The Psychoanalyses and the Psychotherapies.* New Haven: Yale University Press, 1995.

Wanner, Oskar. "Die Moser vom 'Charlottenfels.' " *Schweizer Archiv für Neurologie, Neurochirurgie und Psychiatrie* 131 (1982): 55–68.

Weininger, O. *The Clinical Psychology of Melanie Klein.* Springfield, IL: Charles C. Thomas, 1984.

Widlöcher, Daniel. "L'hysterie dépossédée." *Nouvelle revue de psychanalyse* 17 (1978): 73–87.

Winnicott, D. W. *Collected Papers: Through Paediatrics to Psycho-Analysis*. London: Tavistock Publications, 1958.

——. *The Maturational Processes and the Facilitating Environment: Studies in the Theory of Emotional Development*. London: Hogarth Press, 1965.

Wisdom, J. O. "A Methodological Approach to the Problem of Hysteria." *IJP* 42 (1961): 224–237.

——. "Fairbairn's Contribution on Object Relationship, Splitting, and Ego Structure." *The British Journal of Medical Psychology* 36 (1963): 145–159.

——. "Testing an Interpretation within a Session." *IJP* 48 (1967): 44–52.

——. "Freud and Melanie Klein: Psychology, Ontology, and Weltanschauung." In *Psychoanalysis and Philosophy*, edited by Charles Hanley and Morris Lazerowitz. New York: International Universities Press, 1970.

Wolf, Ernest S. "Disruptions of the Therapeutic Relationship in Psychoanalysis: A View from Self Psychology." *IJP* 74 (1993): 657–687.

Wollheim, Richard. *Sigmund Freud*. New York: Viking Press, 1971. Reprint. Cambridge: Cambridge University Press, 1990.

——. "The Mind and the Mind's Image of Itself." In *On Art and the Mind: Essays and Lectures*, by Richard Wollheim. London: Allen Lane, 1973.

——. *The Mind and Its Depths*. Cambridge, MA: Harvard University Press, 1993.

——, ed. *Freud: A Collection of Critical Essays*. Garden City, NY: Doubleday, 1974.

Wollheim, Richard, and James Hopkins, eds. *Philosophical Essays on Freud*. Cambridge: Cambridge University Press, 1982.

Wolman, Benjamin, ed. *Psychoanalytic Techniques*. New York: Basic Books, 1967.

Wolstein, Benjamin. "Ferenczi, Freud, and the Origins of American Interpersonal Relations." *Contemporary Psychoanalysis* 25 (1989): 672–685.

Wortis, Joseph. *Fragments of an Analysis with Freud*. New York: Simon and Schuster, 1954.

Yorke, Clifford. "Some Suggestions for a Critique of Kleinian Psychology." *The Psychoanalytic Study of the Child* 26 (1971): 129–155.

——. "Anna Freud and the Psychoanalytic Study and Treatment of Adults." *IJP* 64 (1983): 391–400.

Young, Allan. *The Harmony of Illusion: Inventing Post-Traumatic Stress Disorder*. Princeton, NJ: Princeton University Press, 1995.

Young-Bruehl, Elisabeth. *Anna Freud: A Biography*. New York: Summit Books, 1988.

Young, Robert M. "Freud: Scientist and/or Humanist." *Free Associations* No. 6 (1986): 7–35.

——. *Mental Space*. London: Process Press, 1994.

Zetzel, Elizabeth R. "Ernest Jones: His Contribution to Psycho-Analytic Theory." *IJP* 39 (1958): 311–318.

——. *The Capacity for Emotional Growth*. London: Hogarth Press; New York: International Universities Press, 1972.

Index

Page numbers in **bold** represent whole chapters devoted to that topic.
Where unspecified Freud refers to Sigmund, rather than Anna.

For Product Safety Concerns and Information please contact our EU
representative GPSR@taylorandfrancis.com
Taylor & Francis Verlag GmbH, Kaufingerstraße 24, 80331 München, Germany

www.ingramcontent.com/pod-product-compliance
Lightning Source LLC
Chambersburg PA
CBHW070356270326
41926CB00014B/2570